Birgit Spengler, Babette B. Tischleder (eds.)
An Eclectic Bestiary

**Human-Animal Studies** | Volume 20

**Birgit Spengler** is Professor of American Literature at the University of Wuppertal, Germany. She is the author of two books, *Vision, Gender, and Power in Nineteenth-Century American Women's Writing, 1860-1900* (2008) and *Literary Spinoffs: Rewriting the Classics - Re-Imagining the Community* (2015). Her research focuses, among other things, on articulations of states of exception, bare life, and precarious being in contemporary American literature and other cultural media.

**Babette B. Tischleder** is Professor of North American Studies and Media Studies at the University of Göttingen. Her books include *The Literary Life of Things: Case Studies in American Fiction* (2014) and the coedited volume *Cultures of Obsolescence: History, Materiality, and the Digital Age* (2015). Her research focuses, among other things, on the ways that critical and creative practices tackle present ecological troubles and our endangered futures.

BIRGIT SPENGLER, BABETTE B. TISCHLEDER (EDS.)
## An Eclectic Bestiary
Encounters in a More-than-Human World

[transcript]

**Bibliographic information published by the Deutsche Nationalbibliothek**
The Deutsche Nationalbibliothek lists this publication in the Deutsche Nationalbibliografie; detailed bibliographic data are available in the Internet at http://dnb.d-nb.de

© 2019 transcript Verlag, Bielefeld

Cover layout: Maria Arndt, Bielefeld
Cover illustration: Babette B. Tischleder, Berlin, 2019, © Babette B. Tischleder

Print-ISBN 978-3-8376-4566-8
PDF-ISBN 978-3-8394-4566-2
https://doi.org/10.14361/9783839445662

For **Susanne Opfermann,**

"doctor mother" and mentor

dog mother and significant human

companion and partner

colleague and collaborator

dear friend

and so much

more

# Contents

INTRODUCTION

**Multispecies Chronotopes: Keywords for Thinking Creatively Beyond the Human**
*Babette B. Tischleder* | 11

VEGETAL LIFE AND PLANT POETICS

**Cleveland Select**
*Judith Fetterley* | 33

**Blood on the Kitchen Table**
*Ulla Haselstein* | 43

**Flowers**
*Kirsten Twelbeck* | 53

**Arboreal Encounters in Richard Powers's *The Overstory***
*Birgit Spengler* | 65

PHOTO SERIES #1

**The Lives of Trees**
*Birgit Spengler* | 91

## Sonic Bugs and Lyrical Beasts

### Skunk
Karen L. Kilcup | 107

### "The Citizenry of All Things Within One World": Mary Oliver's Poetic Explorations of Kinship
Katja Sarkowsky | 109

### Strange Animals in Stylish Habitats: Marianne Moore's Poetry Revisited
Sabine Sielke | 123

### The Beetles—Greatest Hits: The Rhythm 'n' Sound of Insects
Bernd Herzogenrath | 141

### Robert Lowell's Hidden Cats: From *Lord Weary's Castle* to *Dolphin*
Astrid Franke | 151

### Zoological Encounters
Susanne Scharf | 161

## Photo Series #2

### Urban Animals
Babette B. Tischleder | 163

## Political Ecologies in a Multispecies World

### Notes on Thoreau's Posthuman Democracy
Johannes Voelz | 181

### Sacred Pact or Overkill? Human-Bison Relations in North American Mythologies
Gesa Mackenthun | 195

### Hands: Transdifferent Encounters between Human and Nonhuman Animals
Helmbrecht Breinig | 211

**Immanence Is Bliss: The Ecological Imagination in Thomas Pynchon's *Gravity's Rainbow***
Magda Majewska | 225

**The Decline of Humanity in a Post-Animal World: The Animal Motif in Cormac McCarthy's *The Road***
Yvonne Wiser | 241

### Art Work

**Uninvited Collaborations with Nature**
Nina Katchadourian | 255

### With and Beyond Nonhumans: Encounters, Empathy, Entanglements

**"Strange Matings" and Cultural Encounters: Octavia Butler's Fiction as "Companion Species" to Theory**
Maria Holmgren Troy | 263

**More Than Human? Dracula's Monstrosity**
Susanne Scholz | 277

**"Revealing the Wellsprings of Power": An Essay on the Social Function of Humor in "The Wonderful Tar-Baby Story"**
Christa Buschendorf | 291

**Empathy with the Animal**
Christine N. Brinckmann | 303

**Martin Usborne's Dogs: On Entangled Empathy in *The Silence of Dogs in Cars* and *Where Hunting Dogs Rest***
Claudia Lillge | 311

**Paws of Courage: The Heroization of Dogs in Contemporary American Culture**
Simon Wendt | 321

**Acknowledgements** | 335

**Biographical Notes** | 337

# Introduction: Multispecies Chronotopes— Keywords for Thinking Creatively Beyond the Human

Babette B. Tischleder

> There are these two young fish swimming along and they happen to meet an older fish swimming the other way, who nods at them and says, "Morning, boys. How's the water?"
>
> And the two young fish swim on for a bit, and then eventually one of them looks over at the other and goes, "What the hell is water?"
>
> —David Foster Wallace

We live in a more-than-human world, a fact we pay little attention to in our daily lives. We share the Earth with four-legged companions, with pigeons and penguins, rats and roaches, rivers and volcanoes, fireflies and water bugs. And even if we attend to pets and leaves and blossoms with pleasure, our cities are full of wildlife that more often than not goes unnoticed: not only the weeds, trees, and flowers that stretch their bodies out of the fissures of the pavement, or the swift sparrows that try stealing crumbs from your saucer when your mind is elsewhere, but also the smart-ass crows that watch you closely as they organize their communities, or the daring squirrels that climb up six floors on ivy and vine, balancing over balcony railings to find nuts and take a sip of water spared by potted plants. These are only some of our fellow urban dwellers in the street, in trees, on garbage cans and window sills, and in the sky, fighting over and feasting on our leftovers and occasional treats.

Urban wildlife also includes the shy figures of the night: foxes in Berlin, coyotes in Chicago, black bears in Reno, falcons in Manhattan, owls in Toronto, turtles in Athens, raccoons everywhere. If we think they are visitors on an aberrant path, or just passing through, we are mistaken: cities are their habitats as much as they are ours, and wild animals have been urban residents for quite a while. In fact, cities have become safer habitats for survival than many rural areas, and they are home for a large diversity of nonhuman species: city centers, residential neighborhoods and suburbs alike are places where not just squirrels, ducks, rats, and rabbits live, but also varieties of wild canines, bats and boars, and many species of birds, including hawks, herons, and eagles. Urban areas are where they roam, sleep, scavenge, hunt, mate, and raise their young ones.

Even less frequently, we consider cohabitation in terms of our intestinal faunas, the microbes in our guts and wrinkles, the dirt and debris that lives in the shadow of our daily existence, or the short lives "granted" to the cows and chickens and fish that end up on our plates. We humans are by far the greediest animals on the planet, claiming more resources, lives, and territories than all other species combined, and leaving much of our Earth depleted, thereby destroying and shrinking the habitats of other fellow creatures that, like us, have no other place to go.

Last but not least, there are the earthbound ecosystems we call flora—even though habitats for all living creatures, they are much more than just "environments" that provide food and shelter for amphibians, mammals, birds, fishes, and reptiles: they are complex living beings and systems of their own. Plants, to use a very general term for a highly diversified group of non-animal beings, have their own forms of sociality, exchange, and support. They "tell" their own stories and communicate with one another through complex channels and networks—subterranean, biochemical, airborne. Trees, for instance, form a "wood wide web," an undergound network made of fungi that allows plants to communicate with and support one another. But, sadly, their communication goes mostly unheard by those who consider vegetal life merely food, ornament, recreational space, building material, energy supply, or capital, even if people are becoming increasingly fascinated by, for instance, "the hidden life of trees" (Wohlleben).

The idea of this volume is to redirect the attention of our readers to the diverse life forms and rich more-than-human "cultures" of our multispecies world. The book offers essays, literary criticism, autobiographical pieces, poems, and photographs that represent and reflect a wide spectrum of human and nonhuman beings, which have lives of their own and thrive in ways that can suggest new ideas regarding the challenges of dwelling together, indeed sharing the same Earth. A crucial question guiding our efforts, and the efforts of those we follow, is how scholars of the humanities, writers, and artists can, in and through their work, contribute to the "arts of living on a damaged planet" (Tsing et al.).

The essays in this volume provide different angles to give at least partial answers to this question; they explore the shared worlds—the social, physical, and emotional entanglements, the literary, aural, and visual imaginaries, and they rethink the conceptual boundaries between the human and the nonhuman. By attending to fiction and nonfiction, photography, art, and poetry, the contributions show how common categories that neatly distinguish between people and "beasts," flora and fauna, the living and the dead, are often at odds with actual and imaginary forms of cohabitation, collaboration, and exchange. Offering a whole range of critical, theoretical, and creative approaches, and engaging with historical and satirical as well as fantastic and speculative ways of building more-than-human worlds, the chapters partake in contemporary debates in the fields of *human animal studies, critical plant studies,* and *the nonhuman turn.* Our contributors take up the critical concerns in these fields and focus on larger-than-human forms of sociality and solidarity as well as the ecological damage already done and on the horizon. They challenge long-held assumptions, hierarchies, and economies that have characterized the self-conceptions and views of "others" and "nature" in the Western world. Together, they offer fresh perspectives for thinking through the diverse and entangled life forms that make up our shared planet.

This book appears at a time when scholars in many fields are paying increasing attention to what geologists have come to call the Anthropocene, a geological age in which human impact has modified not just the face of the Earth but is prone to put into jeopardy all earth-bound forms of existence, even if in different degrees. Habitat loss has become an alarming fact for an increasing number of our planet's populations, nonhuman as well as human, and many more habitats are on the verge of disappearing due to rising ocean levels, large-scale deforestation and desertification, ongoing industrial, agricultural, and nuclear pollution, and other ecologically hazardous developments. These problems will not arise someday in the future. They are happening and they concern us now: the rapid extinction of species and declining biodiversity, global warming and climate change, the acidification of oceans, which are becoming "home" to more plastic than fish; the local and global effects of a runaway corporate capitalism and the concomitant, ever-growing waste production. Moreover, there is the still largely uncontrolled exploitation of the planet's "resources" through mining, fracking, and quarrying (from fossil fuels to precious metals, minerals, and rocks), industrial livestock farming and agriculture, where cows, pigs, birds, sheep, and fish are raised to be killed, and where bees and other insects and more birds and more fish and other critters die as bycatch and "collateral damage." And let's not forget the rapid decimation of rain forests, the shrinking of lakes, rivers, and intact marine ecosystems, including unique habitats like swamps, coral reefs, and mangroves and their populations—species that cannot survive elsewhere. The rapid cycles of our consumerism, endorsed by neoliberal ideologies and promoted in the name of progress and convenience, are built on systematic obsolescence, not just the obsolescence of daily disposables (such as coffee or dinner to go) and the short-lived fashion cycles of gadgets, clothes, and architecture, but the coldly calculated obsolescence of the lives of others—the exploitation of human labor and nonhuman bodies that are utilized, eradicated, poisoned, deprived of their subsistence, left to die or killed for consumption and economic profit (see Tischleder et al. *Cultures of Obsolescence*).

What follows is not *about* the disconcertingly unsustainable ways in which people treat their fellow creatures and the land, air, and oceans of this planet, though this is an important context. The different encounters between humans and nonhumans addressed in the book call for a more nuanced attention to other-than-human forms of being-in-the-world. There is no way we can consider the life of plants in our backyards, the vegetal nature of our bodies, or the love of gardening, without recognizing the singularity of manifold life forms and our existential dependence on them. Contemplating the lives—the fear, joy, and pain, the style, skills, and intelligence—of nonhuman animals and plants, telling their stories, reflecting on our interactions with them, involves apprehending both that which we have in common with them and the way nonhuman life exceeds us, and it entails seeing our own pleasures and vulnerabilities reflected in their bodies and faces. Contemplating the life of others, then, requires both empathy and the recognition that there are many dimensions of the other that are in fact beyond our apprehension.

Trying to get in the footprints and "mindsets" of other animal and vegetal life forms, then, is an exercise in inhabiting our larger-than-human world in a more balanced way. It means paying heed and respect to a world that is not ours alone. In view of humanity's considerable geological and ecological impact, this book means to direct attention to the ways we share the Earth with other creatures, and it considers how much we rely upon more-than-human cycles of exchange, which enable and sustain all terrestrial life forms. The volume is divided in four sections that deal with vegetal life, poetry and music, political ecologies, and questions of thinking with and beyond the nonhuman respectively. There are, in addition to these sections, two series of photographs, Birgit Spengler's "The Lives of Trees" and my "Urban Animals," as well as a selection of photographs that present work by the artist Nina Katchadourian: "Renovated Mushrooms" and "Mended Spiderwebs." Rather than presenting an overview of the four thematic sections and individual essays, the remainder of the introduction offers a glossary of eleven keywords that constitute relevant concepts discussed throughout the book. Given the eclectic nature of this bestiary, it serves to consider the intellectual, ethical, and practical challenges to understanding a multispecies world through key concepts raised by single contributions. The glossary constitutes an incomplete "alphabet" that aims at pointing out the connections and correspondences between individual chapters and thus draws attention to the book's internal dialogism.

**Keywords**

**A is for anthropocentrism.** The world we live in is focused on human affairs, and this is true for our day-to-day lives and for academic thought, whether in the humanities, in politics, history, psychology, or economy. Our value systems and notions of the good life, our senses of democracy, justice, and equality as well as ideas of property, efficiency, sustainability—diverse as they may be, are usually restricted to human societies and culture. As a challenge to our vicissitudes and value systems, let's for a moment assume that we extended the inalienable rights of life, liberty, and the pursuit of happiness to cows, chickens, dolphins, rhinos, and orangutans, or, more "radically," to bees, trees, or rivers. This would throw into disarray our legal systems, beliefs, and modes of living. It would also entail acknowledging that most people are complicit with systems of industrial mass murder, large-scale theft, annihilation, and waste. You may object that this is only a thought-experiment: our lives and social being cannot be compared to those of other creatures; their lives count too, but less somehow. That we usually disregard the fact of a more-than-human sociality, that we cannot or do not want to face what equality among all earthbound creatures would entail, is part of holding onto our anthropocentric worldviews and privilege. Yet we should not forget that these worldviews inform our practice of treating nonhuman beings—as resources, property, pets, capital, and food. One aim of the book, then, is to unsettle our perspectives and to suggest ways of imagining the world that go beyond this anthropocentric frame of mind. This begins with our willingness to acknowledge that frame in the first place.

Minding our own mindsets does not mean "apologetically distanc[ing one-] self from a human positionality," as Katja Sarkowsky writes in her essay; it rather entails distinguishing between "the inescapability of a human perspective" and "the inevitability of human dominance." Non-anthropocentrism, moreover, can be found in the original, playful, and strange aesthetic modes of literary texts and visual arts that either hyperbolize or defamiliarize prevalent human perspectives, such as the raccoon in Gregory Blake Smith's short story "Hands" that Helmbrecht Breinig discusses, or the types of mimicry that Sabine Sielke takes into view in her interpretation of Marianne Moore's poetry. Breinig shows how the raccoon's agency interferes not only with the human narrator's daily affairs (garbage in particular), but challenges the very distinctions between wild and civilized, protagonist and antagonist, and human and nonhuman bodies, thus making visible the human character's animality and the raccoon's human features. How lyrical language can be a powerful "tool" to unsettle our anthropocentric view is further demonstrated by the poems and artwork in this volume. Karen Kilcup's "Skunk," Susanne Scharf's "Zoological Encounters," and Marianne Moore's poems, which Sielke discusses, are all witty and playful attempts to pay heed to other animals' idiosyncratic nature—a nature that calls, above all, for our respect. Nina Katchadourian's "Mended Spiderwebs" constitute a beautiful yet ultimately futile attempt at mending what spiders can do so much better, reminding us in a humorous way that the architectures of the nonhuman world might serve as models for our enterprises and affairs rather than the other way around.

**B is for bestiary.** We understand *bestiary* as a term for a heterogeneous collection of real, allegorical, fabulous, and imaginary animals and non-animal creatures. As a working term, *bestiary* invites thinking through and with plants and animals, reflecting on the allegorical and metaphorical dimensions of living beings as well as on human characteristics represented through figures of fantasy, tricksters, monsters, and vampires. Following the lead (and laughter) of Michel Foucault in *The Order of Things*, I will in the following consider the multispecies "beasts" of our bestiary along some of the categories of Jorge Luis Borges' humorous list of animals in "a certain Chinese encyclopaedia" (Foucault xv): first, "(f) fabulous"—the contributions by Christa Buschendorf and Susanne Scholz, each in their own way, are concerned with how fiction and folklore have always provided means for imagining historical power relations and cultural hierarchies, as well as offering occasions to assess the role and place of humanity as species among species. Buschendorf's "Revealing the Wellsprings of Power" examines the function of African American folk tales, known as Uncle Remus tales, that circulated in oral form among slaves, and became available in written form through Joel Chandler Harris. The figure of Brer Rabbit, a physically weak yet witty animal, embodies those intellectual and social faculties that enslaved people needed to survive. There is, however, no guarantee that the cunning trickster figure will succeed in escaping the symbolic violence and racism that threaten his social standing. Nevertheless, the animal nature of the trickster serves as a vehicle for strong emotions and aggressions that would be improper for "civilized" human figures.

While the African American animal figures thus have a liberating potential, the nonhuman vampire in Bram Stoker's *Dracula* apparently has no such emancipating traits. Referencing Judith Halberstam's work on gothic horror and technologies of the monstrous, Scholz discusses the parasitic mode of the vampire who takes on a human disguise, right at the historical moment when people gained insights into their own animal nature. The figure of the vampire that passes as human carries within him the bloodsucking danger of contagion and pollution—a threat, above all, to the "pure" social body. Both Stoker's Dracula and the notorious Nosferatu in Murnau's 1922 movie, pose a threat to society from within, but they are also part of a popular anthropology that is challenging what it means to be "truly" human.

Another, less graspable, monster that "haunts" this book is one whose nature is all-too-human. In Yvonne Wiser's reading of Cormac McCarthy's *The Road*, what is called the monster has no palpable traits and is defined by emptiness rather than presence; the novel is characterized by the total lack of nonhuman animals in the Western landscape that forms its setting. Wiser reads the horror of this absence as a form of monstrosity that throws into relief the critical state of humanity whose ruthless supremacy on planet Earth no longer allows any other species to survive. An equally dark chapter of disconcerting absence and death addressed in the book comes in the form of a photograph from the 1870s that shows hundreds of buffalo skulls piled up to form a huge mountain of skeletal remains, presided over by a comparatively tiny human figure standing on top (see fig. 2., p. 202). Gesa Mackenthun's "Sacred Pact or Overkill" tackles the historical representation of the bisoncide and related anthropogenic impact on the North American megafauna by critically analyzing a direction of scholarly discourse that promotes a form of "Neo-Savagism" by casting doubt on the popular image of Native Americans as ecologically concerned people. Given that this animal genocide constitutes a historical monstrosity that, in its disturbing realness, goes beyond allegory, Mackenthun's essay clearly falls out of the "fabulous"-taxonomy and should be granted a category of its own; hence I propose "(h) historical atrocity."

Borges' category "(g) stray dogs" fits well both for Claudia Lillge's chapter on the work of photographer Martin Usborne and the photograph of the young dog mother in Dehradun, India, in my "Urban Animals" series. More generally, the beasts in this book can be classified according to category "(j) innumerable," if only for the reason that those thought with and mused upon here evoke so many others elsewhere. Lillge's discussion of Usborne's photographic framing of a Spanish Galgo (hunting dog) in a scene that, in color and style, is meant to evoke Diego Velásquez's still-life painting, justifies including category "(k) drawn with a very fine camelhair brush," or what comes closest to it at a time when pets and other animals are becoming popular categories on platforms like Instagram and YouTube. Borges' category "(l) *et cetera*" is appropriate since the creatures collected in this bestiary include many hybrid and fantastic ones that don't fit any of the other categories: consider, for instance, the Uroboros and the dodo, an extinct Mauritius bird, in Magda Majewska's meditation on Thomas Pynchon's ecological concern with plastics and harmful anthropogenic impact in the 1970s. The Uroboros, a figure representing the natural life cycles, is juxtaposed with plastics, a valuable material in rocket technology, yet one that is "indigestible" in biological terms. The dodo bird, which has only "survived" as a specimen in the Oxford University Museum of Natural History, constitutes the first documented case of extinction due to human influence: the last dodo was seen in 1662.

Borges' "Chinese encyclopaedia" ends with the letter "(n)" for animals "that from a long way off look like flies." It is a category that corresponds, in a certain sense, to Bernd Herzogenrath's essay "The Beetles—Greatest Hits," though Herzogenrath is more concerned with sound than flies. His attention is directed to the smallest species represented in this book—insects such as beetles, cicadas, and fireflies who have inspired and resonate strongly in contemporary "bug music." It makes insect sounds and rhythms audible in human compositions and thus creatively expands our common concepts of what constitutes music. In order to accommodate another variety of animals missing in the encyclopaedia, I suggest the category "(s) glossy sea creatures dressed in stylish words"—a category custom-tailored to fit the essay by Sabine Sielke—"Strange Animals in Stylish Habitats," which leaves lyrical cats and dogs behind in order to cast a fresh feminist look at Marianne Moore's lyrical poem "The Paper Nautilus." This poem brings together the poet's interests in poetry and biology, maritime habitats and mothering, and the complex interrelation between creative production, the sea, and poetry as dwelling place.

**C is for companion species.** If we think of companions from the animal kingdom, dogs and cats usually come to mind first. Donna Haraway has coined the expression, and her *Companion Species Manifesto* (*CSM*) provides a visceral sense of the intimacy she shared with her beloved companion Cayenne:

*There must be some molecular record of our touch in the codes of living that will leave traces in the world, no matter that we are each reproductively silenced females, one by age, one by surgery. Her red merle Australian Shepherd's quick and lithe tongue has swabbed the tissues of my tonsils, with all their eager immune system receptors. Who knows where my chemical receptors carried her messages, or what she took from my cellular system for distinguishing self from other and binding outside to inside?* (2)

The *Manifesto* begins with a love story, a personal account, that is nonetheless put in historical perspective right away: "This love is a historical aberration and a naturalcultural legacy" (3). In other words, dogs and humans are what they are because they have coevolved. Adopted as pets, dogs, cats, hamsters, and parrots share their lives with people and more or less depend on them for food and shelter. But the question remains how this companionship defines us? Haraway clearly suggests that the relationships are mutual and that our nonhuman companions impact us at least as much as we impact them. All over the world, dogs have been bred and raised for particular jobs—hunting, herding, guarding, patrolling, and so on—and, if in the Western world, many have become pet owners' best friends, they are still widely employed and trained for particular tasks: they work for the police, are part of rescue teams, do sentry and scouting jobs; they are service dogs for people with physical disabilities and serve as "professional" companions for those in psychological need. In the chapter "Paws of Courage," Simon Wendt discusses the importance of dogs employed in the military service in Iraq and Afghanistan and as rescue dogs in the wake of September 11, 2001. Their service, however, goes far beyond any practical job description. Their labor is both physical and emotional, and they also "do" considerable cultural work: as subjects of heroization, their interaction with people is interpreted as one way in which "humans use animals to make sense of their world" (Wendt). In other words, the heroic deeds and agency of canines are subject of a cultural discourse that reflects back on the values and hierarchies of US-American society. Heroization is just one way in which characteristics traditionally deemed human are articulated through the agency of nonhuman animals and through human-animal relations—here military or civil camaraderie—so that social values like courage, loyalty, companionship, and altruism are embodied by dogs while valued by people. Presenting these "heroic" character traits serves to both naturalize these values and to idealize them in the service of nationalist (war) interests.

Companionship can be exploited ideologically in many different ways, and it may be a long way from the kind of "biosociality" and "partners in crime" that Haraway has in mind when exploring the human-canine coevolution and cohabitation (*CSM* 5), to the idealized "paws of courage." Haraway's manifesto stresses the reciprocal character of human-canine relationships: rather than part of a human history of domestication, according to recent research, the coevolution might have been initiated by dogs rather than people—an "unending dance of distributed and heterogeneous agencies," which has instigated naturecultures more complex than we have imagined (*CSM* 28).

That Haraway's conceptualizations of interspecies love can be made productive in relations other than those between humans and canines, becomes clear in Maria Holmgren Troy's "'Strange Matings' and Cultural Encounters: Octavia Butler's Fiction as 'Companion Species' to Theory." Troy reads Butler's science fiction alongside Haraway's meditations on the encounters between species, reflecting on how significant otherness plays into the intimate relationships between human characters and the members of an alien species. Rather than offering an abstract conceptualization of intimacy, Haraway embraces the tactile and the sensory in thinking the nonverbal interactions between humans and other critters. Focusing on these nonlinguistic forms of accommodation and communication, Troy reads Butler's short stories as a form of theory that thinks interspecies relationships within the alien setting of a fictional storyworld. Fiction might be a starting point for rethinking the bonds we forge with nonhuman companions (many others creatures besides dogs)—a thinking-with that needs neither our culture's "infantilization of dogs," as Haraway calls it, nor their heroization but the recognition of their difference as subjects in their own right.

**E is for empathy and entanglement.** Empathy is one of the most crucial concepts around which the reflections on encounters between various beings in this volume revolve. In a general sense, *empathy* defines the "ability to share someone else's feelings or experiences by imagining what it would be like to be in that person's situation." While the *Cambridge Dictionary* considers empathy an ability, *Merriam Webster*'s entry emphasizes "the action of understanding, being aware of, being sensitive to, and vicariously experiencing the feelings, thoughts, and experience of another without having the feelings, thoughts, and experience fully communicated in an objectively explicit manner." Whether described as action or imagination, empathy depends on a form of communication that is based on intuition. Such an understanding of two separate beings—psyches, bodies, minds—that overcome, to a certain extent, the distance between them through an empathic relation is rather different than Lori Gruen's notion of "Entangled Empathy":

> a type of caring perception focused on attending to another's experience of wellbeing. An experiential process involving a blend of emotion and cognition in which we recognize we are in relationships with others and are called upon to be responsive and responsible in these relationships by attending to another's needs, interests, desires, vulnerabilities, hopes, and sensitivities. (Gruen 3)

Gruen's notion of empathy is entangled indeed, and it emphasizes the bonds between different beings through a heightened attentiveness and responsiveness, an attitude and ability that combines emotional intelligence with an ethical thrust, or what Haraway has termed "response-ability" (*Staying* 2). This kind of empathy foregrounds a mutual connection that applies equally to the bonds between beloved companions, friends, and kin, as to less intimate relationships. Many chapters in this book shed light on the wide range and specific dimensions of empathetic response-ability: Christine Brinckmann's and Claudia Lillge's essays both explore the role empathy plays in the reception of photographic and cinematic images. In Brinckmann's essay, empathy extends beyond the cognitive and emotional registers to include "affective mimicry" and "motor mimicry"—intuitive responses to (moving) images that are independent of either sympathy or moral (dis)approval, but involve our bodily reactions and rely on the specific modes of visual presentation rather than anatomical likeness. Brinckmann explores in detail how images can elicit empathy with animal bodies with whom we share little physical resemblance, including horses, herons, and millipedes. Lillge's essay on Usborne's photography is also concerned with the emotional entanglements that images can trigger—imaginary "contact zones" that elicit empathy with lonely canines through their aesthetic appeal and suggestive iconographies.

**K is for kinship.** Kinship is another crucial term for rethinking the relations we forge with other beings, be they human or nonhuman, animal or vegetal. Haraway has coined the phrase "making kin" in an appeal to her fellow humans, suggesting that kinship extends far beyond the bonds we maintain with family members and relatives. In fact, if we begin to see more distant living beings as our kin, we can no longer ignore the kinds of being-in-the-world that often seem other and remote, but are closely entangled with our own. In this sense, then, kinship is about response—or "response-ability"—the willingness to open up our minds and senses to other forms of being: "The task is to make kin in lines of inventive connection as a practice of learning to live and die well with each other in a thick present" (*Staying* 1). Hence "making kin" is a task: a practice of entering connections and rethinking relations; it is an urgent appeal to recognize and respond to our connectedness with other life forms and organisms, and to understand that this "withness" is the only way we can face many terrestrial troubles. "What shape is this kinship," asks Haraway, "where and whom do its lines connect and disconnect, and so what? What must be cut and what must be tied if multispecies flourishings on earth, including human and other-than-human beings in kinship, are to have a chance?" (2).

Katja Sarkowsky's chapter "The Citizenry of All Things Within One World" explores kinship in Mary Oliver's poetry as a connection that crosses species and is able to recognize the commonalities between, as Oliver suggests, people, camels, grass, and maple trees. Sarkowsky attends to poetic scenes that present a variety of kinship relations between humans and nonhumans, allowing us to perceive new forms of sociality that bring together notions of kinship and citizenship in a larger-than-human world. The contributions by Astrid Franke, "Robert Lowell's Hidden Cats," and Johannes Voelz, "Notes on Thoreau's Posthuman Democracy," equally reflect on kinship as a concept that permits us to see unexpected alliances and forms of conviviality; Lowell's poetry (Franke) and Thoreau's nature writing (Voelz) are the contexts for reconfiguring the relation between kinship and strangeness, responsiveness and responsibility, and for apprehending fellowships and practices of living and dying that are shared across species. That even science, when done with humility and respect for the reciprocity that characterizes all inquiries across species boundaries, can initiate new forms of kinship is one promising prospect of Breinig's "Hands."

**P is for plant studies.** Plants that prefer Mozart over Beethoven, plants that are able to process and pass on neurobiological information to fellow plants via fungal networks, plants that display specific behaviors—these examples display a new interest in plants as a field of studies that is no longer restricted to the sciences but attracts the attention of scholars in the humanities as well. Michael Pollan even speaks of "a radical new paradigm in our understanding of life," referring to the field of plant neurology: "Its proponents believe that we must stop regarding plants as passive objects—the mute, immobile furniture of our world—and begin to treat them as protagonists in their own dramas, highly skilled in the ways of contending in nature" ("Intelligent"). As Birgit Spengler discusses in greater depth in "Arboreal Encounters," it is particularly the temporal dimension that distinguishes plants from animals, and because their lives unfold on so vastly different time scales their intelligence has not been appreciated accordingly. In recent times, however, some scientists read certain behaviors of plants as indicative of "learning, memory, decision-making and intelligence"; whether or not these terms are appropriate for non-animal beings, remains controversial, but these question have become subject of serious debate (Pollan, "Intelligent").

"The ancient relationship between bees and flowers is a classic example of what is known as 'coevolution'," writes Pollan in an earlier book, *The Botany of Desire* (2001). Here the question of intelligence is not yet a concept that guides his understanding of plant-animal co-evolution: "In a coevolutionary bargain like the one struck by the bee and the apple tree, the two parties act on each other to advance their individual interests but wind up trading favors: food for the trees, transportation for the apple genes. Consciousness needn't enter into it on either side, and the traditional distinction between subject and object is meaningless" (xiv). Pollan sets out to present "a plant's-eye view of the world," as the subtitle of his book announces, and, at the beginning at least, it seems that the world works well without human animals and their categories of distinction. Humans nevertheless have their own co-evolutionary histories when it comes to apples, potatoes, tulips, or marijuana, all of which are discussed in Pollan's book. While his account is one that presents a rather optimistic outlook on animal-vegetal coevolution, the contributions in this volume also take into account the dark side of plant studies and stories.

It is indeed a comforting idea that trees are sturdy, stable, and steadfast, that they not only outgrow, but will survive us, even if they have already lived for a hundred or several hundred years before individual humans saw the light of day. In this sense, trees are more than living creatures that we like to look up to, quite literally, for their stamina and longevity. Whether as individuals or as forests, they are often embraced (literally by so-called tree-huggers) as emotional bulwarks in our restless time, when dynamics of obsolescence rather than permanence set the tone and pace of our lives. But trees too can break (prematurely), as Judith Fetterley tells us in "Cleveland Select," and they can break hearts as well. Fetterley explores her own attraction and attachment to trees—one in particular—for their splendor and capacity to provide shade, protection, shelter, beauty, and fruit—unfolding the larger story of her own physical and emotional entanglement with the lives of particular pears, maples, magnolias, and spruces. Her essay is as much a love story as it is a meditation on loss—"gardening is not for the faint of heart"—critically reflecting on the romanticism with which humans idealize and anthropomorphize these beings.

Trees, like us "children" of the Anthropocene, constitute no "natural" counterbalance to human existence, but have to bear up against many forms of stress themselves, including the challenges of human (nursery, landscape, tree growing) industries. In her essay, Spengler tackles the anthropocentrism of human chronotopes by juxtaposing them with plant-based time-spaces. Combining a theoretical reflection on the complex lives of trees with a close reading of Richard Powers's novel *The Overstory*, Spengler demonstrates how the narrative organization of the novel itself is inspired by the deep temporal dimensions and interconnected systems of trees rather than by human biographies and trajectories. Hence trees constitute not only a diegetic focus of *The Overstory*, but its novelistic form follows and articulates the non-animal temporalities and cyclical spatialities that characterize the growth of trees, thus unsettling anthropocentric notions of the world.

Kirsten Twelbeck and Ulla Haselstein both offer creative visions of plants that inspire poetic forms of thinking inside and outside human schemes. In "Flowers," Twelbeck brings to cultural and political life a wide variety of flowers. Attending to the "mute eloquence" and expressive floral semantics of nineteenth-century American texts, Twelbeck shows how roses, jasmine, marigolds, petunias, and a number of other species contribute to cultural practices and ceremonial expressions closely related to pressing cultural issues, from life's transience and gynecology to gender relations and racial politics. Haselstein's "Blood on the Kitchen Table" is dedicated to a section from Gertrude Stein's *Tender Buttons*: Haselstein shows how the materiality of language and the sound and varying positions of words on the page are closely tied to the materiality and creative space of the kitchen, revealing unexpected resonances between the practices of chopping, cooking, thinking, and writing. Her critical practice constitutes a playful engagement with and mimicry of Stein's creative compositions.

**T is for thinking with.** "Thinking with" is different from "thinking about." "Withness" has become a crucial category for our critical engagements with other species because scholars in both the humanities and the sciences are moving away from thinking the world as populated by individuals who supposedly think and feel independently from others. In the introduction to the volume *Thinking with Animals: New Perspectives on Anthropomorphism*, the editors Lorraine Daston and Gregg Mitman make clear that anthropomorphism is much more than the projection of "human" ideas and emotions onto animals. Anthropomorphism used to be "a term of reproach," but these thinkers embrace it as a way of thinking about relations: "humans assume a community of thought and feeling between themselves and a surprisingly wide array of animals; they also recruit animals to symbolize, dramatize, and illuminate aspects of their own experience and fantasies" (2). Thinking with animals, however, still includes thinking about them; thus animal activists try to lend nonhuman creatures a voice to represent their rights, especially when they live in captivity, or are exploited in the name of science, or raised exclusively to be killed and become food. That thinking with is as much a matter of the heart as it is one of the mind is a premise shared by many scholars in the field of animal studies: "Thinking with animals can take the form of an intense yearning to transcend the confines of self and species, to understand from the inside or even become an animal" (Daston et al. 7). Charles Foster's *Being a Beast*, a book based on the author's immersive attempts to live for a couple weeks respectively the lives of a badger, an otter, a fox, and a deer, is one of the most radical expression of this human yearning and the desire to put it into practice.

**U is for urban animals.** The first animals that come to mind when thinking of urban animals in Northern cities are our domestic companions, then pigeons and squirrels; then one might think of mice and rats and bunnies and crows. There are, as suggested above, many more nonhuman city-dwellers, four-legged and winged ones, insects, with tails and without, and in warmer regions, we encounter yet other wild species that populate the streets, roofs, parks, and many other niches that make great urban homes: cows, monkeys, geckos, lizards, parrots, and so on. The nonhuman creatures in my photo series are all "wild" animals that I came across in their urban habitats; none of them have significant human others as owners who provide shelter and food for them. Of course, their lives are not independent from those of people since they share the same streets with us: human and nonhuman paths cross, even if people are often little aware of these wild citizens. Coyotes in Chicago, for instance, not "naturally" nocturnal, have learned to avoid direct encounters with human and domesticated animals by living their active lives at night, travelling along major thoroughfares, such as Lake Shore Drive, when there is less traffic, and by keeping a low profile during the day, when humans are out and about. I was not fortunate to encounter a coyote, but friends told me about sightings of these wild Chicagoans while walking their dogs at night. It is quite remarkable that coyotes have become permanent residents of this major metropolis (as of other North American cities)—a development of urban naturecultures in which coyotes usually navigate around people with little interferences. Gavin Van Horn's appreciation for urban wildlife has culminated in a fascinating recent study, *The Way of the Coyote: Shared Journeys in the Urban Wilds*, which, part memoir, part scientific study, explores the how the paths of coyotes, humans, and other animals traverse and intersect, thereby retracing the map of Chicago to chart new ways of connecting and cohabiting. That daylight encounters with this wild species in the city are rather rare, is also due to the coyotes minding their own "business." They excel at circumnavigating people, while making good use of our infrastructures, garbage, and leftovers, but also hunting other wild animals, such as squirrels, rats, and mice. The latter offers a "natural" transition to the next keyword.

**V is for vermin.** Vermin are not a species, the term denotes a classification, a label expressive of human disgust for animals that are considered "harmful" and/or "objectionable," or a competition to what people think is theirs alone: crops, fruit, livestock. In fact, the concept of vermin is not scientific, but reflects an anthropocentric attitude toward certain kinds of nonhuman animals that are seen to be anything from distasteful (at best) to revolting and loathsome. Some vermin are seen to be repulsive because they prey on us (lice or fleas), or on our "things" (locusts, snails, mice, rabbits, and other so-called "pests"). Even if they stay out of our hair, they compete with us and our companion species because they like what we like. We detest mice, moths, pigeons, rats, and roaches because they seem to be in our way and trespass into what we consider our territories. Human animals have little compassion even for fellow mammals when they are deemed vermin. In fact, we have invented entire arsenals to exterminate them: whether poisoning or breaking their necks or both, humans have decided that, unless they serve in our labs or (sometimes) as pets, mice and wild rabbits and rats are, above all, a nuisance. On signposts in Chicago you can find the entire spectrum of human love and loathing in close proximity: instructions of how to handle and secure your garbage so not to feed rats are posted right next to posters promising rewards for bringing back a beloved cat.

Yet right next to humans, domestic cats (including strays) are among the most dangerous predators of contemporary naturecultures that—unless they live exclusively in houses or apartments—are likely to hunt not just "vermin" but all sorts of birds, while they care less for the edible leftovers in our garbage bins than do mice, rats, and raccoons. This may give us some "food" for rethinking our classifications and value systems regarding nonhuman animals more generally. Hal Herzog has explored the curious distinctions that characterize our ways of treating nonhuman mammals and birds in his book *Some We Love, Some We Hate, Some We Eat: Why It's So Hard to Think Straight About Animals* (2011). This is a study that poses important questions through a cross-cultural approach: Why can a puppy be regarded as a family member in Kansas, a pariah in Kenya, and lunch in South Korea?" "What can we really learn from experiments on mice?" Clearly, the questions the book poses reflect not only on animal ethics, or the nature of the distinctions that lead to us to treat some as friends, other as foods, and still others as vermin. Ultimately these distinctions challenge us to ask how we can maintain loving relationships with some fellow creatures, including people, while considering others as unworthy and disposable. On a more visceral level, however, we encounter vermin as a disagreeable proximity with other bodies; such encounters can turn empathy into disgust, as Brinckmann shows in her essay—a visceral reaction, rather than a conscious response, to the lives of other animals.

**Y is for Yuman.** The protagonist and first-person narrator of George Saunders's darkly humorous tale *Fox 8* has learned to speak "Yuman" by hiding near the open window of a house where a mother reads bedtime stories to her kids. Attracted by "the most amazing sound" of the "Yuman" voice that sounds like "prety music" to him, he is "fast and nated by these music werds" (3). Returning "nite upon nite," the observant fox over time acquires a pretty good command of Yuman and also learns about "luv": "When done, she wud dowse the lite, causing dark. Then, due to feeling 'luv,' wud bend down, putting snout and lips to the heds of her pups, which was called 'goodnite kiss.' Which I got a kik out of that! Because that is also how we show our luv for our pups, as Foxes!" (4). The fox's identification with the bedtime ritual is moving, but his good feelings and hope after witnessing Yuman "luv" is also alarming for the human reader, who is alert to the "danjer" involved (3). Taking the treatment of "pups" as an expression of a general Yuman friendliness toward the world—"hope full for the future of Erth"—indeed indicates that trouble is in store (4). This trouble comes in the form of "The Mawl" named "FoxViewCommons," as Fox 8 learns when speaking to a dog in a car in a place called "Par King" (his command of Dog is "decent," as he tells us) (15). Fox 8 tells his fellow foxes about the "Fud Cort" he'd like to explore, but the leader of the pack is skeptical—"What is Fud Cort anyway, sounds danjerus"—and advises Fox 8 to stay away (19). The latter, however, tries to convince his fellow foxes, assuring them, "Yumans are nise, they are cul" (20), and the next day, against the better advice of the elders, Fox 8 and his friend Fox 7 take off, resolved to find the "Mawl's" "Fud Cort."

Fox 8 is a self-conscious storyteller, since stories—fables and fairytales as well as overhearing Yuman conversations and talking to dogs—have taught him about "Yung Yumans," "Old Yumans," and Yuman-owned dogs and their (story)worlds (27). And Fox 8 has learned that narratives work by appealing to their readers' feelings and playing with their expectations. Accordingly, he has been preparing "the reeder" for something to happen and announces a twist of the plot explicitly: "Then it happened" (29). Rather than giving away how the story develops from here, my brief account of this witty satire should give you a taste of the effectiveness of Saunders's craft: by presenting the encounter between Yumans and Nonyumans through the perspective of a fox, the tale effectively reflects on the inherent "danjers" of Yuman culture (3). Even though

Fox 8 has a "reputashun as dreamer" among his own peers, we shouldn't brush aside his point of view as purely naive (19). In fact, his "naïveté" is founded on a saneness that allows one to see the craziness and cruelty of Yuman institutions in the first place.

Saunders's narrative focalization through Fox 8 has a similar effect as Tolstoy's horse point of view in his short story "Kholstomer" (1886). Presenting the concept of private property through the viewpoint of a horse that marvels at the meaning of the phrase "his own" is an effective way of criticizing such concepts through defamiliarization. Considering the enigmatic nature of possessive pronouns, the horse infers, "I saw that people thought there was some sort of connection between me and the stable. At the time I simply could not understand the connection" (Tolstoy cited in Shklovsky 779). Not unlike Saunders's fox, Tolstoy's horse tries hard to unravel Yuman language, straining to grasp how it works as a powerful tool to define social relations among them: "The words 'my horse' referred to me, a living horse, and seemed as strange to me as the words 'my land,' 'my air,' 'my water'" (779). Here a horse that explains to us Yumans what it means to own or to be owned; in the contemporary narrative a fox who hopes to find food in a "fud cort," which seems "natural" to him, given that he also lacks any understanding that things in "mawls" come with a price tag, and that nothing in neoliberal economies is ever for free—neither snacks, nor land, nor air, nor water. Tolstoy and Saunders both narrate the stories from an animal perspective to call human ownership of "nature" into question. And the latter makes us anticipate early on that the fox will learn his lesson the hard way: even if two people in the "Mawl" will "drop a bit of fud" at him and his friend—"karmel korn, sevral parshul biskits, plus a pare so fresh it did not even stink" (28)—Yumans do not generally share, care, respect, or even notice, the nonhuman creatures whose habitats were destroyed in the course of building what now is ironically called "FoxViewCommons":

Week upon week the Truks kep werking. These Yumans sure cud werk. They werked and werked until soon a hole forest is gone. . . . Terns out, what they were making is: sevral big wite boxes, with, written upon them, mistery werds. Upon my reeding of these werds, my felow Foxes looked at me all quizmical, like: Fox 8, tell us, what is Bon-Ton, what is Compu-Fun, what is Hooters, what is Kookies-N-Cream?

But I cud not say, those werds never being herd by me at my Story window. (14)

Fox 8 can only speculate about the purpose of these strange boxes and the meaning of enigmatic words, which, for Yumans familiar with the U.S.-American commercial landscape, are fairly easy to identify as actual or fictional brand names, evoking the bleak vista of strip malls with their chain stores and restaurants. While the foxes are mystified, the effect on the reader can be equally perplexing, yet in a different way. The reading experience is a complex one, producing multiple layers of unsettling comprehension: the easy identification of familiar tokens of American consumer culture via "mistery werds" is paired with the much harder realization of the dark realities and "collateral" damage that comes with the expansion of this culture: the familiar American names are embedded in an unfamiliar language: the (mis)spellings require a more than cursory attention by the reader and her willingness to make the "werds" sound, that is, to read them aloud (at least in the mind) in order to grasp their meaning. Hence the materiality of sounding becomes a crucial part of the reading process, a form of reception that resembles that of Fox 8's initial eavesdropping on fables and stories read aloud by the Yuman mom. Storytelling, then, is a process that constitutes making and unmaking at the same time; we simultaneously see more and less than the nonhuman protagonist, and his language and epistemology demand that we stop and think to be able to follow.

Even though the fox's rendering of scenes seems pretty straightforward at first, our material resonance with his "werds" produce repercussions far beyond simple meanings, making palpable the sensory and imaginative multiplicity of a more-than-human practice of worlding. As Shklovsky writes of the image (be it literary or visual or both): "An image is not a permanent referent for those mutable complexities of life which are revealed through it; its purpose is not to make us perceive meaning, but to create a special perception of the object—*it creates a "vision" of the object instead of serving as a means for knowing it*" (781). In a similar fashion, a seemingly simple question, posed by a fox after he's experienced the loss of his friend at the hands of a Yuman, in a way no Yuman storybook could have prepared him for, makes his "werds" resonate far beyond the confines of the story. It is a story, then, that defies being a parable, and a protagonist who defies serving as allegory by asking: "I wud like to know what is rong with you peeple?" Upon closing his "leter" that asks us for some kind of "eksplanashun," he leaves his readers with a clear appeal (44, 48):

If you Yumans wud take one bit of advise from a meer Fox? By now I know that you Yumans like your Storys to end hapy?
If you want to your Storys to end happy, try being niser.
I awate your answer.
Fox 8   (48-49)

We are left with the uneasy sense that this is not a goodnight story, nor a book we can put aside because the animals in it go to sleep with the Yung Yumans, once the lights are dimmed. At stake is rather the way we are telling—living—our own stories, individually and collectively. And the question posed extends beyond Fox 8—the character, the book, the vision. We Yumans owe an answer.

**Z is for zoomorphism**: Unlike anthropomorphism, zoomorphism suggests the longing to understand and to embody a nonhuman form of living: Foster's *Being a Beast* is maybe the most physically engaged way of trying to slip into the skin, paws, and appetites of a badger and other nonhuman animals. On a more philosophical plane, it is a question that asks, "what is it like to be a . . . ." Thomas Nagel's 1974 essay "What is it Like to Be a Bat" prominently poses this question, setting out from the realization that, even if we will never be able to really understand the sensory apparatus and corporeal being of a bat, we need to assume that "being a bat" is indeed a very different way of experiencing and navigating the world than that of two-legged or four-legged mammals who rely primarily on their eyes, ears, noses, and sense of touch (even though the range of senses here also varies considerably, if we take into consideration a bear's excellent nose or a falcon's keen eye).

The longing to experience what it is like to be another animal is part of the way in which etiologists understand other animals, how they fathom the sociality, emotional make-up, and relationships of the beings they observe and describe. "The yearning to understand what it would be like to be, say, an elephant or a cheetah scrambles the opposition between anthropomorphism and zoomorphism, that is, between humanizing animals and animalizing humans. This extreme form of thinking with animals is the impossible but irresistible desire to jump out of one's skin, exchange one's brain, plunge into another way of being" (Daston et al. 8). Zoomorphism, then, is not the opposite of anthropomorphism, but must be considered along a continuum with its companion term. Both anthropomorphism and zoomorphism can express the desire to expand the range of our own bodies and imagination and to think with animals to comprehend other forms of being-in-the-world and to "thicken" our own experiential range by seeing and sensing and reading in fresh, nonhuman ways. In any case, the ban on anthropomorphism needs to be lifted because we will never be able to slip out of our skins. Even those among us who restrict themselves to the diet and earthy shelter of a badger, need to rely on their own bodies to perform emotional and physical zoomorphism. The authors of this book—in the limited scope that poetry, photography, novels, and nonfiction allow—all engage in such intellectual (meta)morphisms, inviting our readers to experience with them the pleasure, pain, humor, and strangeness that can turn exploring the lives of others into an extraordinary journey.

## Works Cited

Bennett, Michael and David W. Teague. *The Nature of Cities: Ecocriticism and Urban Environments*. University of Arizona Press, 1999.

Braitman, Laurel. *Animal Madness: Inside Their Minds*. Simon & Schuster, 2015.

Calarco, Matthew. *Thinking through Animals: Identity, Difference, Indistinction.* Stanford University Press, 2015.

Daston, Lorraine and Gregg Mitman, "Introduction: The How and Why of Thinking with Animals." *Thinking with Animals: New Perspectives on Anthropomorphism.* Columbia University Press, 2006, pp. 1-14.

Foster, Charles. *Being a Beast: Adventures across the Species Divide.* Metropolitan/Henry Holt, 2016.

Foucault, Michel. *The Order of Things.* Pantheon, 1970.

Gruen, Lori. *Entangled Empathy: An Alternative Ethic for Our Relationships with Animals.* Lantern Books, 2014.

Haraway, Donna. *The Companion Species Manifesto: Dogs, People, and Significant Otherness.* Prickly Paradigm Press, 2003.

---. *When Species Meet.* University of Minnesota Press, 2008.

---. *Staying with the Trouble: Making Kin in the Chthulucene.* Duke University Press, 2016.

Herzog, Hal. *Some We Love, Some We Hate, Some We Eat: Why It's So Hard to Think Straight About Animals.* Harper, 2010.

Kirksey, Eben et al. "Multispecies Studies: Cultivating Arts of Attentiveness." *Environmental Humanities*, vol. 8, no. 1, 2016, pp. 1-23.

Lorimer, Jamie. *Wildlife in the Anthropocene: Conservation after Nature.* University of Minnesota Press, 2015.

Nagel, Thomas. "What Is It Like to Be a Bat?" *Philosophical Review*, vol. 83, no. 4, 1974, pp. 435-50.

Pollan, Michael. *The Botany of Desire: A Plant's Eye View of the World.* Random House, 2001.

---. "The Intelligent Plant." *The New Yorker*, December 23, 2013. newyorker.com/magazine/2013/12/23/the-intelligent-plant.

Saunders, George. *Fox 8: A Story.* Illustrated by Chelsea Cardinal, Random House, 2018.

Shklovsky, Victor. "Art a Technique." *The Critical Tradition: Classic Texts and Contemporary Trends*, edited by David H. Richter, 3rd edition, Bedford/St. Martin's, 2007, pp. 775-84.

Tischleder, Babette B. and Sarah Wasserman, editors. *Cultures of Obsolescence: History, Materiality, and the Digital Age.* Palgrave Macmillan, 2015.

Tsing, Anna Lowenhaupt et al., editors. *Arts of Living on a Damaged Planet: Ghosts of the Anthropocene.* University of Minnesota Press, 2017.

Van Horn, Gavin. *The Way of Coyote: Shared Journeys in the Urban Wilds.* University of Chicago Press, 2018.

Wallace, David Foster. *This Is Water: Some Thoughts, Delivered on a Significant Occasion About Living a Compassionate Life.* Little, Brown, 2009.

Wohlleben, Peter. *The Hidden Life of Trees: What They Feel, How They Communicate.* Greystone Books, 2016.

**Vegetal Life and Plant Poetics**

# Cleveland Select

*Judith Fetterley*

It wasn't supposed to come down. Yes, it was a Callery pear, but it was not the "Bradford" pear, the Callery cultivar that had been for a few years the darling of city planners and landscapers alike, planted along city streets because of its tolerance of bad air and dry conditions, planted in residential neighborhoods because of its ornamental qualities, planted extensively in my own Capital District Empire State Plaza because of its willingness to be trimmed into formal boxy symmetrical rows to reflect the Plaza's architecture. Half the yards in my neighborhood had a "Bradford" pear.

I could see why. I moved into my new suburban neighborhood in the springtime and was greeted by the spectacular sight of many Bradford pears in full bloom. True, its spring blooms smell a bit like cat piss, but the Bradford leafs out early and covers itself with a host of small fluffy white flowers that create the illusion of a snow storm in May. In summer I saw the leaves turn a dark and glossy green; they held that color throughout the summer, no matter the heat or drought. Walking in my neighborhood that fall, I saw those same Bradford pears ablaze with gorgeous colors—dark red, yellow, orange.

The Bradford pear does not look like the tree I learned to draw in kindergarten, with a tall single main trunk and staggered branches coming off at 45 degree angles on alternate sides. Instead, the Bradford has a short base with branches that grow up and over at tight angles so that, when mature, it looks like a brandy snifter and could even be said to resemble a pear. This growth pattern gives it a lovely, symmetrical, uniformly rounded form. When it reaches maturity at 25 feet with a canopy of 25 feet as well, the tree is architecturally splendid and indeed unique; no tree is quite like it. Combine all these features and add in the fact that the Bradford has no insect or disease problems and you have a landscaper's and home owner's dream-come-true tree.

I was smitten, I determined to have one myself. Then came a severe September thunderstorm—the kind we get in my corner of the world, the kind that brings huge gusts of wind—and I saw a different side of the Bradford pear. I saw that there is a reason for the pattern of our kindergarten tree. The branch structure that makes the rounded canopy shape of the Bradford pear so pleasing, those branches angled sharply upward from the trunk, makes the tree weak and thus susceptible to storm damage, whether from wind or from ice. In my neighborhood whole trees were down; others had lost large limbs. In some yards the force of the wind had ripped all the branches off one side, leaving a large gash and a now lopsided tree, its carefully cultivated symmetry gone.

I reconsidered. I called the landscaper who had planted most of the trees in our neighborhood. He admitted to having been seduced by the perhaps too many virtues of the Bradford, told me of the despair filling the landscape business as the industry saw the Bradford coming down again and again. "But," he said, "we now have a cultivar that does not have the same structural problems and will not come down. Let's plant a 'Cleveland Select.'"

I did. I called it "the cocktail tree" because, even when first planted and quite small, it provided shade for two people on our patio at four in the afternoon when the western sun was strongest and the need for a glass of wine the greatest. Over the years it doubled in size, then doubled again, and then again. Eventually it shaded the whole patio. Like Xerxes in Handel's opera, I would sing to it, "Ombra mai fu di vegetabile, cara ed amabile, soave più." ("Never was a shade of any plant dearer and more lovely, or more sweet"). Though no counter tenor, I have a decent enough tenor voice and I can even sound a bit Italian, enough so that the neighbors did not complain of my braying or my accent. As I sang I recalled my little girl self in Toronto, learning to play on the piano her first piece of real music, the so-called "Largo" from the opera *Xerxes*, heavily edited for childish fingers but planting in me a love for music as deep as my love for this tree. I completely identified with Xerxes who, as Herodotus tells us, fell in love with a tree while on his way to, as he hoped, conquer the Greeks (he didn't):

Passing from Phrygia into Lydia, he came to the place where the roads part; the road on the left leads to Caria, the one on the right to Sardis; on the latter the traveller must cross the river Maeander and pass by the city of Callatebus, where craftsmen make honey out of wheat and tamarisks. Xerxes went by this road and found a plane-tree, which he adorned with gold because of its beauty, and he assigned one of his immortals to guard it.

I did not grow up with a special tree in my life. We had a cherry tree in our backyard and I have pictures of my brother and me hanging out in its branches. We climbed it but we didn't love it. It wasn't the double weeping cherry tree that plays such a large role in George Meredith's *The Egoist* or the one that brought me to tears every spring as I walked the Swarthmore College arboretum. It was just a tree and we were supposed to get to the cherries before the birds but we never did. Scraggly Lombardy poplars lined the side of one of our neighbor's yards and my mother explained that they were meant to be in sunny Italy, not suffering through our Canadian winters. Across the street a neighbor had planted a mountain ash whose orange berries I remember vividly, being obsessed by color even then, but it fell victim to the common ash diseases (cankers, fire blight, leaf spot) and turned ugly.

I remembered this tree in particular when I first encountered Joyce Kilmer's poem called "Trees." We had just moved from Canada to Indiana and a friend of my mother's had given my brother and me a book of American poetry as a "welcome to the United States" gift. My mother, who had embarked on reading aloud to us the novels of James Fenimore Cooper, offered me 50 cents if I would read this anthology to myself (it was the early fifties and two quarters were worth something), so I did. I was only ten, but still I wondered if Joyce Kilmer had ever encountered a mountain ash, a Canadian-planted Lombardy poplar, or our rather ragged cherry tree. In this very anthology I encountered poems I thought more beautiful than any of these trees. Years later I would wonder if Joyce Kilmer had ever bothered to look closely at a city street lined with trees mangled to allow for power lines to pass safely through them, or if he had ever walked in a forest like the one my father inherited. For every tree the forester told us to save, we trashed at least ten whose shape or health made them worthless for timber and for viewing. If one ever bothers to look closely at a landscape, be it urban, suburban, or forest, she will discover that most trees are actually unattractive.

No wonder then, that as a young adult, married and living in Philadelphia, my husband and I bought a house in the Main Line suburbs because I fell in love with the twin American elms that graced the front lawn. Coming home from work each day that first winter to these trees, I could actually tolerate repeating some of Kilmer's lines: "A tree that looks at God all day / And lifts her leafy arms to pray; / A tree that may in summer wear / A nest of robins in her hair; / Upon whose bosom snow has lain; / Who intimately lives with rain." The way the branches of these elms moved in the wind looked some days to me like prayer, other days like dancing. I began to understand why Druids worshipped trees. But in the spring when they should have begun to leaf out, I discovered that my beloved elms were already almost dead, a victim of the disease that has destroyed the American elm forever.

My husband and I soon separated and moved, I back to Philadelphia, and then to Albany, New York; he to another suburb. An urban dweller until I moved, many years later, to the suburb where I first encountered the Bradford pear, I had no other tree to equal my beautiful and doomed elms until I planted *Pyrus calleryana* "Cleveland Select." This was my very own perfect tree and a match for any poem. Each spring it gave me blossoms, each summer it gave me shade, each fall it shed enough of its gorgeous colored leaves to make two bags of leaf mulch for my winter patio garden. "You may not know this," said the instructor of the class in Soil Science that I took as part of my Certificate in Garden Design, "but our job as humans is to keep the soil microbes happy. In winter, this means warm. So cover your soil if you want to save your soul!" And so, with the help of my pear tree, I did. And with the help of my pear tree I survived winter's depression. Sitting at my kitchen table I could look out the sliding glass doors leading to the deck, across the patio, to the tree beyond both and in the uplift of black bark that filled the frame created by the doors I could watch the little birds land on my tree and take off as they picked away at the remaining fruit.

I believed I had found a cultivar with all the virtues of the Bradford but without its structural problems. I don't know why I thought that. Cleveland Select looked just like the Bradford and had its magnificent brandy-snifter structure. Like so many gardeners, I was hopeful. Gardeners are the most hopeful people I know. When the temperature is below zero and the snow above eye level, we set out for a class on hot new perennials for "summer sizzle." No matter how bad the weather last year, no matter the unusually warm spring that teased out blossoms only to be killed by an "unprecedented" late frost, no matter that summer brought flood or drought, no matter the winter ravages of bark-eating rabbits or root-gnawing voles, no matter the disasters suffered, we approach the new season with hope, believing that this time spring will be perfect. Henry Mitchell, who made his mark in garden writing by being cranky, observes, "The kind of innocence that is best lost quickly is the simple-minded belief that spring will be lovely. It will not. It will be dreadful." Nevertheless, we believe. This hopefulness is a virtue until it isn't. When an October "tornado" tore a path through my garden and found Cleveland Select in its way, my hopefulness proved a liability.

On the day my pear tree came down, I was visiting Sara, with whom I had just begun a relationship. Sara and I had reconnected in a class on red wine, given at the local high school, each class followed by a trip to a local wine store and a "tasting." We had known each other years before, but when her partner left her to become partners with my housemate, my house was no longer a place Sara wanted to be. But at the "tasting," we discovered again our mutual interest in late night movies and the Metropolitan opera. One thing led to another and here we were a year and a half later embarking on a late-in-life romance. I had also that day had my first physical therapy appointment to try to repair the damages of a herniated disk in my lower back, the result of stress over the "divorce" of my two best friends and my attempt to move ten yards of compost myself.

Despite the continuing pain, I was feeling somewhat encouraged by the therapist's prognosis. I was ready to begin daily walks, start an exercise program, and strengthen my "core" (the mantra of all physical therapists, though I was not entirely sure what it meant). When I returned home that Friday afternoon in late September from visiting Sara, I did not at first understand what I was seeing. Something out my kitchen window looked different but I couldn't decode it. Minutes later, when I did get it, I pretended I hadn't, and, seconds later, when I could no longer pretend, I told myself I could not do anything about it anyway. Sara was coming for dinner, and I had strict instructions from my therapist to be careful with my back. I had a friend coming next week to help me take down the garden, she and I can deal with it then, I thought. Five minutes into preparing the meatloaf, it hit me: my pear tree had split in two and half of it had fallen on my tree peony, my cutleaf Japanese maple, and my dwarf Hinooki cypress. I had to get it off them now.

For the next two and a half hours, in the wind and the rain, I lopped and sawed and sawed and lopped trying to save *Paeonia* Shimadaijan, my tree peony, whose red flowers in June are almost obscene, they are so lush and so large; *Acer palmatum, var. dissectum* Green Lace, a cultivar of the cutleaf Japanese maple that is hard to find since most nurseries carry only the generic Viridis; and *Chamaecyparis obtusa* Hinooki, difficult to establish and slow growing, but after ten years finally showing its magnificent form. Forgetting Sara's dinner, forgetting my herniated disk, forgetting the miserable weather, I worked like one trying to free trapped persons from wrecked buildings. As I reached each plant and found it broken, I too broke down like rescuers who find only dead bodies. When my saw snapped, I began to curse. "Not one," I cried, "you didn't leave me even one." I guess I was screaming at God, but I don't believe in God and for a long time have said "Mother" Nature is a backyard abortionist. When I could no longer see, I went inside, called my friend to come the next day, picked up where I left off preparing the meatloaf, and began to drink.

My garden helper friend, Susan, came on Saturday bringing her own saw and an extra, and for the next five hours we cut up and removed the half of the tree that had fallen, then cut down, cut up and removed, the half of the tree that was still standing, the gashed trunk exposed and sickeningly raw, making me want only to get it down. For five hours I had my beloved tree face to leaf and saw at close range that the fall foliage was more lovely than I had known— leaves gray green on the back; maroon, orange, yellow on top; each leaf intricately patterned, almost round but with scalloped edges. And for the first time I noticed up close the gray green yellow fruit, the size of a cranberry and hard, with a fuzzy matte finish, the fruit that the birds and the squirrels devour in the winter. For five hours, as I prepared each branch to be laid by the side of the road where the town's chipper could find them and turn them into the wood chips I would use next spring to make the paths in my garden, I mourned my Cleveland Select.

I tell everyone I know that gardening is not for the faint of heart. When I retired from my academic job of 30 years, I started a small perennial garden design business that I called Perennial Wisdom. I warn Perennial Wisdom customers, "Do not start down the garden path if you are not prepared to lose what you love." I have called gardening a spiritual practice because it can teach us to have connection without attachment. This stance, the Buddhists say, offers the key to spiritual growth and ultimate happiness. And true to my own teaching, I loved and lost and continued to plant again as larch and maple and dogwood and linden went down and I believed I had achieved enlightenment. But when Cleveland Select came down, I lost the smugness of my assumption that I had achieved such spiritual heights. I was forced to acknowledge that there were some connections whose loss I could not survive, whose loss might kill my love for my garden and for gardening. When I first moved into my newly built suburban home, I planted four blue spruces along the back line of my property. Over the years they have grown majestically to form a green fence between my neighbor's property and mine. At a concert one summer night before my pear came down, as I listened to Schubert's ninth symphony, I had a vision of my spruces holding "hands," lifting up their lower limbs, joining them together, and dancing forward and back, full of the joy of being in my garden. Clearing out the wreckage of my beautiful Cleveland Select, I made a secret vow to myself, signed with the blood from the cuts I suffered reducing my tree to brush. I spoke aloud to whatever forces were listening: "I will leave this garden if anything happens to those blue spruces. I will not plant again. I will not love again and lose."

Thanks to early cherry and mountain ash, I never expected all trees to have poetry-inspiring shapes. I did not discover how truly difficult it is to get a majestic oak or spreading maple, however, until I moved to Columbine Drive and had the chance and the need to plant trees. The tree growing industry, the nursery industry, and the landscape industry all conspire to produce and plant unattractive and unsound trees. Instead of educating their clientele, they bow to its desires. No one, it seems, wants to pay $700 for a sapling, a thin stick that sits in your yard and takes two or three years to develop into something you might call a tree. So in order to create the fullness that attracts customers, growers will cut a tree's "leader," the primary growing branch that keeps shooting straight upward. This stimulates the side branches to bush out, making a young tree look big and worth the several hundred dollars nurseries charge for it. The practice also produces a plant that after two or three years is structurally unsound and aesthetically unattractive. It has taken Ben, the environmentally sensitive landscaper who defies the practices of the industry and whom I was lucky enough to find in time, five years of pruning to undo the effects of this practice, to get the side branches under control and to re-establish a leader for my maples. It would have been a lot cheaper to have bought a sapling, even for $700.

While I had no illusions about trees being naturally beautiful, I came to realize as I began my suburban adventure that I expected trees to be a certain way. Suffering perhaps from a residual Joyce Kilmer effect, I retained the romantic notion that trees represented a life without stress in a stress-filled world. I thought of them as an oasis of calm, the symbol of a state of being that I longed for but could not attain due to the stresses in my own life. I imagined, however, that I could achieve some relief from stress simply by having them in my garden and looking at them. My trees, I assumed, would grow steadily and peacefully, at ease and in harmony with their surroundings. I was prepared for botrytis on the peonies, Japanese beetles on the oak leaf hydrangeas, aphids on the lupines, but losing a Pagoda dogwood to the stress of being planted in a dry spot and not being sufficiently watered? No way was I prepared for that.

One fall day, working with Ben, it hit me that trees, like me, live lives of constant stress. I was looking at the leaves of my sugar maple and noticing a bit of brown curling at the edges. "Look at this, Ben," I said, "what's up with this?" He studied the tree, then said, "Well, this summer has been kind of hard on trees. We haven't had a lot of rain, and it's been very hot. That can stress them out. This tree looks a bit stressed to me." We moved on to the red maple in a different part of the yard, but some trace memory nagged at me. Wait a minute, I thought, didn't we have this same conversation last year when I pointed out early leaf drop on the red maple? Didn't Ben say that the tree looked stressed and no wonder, because the summer had been so wet and cold? Then it hit me that every fall since Ben and I have been working together we have had a version of this conversation. By now we had reached the red maple. Squinting, I looked up at it, carefully scanning the crown. "Looks stressed to me," I observed, trying to sound as much like Ben as possible. "Yes, it does," he replied, and we moved on to the yellowwood.

It took me awhile to absorb the lesson that trees, like me, are alive and hence experience stress—from disease, from other living creatures, from the environment, from the practices of the industry that grows them for commercial purposes. Marauding teenagers broke my paperbark maple in two the night of their high school graduation. Voles got my weeping Siberian pea tree. Perhaps I killed my Japanese maple by not disinfecting my pruning shears after I pruned the Merrill magnolia. The maple died from verticillium wilt, a virus that clogs the tree's vascular system and starves it to death, but the magnolia died from scale. Still, it could have also been infected with the wilt fungus. I lost my pagoda dogwood because the nursery that sold it to me neglected to mention it would not survive in the location I chose for it. Dogwoods need water, lots of water. To plant a dogwood in a dry spot such as the one I chose was to subject it to a level of stress that proved lethal.

Selling people trees that are likely to die from stress is built into the nursery business. It is hard to keep ahead of growing roots; many producers don't even try. Virtually any tree found in a nursery will be stressed already by roots that grow in circles instead of out. I lost a little leaf linden, one of the first trees I planted, to another autumn storm that broke it off at the point where trunk meets root. When I investigated the remaining stump, I found it shaped like the point of a pencil, the trunk so constricted and narrowed by girdling roots that it just snapped off. Recently, I lost a weeping larch. When Ben and I dug it up, we found the roots growing round and round the trunk instead of out and into the yard. "Choked itself to death," said Ben in disgust.

We could not have saved it. By the time its leaves make a tree's distress visible to the average gardener, the tree is already past recovery. No matter how much I care, my eye cannot discern the girdling roots beneath the ground nor the virus spreading beneath the bark. I can see and treat the mildew on my lilacs; I can pull the sawfly larvae off my Mugho pine and squish them to death; I can shake salt onto my Hosta-eating slugs; but my trees put me face to face with my limitations as a caregiver. The stress of trying to keep my trees alive has made me vulnerable to a new kind of charlatan.

Today's snake-oil salesman is the one who claims, "I can save your tree." In an effort to preserve a sugar maple, I had such a one come to my house. He came highly recommended; even Ben thought well of him. I neglected to inquire his fee. He examined each tree I had on my property and found something wrong with all but one of them. He spoke at length of solutions, then pronounced the problems to be either too hopeless (in the case of the maple it was girdling roots too large to cut); or too complicated (soil analysis would no doubt reveal that Serbian spruces needed a higher pH but, of course, it is not possible to replace the soil of an already growing large tree); or too expensive (hundreds of dollars to move a tree that was getting too wet to a place that would be drier). He noticed my newly dead weeping larch, which I had kept as a reminder of my insight about trees and stress. He asked if he could have it to show other clients what a really bad case of girdling roots looks like. I demurred. On leaving, he checked my Bristlecone pine and announced that it had an infestation of the woolly adelgid. I murmured something about white gum-like spots on the needles being part of the charm of this particular tree, but was advised to spray and spray heavily. He glanced at the spot nearby where my Japanese maple had succumbed to verticilum wilt, pronounced that the virus was rare in Japanese maples, and told me to go ahead and plant another. Then he gave me his bill. I will not reveal what this visit from the medicine man cost me, but I could have replaced more than one of my lost trees with the sum.

My losses have given me a healthy respect for established, living, mature trees, whether ugly or beautiful. They have also given me respect for the gardener, like myself, who is willing to take on the challenges trees present. Trees cost a lot up front, they take a long time to develop, and they become exponentially more valuable as they mature. When even an adolescent tree dies (and I will not live long enough to see any of my trees as adults), it leaves a large hole in your garden but, more importantly, it leaves a large hole in your heart. For trees are not interchangeable. When I lost my *Acer saccharum*, I could have gotten another but it would not have been the same sugar maple as the one I lost.

When my cat died, I told the children we would have to wait a whole year before we could even think about getting another. I lectured them on the damage we do to our souls when we short circuit mourning for something we love by instantly replacing it. Within days of removing the last traces of Cleveland Select, however, I realized that I could not survive my own winter's downing nor next summer's sun without a tree in the same spot. I had to replace it immediately. But with what? Surely I would not be so stupid as to choose another Callery pear. There are many trees to choose from, I said to myself, many options for the sadder but wiser gardener. I went on-line, I read and re-read *Trees for the Small Garden*, I consulted Dirr's *Manual of Woody Landscape Plants*. Ben suggested an *Oxydendrum*. I went to the Landis arboretum to see one; I rejected it immediately. I have confidently told my customers that there are always native alternatives to the foreign invasives they want me to plant for them. I have handed out lists, recommended books to read, discussed the many virtues of the native alternative and even persuaded some people to let me plant a native holly instead of the Japanese barberry. But as I sought an alternative to the Callery pear, listed in *Native Alternatives to Invasive Plants* as itself a foreign invasive, I discovered something rather disturbing: sometimes there really are no alternatives.

I didn't want to plant another Callery pear. I didn't want to have another tree come down. I didn't want to be ten years older and still have no tree in my winter window or shade on my summer patio. But neither did I want the scraggly native serviceberry or the clump forming native fringe tree or the disease-ridden native hawthorn. I wanted a tree just like the Callery pear—one with an upright shape, yet spreading, but not too spreading; large enough to shade the patio but not so large as to reach the deck. I have an extensive garden around my patio. Few trees look good in the middle of a garden and even fewer let you plant underneath them. The Callery pear does both. Then none of the native alternatives had the four season interest of the pear, essential to me because I would see this tree every day from inside and outside. And since verticilium wilt took down my Japanese maple and scale destroyed my magnolia, I found the disease and pest free attribute of the Callery pear irresistible.

Finally I called Ben and gave him the news that I wanted, no, needed another Callery pear. A week or so later he came back with a young tree. "I picked the one with the best structure," he said. "It doesn't have the same fall color but it has held up better than 'Cleveland Select' in strength tests." "Yes," I said. "I saw the report on the New Jersey highway test. It gives *Pyrus calleryana* 'Aristocrat' the best marks for structural strength." "They all come down in twenty years," said Ben, forgetting that he was about to plant another Callery pear for me, "and most of them don't last more than ten."

Ten years later my tree is still standing. It is not the same tree as the one I lost. It provides the needed shade and the resting spot for birds as they eat its fruits, but it does not have the same magnificent fall color, nor does it have the same brandy snifter structure. It fills the frame made by my sliding glass doors and keeps me from going down in winter, but I do not sing to it in summer. I no longer have a tree I wish to adorn with gold and there is no guard I can set to protect it. But perhaps my own structure is stronger now that I am no longer devoted to a single tree. Having learned not to replant a Japanese maple in the site where one went down to verticilium wilt or a Merrill magnolia that is subject to scale, and having learned to allow only Ben to choose and plant a tree for me to ensure no early death from girdling roots, I now am blessed by two healthy paperbark maples, a Japanese *Stewartia* with good fall color, the Seven Sons *Heptacodium* which puts forth a mass of white blooms in August, a fastigiated sweetgum that fits its space, and a Serbian spruce that has actually survived.

This spring we had a scare. The pear tree did not bloom and it was late leafing out. We thought it might have died from last summer's drought and the following dry fall. We immediately made plans to move our sitting area to the shade of the Heptacodium. We agreed we would plant no more Callery pears. We called Ben who fertilized the tree and said, "Give it another few weeks. It may be fine. If not, we will plant a little leaf linden." The tree came back, we have more shade than ever, but a warning note has been struck.

When I lost Cleveland Select, I vowed I would leave my garden if anything happened to my spruces, but now I know I probably won't. The spruces are doomed, victims of the needle cast fungus that is rapidly decimating their population. I am keeping them alive for now by annual fertilizing and spraying. The last time Ben and I treated them, he noticed a line of woodpecker holes almost completely surrounding on the spruces. "Better get a baffle, fast," he said. "The sapsucker has almost completely girdled this baby." I got a baffle, a piece of tinfoil that flutters in the wind, but I take a dim view of its dissuading any pecker of wood from gouging my tree. If the bronze birch borer can find its way to a white birch when it is stressed and vulnerable, I suspect my sapsucker knows the way to my stressed blue spruce.

Sara and I talk about aging in place. I know I will not see "Aristocrat" mature. I know it could come down in a severe storm. I know that getting old means just one loss after the other, making it harder and harder to stay vital, connected, loving. But I say, "I just read an article in the latest issue of *The American Gardener* about hedges. Did you know that hedges, in addition to marking property lines and creating privacy, can also 'provide wildlife habitat, sequester carbon, and control soil erosion?' If the spruces go, let's create a hedgerow. What do you think, dear?"

# Blood on the Kitchen Table

Ulla Haselstein

I.

Only rarely have critical discussions of Gertrude Stein's *Tender Buttons* (1912) produced readings of individual texts. Resisting to interpretation, all these portraits of things seem to make the same point of contingency, indeterminacy or presymbolic *jouissance* (Murphy). Randa Dubnick explained *Tender Buttons* as "a change from mimesis of external reality to mimesis of the present moment of consciousness with an object" (28). Neil Schmitz had earlier made the same point:

*Tender Buttons* records, moment by moment, the play of the mind with the world before her [Stein]. But since the writer is not fixed, writing from a position, from a clarifying knowledge of the nature of things, and since the world (carafes, cushions, umbrellas, mutton, celery) is also in process, presenting only phases and attributes in their time and place of existing, nothing can be named and then classified, given as real. Everything is contingent, changing as it moves and the mind moves. (1206)

Marjorie Perloff did not shrink away from reading *Tender Buttons*, but she argued that the texts lend themselves to the filling in of the gaps "in whatever way suits us" and re-iterated Schmitz's argument, replacing contingency by indeterminacy (106). All authors refer at some point to Richard Bridgman, whose analysis set the course for later criticism; resonances of his interpretation are discernible in Schmitz's, Perloff's, and Dubnick's work. Bridgman wrote:

Her practice was to concentrate upon the object as it existed in her mind. Her imagination was stimulated then not by the object's particular qualities alone, but also by the associations it aroused, by random interruptions of the act of composition, and by the words as they took shape upon the page.... [A]ll of these made up the object's full and authentic existence insofar as it had any reality for her. The object could not be separated from its context. It was entangled in an infinite web of relationships.

If illuminated from a single source, fixed in a specific position, and viewed from one perspective only, the object would inevitably be falsely conceived. Gertrude Stein perceived that it was immersed in a continuum of sound, color, and association, which it was her business to reconstitute in writing. (124)

Bridgman summarizes Stein's description of how she wrote *Tender Buttons*, but fails to address the experimental context with its relation to Cézanne's painting and Bergson's writing. Stein had declared,

I used to take objects on a table, like a tumbler or any kind of object and try to get the picture of it clear and separate in my mind and create a word relationship between the word and the things seen. ("Transatlantic" 25)

The first step was to inhibit the automatic mode of seeing by paying attention to the process of visual perception. Instead of habitually recognizing a familiar object, she attended to her visual perceptions and retraced the outlines of the object perceived. She registered the colors of the thing, its spatial configuration and its relation to other things, the line which seems to delimit the object, the properties that visually suggest its weight, and the regularities or irregularities of its form. This decomposition of the image was then turned into a recomposition whose final result was the formation of a "clear and stable" mental image of the object (Stein used the term "picture" to identify this process as a painter's mode of seeing).

Nineteenth-century psychological experiments on perception recognized that seeing is a habitualized process of mental construction: visual perceptual data of an object are computed and compared with memory images of this object and other similar objects. Once a sufficient amount of resemblances has been determined, the object is identified as a specimen of a certain class, and its resemblances to other objects are forgotten.[1] Ernst Gombrich characterized this process as the "reading" of the image of the object, adding that "reading an image may perhaps be better described as testing it for its potentialities, trying out what fits" (190-91). But the serial testing for matches between perceptions and memories is only one side of the mental process. Referring to experiments by Stein's teacher Hugo Münsterberg, Bergson characterized the other side as imitation: testing leads to a projection "identical with or similar to, the object on which it comes to mold itself," with the effect that "we are no longer able to discern what is perception and what is memory" (102). He summarized his argument by stating that "the progress of attention results in creating anew not only the object perceived, but also the ever-widening systems with which it may be bound up" (Bergson 105). Scientific experiments on visual perception instigated Cézanne's conceptualization of painting as *réalisation*, as a recreation of the process of seeing objects by inhibiting the habitual recognition of the object, on the one hand, and by inventing techniques to make the viewers experience the process of de/recomposing the perceptual image of the object, on the other. Cézanne's paintings direct the viewers' attention to the process of seeing and make them aware of the constructive cognitive processes involved in seeing. The paintings are not so much visual representations of things than compositional reenactments of perceptual and intellectual processes whose habitual performance installs the subject in a position of control over things, while Cézanne's pictorial performance effects a contemplation of things.[2]

Stein's second step in producing her portraits of things consisted in creating a "word relationship between the word and the things seen." Paying attention to seeing the object in the sense of "trying out what fits," she followed Cézanne's example, recreating this process in the medium of language. In adapting his concept of *réalisation* to writing, she had to work with visual, but also with linguistic, signs whose link to the object is not perceptual but conventional.

As nineteenth-century experiments showed, reading is a process, not a series of single steps. Readers observe a few characteristic marks on the page and fill the gaps with memory-images "which, projected on paper, take the place of the real printed characters and may be mistaken for them" (Bergson 103)— memory-images that synthesize the knowledge of orthography, typography, grammatical rules with knowledge about the world. *Tender Buttons* makes readers aware of this process by blocking it. Using the title as a conceptual frame for the portrait, Stein decomposed the concept into series of verbal "data," some of which refer to the visual qualities, the functions, or the various classifications of the thing, while others refer to visual qualities, functions, or classifications of things that share a feature or two with the visual image of the thing, and yet others refer to the verbal concept of the portrayed thing (by puns for instance). To compose the portrait, Stein made selections from the assembled corpus of data, choosing words that can be visually or conceptually linked to each other.

Reading a text from *Tender Buttons* means testing the elements of the portrait for their potential similarities to the image and the verbal concept of the thing, by "trying out what fits." Descriptive terms are rarely used in the portraits; instead, many verbal "data" are submitted to well-known poetic devices such as metaphor and irony, which refer to an object by way of a similarity with other objects, or of alliterations, assonances, and rhymes, which are built on sensory similarities between words to suggest a link to the concept of the thing.

I try to call to the eye the way it appears by suggestion the way a painter can do it. This is difficult and takes a lot of work and concentration to do it. I want to indicate it without calling in other things. (Stein, "Transatlantic")

Stein emphasizes that writing *Tender Buttons* was a process of careful textual construction, not a recording of a play of her mind.

A painter of still lifes works with lines, forms, and colors, and combines them to suggest an object to the viewer, who in seeing/reading the painting by "trying out what fits" will come to a predictable result, but may or may not notice the difference art makes in the process. Stein did not leave the process of reading *Tender Buttons* to chance but gave it a direction by the title of each portrait. The reader will work with the words and sentences of the text, "trying out what fits" the object named in the title, and in the end will come up with a predictable result: she will have found some links to the object, and some links to other objects which have a trait or two in common with the named object, and some links between the words of the text. Neither the process of composition nor the process of reading is contingent, nor are they designated to produce indeterminacy. And while there are certainly parallels to Shklovsky's famous essay "Art as Technique" (1914), the goal of *Tender Buttons* is not to rediscover the object. Rather, the text calls attention to the fact that speaking permits more than conventional practices of signification, and it shows that these practices are held in common with other speakers as the foundation of a common knowledge about the world.

## II.

The following text is listed under the second rubric of *Tender Buttons*, "Food."

VEGETABLE.

What is cut. What is cut by it. What is cut by it in.

It was a cress a crescent a cross and an unequal scream, it was upslanting, it was radiant and reasonable with little ins and red.

News. News capable of glees, cut in shoes, belike under pump of wide chalk, all this combing. (53)

"What is cut." The first sentence can be read as a definition of a vegetable. But as it turns out, it defines this portrait of a vegetable as well.

The first sentence of the text starts off a series of almost identical sentences. Their grammatical status hovers between a question and a relative clause whose main clause is missing, if the title does not serve in that function. The second sentence adds two small words and the third sentence another small word to the previous one. But each time, a truncated sentence is the result. The second and the third sentence were obviously submitted to cuts; that the first sentence was cut up as well is strongly suggested by the serial structure. In fact the cut in the first sentence appears to be the deepest, precisely because the sentence makes sense as it is, and the cut is only inferred by the subsequent sentences. That the series of relative clauses can also be read as questions implies a self-referential comment, since the meaning of each sentence becomes the more enigmatic the more words are added (perhaps to make up for the cuts). The reader's filling in of the gap is thus anticipated by the text and is figured as a repetition of the writer's technique of cut and paste.

"What is cut by it." The reference of the pronoun is unknown, an indication that a sentence or even a paragraph has been cut. At the same time, it is clear that it is not the name of the person who does the cutting that has been cut, but the instrument used for cutting. "What is cut by it in." The place where the cuts are done is also cut out. Since vegetable is the object of this portrait, a kitchen immediately suggests itself (which was Alice Toklas's domain, if one wants to read *Tender Buttons* biographically—Stein did not cook). But given the cuts of the portrait text, the writer's study is an equally suggestive solution. In both work spaces different cutting tools are used: a kitchen knife, scissors—instruments that are connected to women's work, such as cooking and sowing, but that can mutilate, even kill.

The first line or paragraph of the portrait thus mentions and displays a defining aspect of a vegetable, namely its being cut for cooking. Grammar and typography are thus used by Stein for "data." The filling in of the gaps brings out a similarity between a writer's and a cook's work, and the reader will inevitably attempt to stabilize this connection by finding more clues along the same line. A vegetable thus becomes an object to think with, a metaphor in which the semantic fields of cooking and writing converge. The cutting of vegetables is a step in the preparation of a meal. And if cooking is like writing, defining the latter as a selection and combination of words is not enough: VEGETABLE points to the importance of the cutting up of sentences in writing. In contrast to speaking, where a correction cannot efface a previous utterance, textual revisions can cut out words and replace them with other words without leaving a trace. Like a dish, a text is the result of numerous cuts—but also of stirring, mixing, fusing.

But that is not all. Due to the impact of the title, the repetitions of the word "cut" in the first line in conjunction with the brevity of the sentences evoke the sound of chopping up vegetables in the kitchen: *cut/cut/cut*. And this observation triggers the discovery of more similarities in the next paragraph. For neither vegetables nor sentences endure the ordeal of being cut silently. The sounds in the alliterative chain "cress"—"crescent"—"cross" render the vegetable's pain audible and culminate in "an unequal scream." Suggesting a link between the cutting of *cress* and the Passion of *Christ*, the text makes the reader aware that a preparation of a meal is a practice of violence. And the vegetable does not sacrifice itself, but is sacrificed—not to God, but to hungry human beings (but then of course Gertrude Stein may self-ironically imagine herself as Alice Toklas's God, if we remain within the biographical context). The discursive boundaries between the handling of vegetables in the kitchen and the world religions of Christianity and Islam symbolized by the crescent and the cross are broken down, while the cutting up of a vegetable and the work of the guillotine (as a more contemporary version of public execution) make an uncanny fit. But, of course, it could just as well be a banal kitchen accident that is melodramatically inflated here—somebody cuts herself (an inference from convention) in or *across* the finger while cutting a vegetable, and then utters an "unequal scream." Then the text pivots on the comparison of human pain and the pain of the vegetable, calling into question the same discursive fault line as that between "cress" and "cross."

While the two religions offer the prospect of resurrection ("upslanting"), there is only a very mundane transubstantiation that awaits a chopped vegetable, and the writing of a portrait resurrects the vegetable only to immortalize the chopping. The more profane scenario can accommodate "upslanting" as well: the cook cuts herself in the finger and holds it up to stop the bleeding. In which case the traces of the accident are readable as "little ins and red."

But the suggestiveness of the words are not exhausted yet, for reading may require cuts and additions as well: with a cut, "scream" is transformed into *cream*, a word that has its place in the cooking of vegetables, while *crass* can be added as a latent word that fills the semantic abyss between the words "cress" and "cross" by pointing to it. Another word one might add to the chain is *crisscross*, which would refer to the materiality of the portrait text before it was printed and consumed in reading, and figuratively to the structure of the portrait as produced by intersecting associative chains.[3] "[R]adiant" and "reasonable" constitute an alliterative pair; the latter term rhymes with the portrayed object, while the former resonates with the word *radical*, whose etymology leads to the Latin word for root, which in turn constitutes a semantic link to *vegetable*. To be sure, vegetables are an entirely *reasonable* food; but in Stein's textual cooking, they become *radiant* and, like x-rays, bring out otherwise invisible words. As Mina Loy wrote in 1923, Stein was "the Curie of the laboratory of words."[4]

In the light of crucifixion, the cutting of vegetable appears as a sacrificial ritual as part of the routines of everyday life. Note that "ins" is an anagram of *sin*; perhaps the accidental cutting of the finger could be regarded as an act of divine justice. Either way, "red," the color of blood, fits into the semantic constructions created by filling in the textual gaps. As the sole descriptive term of the entire portrait, "red" is radiating in all directions: it is the key to both the martyrdom of the vegetable and the cook's bleeding that the portrait permits to be *read*. Many years later Toklas wrote in *The Alice B. Toklas Cook Book*, "[b]efore any story of cooking begins, crime is inevitable"—a remark that stresses the unlawful violence of cooking and writing and carries the notion of punishment with it (34).

In the last paragraph of the portrait, the reader's "trying out what fits" must deal with some unyielding "data." The general focus shifts to self-referential comments on the construction of the text. The text is "[n]ews," and its composition is designed to give pleasure ("glees"). Taking the chain "cress"—"crescent"—"cross" as a model, "glees" can be seen as a replacement of *glues* that rhymes with "cut in shoes," which, if read as a substitute for *cut and choose*, could characterize Stein's method of composition. But then "shoes" could also serve as a proxy for *chews*, reminding the reader that a vegetable is chopped in order to be eaten, while the portrait of the vegetable is cut up in order to be metaphorically chewed on. The archaic term "belike" may be another instance when the gluing must be reversed, and a cut must be made: the result would be *be like*, which highlights the principles of analogy and of acoustic and semantic similarity that make up the text and provide a conceptual framework for it. But "belike" can also be read as a transmutation of *black*, and then the enigmatic phrase "under pump of white chalk" can be taken as yet another allusion to the text's overall design and structure: readers are called upon to discover the lost black under the *pompe funèbre* of the whiteness of the page, as the site for all the words that were written and then cut out again in the process of composition. The same enigmatic phrase could also refer to school: in first grade, children used to learn to write by applying white chalk on a blackboard, which allowed them to wipe out what was written without a trace. Another possibility concerns the place that was so often presented in cubist *papier collés*, namely the Parisian café, where today's specials are written with chalk on a blackboard; Stein might thus allude to similarities and differences between these works and her own. And then the phrase might also refer to a treatise from antiquity that addressed the way that language impinges on visual reference: "Even if we drew one of these Indians with white chalk, he would seem black, for there would be his flat nose and stiff curly locks and prominent jaw to make the picture black for all who can use their eyes," the Pythagorean sage Apollonius once said, as quoted by Philostratus, as quoted in turn by Gombrich (155).

And then the climax: Advice is given to the reader, who must carefully go through the text ("all this combing"); but, of course, "combing" can also be regarded as a self-referential *combining* mutilated by another cut. "Combing" could also refer to Stein's friend and competitor Picasso, who in his *papier collés* frequently used a steel comb to create visual suggestions, of hair for example (see Daix). In yet another variant, "all this combing" brings about a *coming* of the object—a *Second Coming* of the vegetable, should its resurrection as a textual object be achieved—and/or the *coming* of Alice Toklas, for whom cutting vegetables for cooking presumably constituted a practice of religious devotion and erotic pleasure. Or indeed the ecstatic *coming* of Stein in writing this portrait, and perhaps even the *coming* of the reader who enjoys herself in filling in the gaps and surrounding the text by a heap of interlinked words.

This is not a presymbolic *jouissance* however, but the pleasure rendered by a self-reflexive combinatory activity, a working with clues and glues. To be sure, some of the suggested fillings of the gap —the Apollonius quote for instance— are rather exotic. But the point of *Tender Buttons* is not to recover Stein's associations, but to experience how similarity as a fundamental mechanism of *recognition* can also be used to discover connections between things or practices that are discursively and practically kept apart.

## III.

Reading VEGETABLE produces some rather uncanny effects. The text *cuts across* discursive barriers that construct reality as made up of different times, spaces, and social practices: it needs just cutting or pasting a word or two, and the cutting of vegetable will inevitably be read as a ritualist killing. The similarities between cooking and writing figured by the cutting of a vegetable are the most consistent throughout the text, but it is the religious value of the word *cross* (supported and reinforced by *crescent*) that in conjunction with *cut* and *unequal scream* produces the most powerful fit. The similarity between chopping up a vegetable and executing a human being is as irrefutable as it is unsettling.

As categorial and ontological differences are overridden by similarities, questions come up that otherwise remain unasked because they are systematically cut out. The Bible (Gen 1.28) defined the position of human beings on earth as having been given dominion by God over every living thing. In the course of the nineteenth century, Christian belief in a divine act of creation gave way to the evolutionary law of nature. But once "Nature, red in tooth and claw" was invoked to legitimize the human dominion over other life forms, life on earth was constructed as a competition of predators (Tennyson 166). Realizing the similarity between the cutting up of a vegetable and a sacrificial killing implies a change of perspective. Eating is inevitable, if humans are to live. But what are the ontological premises implied in this fact, and what environmental ethics follow from it?

One might be tempted to read VEGETABLE as an instance of modernist primitivism, as a poetic recuperation of a mindset in which the categorial and categorical differences between words, things, and life forms were more permeable. But Stein described the process of composition of *Tender Buttons* as a rigorous conceptual activity of a working with words that rested on making different cuts than those that are made habitually: "It is devilish difficult and needs perfect concentration, you have to refuse so much and so much intrudes itself upon you that you do not want it, it is exhausting work" ("Transatlantic" 29). *Tender Buttons* is neither nostalgic nor subversive, neither sentimental nor accusatory, but experimental. The texts require no other resource than attention—attention to language, to the perceptions of the object, and to the mechanism of one's own consciousness. The discoveries of unrealized or repressed connections can be reproduced by anyone, anytime.

## Notes

**1** | Cf. William James's observation, "the mind makes continual use of the notion of sameness" (1: 460).
**2** | For the relation between Cézanne's and Stein's work see my "Learning from Cézanne" (2016).
**3** | Stein wrote her texts in "French school-children's criss-cross note-books" (Imbs 152).
**4** | See my reading of Loy's portrait of Stein in "The Intermedial Experiments of Modernist Portraiture" (2008).

## Works Cited

Bergson, Henri. *Matter and Memory*. Zone Books, 1991.
Bridgman, Richard. *Gertrude Stein in Pieces*. Oxford University Press, 1970.
Dubnick, Randa. *The Structure of Obscurity: Gertrude Stein, Language, and Cubism*. University of Illinois Press, 1984.
Gombrich, Ernst H. *Art and Illusion: A Study in the Psychology of Pictorial Representation*. Phaidon, 1960.
Haselstein, Ulla. "The Intermedial Experiments of Modernist Portraiture: Mina Loy and Gertrude Stein." *American Studies as Media Studies*, edited by Frank Kelleter and Daniel Stein. Winter, 2008, pp. 169-80.
Haselstein, Ulla. "Learning from Cézanne: Gertrude Stein's Working With and Through Picturing." *Picturing: Perspectives on American Art*, edited by Rachael DeLue. Terra Foundation, 2016, pp. 150-72.
Imbs, Bravig. *Confessions of Another Young Man*. Henkle-Yewdale House, 1936.
James, William. *Principles of Psychology*. Dover, 1950. 2 vols.
Loy, Mina. "Letter to the Editor of The Transatlantic Review." *The Critical Response to Gertrude Stein*, edited by Kirk Curnutt. Greenwood Press, 2000, pp. 178-82.

Murphy, Margueritte S. "'Familiar Strangers': The Household Words of Gertrude Stein's *Tender Buttons*." *Contemporary Literature*, vol. 32, no. 3, 1991, pp. 383-402.

Perloff, Marjorie: "Poetry as Word-System: The Art of Gertrude Stein." *The Poetics of Indeterminacy*. Princeton University Press, 1981, pp. 67-108.

Schmitz, Neil, "Gertrude Stein as Post-Modernist: The Rhetoric of *Tender Buttons*." *Journal of Modern Literature*, vol. 3, no. 5, 1975, pp. 1203-18.

Stein, Gertrude. *Tender Buttons*. Sun and Moon Press, 1991.

Stein, Gertrude. "A Transatlantic Interview." 1946. *A Primer for the Gradual Understanding of Gertrude Stein*, edited by Robert Bartlett Haas. Black Sparrow Press, 1971, pp. 11-35.

Tennyson, Alfred. "In Memoriam A.H.H." *Selected Poems*. Penguin, 1991, pp. 130-224.

Toklas, Alice. *The Alice B. Toklas Cook Book*. Anchor, 1960.

# Flowers

Kirsten Twelbeck

## Mute Eloquence

In the early nineteenth century, an author who simply identifies herself as "a Lady" instructs American readers how to "make the most" of those short-lived, withering "objects which surround us"—the queendom of flowers. First published in 1829, *Flora's Dictionary* becomes a phenomenal success. It is printed several times, culminating in the lavishly illustrated 1855 edition, a beautiful gift book featuring mixed bouquets with flowers of all colors and shapes. In the accompanying explanations, readers learn that yellow acacias convey a concealed love, that jasmine breathes elegance, and that zinnias announce absence. They are also informed that the author's name is Elizabeth Washington Gamble Wirt. As she proudly claims in the preface, she has written the book for the sole purpose of entertaining her family (she is a mother of ten). Yet for the nineteenth-century "true woman," entertainment is also thoroughly educational: listing more than 200 flowers, *Flora's Dictionary* acknowledges the value of botanical categorization while sharing the common admiration of a blooming earth. The actual impetus for the book, however, is a patriotic, transcendentalist longing for "something sacred" to take root in American conversations (Gamble 16). Arranged in the strict alphabetical order of an encyclopedia, *Flora's Dictionary* draws on Middle Eastern and Asian symbolism, scours through British poetry, fantasizes about the popular names of flowers and their botanical definitions, alludes to their scent, look, and medical virtue—all to build associations that aim at replacing "those awkward and delicate *declarations*" of American men with something reminiscent of the "mute eloquence of the eastern lover" (Gamble 16).

## Unfolding

Of course, the language of flowers is not for everyone. In the nineteenth century, few whites believed that a black person, a slave even, could own the capacity "to stamp intelligence and expression on a simple posy" (Gamble 17). It must have been a provocation, or, for some, a moment of triumph, to observe that "the whole front" of Uncle Tom's legendary cabin "was covered by a large, scarlet bignonia and a native multiflora rose, which, entwisting and interlacing, left scarce a vestige of the rough logs to be seen" (Stowe 20). Danger and beauty reside side by side on the plantation, and it is the slave woman's garden that cautions us against the sentimentality of the scene: the "various brilliant annuals, such as marigolds, petunias, four-o'clocks" exude a negative mix of trouble (marigolds), anger (petunias), and timidity (four-o'clocks). What drives Aunt Chloe, the gardener of this "neat garden-patch"? Is the "cook," which she "certainly was, in the very bone and center of her soul," also a healer who works with the magical power of flowers that she knows will "unfold their splendors" (Stowe 20)? In the mid-nineteenth century, homeopathy was more popular in the United States than in Europe, and, like many of their time, the Beecher family relies on homeopaths, hydropaths, and other alternative doctors. Is Aunt Chloe's gardening scheme based on the "like cures like" *(similia similibus curentur)* principle? Or is her flower bed a far cry from a medieval belief in magical spells, but a protective ring to fend off the collective fears of the slave community? Or is it simply a sign for the white reader, a hint at the dark things to come? Whatever the motivation: Chloe appropriates and continues the latest fad that was also further popularizing *Flora's Dictionary*: some editions included blank pages in several colors, inviting readers to contribute their own pressed specimens. Chloe's marigolds, however, are alive, nodding their heads—a black woman's thoughts planted on a white man's property. Chloe seems to know the strengths and limits of her art when she exclaims that "Mas'r George is such a beautiful reader" (27). In the lives of slaves, listening can bring relief. Yet ultimately, literacy is a matter of survival, not beauty.

## Ceremonies

Shortly after Harriet Beecher Stowe had, according to rumor, caused the American Civil War, Dorothea Dix was appointed the Union's Superintendent of Army Nurses. At the time she was known as a tireless crusader for improving the lives of the mentally ill but also as a writer of didactic fiction. Only once did she break out of the moral norms that governed her stories: in 1829 she followed the same popular fad as *Flora's Dictionary* and published *A Garland of Flora*. The book was not only a commercial failure but led Dix to abruptly end her career as a writer. In the self-denigrating manner that was so typical for her gender, she admits that *A Garland of Flora* is an embarrassing example of a woman's "scribbling" and an instance of those "'degenerate days'" that her gender spends in the limelight of the public sphere. More than thirty years later, Dix resolves what had been her personal conflict by combining the idea of respectable womanhood with the concept of female usefulness. While she helped the profession of nursing become a widely accepted female occupation, she set standards that prevented young, good looking, and ambitious women from helping with the wounded. Esther Hill Hawks, for instance, fell victim to those standards. She was one of only a few American women with excellent credentials, including a medical degree. But she was under 30 years old, not a mother, and certainly not "plain looking" enough to become a nurse (a position she had applied for after being turned down as a doctor). Having exhausted all other possibilities to significantly contribute to the Union's cause, she eventually joined an early post-slavery experiment and traveled to the South Carolina Sea Islands—a region that had already been liberated in 1861. Yet instead of working as a missionary (as many others did), she became a doctor in the black hospital of Beaufort. It was here that she learned that many contraband women were raped by Union soldiers stationed there and/or forced into relationships with the officers. And she also came to understand that the few white women residing on these islands were not safe from the "brutal lusts of the soldiers" (Hawks 34). Hawks's diary bears witness to a situation that is rarely talked about. But it also conveys a white woman's alienation from her own culture. After being forced to leave her work as a doctor in the Beaufort hospital, her entries betray an identification with the black community that goes far beyond the widespread appropriation of slavery in the rhetoric of nineteenth-century feminism. Shunned by whites who refused to acknowledge her as a professional doctor, she sought—and found—recognition elsewhere, among the Gullah population. In her diary, the white doctor and teacher is showered with flowers, fruit, and songs that become ideal carriers of provocative, interracial, and feminist messages. The events described appear archaic: the flowers remain unspecified, whether they come singly or in a bouquet is not mentioned. Rather than expressing the dreams and fears of America's emerging white middle class, they serve as ceremonial offerings that distinguish the African American givers as members of a different culture with a more pleasant model of social interaction:

Two of my girls (in my first class) Salina and Rose, came to see [sic] last night and brought, one a can of peaches, and the other a half dozin [sic] eggs—they had just bought them out of their own money and of their own accord—dear girls—it is pleasant to be remembered so kindly. Some of them are constantly bringing me something—which they think I shall relish—and the little children are constantly running in with flowers! (118)

By accepting flowers, fruit, and eggs in exchange for her teaching and support, Hawks replaces Dix's nineteenth-century ethics of female modesty and sacrifice with an earlier and ultimately joyful economy of exchange and mutual recognition that is quite remarkable for her time.

The transitory character of these gifts is significant: Hawks's fantasies of leadership include the promise of a fabulous ceremony in which signs of interracial respect are perpetually renewed. The seemingly endless stream of flowers and songs signals a "democracy in action"—a social contract based on mutual recognition and constant reassurance that firmly acknowledges the many individual stories of rape, exploitation, and cross-racial courage.

## Spring

Bearing large clusters of fragrant purple or white that fade as quickly as they have appeared, lilacs are among the most opulent and ephemeral of flowers. According to *Flora's Dictionary,* lilacs stand for the pure and undefined—a sign of youth and of "the first emotions of love" (134). In his famous elegy for Lincoln, Walt Whitman mourns not only his personal loss of the late President ("him I love") but the nation's bereavement of its "Captain," as he calls him elsewhere ("When Lilacs" 255). Withering away but "ever-returning," the perennial lilac resembles that "drooping star in the west"—a natural spectacle of death and resurgence that repeats itself, over and over again, before the unbelieving eyes of a nation that has already witnessed too many deaths (255). This time, the transience of human grandeur and natural beauty are tied to both personal regret and collective trauma, and there is a yearning to snatch from death a permanent "likeness" (a paradox that drove Whitman's lifelong fascination with photography). Whitman's poetic lilacs are there to last and yet also to fade, "I mourn'd, and yet shall mourn with ever-returning spring" (255). The President's untimely death appears unnatural; unlike lilacs, he shall not return to drench the land in a purple haze (in Christianity, a color signaling a state of transition and change). And yet his legacy will guide the nation—lovingly entangled with that trinity of "lilac and star and bird twined with the chant of [the poet's] soul" (262).

## Rose

Henry Ward Beecher heard about the President's assassination on his journey home, after holding his soon-to-be famous speech at the raising of the Union flag at Fort Sumter. Lincoln had personally asked him to find words of consolation for the Southern population. On a symbolic level, he not only proclaimed a new era of national reconciliation but provided closure to the then popular narrative that the war had been caused by his sister Harriet. The latter was soon to grow so fond of the South that she purchased a plantation and celebrated, in *Palmetto Leaves* (1873), the abundance of yellow jessamine (grace, with tenderness and sense combined) and magnolia (perseverance) that grew in her new home state, South Carolina. Her brother's name, of course, was associated with less flowery items: in the late 1850s he had famously sent twenty-five rifles (counterbalanced by twenty-five Bibles) to Kansas, to an antislavery group that opposed the Kansas-Nebraska Act. In 1868, however, Henry had abandoned the revolution. His first and only novel, *Norwood*, features an imaginary New England community, the "brood-combs" (sic) of an ideal America (Beecher 4). The central female character is named after the queen of flowers—Rose is an extraordinarily intelligent artistic and medical talent. Before the war she studies under the zoologist Louis Agassiz; during the war she expertly performs surgery on a wounded soldier (something that is historically unheard of), and for some time afterward she helps nursing veterans. Coming of age during the Civil War, she knows instinctively where she belongs when peace is about to arrive. The bright and beautiful Rose turns into a self-contented flower lady—taking endless rounds in the garden she has created just outside of her father's library. Rose is ever eager to converse with her father's visitors who praise her for knowing "every plant that grows in this region in the same easy and natural way that she knows all her neighbors. She can tell me the floral calendar of every month. She knows the structure of plants—vegetable physiology, of course; but, in her way of conceiving things, plants have a domestic life" (199-200). After the narrative has repudiated all possible allusions to a feminist logic of female independence, Rose comes into the full bloom as is implied by her name: when she eventually marries a man similar to the young Beecher himself, she happily declares that from here on she will be "a naiad to every rill in your soul; and if your heart were deep as the ocean, I will be the sea-nymph, and gather white corals from the very depths, and bring out hidden treasures from its caves!" (542). Entirely self-sufficient and without a trace of that stubbornness and regret that marked her antebellum sisters, this queen of flowers is the emerging nation's ideal citizen—a constant inspiration to her husband who builds his authority on what is seen as the natural consent of the governed, among them northern blacks and freedmen who prefer to live behind fences.

Meanwhile, Esther Hill Hawks sets up the first interracial school in Smyrna, Florida, and continues to receive flowers from her students (Winslow Homer's 1875 painting "Taking a Sunflower to the Teacher" comes to mind here). When the school is set on fire a few years later, she moves back North and starts her own medical practice, specializing in gynecology.

## Granite

In the early 1880s, almost ten years before the story was published as a book (*Mizora*, 1889), the *Cincinnati Examiner* printed a couple of installments about an unknown country where "[a]nimals and domestic fowls were long extinct," thus causing a "weird silence" (Lane 54). The anonymous author of this strange scene was a middle-aged schoolteacher named Mary Bradley Lane; a woman we know little about to this day. If she seems radical now, she was certainly back then, and yet her views were deeply informed by the scientific debates, philosophical struggles, and collective needs of a restless era. In *Mizora* nature must be tamed to allow for aesthetic appreciation. This is not to ignore that in the late nineteenth century, the death of species, including birds (some of which were hunted to extinction for their feathers), was followed by a nationwide call for responsive policies. And yet the desire for tranquility and structure was excessive: still haunted by images of natural destruction wrought by war, Lane's audience was spared the more threatening aspects of America's landscapes and could find consolation in the "glorious atmosphere" of a feminized picturesque idyll, lying "asleep in voluptuous beauty" (15). Once we move beyond this "enchanted territory," the description centers on the ordering perspective and symmetry of a European garden (15). Carefully arranged and highly artificial, it is organized around a defining center, a marble structure that houses a gigantic college, framed by stairs, fountains and water basins. It is here, right below the rim, that "a wreath of blood red roses, that looked as though they had just been plucked from the stems" meets the eye of the narrating "I" (64). She, the visitor from the real world, reacts stunned—not scandalized—upon realizing that the queen of flowers is not a temporary ornament but "the work of an artist, and durable as granite" (64). Not much is left of that "blush of bashfulness" that *Flora's Dictionary* attaches to the red rose's "angel whiteness."

If traditional beauty is eternal in *Mizora*, and nature is an "effect" of "something charming," they are both brought about exclusively by superior female talent and skill (17). Home to a tribe of hyper-intelligent blonde women, the land of *Mizora* is run by coordinated collective talent that in its organization resembles a beehive: the blondes study and experiment enthusiastically in order to develop their all-female nation further. In their version of the pursuit of happiness, everything falls into place.

Their population is the result of (a not-so-)natural selection—the Civil War and its even more chaotic aftermath had laid bare the enormity of men's inherent inferiority, kicking off a long process of natural selection which eventually led to the extinction of the male gender. Freed from male disaster and from the restraining effect of the "dark race," the novel's Darwinian victors discover "the secret of life" in their laboratories, which allows them to produce ever new daughters for their nation (92, 103). This ultimately helps them abandon the toilsome lives of their ancestors: the pairing of female sensibility with science makes even trimming an unruly rosebush into a desired form and its flowery abundance appear excessive and rude. It is through art (especially sculpture) that the daily battle against the vegetable kingdom can be won, and through modern technology that the dust in the living room can be banished. Ironically, racial segregation is no longer necessary in the eugenic feminist state: with its emphasis on natural selection and natural hierarchy, the Mizoran universe is surprisingly similar to Beecher's *Norwood*; a "cosmic success story" where everything falls into place. Yet while in the minister's novel, a gang of happy freedmen allows for a leisurely, inspirational lifestyle in the white village, it is little machines that enable the essentially posthuman world of the monumental blondes.

There is, of course, a dystopian impulse in the Mizoran notion of human-centered, proto-fascist biopower—even their awestruck visitor decides to leave after fifteen years of admiration: she is, after all, a brunette, and dearly misses the non-rational dimensions of the human, our animal side, which the Mizorans eliminated so successfully, along with all the roses.

## Color

Although Reconstruction was officially over, the state of political instability continued: sectional relations were fragile, economic suffering was widespread, and former slaves still flocked to the cities, looking for safety from white supremacist violence, but also for work and community. In the late eighteen-seventies, Walt Whitman traveled to Philadelphia and collected "queer, taking, rather sad" impressions of a tramp family, consisting of a wife whose "figure and gait told misery, terror, and destitution," and "a real hermit, living in a lonesome spot, hard to get at, rocky," who does not reveal "his life, or story, or tragedy, or whatever it is" (*Specimen Days* 115, 116, 131). When Whitman reaches his destination, the densely populated Chestnut Street in downtown Philadelphia, he lists:

The peddlers on the sidewalk ("sleeve-buttons, three to five cents")—the handsome little fellow with canary-bird whistles—the cane men, toy men, toothpick men—the old woman squatted in a heap on the cold stone flags, with her basket of matches, pins, and tape—the young negro mother, sitting, begging, with her two little coffee-color'd twins on her lap—the beauty of the cramm'd conservatory of rare flowers, flaunting reds, yellows, snowy lilies, incredible orchids, at the Baldwin mansion near Twelfth street . . . . (128)

Cursory as it may seem, the street scene is carefully conceived as it refuses to isolate race relations from the larger kaleidoscope of precariousness. And yet the emblematic family of three mentioned here oscillates between belonging and marginalization. Symbolically placed at the lower end of a society that struggles economically, and wholly dependent on the support of others, the "young negro mother" of twins (signaling her fecundity) is the least hopeful of those who try their luck on Chestnut Street. Powerfully juxtaposed against a description of the "conservatory of rare flowers" and "the Baldwin mansion," her misery suggests a racial dimension that complicates this seemingly harmonious picture of multifaceted poverty and individual effort. In a metonymic shift, the image of the black mother with her children is captured in the metaphorical conservatory, waiting to be admired just like the "incredible orchids" of the wealthy.

As has been argued with regard to the poetic figure of the "black whale," Whitman warranted particular attention to color as metaphor, and there is often a strong racial component to this usage (Beach 55-100). Immediately linked to the black mother and her "coffee-color'd twins," the "rare flowers, flaunting reds, yellows, snowy lilies, incredible orchids" invoke popular definitions of the shades of blackness that circulated in nineteenth-century America and that were often associated with the names of flowers. (The antebellum folk song "The Yellow Rose of Texas" comes to mind here: "There's a yellow rose in Texas, that I am going to see / No other darky knows her, no darky only me˙). In Whitman's street scene, despair and poverty, beauty and abundance, but also exoticism and a sexualized lack of constraint are intertwined. The metaphor is dense and multilayered: cast as an exhilarating spectacle of otherness, the black family beautifies a new, lively, and diverse America. And yet the ensemble is strangely removed from the bustling street scene; it appears "cramm'd in" the conservatory of the rich white man's mansion: after all, this nineteenth-century tableau vivant puts on display the "rare flowers" of slavery and miscegenation. Whitman, who could never bring himself to fully welcome African Americans as part of his postwar democratic vision, left it to his readers to decide whether, and to what degree, this "exotic" constellation would be free from the trauma and economic deprivation that, years after the Emancipation Proclamation, continued to separate them from the hopes and opportunities of white Americans.

## Beguiling Scents

By including orchids as exotic objects of contemplation, Whitman deviated from his usual repertoire of native species. This is not to say that he did not seek inspiration outside the confines of his country—he was, in fact, fascinated by the mystical and spiritual traditions of Asia, and Indian thought in particular helped him on his quest for wholeness and for the spiritual re-invigoration of the American self. Whitman lived long enough to observe how American sensationalist media turned to urban Chinatowns to cater to their readers' desire for a pleasurable thrill. But by 1898, when his country annexed Hawaii and decided to join Europe's imperialist venture into Asia, the "good gray poet" lay buried in Camden (he had died in 1892). It fell upon a younger generation, one that was born after the Civil War, to cast a critical eye on this late nineteenth-century hunger for an obscure East. In Frank Norris's *The Octopus* (1901), a city club for the nouveaux riches seeks to fill the spiritual void that it has created by inviting a fakir for a leisurely teatime. One of their favorite guests is a Japanese youth who "delivered himself of the most astonishing poems, vague, unrhymed, unmetrical lucubrations, incoherent, bizarre" (Norris 157).

What Norris worries about is not the "real" Asia of trade and commerce (although transpacific expansion is clearly an issue in *The Octopus*) but what Americans make of the new frontier, west of California. How exactly are they affected, as individuals and as a collective, by the transpacific endeavor? In *The Octopus* they lose their sense of belonging to either place or time. While urban elites flock around the latest yogi to circumvent social responsibilities at their very doorstep, the less privileged are personally doomed. For them, the dream of the Orient brings individual development to an untimely halt. The tragedy unfolds in the subplot involving Vanamee: the shepherd, in this wheat-growing community that most of the book focuses on, is traumatized by the rape and murder of his beloved Angéle, the daughter of a flower farmer. A recurring, oriental-looking apparition dominates the deserted lover's mind and spirit, and he avails himself of telepathic prayer to conjure up the ever-same nightly encounter:

She came to him from out of the flowers, the smell of roses in her hair of gold, that hung in two straight plaits on either side of her face; the reflection of the violets in the profound dark blue of her eyes, perplexing, heavy-lidded, almond-shaped, oriental; the aroma and the imperial red of the carnations in her lips, with their almost Egyptian fullness; the whiteness of the lilies, the perfume of the lilies, and the lilies' slender balancing grace in her neck. . . . The folds of her dress gave off the enervating scent of poppies. (72)

Repeated at various moments in the novel, the scene performs narrative trauma by linking the apparition to an exaggerated visual and olfactory impression of flowers. Vanamee falls prey to the multi-sensual power of an abysmally beautiful bouquet: a mix of presumed innocence (roses), "female love" (violets and carnations), "purity" and "sweetness" (lilies), whose scent is superimposed by the perfume of poppies—a plant associated with consolation and death (according to *Flora's Dictionary*), but also with San Francisco's opium dens. Unsurprisingly, this story about dangerous blooms ends in addiction: when Vanamee eventually meets Angéle's daughter, who looks just like her mother, his obsession transforms into madness. For him who fails to understand the multiple meanings of flowers, there is no love, no home, and no sanity.

## Into the Open

In the nineteen-twenties, the language of flowers was no longer à la mode, but roses continued to be roses, and baby girls were still given names such as Daisy, Heather, and Violet. Gertrude and Georgia deviated from the established floral scheme, and it may in fact have made it easier for them to use flowers to break with the dead forms of the past. Let us not repeat Gertrude's famous repetition or resort again to discussing what flowers and vaginas have in common. O'Keeffe had mocked the persistently male gaze of her critics during her lifetime by referencing Alfred Stieglitz's famous *Portrait of O'Keeffe*, a collection of approximately three hundred photographs that her husband took over a period of more than twenty years. Initially, these (often nude) portraits threatened to destroy the career of the young woman, but she soon managed to use them as inspiration for a particularly creative, cross-media dialogue with her husband. One can easily find, in the black-and-white *Portrait* photographs, the model for O'Keeffe's "Alligator Pears"—two greenish fruit that protrude seductively, not from a leisurely-worn nightgown but from a folded piece of pure white fabric.

One way of looking at O'Keeffe's oeuvre is by concentrating on her experiments with form and color. Flowers were just a beginning, before she ventured into the open landscapes of New Mexico with its shades of white, brown, red, ochre—and a blue "that will always be there as it is now after all man's destruction is finished." The sparseness of that landscape allowed her to combine a ram's head with a single blue morning glory or a white hollyhock, and a bleached cow's skull with two calico roses. These flowers, as well as their replications, do not decorate what remains of an animal after death, but lend new meaning to it simply by sharing the same space—a seemingly white surface, often hovering above the glorious colors of a mountain that talks and sings to us, to you.

## Works Cited

Beach, Christopher. *The Politics of Distinction: Whitman and the Discourses of Nineteenth-Century America*. University of Georgia Press, 1996.

Beecher, Henry Ward. *Norwood: Or, Village Life in New England*. 1868. Charles Scribner, 2010.

Brown, Thomas J. *New England Reformer*. Harvard University Press, 1998.

Daly, Ann. "Line, Color, Composition." *The Smart Set*, vol. 1, no. 4, 2016, thesmartset.com/line-color-composition.

Folsom, Ed. "The Vistas of Democratic Vistas: An Introduction." *Democratic Vistas: By Walt Whitman*. University of Iowa Press, 2010. pp. xv-lxvii.

Gamble, Elizabeth Washington. *Flora's Dictionary*. Fielding Lucas Jr., 1832.

Hawks, Esther Hill. *A Woman Doctor's Civil War: Esther Hill Hawks' Diary*, edited by Gerald Schwartz, University of South Carolina Press, 1984.

Hendrik, Joan B. *Harriet Beecher Stowe: A Life*. Oxford University Press, 1995.

Lane, Mary Bradley. *Mizora: A Prophecy: An 1880s Radical Feminist Utopia*. 1889. Edited by Jean Pfaelzer, Syracuse University Press, 2000.

Norris, Frank. *The Octopus: A Story of California*. 1901. ReadaClassic, 2011.

O'Keeffe, Georgia, "About Painting Desert Bones." *Georgia O'Keeffe: Paintings, An American Place*, 1944, n.pag.

Rathbone, Belinda, et al. *Two Lives: Georgia O'Keeffe & Alfred Stieglitz: A Conversation in Paintings and Photographs*. Harper Collins, 1992.

Stowe, Harriet Beecher. *Uncle Tom's Cabin*. Wordsworth, 1995.

Whitman, Walt. *Specimen Days & Collect*. 1882. Dover, 1995.

---. "When Lilacs Last in the Dooryard Bloom'd." *Leaves of Grass*. David McKay, 1891, pp. 255-62.

# Arboreal Encounters in Richard Powers's *The Overstory*

Birgit Spengler

> To be human is to confuse a satisfying story with a meaningful one, and to mistake life for something huge with two legs.
> —Richard Powers, *The Overstory*

> Time is the shape of an old oak as the winds caress and sculpt the bark.... Time is the trunk that splits apart in great age to accommodate the tempest. Evidence of time is revealed in the furrowed bark of an ancient tree, gnarled, crooked, and beautiful.
> —Beth Moon, *Ancient Trees*

In his 2013 book *Plant-Thinking*, Michael Marder calls for an extension of the attention that has been directed to "the question of the animal" (1) in order to encompass "non-human, non-animal living beings" and to overcome "the absence of the will to think through the logic of vegetal life, beyond its biochemical, cellular, or micro-molecular processes and ecological patterns" (2). Rather than relegating such life forms to the lower levels of taxonomic orders or reducing them to the status of resources to be exploited, Marder asks: "How is it possible . . . to encounter plants? And how can we maintain and nurture, without fetishizing it, their otherness in the course of this encounter?" (3). Marder's philosophical intervention for a new commitment towards vegetal life resonates with the work of ecofeminists such as Donna Haraway, who also demands a reconceptualization of our relation to the nonhuman world and a greater degree of "response-ability on a damaged earth" (*Staying* 2). For Haraway, one way to achieve this goal is to engage in what she describes as "tentacular thinking" (5) and "sympoietic threading, felting, tangling" (31)—cognitive and material ways of relating to the world that should replace notions of human exceptionalism and "bounded individualism" (5) since the latter have proven to be unsustainable for our ecosystem and the many "critter[s]" that inhabit it (61).[1] As Haraway points out, to "make kin in lines of inventive connection" is a necessity in order "to live and die well with each other in a thick present" (1). And it is the very "thickness" of this present, which Haraway captures through the concept of the *Chthulucene*, and its "myriad temporalities and spatialities and myriad intra-active entities-in-assemblages—including the more-than-human, other-than-human, inhuman, and human-as-humus"— that need acknowledgement in the first place in order to cultivate more sustainable forms of human-nonhuman interaction ("Anthropocene" 160).

As Haraway's emphasis on "myriad temporalities," "spatialities," and "intra-active entities-in-assemblages" indicates, ushering in such a paradigm shift depends on unsettling anthropocentric notions of world, including conceptualizations of time and space that are at the core of our present political order and the exploitative-extractive economies that have shaped Western modernity.[2] Mary Louise Pratt has recently drawn attention to the potential of Mikhail Bakhtin's concept of the chronotope for projects like this, suggesting that the chronotope can function as "a device, and an invitation, for Western-identified subjects to resituate themselves in the space-time-matter of the planet" (G171). If we consider the chronotope a historically variable "configuration of time and space that generates stories through which a society can examine itself" (Pratt G170), and our contemporary chronotopes as primarily anthropocentric, it does not seem far-fetched to ask how attempting to think time and space from a nonhuman perspective—for example, the point of view of plant life—might change the stories we tell, the ways we construct reality, and help generate new forms of "response-ability" towards the nonhuman world as well as human life forms.[3]

In my contribution to this volume on encounters in a more-than-human world, I will read Richard Powers's 2018 novel *The Overstory* as an attempt to foster such reimagining. I will argue that *The Overstory* examines possibilities for a new ontology of human and nonhuman lives by juxtaposing and negotiating human- and plant-oriented chronotopes. These alternative imaginings emerge through the novel's exploration of the agency of trees, through dramatizing the sympoietic entanglements of vegetal and non-vegetal live forms, and through conceptualizing time and space in ways that destabilize an exclusively anthropocentric perspective. Before focusing on Powers's novel, I will introduce Bakhtin's concept of the chronotope and briefly explore the ways in which recent plant research may provide a basis for unsettling conceptualizations of time, space, and being-in-time-and-space that inform notions of human exceptionalism, bounded individualism, as well as the political and economic practices that have accompanied them in Western modernity. I will then turn to the ways in which *The Overstory* constructs the agency of trees and the entanglement of life forms as ways of decentering such anthropocentric concepts and attitudes. In the final section of my essay, I will return to the chronotope to argue that Powers's novel prods its readers to reimagine time and space in more- (and other-) than-human terms.

## Bakhtin's Chronotope

Bakhtin introduces the concept of the chronotope in his essay "Forms of Time and of the Chronotope in the Novel" (1937/38, 1973). The term chronotope literally means time-space and is used by Bakhtin to describe "the intrinsic connectedness of temporal and spatial relationships that are artistically expressed in literature":

In the literary artistic chronotope, spatial and temporal indicators are fused into one carefully thought-out, concrete whole. Time, as it were, thickens, takes on flesh, becomes artistically visible; likewise, space becomes charged and responsive to the movements of time, plot and history. This "intersection . . . and fusion" of indicators characterizes the artistic chronotope. (84)

It is this "intrinsic connectedness," as well as the "intersection" and "fusion" of time and space emphasized by Bakhtin which turn the chronotope into a useful conceptual tool for a culturally informed literary analysis. The time-space arrangements that Bakhtin refers to in terms of the chronotope are not just the basis for any fictional conceptualization of "world," but also the interface between a work of fiction and its cultural context. As Bakhtin emphasizes, historically specific configurations of time and space shape fictional texts as well as the cultural contexts from which they arise: "All the novel's abstract elements—philosophical and social generalizations, ideas, analyses of cause and effect—gravitate toward the chronotope and through it take on flesh and blood, permitting the imaging power of art to do its work" (250). The chronotopic makeup of a literary text therefore has far-reaching implications. It reflects the *episteme* that informs a text—its epistemological and ontological presuppositions as well as the scientific, political, social, and cultural discourses that shape it. As Bakhtin scholar Sue Vice puts it, through the model of the chronotope, Bakhtin insists "on a social and political reading of time and space" (209). Bakhtin's genealogy of chronotopes therefore also reflects changing conceptualizations of subjectivity and world.

Since the chronotope foregrounds the historicity and discursivity of our conceptualizations of time and space, and with them the situatedness of human beings and human knowledge, it seems to be ideally suited for the project of a repositioning of "Western-identified subjects . . . in the space-time-matter of the planet" that has been demanded by ecofeminists (Pratt G171). Specifically, the chronotope presents itself as an analytical tool for investigating the discursive and ideological implications of time-space arrangements on a representational and conceptual level and for opening up alternative imaginings of space and time that may contribute to re-situating ourselves on a planetary scale.[4]

Finally, the chronotope is also a concept that emphasizes the continuities between the human(-made) and "world" and, therefore, the fundamental relationality of existence. Bakhtin argues this point explicitly regarding the relationship between products of the human imagination and "world," that is, between literary and extra-literary chronotopes: the "actual chronotopes of our world" and "the reflected and *created* chronotopes of the world represented in the work" are "indissolubly tied up with each other and find themselves in continual mutual interaction; uninterrupted exchange goes on between them, similar to the uninterrupted exchange of matter between living organisms and the environment that surrounds them" (253, 254). By emphasizing "mutual interaction"—a process of exchange that goes in both directions—Bakhtin moves beyond a mimetic concept of literature and grants art a potentially world-changing power. And yet, as products of the human imagination, artistic chronotopes are themselves an expression of the fundamentally chronotopic nature of our existence. Rather than being "bounded individuals," our imaginative as well as our physical life involves us in forms of exchange and interspecies interdependencies, from the bacteria that live within our bodies to the trees that make life on Earth possible by producing oxygen and that have provided the material basis for dialogic exchange between and across generations of human animals.

## Plant Life and the Renarrativisation of World

A change of our relationship to the biosphere and any attempt to save the life forms currently existing on Earth requires more than a change of the stories we tell. Nevertheless, considering "the time-space matter of the planet" on a nonhuman scale and taking into account what we know today about the agency of nonhuman life forms may go a long way towards the ontological re-orientation that ecofeminists, plant philosophers, and environmental activists demand in order to develop sustainable ways of "living on a damaged planet."[5] As Elizabeth Grosz succinctly puts it, narratives can "enable us to surround ourselves with possibilities for being otherwise" and to *think* these possibilities in the first place (78).[6] It is therefore little surprising that philosopher and eco-feminist Val Plumwood calls for a "renarrativisation" of our place in and a "re-animating" of the world that acknowledges the "fluidity of the human," a "flowing on into the non-human, both at death, and in historical, evolutionary terms from non-human as well as human ancestors" (125, 121).[7]

Both fictional and scientific narratives can provide forms of and incentives for such renarrativisation. What is known today about the lives of trees and plants can have a large-scale effect on how we think time, space, and the relationality of existence, if we allow these insights to unsettle long-held certainties about the ostensible distinctions and hierarchies between human and so-called vegetal life in terms of agency and forms of intelligence.[8] For example, recent work in the field of biosemiotics "conceives of language as an evolutionary response" or form of "world making" that humans share with other forms of life and through which "beings bring forth their lifeworlds (or *Umwelten*) in dynamic conjunction with the lifeworlds of other entities" (Gagliano et al. xix). This extended and non-anthropocentric concept of language includes forms of expression such as "sensuous, bodily, and material forms ... that most animate and inanimate beings possess," and it helps us to move away from an understanding of language as something unique to human and, potentially, animal life, and to acknowledge the ability of worldmaking through communication with one's surroundings pertaining to other life forms, including plants (xx).

Communicative processes and social networks among plants are also at the center of Peter Wohlleben's popular scientific account of the *Secret Lives of Trees* and the work of botanists, biochemists, and forest ecologists such as Diana Beresford-Kroeger and Suzanne Simar.[9] Wohlleben elaborates on recent insights into the ability of plants for language by detailing various mechanisms of tree communication, but he also discusses what might be described as social behavior among trees, as well as processes associated with learning and memory. For example, Wohlleben describes the ways in which nutrients are being exchanged among networks of trees, thereby helping to sustain members of the community that run short, he reports on 400- to 500-year-old tree stumps still supplied with sugar by their network (10), and he explains the symbiotic and mutually beneficent relationships among trees and fungi (50-55). Wohlleben also accounts for learning processes among trees (46-47) and discusses tree communication (or "language") via mycorrhizal systems of roots and fungi, aerosols such as ethylene, as well as other chemical and electric forms of signaling (14-20). While Wohlleben's sustained anthropomorphization of trees does not exactly move beyond the human, it effectively challenges ideas of human exceptionalism and fosters a greater appreciation of nonhuman life forms.

Plant neurobiologists are going a step further yet and suggest that even though plants do not have neurons and brains, they seem to have structures that fulfill analogous functions and emit neuro transmitters such as serotonin (see Pollan, "Plants"). If considering the emission of a chemical and the purposeful movement of roots as behavior, it is indeed justified to speak of "plant behavior." Similarly, if intelligence is defined broadly in terms of a problem-solving ability, we will discover more continuities between human and nonhuman forms of life than we may care to admit.¹⁰ Granting such communicative abilities, intelligence, and forms of agency to trees and other nonhuman, non-animal life beckons us to reconsider the ways we coexist and engage with the other-than-human because it renders ostensibly stable distinctions between "us" and "them" fuzzy. The life forms of trees and other plants—their longevity, movement in space and time, and ability to make connections—may therefore provide the basis for a new episteme, one that reconsiders the place of the human and nonhuman in the "time-space matter of [our] planet," to once again use Pratt's apt phrase.

If recent research in plant neurobiology and biosemiotics provides an important scientific basis for "surround[ing] ourselves with possibilities for being otherwise" (Grosz 78), fiction, too, can contribute in important ways to transforming our "ecosocial imaginary" (James, "Plant" 253). One important way of doing so lies in the potential of fiction to reimagine time and space and reflect on the possibilities of time-space arrangements that present alternatives to dominant ways of conceptualizing our being in the world.¹¹ While there is no place beyond discourse, the potential of the fictive lies in its ability to give shape to the imaginary and thereby challenge the (ostensibly) historically given by moving beyond what passes as mimetic in a specific place and moment in time: this would be one way in which fictional chronotopes interact with and potentially impact extra-literary time-spaces according to Bakhtin.¹² On the basis of emergent discourses, works of the imagination such as fictional texts may reflect upon potential paradigm shifts and help bring them about. Fictional texts (among other forms) can therefore contribute in important ways to a renarrativisation of world, a reconsidering of our relationship to the biosphere, and to the remaking of kin.¹³

## The Agency and Language of Trees in *The Overstory*

Inspired by the recent insights of foresters, dendrologists, and scientists such as Wohlleben, Simard, Beresford-Kroeger, Trewavas, and Gagliano, *The Overstory* offers a rich appraisal of tree agency that unsettles long-cherished certainties concerning the distinctions between human and nonhuman life forms. In particular, it is through the discoveries of Patricia Westerford, a forest ecologist, that the novel introduces recent scientific insights about the "lives" of trees and imbues nonhuman, non-animal life with its own agency. In the course of a lifetime of research dispersed over 500 pages, Patricia becomes the novel's most explicit proponent of a reconsideration of plant life, for example, when she discovers that trees are social beings that share and trade nutrients and that communicate via "airborne aerosol signals" to warn other trees of attacking species and to build up a form of immune system that can help the collective survive (Powers 137, 126).¹⁴ Scientific insights such as these have an enabling function, familiarizing the reader with forms of plant agency and promoting the above-mentioned disposition requested by Marder "to think through the logic of vegetal life" (2). By depicting a scientist disposed to do this type of thinking, *The Overstory* lends ontological weight to it and renders it more acceptable. Patricia's initial ostracism from the scientific community and her rehabilitation some twenty years later model a reader's possible change of mindset, if not a larger paradigm shift.

Perhaps more importantly than providing new knowledge about trees, lending scientific weight to it, and modeling a change of scientific paradigms, numerous passages in *The Overstory* illustrate the consequences of such an understanding of our environment. In this way, the implications of a world imbued with nonhuman agency become imaginatively and emotionally available for the reader. Thus, a forest turns into a time-space in which constant micro activities bespeak the agency of vegetal life—an agency that usually remains hidden below the relatively coarse levels of human perception due to its diminutive scale and the relative slowness of change: "Clicks and chatter disturb the cathedral hush. The air is so twilight-green she feels like she's underwater. It rains particles—spore clouds, broken webs and mammal dander, skeletonized mites, bits of insect frass and bird feather. . . . Everything climbs over everything else, fighting for scraps of light" (134). Sections like this in the novel present the forest as an animate world shaped by the sounds, matter, and activities of nonhuman life. Their great degree of immediacy does not simply make scientific knowledge accessible on a cognitive level, but renders its implications palpable for the reader, offering a mediated form of encounter with plants that may, in turn, affect her future experiences of encounter.

While Powers tends to place the reader in proximity to a character's experience, *The Overstory* occasionally leaves it open whose perceptions are rendered and, at times, approaches the non-focalized stance that purports to convey an accepted or superior knowledge of world:

High up, *beyond* his sight, rocky outcrops crawl with manzanita, shedding their curling, crimson barks. Bay laurels rim the logger-made meadows. Canyons thicken with orange madrone peeling to creamy, clammy green. Coast live oaks like the one that crippled him gather on the crags. And down in cool riparian corridors smelling of silt and decaying needles, redwoods work a plan that will take a thousand years to realize—*the plan that now uses him, although he thinks it's his*. (111; italics mine)

The novel's movement between different types of focalization and degrees of distance has two important effects. First of all, passages like the above transform the impression of an agency of nonhuman life forms from a subjective experience to an ostensible "truth" by assigning descriptions of an agentive natural world to a neutral or omniscient center of focalization, thereby investing them with an authority that moves beyond the limitations and potential erring of an individual character's perceptions. Secondly, by rendering the lines between interior, zero, and external focalization deliberately and strategically "fuzzy" in selected passages of the novel, Powers employs the resulting ambiguity to effectively withhold a stable or even unequivocal basis of knowledge. This lack of positivism is, in turn, the de facto basis for any epistemic shift.[15]

A different dimension of the "agency of nonhuman matter" (James, "Narrative") is foregrounded in the epigraphic introductions preceding the four sections "Roots," "Trunk," "Crown," and "Seeds." Set off typographically from the main text, these sections also disrupt its chronological progression and take up issues such as the communication of trees, their "narrative agency," as well as matters of time, space, and mobility.[16] For example, the first introduction, which cannot be precisely located in terms of time, takes up Plumwood's bidding to think about nature "in the active voice" (126) by moving between passages that anticipate Patricia's later insights into the biochemistry of tree communication and those that take the idea of tree communication more literally and translate the potential—and timeless—"messages" transmitted by trees through physical and biochemical processes into a quasi-human voice.

This "active" voice communicates what might best be described as a "tree ontology"—insights that prod the reader to imagine how the world may "look" or "feel" from the perspective of trees and may therefore trigger a re-orientation of the reader's understanding of world along the lines envisioned by ecofeminists: "In re-animating, we become open to hearing sound as voice, seeing movement as action, adaptation as intelligence and dialogue, coincidence and chaos as the creativity of matter" (Plumwood 125). This rendering of nature in a—literally—active voice may, of course, seem overly anthropomorphizing. As, for example, John Bennett argues in response to Plumwood, "[m]any diverse approaches are needed, but in terms of cognitive change in our knowledge, beliefs, attitudes and articulated values, it is not necessarily a re-animating intentionality . . . that we need, but a realisation of the ontology of natural processes, and this sense of our belonging." *The Overstory* attempts to have it both ways: suspend readers' epistemic disbelief in talking trees and harnessing the ideas—or words— "voiced" by trees into the service of bringing into being a new ontology.

In addition to introducing trees in "the active voice" by addressing the biochemical dimension of tree communication and offering anthropomorphizing acts of "translation," the epigraphic sections introduce the idea of a physical and material narrative agency of trees as yet another dimension of their communicability. According to Erin James, this focus on the narrativity of organic and inorganic matter—for example, rocks or tree rings—is one way to challenge traditional ideas about narrativity in the service of unsettling anthropocentrism

("Narrative"). In *The Overstory*, the narrative agency of trees includes fleeting as well as durable forms of narrativity that can provide encompassing stories to those whose reading skills are apt enough to decipher them: "the spruces pour out messages in media of their own invention. They speak through their needles, trunks, and roots. They record in their own bodies the history of every crisis they have lived through" (356). The novel thus presents tree language in terms of a complex semiology that includes the visible and invisible, minuscule particles as well as large-scale physical movements, fleeting signs as well as the durable manifestation of events—signals more elaborate and "hundreds of millions of years older" than the "crude senses" of human beings (356). These include scent in the air, the distribution of pollen, the movement of branches and leaves in the wind, and evergreen tips of spruces that "sketch and scribble in the morning sky" (3, 356).

The mediality of tree language and the narrative agency of trees is most central in the introduction to the section "Trunk," in which a wooden desk turns into a "text" to be deciphered:

The grain under his fingers swings in uneven bands—thick light, thin dark. It shocks him to realize, after a lifetime of looking at wood: He's staring at the seasons, the year's pendulum, the burst of spring and the enfolding of fall, the beat of a two-four song recorded here, in a medium that the piece itself created. The grain wanders like ridges and ravines on a topo map. Pale rush forward, darker holding back. For a moment, the rings resolve from out of the angled cut. He can map them, project their histories into the wood's plane. And still, he's illiterate. Wide in the good years—sure—and narrow in the bad. But nothing more.
If he could read, if he could translate. . . . If he were only a slightly different creature, then he might learn all about how the sun shone and the rain fell and which way the wind blew against this trunk for how hard and long. He might decode the vast projects that the soil organized, the murderous freezes, the suffering and struggle, shortfalls and surpluses, the attacks repelled, the years of luxury, the storms outlived, the sum of all the threats and chances that came from every direction, in every season this tree ever lived. His finger moves across the prison desk, trying to learn this alien script, transcribing it like a monk in a scriptorium. He traces the grain and thinks of all the things this antique, illegible almanac could say, all the things that the remembering wood might tell him, in this place where he is held, with no change of seasons and one fixed weather. (155-56)

Granting trees (a limited) narrative agency destabilizes categorical distinctions between human and nonhuman life forms. The narratives that are being yielded, however, differ drastically from the stories that have been the focus of Western traditions. They would require us to reconsider notions of character, events, time, space, and plot as well as their role and function in the stories we tell. Perhaps most importantly, the narratives recorded by trees foreground their situated and communal character: they may tell the life story of an "individual" tree (if such a thing exists), but always tell a story of multiple dependencies, entanglements, and relationality.

## Creative Liasons: String Figures in the "Wood-Wide Web"[17]

As argued above, *The Overstory* shares with contemporary ecocritical philosophers an interest in the question of how to rethink and reestablish community on a basis that goes beyond notions of human exceptionalism and bounded individualism. In addition to presenting trees as agentic and communicative beings, this concern also expresses itself through the novel's use of entanglement as a motive and structural principle. Such entanglements resemble Haraway's concept of the "string figure" and related modes of "tentacular thinking," which exemplify processes of "sympoiesis" or "making-with" in Haraway's terminology (*Staying* 3, 5).[18] Haraway uses the string figure to denote three related, but distinct phenomena: it is (a) a concept, "theoretical trope" (31), and mode of inquiry that emphasizes connections and entanglements between different "critters" and life forms; (b) a term for the sympoietic phenomenon that triggers such tracing; and (c) a model for collaborative efforts and engagement with others (3). In its three dimensions, the string figure stands for our "response-ability" (2) and connectivity: whether, how, and with whom we "make kin" will determine the future of the planet.

Different types of string figures shape *The Overstory* on a formal and on a thematic level. While the novel as a whole can be read as a string figure in terms of a mode of inquiry, the string figures created by trees through processes of sympoiesis—both through entanglements with other trees and through modes of collaboration with or connections to other species—are a central focus of the text on a thematic level while also functioning as a model for other collaborative efforts in the diegetic world.

As outlined above, Patricia Westerford's scientific work revolves around the communication between trees as well as other forms of what could be called their "social" behavior, including the exchange of nutrients and aerosol warning systems that help the collective survive. However, the sociality and entanglements of trees go far beyond occasionally helping out a fellow tree. Douglas firs, for instance, grow lateral roots that connect with one another when their tips make physical contact, thus joining "their vascular system" and effectively turning them into a single organism—an interspecies organism in fact, because the trees' roots are infused by fungi in such a way as to make it "hard," if not impossible, "to say where one organism leaves off and the other begins" (Westerford 142, 141):

Networked together underground by countless thousands of miles of living fungal threads, her trees feed and heal each other, keep their young and sick alive, pool their resources and metabolites into community chests. . . . Her trees are far more social than . . . suspected. There are no individuals. There aren't even separate species. Everything in the forest is the forest. Competition is not separable from endless flavors of cooperation. (142)

Such insights about vegetal life forms unsettle deeply ingrained ideas of bounded individualism that are at the core of modern Western conceptualizations of self.[19] Hence, the destabilization of the hierarchies that inform our attempts at ordering the world, and which occurs when ostensibly inanimate matters assert their agency, creates an experience of the uncanny:

She sees why her kind will always dread these close, choked thickets, where the beauty of solo trees gives way to something massed, scary, and crazed. When the fable turns dark, when the slasher film builds to primal horror, this is where the doomed children and wayward adolescents must wander. There are things in here worse than wolves and witches, primal fears that no amount of civilizing will ever tame. (135)

The primal horror of this scene does not lie in that which may be hidden by the "close, choked thickets," but in the secret fear, if not repressed knowledge, that human mastery of nature and the projection of a human-devised order onto nature cannot do justice to the "thickness" of world. The "massed, scary, and crazed" is the surplus of "world" that cannot be mastered, named, or tamed, and the dense forest signifies the return of this repressed knowledge. What would be more effective in further repressing this uncomfortable inkling than putting the axe to the tree and clearing out the thick "understory"?

Rather than performing such cropping, *The Overstory*'s structure and plot recreate the entangled life forms of trees in order to promote a more-than-human frame of orientation, but suggesting that human lives, too, follow patterns that more closely resemble the ontology of plant life than traditional ideas about "plot" or "story," which tend to carry a teleological impetus. This use of tree life as a sense-making strategy is foregrounded by the titles of the novel's four sections. "Roots" introduces the reader to nine characters in eight short stories or chapters that appear to be unrelated other than through their shared thematic concern and the individual characters' "entanglements" with trees. Fittingly, the chapters' or stories' deeper coherence at first remains largely "below ground," unstated, submerged, functioning like the root system of trees, which are connected by "[m]ats of mycorrhizal cabling" that "link trees into gigantic, smart communities spread across hundreds of acres" (218). The "Trunk" that evolves from these roots brings ostensibly separate threads or stories more closely together by rendering their subliminal, subterranean connection manifest. "Crown" depicts the results of this coming-together and leads to the dispersal of the protagonists and their ideas in the final section, "Seeds."

If the novel's structure thus resembles a string figure by depicting the entanglements of various human and nonhuman forms of life and by using the non-teleological and non-individualistic life form of trees as an underlying pattern, its first section, "Roots," also fleshes out the idea of interspecies entanglement on a less abstract level. As shown in its eight chapters, each of the main characters' lives is entangled with a tree or trees, thus essentially presenting a string figure: an American Chestnut tree planted in Iowa by Norwegian immigrants will become an artistic inspiration to their descendant, Nick Hoel, and a symbol of his life as the lone survivor of a family tragedy; a Mulberry tree's surrender to blight drives Mimi Ma's father into suicide; a banyan tree saves the life of airforce pilot Douglas Pavlicek and turns him into a tree activist later on. And while an oak is involved in an accident that leaves Neelay Mehta crippled at age 11, his encounters with trees two decades later turn him into the highly successful inventor of a computer game that will attempt to train players to a new world view—a cultural medium that, not unlike literature, can harness the imaginary's innovative potential and denaturalize learned patterns of behavior and perception, including those of space and time. Ray Brinkman and his wife Dorothy, a childless couple, decide to plant a tree every year at their wedding anniversary; Patricia Westerford dedicates her life to the study of trees; and Adam Apich, who has a boyhood attachment to a maple tree—a species associated with endurance—will later on become an expert in "belief perseverance, confirmation, illusory correlation" (232). Finally, Olivia Vandergriff, a college student, begins to hear the voices of trees after a near-death experience and is summoned by them to come to their aid.

The entanglements between different characters, storylines, as well as human and nonhuman life forms become more obvious in the sections "Trunk" and "Crown." As Olivia, Nick, Mimi, Douglas, and Adam become tree activists to protect old-growth forests in the Pacific Northwest, their lives become more closely interwoven. And although their paths never cross those of the activists, the lives of intellectual property lawyer Ray and his wife, too, become more closely entangled with trees and tree activism when Ray is forced to lead a near "sessile" life after a stroke and starts to consider the rights of trees. Neelay finds inspiration in the type of worldmaking performed by trees, using it as a model for the virtual world of his final game, which seeks to make an intervention for a more sustainable future. Powers's panorama of characters thus represents a myriad of ways of response-ability to and of becoming entangled with trees: by approaching them on a scientific, artistic, or spiritual level, through activism and legal discourse, by climbing onto, falling into, walking among, or surrounding oneself with trees. And just as the life trajectories of the various characters once again branch out in "Crown," moving further apart, the final section, "Seeds," shows the survivors living through the consequences of their entanglements and scattering their ideas, not the least by potentially implanting them in the novel's readers.

In addition to these modes of interspecies entanglement, the novel also uses the phenomenon of the string figure as model for other types of collaboration that are inspired by the string figures made by trees: for example, the collaboration of activists on behalf of trees and the cooperation between Patricia and her colleagues.[20] As in Haraway, this type of collaboration is part of *The Overstory*'s vision of a more sustainable mode of living, an example of response-ability. It is also the operating principle of the universe created in Neelay's final game, which replaces the capitalistic and individualistic tenor of his previous creations with ideas of cooperation. Entanglement, the novel suggests through these multiple examples, is our primary way of being, despite the semblance of things being otherwise.

Finally, "the matter of paper" serves as yet another example for the modes of connectivity and response-ability represented by string figures and sustained by trees. In particular, it is *The Overstory*'s pronounced intertextual dimension which brings this aspect of response-ability to the fore. As a web of ideas and texts (Barthes speaks of a "tissue of quotations," 146), intertextuality resembles Haraway's string figure and her notion of response-ability to others: it is a way of worldmaking that takes the entangled nature of being into account and works against the concept of self-enclosed entities by suggesting that our ideas do not exist in a void, but are essentially dialogic, and, in fact, rhizomatic in nature—a metaphor that fittingly likens human knowledge production to vegetal being and connectivity. *The Overstory*'s pronounced intertextual dimension therefore makes a conceptual point by presenting the dialogic nature of literature and the human imagination as yet another type of string figure.

*The Overstory* also emphasizes interspecies entanglements through the particular type of intertextual root system the novel establishes on the diegetic level—through texts the characters refer to—and, on the extradiegetic level, through the novel's implicit reliance on a host of contemporary scientific sources on plant behavior and communication. Of course, it is trees that feature most prominently in the novel's intertextual frame of reference: they are at the center of the stories that human beings tell to one another to make sense of the world. The root system or "wood-wide web" (Pollan, "Intelligent") of trees therefore not only provides a conceptual basis for human sense-making strategies, but also in terms of their content. From Yggdrasil (the World Tree) to Ovid's *Metamorphoses*, the forest in Shakespeare's *Macbeth*, and the Tree of Life: *The Overstory*'s intertextual web shows how intricately and persistently the stories we tell about human lives are connected to trees. Even the primary medium that has facilitated the exchange of ideas, and, therefore, human connectivity beyond the bounds of time and place, has its basis in vegetal life and, specifically, trees (see 288). Trees are therefore paradoxically the material basis even for most human-centered conceptualizations of world. In *The Overstory*, there is sympoiesis, "making with" or on behalf of trees on every level.

## Tree Time; or, Imagining the Dendrocene?

The numerous entanglements and string figures presented in Powers's novel challenge the discrete borders and boundaries between human and nonhuman life. They contradict the conceptualization of humans as bounded beings and endorse notions of connectivity rather than human exceptionalism. Such exceptionalism creates states of exception, not the least for human beings themselves, as Patricia's observations suggest: "She sees it in one great glimpse of flashing gold: trees and humans, at war over the land and water and atmosphere. And she can hear, louder than the quaking leaves, which side will lose by winning" (133). By juxtaposing long-term consequences and short-sighted benefits of current ways of dealing with our environment, Patricia's thoughts also implicitly juxtapose two time scales that could be described as geological time—or tree time?—on the one hand and human time on the other. In this final section, I will discuss some of the ways in which *The Overstory*'s chronotopic design enables readers to reimagine time and space from a less anthropocentric perspective—one that decentralizes and de-prioritizes human dwelling on Earth and allows or even invites the resituating of "Western-identified subjects ... in the space-time-matter of the planet" demanded by Pratt (G171).

One way in which *The Overstory* challenges exclusively anthropocentric conceptualizations of time and space is through generic conventions. As a genre, the novel developed in tandem with Western individualism, often focusing on the development of individual subjectivities and lives. The Anthropocene, too, is foregrounding human dwelling on Earth and critically reflects the planet's economic exploitation that has been fostered and justified by teleological ideas of development and progress. While *The Overstory* does not wholly abandon the interest in human protagonists or life stories, the use of the life of trees as an underlying pattern that structures the novel promotes a cyclical, rather than unidirectional, understanding of life at odds with teleological and individualistic designs of story or plot.

This cyclical, non-teleological, and non-individualistic concept is foregrounded in the introduction to section one, when the aforementioned pine tree suggests that "[a] good answer must be reinvented many times, from scratch" (3). The repetitiveness emphasized here is a strategy of tree survival and an example for the type of plant intelligence discussed above: a problem-solving ability.[21] Situated strategically at the beginning of the novel, this expression of tree ontology introduces a conceptualization of life that informs the novel throughout and is further fleshed out in the numerous sections that focus on the agency and entanglements of trees. In line with Bakhtin's ideas on the chronotope, conceptualizations of space and time in *The Overstory* carry implications that go beyond the strictly temporal and spatial: they reflect and express epistemological and ontological presuppositions about the world and may, in turn, alter them. The passages that focus on the lives of tress, tree intelligence, and tree communication interrupt, slow down, and thus serve as a counterpoint to the novel's more human- and plot-oriented features.[22] By balancing and integrating, rather than exchanging, human and arboreal ontologies, *The Overstory* unsettles exclusively human trajectories.

Moreover, even though Powers does not fully abandon human actors and the design of a plot, it is doubtlessly the lives of trees that the novel revolves around. Powers's summary introduction of human lives in the short story-like chapters that constitute the opening section "Roots"—and especially the multigenerational "Nicholas Hoel" and "Mimi Ma"—suggests the relatively minuscule scale of human lives in comparison to the "tree time" that structures the novel formally and thematically. A human life is but a "glimpse" in the overall design of the world that *The Overstory* reveals, and the short story form is an appropriate means to generate a sense of the time scales that are at stake.[23] The fact that the first epigraphic section introduces the ensuing stories and everything that follows through the voice of a pine tree further promotes the contrast between the short stories of human lives and the epic life of trees.[24]

Situated in a place of similar strategic importance as the introductory section of "Roots," the introduction to the final and shortest section of the novel, "Seeds," renders the challenge to human time scales and human conceptualizations of the world even more explicit. This introduction recounts the life of a partly anthropomorphized, partly "dendromorphized" planet Earth in terms of the human time scale of a single day:

*Say the planet is born at midnight and it runs for one day.*
*First there is nothing. Two hours are lost to lava and meteors. Life doesn't show up until three or four a.m. Even then, it's just the barest self-copying bits and pieces. From dawn to late morning—a million million years of branching—nothing more exists than lean and simple cells.*
*Then there is everything. . . .*
*The day is two-thirds done when animals and plants part ways. And still life is only single cells. . . .*
*Plants make it up on land just before ten. . . .*
*Anatomically modern man shows up four seconds before midnight. The first cave paintings appear three seconds later. . . .*

> *By midnight, most of the globe is converted to row crops for the care and feeding of one species. And that's when the tree of life becomes something else again. That's when the giant trunk starts to teeter.* (475, italics in original)

While the creation story provided here follows the idea of chronological order, its placement in the text is unusual: common human sense-making strategies such as religion and myth usually take creation stories as a point of departure, the origin of an explanation of world. Although such creation stories do not necessarily—and not even commonly—start with human creation, humans often constitute the implicit center or rationale of such stories. Being situated close to the end of *The Overstory* (on page 475 of 502), Powers's creation story features human life as a possible end of the world or an afterthought, occurring from 4 seconds to midnight until midnight on the single day that is posited as the metaphoric life span of the planet. It is the factor that makes the "tree of life" "teeter." Within the timescale and overall process of creation presented here, human life is anything but central, even though it may be the cause of an upheaval or destruction of planetary orders. Insofar, "Seeds" is introduced by a "creation" story that asks readers to revise the time-space arrangements transported by more familiar stories of creation, and forwards an interpretation at odds with common non-indigenous, Western mythical and metaphysical explanations of world.

Moreover, this creation story's disruption of the novel's chronological order not only asks readers to reconsider their time scales and ideas about the place of human life on Earth, but also our priorities on a yet more fundamental basis. The story of human creation—if a story that focuses only the 21600th part of its time scale to humans can be described as such—and human sensemaking strategies that are based on such stories, are indeed only an afterword to a time-space or chronotope that is based on life on Earth. The introduction to *The Overstory*'s final section is therefore the most explicit effort to move away from an anthropocentric world view and the establishment of a chronotope that is based on alternative conceptualizations of time and, to a lesser extent, space. How difficult this is, is implied by the anthropomorphizing equation of the life of Earth with a human day—even though it can be argued that this time unit is cosmically defined rather than human. As in Wohlleben, the anthropomorphization of nonhuman life—and the additional dendromorphization of human life—can facilitate a new appreciation of plant life and challenge ideas of human exceptionalism even though it destabilizes and counterweighs rather than fully replaces anthropocentric perspectives.

In addition to the novel's structure and epigraphic sections, the presentation of its diegetic world provides numerous incentives for reconsidering human-centered conceptualizations of time and space. "Nicholas Hoel," the first story or chapter in "Roots," juxtaposes human and arboreal timescales in order to denaturalize what may seem to be simply "given"—that is, time and space—and provides one of the most poignant and beautiful symbols for this re-conceptualization: a flip book with photos of the family's lone chestnut tree. Within a mere 19 pages, this story recounts the lives of five generations of Hoels, covering a time period from the mid-nineteenth to the later twentieth century, and juxtaposes this family history with the growth of a single tree. Late in his life, the first Hoel, who planted the chestnut tree, begins a photographic project which lasts for several generations and encompasses more than 900 images of the lone tree, taken every month on the same day and from the same angle.[25] Outside of the "frame" of these pictures of the family's tree, the "family tree" and its fortunes and misfortunes evolve, as well as the American chestnut's fortunes as a species, which falls victim to a blight and misguided attempts to monetarize its precious wood before the blight destroys it—events that almost completely eradicate the species.

Within the frames of the photographic project "the oldest, shortest, slowest, most ambitious silent movie ever shot in Iowa" evolves, which, after a decade or so, "begins to reveal the tree's goal," showing it "stretching and patting about for something in the sky" (13). After reaching the five-hundred mark, "the time-lapse tree has changed beyond all recognition" (15). And after three quarters of a century, the flip-book has turned into a five-second film (17, 18):

Each picture on its own shows nothing but the tree he climbed so often he could do it blind. But flipped through, a Corinthian column of wood swells under his thumb, rousing itself and shaking free. Three-quarters of a century runs by in the time it takes to say grace. . . .
Neither his grandparents nor his father could explain to him the point of the thick flip-book. His grandfather said, 'I promised my father and he promised his.' But another time, from the same man: 'Makes you think different about things, don't it?' It did. . . .
One more flip through the magic movie, and faster than it takes for the black-and-white broccoli to turn again into a sky-probing giant, the nine-year-old cuffed by his grandfather turns into a teen, falls in love with God, prays to God nightly . . . grows away from God and toward the guitar, gets busted for half a joint of pot, is sentenced to six months in a juvie scared-straight facility near Cedar Rapids, and there . . . realizes that he needs to spend his life making strange things. (18-19)

Through the flip-book's speeding of time, it becomes possible for human beings to see the "life" of the tree, to see movements and developments that are taking place so slowly according to human measurements of time that they are near imperceptible, but which make it possible to visualize—or at least imagine—the agency of trees. At the same time, through the tree flip-book, human life turns into little more than just a fleeting moment—75 years are compressed into five seconds—a way of experiencing human time that may approximate that of a tree if we take trees to be sentient beings. And while the Hoels are imagining that all that is important happens outside of the frame because the photos hide everything that passes on the farm and to the family's human protagonists, the juxtaposition of the tree's evolvement and permanency with the passing generations of Hoels and the fleeting moments of their lives suggests otherwise and challenges traditional notions of what may count as a "story" (16).[26] The flip-book therefore serves as a device that negotiates between human time and tree time. Moreover, just as popular nineteenth-century optical devices such as the zootrope and the phenakistiscope, it anchors human perception in time and space—the body of the observer at a given moment in time—thereby revealing its physiological basis as well as subjective nature (see Crary). Paradoxically, the rapidity of time moving that the flip book "enacts" opens up a dimension of what might be described as deep time—a concept of time in which years are but the equivalent of moments—a geological dimension of time, or, simply, tree time.

The flip-book, then, performs a process of destabilization and delimitation, questioning temporal orders as well as the borders between what is and isn't meaningful—represented, in a symbolic fashion, by the "frames" of the pictures. The question of what the frame of the photos includes and excludes foregrounds and challenges the frames of human perception and self-perceptions.[27] The flip-book, thus, turns into a device that suggests an alternative way of conceptualizing time and, in a less obvious way, space, and it shows how our conceptualizations of time and space are based on and transport far-reaching assumptions about the make-up of the world and the place of the human and the nonhuman within it. The "frames" or boundaries of the photos emphasize the bounded nature of human perceptions—that is its limitations and boundaries. Moreover, the images of the lone tree recall the tradition of portrait photography—a genre that, despite being highly formulaic, is closely associated with individualistic self-stylization if not individualism. The photos, then, liken trees to human subjects while simultaneously challenging the bounded nature of these subjects.

Situated as it is at the beginning of the novel, the flip-book posits an alternative way of conceptualizing time and space—an alternative chronotope. At the same time, it highlights the possible function of art in the process of reconceptualization.[28] As Powers puts it in a voice whose origin remains characteristically fuzzy: "people have no idea what time is. They think it's a line, spinning out from three seconds behind them, then vanishing just as fast into the three seconds of fog just ahead. They can't see that time is one spreading ring wrapped around another, outward and outward until the thinnest skin of Now depends for its being on the enormous mass of everything that has already died" (358). Even though the image of rings used here recalls the idea of boundedness, the spreading of rings—their movement in concentric circles that envelop more and more of their surroundings—suggests not only a replacement of linear time with circular time, and bounded time with the ongoingness of tree time, but it also recalls the delimitation and codependency of life forms, including, in Haraway's words "the more-than-human, other-than-human, inhuman, and human-as-humus" ("Anthropocene" 160).

While its reorientation towards "tree time" may be more apparent, *The Overstory* thus also offers ways of rethinking contemporary anthropocentric conceptualizations of space through its focus on the lives of trees. The networks and entanglements—the "wood-wide web"—function as a relational category, but also in terms of a spatial or spatio-temporal one: entanglements take place in space and time; they can reorient concepts of time through the time span in which they take place, but they also interfere with conceptualizations of space through the distances they breach and connections they establish across distances.

## Conclusion

Even though *The Overstory* remains indebted to realist and human-centered conventions of representing time and space in a number of respects, the novel encourages a reconceptualization of anthropocentric ideas of time and space on a thematic level and finds appropriate formal means to support them. As Bakhtin points out, the chronotopic design of a text is not necessarily—and not even commonly—homogenous or uniform. And since multiple chronotopes can coexist within a given text, it would appear appropriate to think of changes in the chronotopic design of literary texts in terms of evolving changes of and challenges to dominant discursive patterns. By juxtaposing and balancing human as well as nonhuman conceptualizations of space and time, *The Overstory* invites readers to reconsider spatial categories and temporal orientations that divide the world into discrete entities or beings and which promote the exploitative-extractive economies that inform western societies' relationship to the nonhuman and more-than-human world.

At a time that values mobility as never before, in a world that depends, to an unprecedented degree, on an unprecedented amount of movements, and at a historical moment that is also defined by a highly uneven distribution of deliberate and enforced mobility, the "sessile lifestyle" of plants (Pollan, "Intelligent"), may easily seem outmoded, anachronistic, and all but irrelevant: a mode of being that adds to the denigration of plants because it places them at a great distance to human experience. They can neither function as a model for the human status quo nor do they seem to present a desirable alternative. However, the spatial arrangements exemplified by trees challenge the borders of individual being and bounded individualism: Where does one tree or entity begin and another one end? In *The Overstory*—and in our forests—what seem to be individual trees are more likely one single organism, and even a single organism is an organism-that-is-not-one through its exchange and root systems with others. Similarly, ostensibly stationary trees are mobile in the ways in which they retreat and move forward—albeit within a time span that makes movement difficult to discern and that may need a flip book or time-lapse photography in order to be captured. However, trees can move at greater speed by "making-with" wind and animals: "A thing can travel everywhere, just by holding still" (3). As Patricia observes later on in the novel: "The motionless trees are *migrating*—immortal stands of aspen retreating before the latest two-mile-thick glaciers, then following them back north again. Life will not answer to reason. And *meaning* is too young a thing to have much power over it. All the drama of the world is gathering underground—massed symphonic choruses that Patricia means to hear before she dies" (133).

Based as it is on the time-space of trees, *The Overstory*'s chronotopic makeup challenges ideas of bounded being(s) as well as notions of immobility connected to plant life and instead emphasizes entanglements, deep time, and slow, often minute, movement in and through space. In so far as the current political order projects the notion of the individual onto the larger political terrain (that is, the nation-state as a bounded entity with discrete borders), the spatial politics of what could be described as the "dendrocene" also challenge current political borders. In many respects, to pay attention to the "lives" of trees, shows how they foster physical and intellectual processes of "deterritorialization and reterritorialization" (Hannam et al. 2), thereby unsettling long-established certainties and boundaries on the individual, collective, conceptual, and interspecies level. The plural forms of communality and connectivity produced by trees suggest that even that which seems to be separate and immobile, limited to its own discrete place or space, is intrinsically entangled, thus showing the absurdity of drawing lines between different life forms but also between ostensibly discrete spatio-temporal entities such as nation-states, all of which will be impacted by and depend on the kin we make and the possibilities we find for living together on a "damaged planet."

## Notes

**1 |** Haraway's and Marder's philosophical interventions are part of what I consider a broader ethical and relational re-orientation within the humanities and a "post-metaphysical" philosophy (Marder 6). While this re-orientation is most obvious in the context of environmental ethics, human-animal studies, and the budding field of "[c]ritical plant studies" (see Gagliano et al. xvi), it also encompasses more human-oriented philosophical interventions such as Judith Butler's *Precarious Life* and Giorgio Agamben's interrogations of states of exception in Western history.

2 | One notable characteristic of this order is the compartmentalization of Earth and space into discrete spheres of influence, power, and concern—a form of bounded individualism on the state level.

3 | The current state of environmental emergency has been caused to a large degree by modern economic practices. Scholars and scientist have dubbed the age in which humans have caused large-scale effects on the environment the *Anthropocene*. While this terminology captures the magnitude of effects, it falsely assigns the responsibility for such changes to humankind as such as T. J. Demos points out, thus distributing it smoothly and evenly among groups of people and peoples who have been involved in it to very different degrees. I share Demos's reservations towards the way the term distributes responsibility, but consider the theoretical concept of the Anthropocene important since it foregrounds and problematizes anthropogenic impact.

4 | Pratt suggests that the notion of the *Anthropocene* has the potential to usher in "a new chronotope with a multipolar time-space configuration" and that an "[a]nthropogenic chronotope" could be based on a conceptualization of space and time in which "human and nonhuman agency are no longer distinguished, visually or analytically" (G 170; G171). However, since both terms transport notions of human centrality, scholars might do better in devising an alternative terminology.

5 | I am quoting from the resonant title of a volume recently edited by Anna Tsing, Heather Swanson, Elaine Gan, and Nils Bubandt.

6 | As Grosz further points out, concepts are themselves what could be called "relational": they are "modes of address, modes of connection, what Deleuze and Guattari call . . . 'movable bridges'" (78). I am indebted to my own discovery of Grosz's work to Pratt's article "Concept and Chronotope."

7 | Plumwood argues that writers are "amongst the foremost of those who can help us to think differently" and suggests to be on the lookout for passages with "many active, agentic subjects" (126).

8 | See Peter Wohlleben's popular scientific account *The Hidden Life of Trees / Das geheime Leben der Bäume* for an inspiration for this phrase. I would like to thank my mother, Hildegard Spengler, for presenting this book to me.

9 | Films such as Beresford-Kroeger's *Call of the Forest* (2016) and the documentary *Intelligent Trees* (2017) by Peter Wohlleben and Suzanne Simar popularize the research done in the field of plant intelligence by scientists such as Anthony Trewavas (molecular biology, University of Edinburgh) and Monica Gagliano (evolutionary ecology, Biological Intelligence Lab, University of Sydney), who attempts to apply rules of animal behavior and learning to plants.

10 | Other important discoveries concern strategies of resilience in plants, such as Stefano Mancuso's work on plant-specific pain reception, which suggests that plants respond to injury by producing a compound that acts as an anaesthetic. By injecting trees with radioactive carbon and following the spread of it, Suzanne Simar has

discovered that trees are interconnected and send information and nutrients through the network or even trade it with other species. My understanding of plant life has greatly benefited from Polland's account in "The Intelligent Plant."

**11** | See Ursula LeGuin's short story "Direction of the Road" for an example of how literature can challenge dominant and human-centered conceptualizations of space and time and Erin James's perceptive analysis of the use of plant narrators to achieve such unsettling ("Plant"). Erin's article and her guest lecture at the University of Wuppertal have been inspirations to my own thinking about plants and their (narrative) agency.

**12** | This argument builds on Wolfgang Iser's conceptualization of the relationship between the imaginary, the fictive, and the real and on Winfried Fluck's ensuing work.

**13** | In fact, many scientists not only acknowledge, but foreground the role that language and narrative can play to break conceived patterns of thinking. See James ("Plant" 255).

**14** | All subsequent references to *The Overstory* will be given by page number in parenthesis.

**15** | James refers to the narratological concepts of "fuzzy temporality" and "fuzzy spatialization" as two strategies employed by narratives that may help us "think differently" about the Anthropocene and vice versa. Unpublished talk "Narrative and the Anthropocene," University of Wuppertal, November 14, 2018.

**16** | These sections are therefore not epigraphs in a narrow sense of the term—that is, they do not consist of quotations from other literary or non-literary sources. For reasons of brevity, I will refer to them as "introductions" and "epigraphic sections." I will return to issues of time, space, and mobility in the last section of this article.

**17** | I am borrowing the term wood-wide web from Michael Pollan in "The Intelligent Plant."

**18** | As Haraway puts it, "*Sym-poiesis* is a simple word; it means 'making-with.' Nothing makes itself; nothing is really auto-poietic or self-organizing. In the words of the Iñupiat computer 'world game,' earthlings are Never Alone. That is the radical implication of sympoiesis. Sympoiesis is a word proper to complex, dynamic, responsive, situated, historical systems. It is a word for worlding" ("Symbiogenesis" M25). In *Staying with the Trouble*, Haraway further points out: "Bounded (or neoliberal) individualism amended by autopoiesis is not good enough figurally or scientifically; it misleads us down deadly paths" (33). Even though "[a]utopoietic systems are not closed, spherical, deterministic, or teleological . . . they are not quite good enough models" (33).

**19** | See John Fowles's insightful discussion of human and, particularly, modern forms of "ordering" the world through knowledge systems and specific modes of perception in *The Tree*. Fowles suggests that "[e]volution has turned man into a sharply isolating creature, seeing the world not only anthropocentrically but singly, mirroring the way we like to think of our private selves" and associates Linneaus's taxonomy with "our love of clearly defined boundaries, unique identities, of the individual thing released from the confusion of background" (26).

**20** | "Words of hers that she has all but forgotten have gone on drifting out on the open air, lighting up others, like a waft of pheromones" (137). Compare also the "network trading in discoveries" as Patricia's group of scientists is described. The way in which the discoveries about the eco-system of trees are shared is presented in terms that resemble the workings of that eco-system itself: "Together, they form one great symbiotic association, like the ones they study" (141).

**21** | Such is, for example, Stefano Mancuso's definition as described by Pollan ("Intelligent").

**22** | See David Sexton in *The Evening Standard*, who criticizes *The Overstory* on account of its lack of traditional plot when he writes that the stories "never unite effectively into a single plot."

**23** | Raymond Carver associates the genre of the short story with the "glimpse" (34).

**24** | Regarding the idea of *The Overstory* as an epic, see Claire Miye Stanford in the *LA Review of Books*, who describes *The Overstory* as Powers's "environmental epic," as well as Nathaniel Rich in *The Atlantic* and Michael Upchurch in the *Boston Globe*. Reviewing the novel for the *New York Times*, Barbara Kingsolver answers her question "[i]f Powers were an American writer of the nineteenth century, which writer would he be?" by suggesting that "[h]e'd probably be the Herman Melville of 'Moby-Dick,'" a text that has often been described as the U.S.'s nineteenth-century epic.

**25** | Contemporary researchers of plant intelligence like Mancuso also use time lapse photography, albeit of a different kind, as a means of research (see Pollan, "Intelligent").

**26** | Compare Claire Miye Stanford in the *LA Review of Books*: "Here, in the first 20 pages of the novel, Powers sets up a subtle challenge to the reader, and, perhaps, a warning. This novel is interested in what happens *inside* the photos' frames; it will try to make a story of the considerably extended timeline of the trees, not the humans."

**27** | See Butler, *Frames of War*, for an insightful discussion of processes of framing.

**28** | As Ron Charles points out in his *Washington Post* review of *The Overstory*, "Powers is working through tree history, not human history, and the effect is like a time-lapse video."

## Works Cited

Agamben, Giorgio. *Homo Sacer: Sovereign Power and Bare Life*. 1995. Translated by Daniel Heller-Roazen, Stanford University Press, 1998.

Bakhtin, Mikhail M. "Forms of Time and of the Chronotope in the Novel: Notes Toward a Historical Poetics." 1937-38, 1973. *The Dialogic Imagination: Four Essays by M. M. Bakhtin*, edited by Michael Holquist, University of Texas Press, 2006, pp. 84-258.

Barthes, Roland. "The Death of the Author." *Image—Music—Text*. Translated by Stephen Heath, Fontana Press, 1977, pp. 142-48.

Bennett, John. "In Response to Val Plumwood's 'Nature in the Active Voice (*AHR* 46).'" *Ecological* Humanities, vol. 46, 2009, n.p. australian-humanitiesreview.org.

Butler, Judith. *Frames of War*. Verso, 2009.

---. *Precarious Life: The Powers of Mourning and Violence*. 2004. Verso, 2006.

Carver, Raymond. "Principles of a Story." 1981. *Prospect*, Sept. 2005, pp. 32-34.

Charles, Ron. "The Most Exciting Novel About Trees You'll Ever Read." Review of *The Overstory*, by Richard Powers, *The Washington Post*, 3 Apr. 2018. washingtonpost.com.

Crary, Jonathan. *Techniques of the Observer: On Vision and Modernity in the Nineteenth Century*. 1990. Massachusetts Institute for Technology Press, 1992.

Demos, T. J. *Against the Anthropocene: Visual Culture and Environment Today*. Sternberg Press, 2017.

Fluck, Winfried. "The Search for Distance: Negation and Negativity in Wolfgang Iser's Literary Theory." *New Literary History*, vol. 31, no. 1, 2000, pp. 175-210.

Fowles, John. *The Tree*. 1979. Ecco Press, 2010.

Gagliano, Monica, et al., Introduction. *The Language of Plants: Science, Philosophy, Literature*. University of Minnesota Press, 2017, pp. vii-xxxiii.

Grosz, Elizabeth. *Becoming Undone: Darwinian Reflections on Life, Politics, and Art*. Duke University Press, 2011.

Hannam, Kevin, et al. "Editorial: Mobilities, Immobilities and Moorings." *Mobilities*, vol. 1, no. 1, 2006, pp. 1-22.

Haraway, Donna J. "Anthropocene, Capitalocene, Plantationocene, Chthulucene: Making Kin." *Environmental Humanities* vol. 6, no. 1, 2015, pp. 159-65.

---. *Staying With the Trouble: Making Kin in the Chthulucene*. Duke University Press, 2016.

---. "Symbiogenesis, Sympoiesis, and Art Science Activisms for Staying with the Trouble." *Arts of Living on a Damaged Planet*, edited by Anna Tsing et al., University of Minnesota Press, 2017, pp. M25-M50.

Iser, Wolfgang. *Der Akt des Lesens*. 1976. Fink, 1984.

James, Erin. "Narrative and the Anthropocene." Unpublished Talk at the University of Wuppertal, November 14, 2018.

---. "What the Plant Says: Plant Narrators and the Ecosocial Imaginary." *The Language of Plants: Science, Philosophy, Literature*, edited by Monica Gagliano, et al., University of Minnesota Press, 2017, pp. 253-272.

Kingsolver, Barbara. "The Heroes of This Novel Are Centuries Old and 300 Feet Tall." Review of *The Overstory*, by Richard Powers. *New York Times*, April 9, 2018. nytimes.com.

Le Guin, Ursula K. "Direction of the Road." *The Wind's Twelve Quraters & The Compass Rose*. Perennial, 1987, pp. 247-53.

Marder, Michael. *Plant-Thinking: A Philosophy of Vegetal Life*. Columbia University Press, 2013.
Moon, Beth. *Ancient Trees: Portraits of Time*. Abbeville Press Publishers, 2014.
Plumwood, Val. "Nature in the Active Voice." *Australian Humanities Review*, vol. 46, 2009, pp. 113-29.
Pollan, Michael. "The Intelligent Plant." *The New Yorker*, December 23, 2013. newyorker.com.
---. "Can Plants Think?" Radio interview, *Science Friday*, January 3, 2014. sciencefriday.com.
Powers, Richard. *The Overstory*. W.W. Norton & Company, 2018.
Pratt, Mary Louise. "Coda: Concept and Chronotope." *Arts of Living on a Damaged Planet*, edited by Anna Tsing et al., University of Minnesota Press, 2017, pp. G169-74.
Rich, Nathaniel. "The Novel That Asks, 'What Went Wrong with Mankind?" Review of *The Overstory*, by Richard Powers. *The Atlantic*, June 2012. theatlantic.com.
Sexton, David. Review of *The Overstory*, by Richard Powers. *The Evening Standard*, August 2, 2018. standard.co.uk/lifestyle/books.
Stanford, Claire Miye. "Speaking for the Trees: Richard Powers's 'The Overstory.'" Review of *The Overstory*, by Richard Powers. *LA Review of Books*, 10 May 2018. lareviewofbooks.org.
Tsing, Anna, et al. eds. *Arts of Living on a Damaged Planet*. University of Minnesota Press, 2017.
Upchurch, Michael. "A Striking, Visionary Novel About the Environment." Review of *The Overstory*, by Richard Powers. *The Boston Globe*, April 6, 2018. bostonglobe.com.
Vice, Sue. *Introducing Bakhtin*. Manchester University Press, 1997.
Wohlleben, Peter. *Das Geheime Leben der Bäume*. Ludwig Verlag, 2015.

# The Lives of Trees

*Birgit Spengler*

Bristlecone Pine, California

Bristlecone Pine, California

Petrified Wood, Bisti/De-Na-Zin Wilderness, New Mexico

Cross-Section of Tree, Bandelier National Monument, New Mexico

Conifer Bark, Idaho

Charred Wood, California

Driftwood, New Hampshire

Driftwood, New Hampshire

Pacific Madrone, Galiano Island, Canada

Maple, Southern France

Bark, Odenwald Region, Germany

Bark, Odenwald Region, Germany

**Sonic Bugs and Lyrical Beasts**

# Skunk

*Karen L. Kilcup*

Alluring as a kitten,
her perfume like a gun,
she's the painted lady
strolling on the margins
of every rural town
on every summer evening.
Well-endowed, addicted
to browsing, she feeds
wherever she pleases.
Though she has no class,
attired in classic black
and white, she always
makes a statement.
Her tail's the ostrich
plume no lady would wear:
a trigger, a flag
from no known country.
No one ever asks
for her opinion,
and she doesn't care.
She's the citizen
of another stripe,
the dirty secret we admit
only when we must.
Happy voyeurs, we see
our problem is not
to be enticed,
not to come
when she calls.

# "The Citizenry of All Things Within One World": Mary Oliver's Poetic Explorations of Kinship

*Katja Sarkowsky*

> We will be known as a culture that taught and rewarded the amassing of things, that spoke little if at all about the quality of life for people (other people), for dogs, for rivers. All the world, in our eyes, they will say, was a commodity.
> —Mary Oliver, "Of the Empire"

## Nature, Ecocriticism, and Mary Oliver's Poetry

Mary Oliver is certainly one of the most prominent and popular contemporary nature poets in the United States. Her lovingly detailed observations of the natural environment, her admiration and delight at it, and the relation of her spiritual experience of it have gained her a wide and devoted readership. Scholarly responses to her poetry have oscillated between somewhat distanced feminist appreciation (McNew; Bonds), emphatic acknowledgement of her Transcendentalist and romantic roots (Johnson), and critical dismissals of her "deceptively clear" poetry (Moramaro and Sullivan qt. in Johnson 78) as "naïve" in her unwavering, spiritual celebration of nature. Lynn Keller, commenting on the scarcity of human beings in Oliver's poetry, criticizes that "[t]his mode, which elides from the landscape no human other than the privileged speaker in order to find there a source of individual spiritual revelation and renewal, offers another enactment of the problematic 'romantic ideology of wilderness'" and concludes that "the exceptional popularity of Oliver's poetry and work like it speaks to the continuing allure of that ideology" (611). Recent developments in eco-conscious poetry, Keller argues, have given way to "a less organicist understanding that includes urban and degraded landscapes in its concept of environment" (605), and in this context, Oliver's work has indeed often been relegated to a pastoral tradition (Parini 136).

The poem "Of the Empire" quoted at the beginning is, indeed, exceptional in Oliver's work in its direct critique of consumerism, militarism, and the destruction of the environment; most of her poetry's critical potential tends to be implicit. The poem appeared in the 2008 collection *Red Bird,* which includes a number of other obviously political poems such as "Iraq" and "Watching a Documentary about Polar Bears Trying to Survive on the Melting Ice Floes." Despite such examples (including the poem "Do Trees Speak?" in her most recent collection *Felicity),* Oliver has largely remained true to a kind of poetry that indeed focuses on a natural environment seemingly outside social spaces, apparently unscathed by urban or suburban developments, and experienced by an individual speaker as a space of renewal, contemplation, and immersion. However, her poetic ground is emphatically not the wilderness presumably untouched by human interference, it is (mostly) the swamps, ponds, and seashore of Cape Cod, and the occasional fences attest to a human presence. Similarly, the animals that populate her poetry are not only bears, deer, turtles, birds, and crabs, but frequently also pets, especially dogs. As William Cronon has reminded us, "the tree in the garden is in reality no less other, no less worthy of our wonder and respect, than the tree in an ancient forest that has never known an ax or a saw . . . . Both trees stand apart from us; both share our common world" (88). The natural spaces at the center of Oliver's work, we might say, are spaces positioned between the domestic and wilderness.

Yet, in the context of "second wave" ecocriticism (Buell 22) with its focus on a broader understanding of the environment and its emphasis on social ecology and ecological justice, Oliver's poetry may at times indeed appear as anachronistic in its almost total exclusion of urban spaces. This does not mean, however, that it is concerned only with individual emotions. The individual is clearly Oliver's starting point; as for Emerson (whom she deeply admires), the individual is where for Oliver, too, societal change begins. Her "neo-Transcendentalist" perspective, I want to argue, offers ways of thinking about trans-human connections in the contemporary world that, while sharing with posthumanism the view on the human not "as an autonomous agent, but [as] located within an extensive system of relations" (Ferrando 32), does not apologetically distance itself from a human positionality—or pretends that it could. While it does think about "what thought has to become in order to face those challenges [posed by decentering the human]" (Wolfe xvi) and at times seeks to imagine a nonhuman position of perception, or even a merging with other species, Oliver's work is anthropocentric in the sense that it always comes back to a human-individualist position. It is *not* anthropocentric in the sense, though, that would conflate the inescapability of a human perspective with the inevitability of human dominance; here, Oliver's position clearly differs from Emerson's anthropocentrism when he writes that nature "is made to serve . . . . It offers all its kingdoms to man as the raw material which he may mold into what is useful" ("Nature" 21). Her stance might be called with Serenella Iovino an "extended, non-anthropocentric, humanism" (32).

I want to argue in this contribution that Oliver's work offers a perspective on nature, the environment, and the position of human beings in this environment that is place-specific, transcends the pastoral, and that complements the perspectives of contemporary ecocriticism in important ways. Jeannette Riley has read Oliver's Pulitzer Prize-winning volume *American Primitive* (1983) as an example for an eco-narrative, as "a text that enacts ecofeminist tenets through rhetorical strategies that guide readers' ways of knowing, interacting with, and taking responsibility for the worlds in which they live" (82). I regard Oliver less as an ecofeminist than as a deep ecologist in the sense that her poetry affirms the intrinsic value of nature apart from its potential use to human beings and its projection of a return—at least for the speaker—to a "monistic, primal identification of human and the ecosphere" and a "shift from human-centered to nature-centered values" (Garrard 23-24). Despite this difference in categorization, I would like to take my cue from Riley's emphasis on Oliver's poetry as instructing by example and on a responsibility "for the world" that includes the reader, and I want to suggest that, throughout her work, Oliver celebrates human relationality not so much to one another (even though that features more strongly in her poetry than Keller's critique seems to admit), but in a larger framework of a species-transcending kinship. That is, she explores kinship not only between humans, or between humans and animals, but also between humans and plants, rivers, or the sea, very much in line with Donna Haraway's recent call for making "'kin' mean something other/more than entities tied by ancestry or genealogy" ("Making Kin" 161) and for acknowledging "that all earthlings are kin in the deepest sense" (162).[1] *Kinship* is not the term Oliver uses; it is an umbrella term I resort to in order to capture the range of images she explores to emphasize connection and immersion, the relationship between human and nonhuman kin. The term is not unproblematic: in anthropology, *kinship* is a term of social relationality and organization based usually on blood relation and on hierarchy, including heteronormative hierarchies of gender (Tsing 511). In my attempt to conceptualize the kinds of overarching relations I see Oliver exploring in her work, I draw on the figurative meaning of the term, defined in the *OED* as a "relationship in respect of qualities or character" (1541). Seen in this light, the "naturalization" of relationships through the use of kinship as metaphor is a literal one: a relationship grounded in the common participation in the natural environment. For Oliver, I suggest, kinship rests in a shared physicality on the one hand and her assumption of a soul on the other. In "Some Questions You Might Ask," the first poem of her 1990 collection *House of Light*, the speaker inquires about the soul, "Why should I have it, and not the anteater / who loves her children? / Why should I have it, and not the camel? / Come to think of it, what about the maple trees? . . . What about the grass?" (65), defiantly stating *"I believe everything has a soul"* ("Staying Alive" 63). Understanding kinship as emphasizing relation and shared characteristics across differences—rather than as emphasizing the social practice of excluding non-kin—allows for an encompassing conceptualization of kinship as a relation across species that is neither exclusively observant nor headed towards immersion but that continuously revisits the implications of relation for the construction of a responsive and responsible subjectivity embedded in nature not understood as a separate entity.

This relationship is not simply one of being but of becoming and partaking. In some of her writing in the first decade of the twenty-first century, Oliver has used the terms citizenry and citizen to mark such a kinship. While kinship and citizenship do not sit easily with one another as political concepts, as metaphor of connectedness the semantic field of citizenship offers a notion of relationality that imposes a decidedly social understanding upon human embeddedness in nature. Oliver's positioning of the body is crucial in this context, so in a first step, I will briefly discuss how she relates the body, experience, and language before turning, in a second step, to the tension between observation and immersion as ways of both being and speaking in Oliver's work. The tension between these concepts, I argue, captures the oscillation between the acknowledgement of difference and the fundamental fluidity and transformability of the body as nature, both in life and in death. Looking at two kinds of poems and prose texts—those that present a shift from observation to immersion or an oscillation between them and those that present the bodily incorporation of nature by nature—I set out to show how Oliver's rendering of the bodily experience has become both more concrete and more reflexive regarding the porosity of boundaries. Kinship is the kind of connection that acknowledges both, difference and fluidity, and in conclusion I want to look at how the metaphor of citizenry deployed by Oliver shifts towards a more social, less "natural" conceptualization of relationality.

## Of Bears and Birds: Language, Experience, and Bodily Transformation

Despite the heterogeneity of nature writing in the United States and the range of approaches to it, "there is something of a consensus that the blending of scientific, personal, and philosophical perspectives and the tension between those perspectives is intrinsic in and central to nature writing as it is currently practiced in America" (Quetchenbach 2). In a broad sense, this certainly applies to Oliver's work; more specifically, I suggest that the relationship between the speaker and nature in Oliver's poetry is structured by a tension between observation of and immersion in nature, that is, a position that builds on the notion of a human-nature dualism and one that seeks to transcend it. Oliver's nature poems verbalize and thereby mediate experiences that are deeply spiritual and at the same time utterly worldly. Todd Davis has characterized her work as a "fusion of Transcendental, Buddhist, and Christian thought grounded firmly in the earth" (606) and as calling for "a recognition between our bodies and all other forms of physical life, as well as for a firm belief that there is no 'spiritual' element outside the physical element" (610). Experiences—of the natural world, but also of emotions—find a variety of poetic expressions in Oliver's work, from the seemingly concrete and observational to the obviously metaphorical. Metaphor, Hubert Zapf has argued, is the "central mode of ecopoiesis" (142), and this clearly is the case in Oliver's poetry, even at its most concrete.

The oscillation between observation and immersion characterizes the tension within as well as between the poems. The important role of bears in Oliver's prize-winning collection *American Primitive* illustrates both (Bonds 10; Graham 361-65). The first poem of the collection, "August," initially focuses on the pure delight of eating blackberries: "When the blackberries hang / swollen in the woods, in the brambles / nobody owns, I spend // all day among the high / branches, reaching / my ripped arms, thinking // of nothing, cramming / the black honey of summer / into my mouth; all day my body // accepts what it is" (143). The enjambment after "thinking" punctuates both "nothing" and "cramming" in the following line, a juxtaposition of unthinking bodily delight to the workings of the mind, even further emphasized by the insistence that "all day my body // accepts what it is" (143). If the enjambment from "thinking" to "of nothing" shifts the focus from the mind to an unreflective presence, the enjambment from "body" to "accepts what it is" indicates a further transformation.The seeming obviousness of "what the body is"—here a pleasurable physicality—is revealed as insufficient in the next lines, for at least the reader does not know anymore what the speaker's body is and what identity it accepts: "In the dark / creeks that run by there is / this thick paw of my life darting among // the black bells, the leaves; there is / this happy tongue" (143). Not only does the "thick paw" suggest a bodily transformation (or recognition of the body as *what it is?*) into a bear; the shift from personal pronouns to a repeated "there is" suggests a retreat of the speaker toward a position where there is no self-conscious, speaking "I" anymore. Speech remains, though; the final line is both literal and figurative, the "happy tongue" linking, as Bonds has argued, the bear and the poet (11), physicality and language, the concrete and the symbolic.

If metaphor makes physical form fluid in this poem, presenting a transformation that plays with the literal and the figurative, the poem can productively be read in conversation with later poems in the collection, the image of the bear being so prominent in *American Primitive*. "The presence of the bear in 'August' suggests," according to Vicki Graham, "that the transformation of the speaker into a bear in later poems is natural; her own spirit copy, in form of a bear, is already guiding her" (362). However, the proximity of bear and speaker/observer clearly varies in the poems. In "Happiness," the speaker observes a she-bear in her successful search for and enjoyment of honey. The speaker's perspective is clear—"I watched," "I saw" repeatedly stress the distance between the observer and the bear. However, at the same time, a number of words and images link "Happiness" to "August"—the title's happiness, but also honey, tongue, the thickness of the bear's arms. Last but not least, "Happiness" also plays with an imaginative transformation; only here, it is the image of the bear that suggests something other than it is: "I saw her let go of the branches, / I saw her lift her honeyed muzzle / into the leaves, and her thick arms, / as though she would fly— / an enormous bee" (174). In "August," the transformation of the speaker plays with the ambiguity of a literal transformation vs. the figurative rendering of an experience of unthinking pleasure; in "Happiness," the transformation begins as a simile only to then absorb the movement of the bear into the movement of bees; the bear begins to "hum and sway," and then, "an enormous bee, all sweetness and wings" moves "down into the meadows . . . to float and sleep in the sheer nets / swaying from flower to flower / day after shining day" (174). Metaphor transforms the bear "in place" into a bee "out of time."

The fluidity of physical form is clearly highlighted in both poems. Neither unambiguously suggests a bodily transformation of one species into another, but the images used in both emphasize possibility and openness between them. "To merge with the nonhuman is to acknowledge the self's mutability and multiplicity, not to lose subjectivity," argues Graham (353), and I agree. However, already in the poems of *American Primitive*, Oliver explores different nuances and forms of transformation. If in "August" the speaker is immersed in an experience of bliss that finds expression in a language that leaves open the boundaries between identification as and imagination of being a bear, in "Happiness" she remains outside of the observed scene, but also transforms it through observation into one of "imaginative kinship," as Zapf has called it in another poetic context (145).

While Oliver retains the basic tension between observation and immersion within and between poems to explore kinship across different species, its poetic manifestations tend to shift in her poetry of the first decade of the twenty-first century. In *Red Bird* (2008), two poems about the eponymous animal bracket the collection. In the first poem, "Red Bird," the speaker is grateful for the presence of the red bird in winter, "firing up the landscape / as nothing else can do" (1); the red bird serves as a consolation, providing warmth in the cold of winter. As Davis has observed, the two collections *Thirst* (2006) and *Red Bird* are more "overt and raw" (622) in their poetic explorations, most likely in reaction to the death of Oliver's long-time partner Molly Malone Cook in 2005. Read in light of this biographical rupture, both collections very much manifest a struggle with grief, and I suggest that they also present a move away from the earlier fluidity of boundaries between species towards a seemingly more stable perspective on nature's otherness. Less fluid boundaries, however, while changing both perspectivity and the metaphors used, do not change the insistence on a fundamental relation on the basis of corporeality and soul. If anything, the shared inevitability of death adds to the sense of kinship. The closing poem of the collection, "Red Bird Explains Himself," directly answers to the opening poem, as the first sentence establishes: "Yes, I was the brilliance floating over the snow" (78). The bird is given a voice, clearly indicated as such by quotation marks—unusual in Oliver's assignment of voice to animals. Beyond its anthropomorphism, I suggest the "quotation" of the bird's voice also points to a self-conscious use of the image of the bird that can only adequately be understood in dialogue with the opening poem. It picks up on specific lines and words in "Red Bird;" if here "the heart narrows / as often as it opens" (1), in "Red Bird Explains Himself" bird is "the music of your heart, that you wanted and needed" (78), the speaker turning the red bird from observed animal into a metaphor of consolation, of teaching and learning. If "Red Bird" is about looking, observing, "Red Bird Explains Himself" is about listening.

These two pairs of poems—roughly 25 years apart in Oliver's oeuvre—illustrate a shift in the poet's metaphorization of human kinship with nature, particularly with animals. While the earlier poems tend to experiment more openly with the porosity of physical boundaries and with images of bodily transformation, the later poems appear to stress, as Zapf has put it for cultural ecology, "connectivity *and* diversity, relationality *and* difference" (138). In the poem "I will try," the speaker declares "I came, like red bird, to sing," to affirm in the next line that this, indeed, is a simile only: "*But I'm not red bird*, with his head-mop of flame" (75; my emphasis). If by the end of the poem this clear boundary between human and animal appears to be in question again, this is not so much about fluidity as it is about thresholds between inner and outer spaces, and also between life and death. For the speaker is not red bird, but "a woman whose love has vanished" and who is struggling with both her grief and the awareness of her own mortality. The image of the "dark places" of depression seems to veer towards death and resurrection in the afterlife, but it is then interrupted by the speaker's awareness of the present in *this* world: "But this too, I believe, is a place / where God is keeping watch / until we rise and step forward again and— / but wait. Be still. Listen! / Is it red bird? Or something / inside myself, singing?" (75). Images of bodily transformation are replaced by images that link bodies—human bodies, animal bodies—in a kinship based on shared corporeality and the presence of a soul, but that leave the *difference* between them intact.

## "This Other-Creature-Consuming Appetite": Incorporation, Nourishment, and Death

This tension between connection and difference might be seen as the basis of trans-species kinship in Oliver's work; if shared physical existence and the soul provide connection, difference is established by way of concrete interaction and, to put it bluntly, by different positions within the food chain. Diane Bonds has acutely observed that Oliver's embrace of the body of the world often "takes the form of rituals of 'communion' that celebrate the interpenetration of the human and the natural through imagining the actual eating of animals" (10), and this, I suggest, provides a prime example not only for how connection and difference provide the basis for Oliver's understanding of metaphorical kinship, but also for how her metaphors of immersion and observation, which give expression to that kinship, have shifted over the decades.

Bonds's primary example is the poem "Hunter's Moon—Eating the Bear" from Oliver's 1979 collection *Twelve Moons,* in which the speaker addresses the bear s/he will be eating if the hunt is successful: "And I will put you into my mouth, yes. / And I will swallow, yes. / So. You will come to live inside me: / muscle, layers of sweet leaves / hidden in the pink fat, the maroon flesh" (198). As Bonds argues, "[h]er prayer is a verbal ritual in which she accomplishes the incorporation of which she speaks by speaking it" (10). However, in the poem, the speaker imagines the incorporation, the communion, as an act in the future, once the hunt has been successful, not in the present. The act of incorporation is thus doubled: it is spoken and thereby symbolically done before it can be done in the future; speaking the act wills the act and enables, even *makes* the poem (Bonds 10).

The link between the act of eating and kinship is explicated by Robin Riley Fast, who has read this poem as an illustration of a "Native American presence" in Oliver's poetry, a suggested "Native American sense of kinship with nature . . . recalling the ways in which people and animals enter each others' worlds and lives, often by taking the others' form, in American Indian stories" (64). Particularly Oliver's poetry from the 1970s and 1980s has often addressed the violent history of dispossession and genocide of indigenous peoples in the US and its impact upon the present in poems such as "Learning about the Indians" (*The River Styx, Ohio and Other Poems,* 1972) or "Ghosts" and "Tecumseh" (both from *American Primitive,* 1983). Fast has read this engagement as an "imaginative *rapprochement* of Indian ways of being in nature" (59), with "Hunter" clearly illustrating how dangerously close to appropriation such sympathetic imaginings can come at times. With regard to the focus at hand—the eating of animals as one way of ritualistically celebrating a communion with nature, a cycle of life, and kinship across species—it should be pointed out that, much like the imagined transformation into animals (another such rapprochement), such impersonations are present in Oliver's early work much more strongly than in her later poetry. While the trope of devouring and its inextricable connection between destroying and nurturing life remains strong, it shifts towards a more literal mode, in which the depiction of the incorporation resists such a rapprochement.

In the poem "Night and the River," the speaker observes a bear catching and devouring a fish, emphasizing at first the distance between her and the observed animal: "*I have seen* the great feet / leaping / into the river // and *I have seen* moonlight / milky / along the long muzzle // and *I have seen* the body / of something / scaled and wonderful // slumped in the sudden fire of its mouth" (8; my emphasis). The perspective shifts then, the speaker moves from observation to considering her own position and potential identifications in the quotidian spectacle of a nurturing death: "and I could not tell / which fit me // more comfortably, the power, / or the powerlessness; / neither would have me // entirely; I was divided, / consumed / by sympathy, // pity, admiration" (8). While the story "followed me home // and entered my house— / a difficult guest" (9), the speaker nevertheless remains "outside."

While in this poem, the speaker does not do the consuming but only imagines herself as potentially the consumer or the consumed, this is very different in the autobiographical essay "Sister Turtle," originally published in 1999.[2] Here, the narrator observes a snapping turtle laying her eggs. The encounter between human and turtle is described in careful detail, with close attention to what the speaker perceives as the mutuality of acknowledgment. "When our eyes meet, what can pass between us? She sees me as a danger, and she is right" (55). It is early in the morning, "5 a.m.; for me, the beginning of the day—for her, the end of the long night" (55) of reproductive labor. What begins with observation and distance turns into consumption and incorporation. Towards evening, the narrator returns. Carefully, she digs up the eggs, twenty-seven of them, taking thirteen and replacing fourteen in the underground nest. Again, the eggs are described in loving, almost reverent detail, their materiality immediate, tangible, and beautiful. "I scrambled them," continues the narrator. "They were a meal. Not too wonderful, not too bad. Rich, substantial. . . . I ate them all, with attention, whimsy, devotion, and respect" (59).

Seen in this light, "Sister Turtle" presents both, the position of the reverent observer and an imagination of immersion, for while robbing the turtle's nest could of course be read as an act of human exploitation of another species, I claim that it rather presents an act of placing herself in nature and as part of nature; as reflecting, literally, an appetite and a craving for nature. At the beginning of the essay, Oliver challenges the reader by reflecting precisely on this appetite, holding that to "consider Nature without this appetite—this other-creature-consuming appetite—is to look with shut eyes upon the miraculous interchange that makes things work" (49). In the course of the essay, she turns the metaphor of consuming into an act of literal consumption. By entering nature not just as an observer but as a predator, by devouring it, Nature is considered as a relation of interchange; the autobiographical narrator imagines herself not as an exploitative human being but as a fellow animal who in her turn, eventually, will return to nature and provide food for others.

The episode is somewhat disconcerting, and the narrator knows it. She leads up to the devouring of the eggs with elaborate ruminations about her understanding of nature, the philosophers and poets who have shaped that understanding and the possibilities of expressing it, and her observation of the turtles. A long description of two mating turtles indicates the beginning and perpetuation of life, while the narrator's report of the raccoons, who frequently rob the turtle nests and "sniff, and discover, and dig, and devour, with rapacious and happy satisfaction" foreshadows her own unearthing and consummation of the eggs (52-53). While this clearly is a closing of a life cycle (and a closing of the text's own narrative cycle), it also points to the sustenance—the eggs nourish, perpetuate life, as much as their destruction forecloses life. But, as the narrator assures us, "every year, there are turtles enough in the ponds" (53). Life perpetuates itself, and the act of consumption is rather an act of communion; this communion is not just metaphorical—as analyzed by Davis—but also physical. "Sister Turtle" points to an important aspect of considering the relationship between humans and other species: the essay's very title "*Sister Turtle*" suggests kinship across species even in its narrower sense of family relation; only then, in such a relation, can the human predator be imagined as part of the "miraculous interchange that makes things work, that causes one thing to nurture another, that creates the future out of the past" (49).

## "Darling Citizen": Kinship, Responsibility, and the Sociability of Nature

If in "Sister Turtle" Oliver uses the metaphor of family to explore connectivity in difference, there is a discernible shift towards yet another metaphor to capture the sense of trans-species kinship discussed in this contribution. In an essay entitled "The Perfect Days," Oliver uses the "citizenry of all things within one world" (pos. 401) as one such image—"citizenry," the community of citizens. The passage in which she uses the imagery shares its setting and beginning with many others in Oliver's essays and poems: an early morning walk in the woods, a "most casual of moments" (pos. 390) in which the narrator is suddenly seized by a happiness that momentarily has "any important difference between myself and all other things vanish" and strike the narrator with "a sudden awareness of the citizenry of all things within one world: leaves, dust, thrushes and finches, men and women" (pos. 401). While she insists that the moment is not "mystical," the language she uses is clearly one of revelation. Revealed is a deep connection that in the course of this contribution I have called kinship. I take Oliver's metaphor of "citizenry of all things" to entail and to transcend that of kinship. It not only implies a shared basis of physicality and soul, but it also points to the obligations attached to kinship and to a community of equal belonging. Oliver does not use the metaphor of citizenry or the citizen often; when she does, however, as in the example given above, it appears even more striking, for metaphors from the realm of the social rather than from nature are rare in Oliver's oeuvre. The metaphor of citizenship thus moves the connection and difference of kinship from the natural to the social, or, differently put, it explicitly acknowledges that the social is a part of human embeddedness in nature and that nature is inextricably intertwined with the social; in fact, that as a concept it depends on the social. If kinship already indicates that human and nonhuman relations are always already a form of sociability in Oliver's work, her use of the metaphor of citizenship for that sociability adds responsibility as a crucial factor.

As indicated in the beginning, in the terminology of political science *kinship* and *citizenship* do not easily sit with one another, on the contrary. Modern citizenship has usually been seen as ideally overcoming the bonds of kinship understood in terms of blood relations. However, more recent debates on—and metaphorizations of—citizenship have reevaluated the concepts in their relation to one another. In concepts of ecological or environmental citizenship, human ecological obligations have their foundation in human and nonhuman "co-presence" (Iovino) in the world. As Nick Stevenson explains, "an ecologically informed citizenship depends not as much upon 'nature' as upon the links between 'nature' and 'culture.' We need to come to terms with the limits of our bodies, our 'use' of 'nature' and our relationship with other life forms with which we share the planet; it requires a new cultural language within which we might reinterpret ourselves" (70). This responsibility is an individual one, impacts how we live individually and collectively, and has a global scope (Stevenson 74).

This understanding of ecological citizenship as individual or even individualistic is to some extent at odds with more recent focus on ecological justice as social justice, but it captures well the direction of Oliver's use of the term. In the poem "Mornings at Blackwater," the speaker invites the reader to make her own, responsible choices: "the present is what your life is, / and you are capable / of choosing what that will be, / darling citizen" (57). "Darling citizen" is not the address the reader would expect in a poem that, like so many others by Oliver, invite her to Provincetown's Blackwater pond in the morning; a catachresis in its unusual combination of a term of endearment with a term denoting political membership, it jolts the reader from a space of individual choice and appreciation into one of responsibility and sociability.

While Oliver's use of citizen and citizenry as metaphors for a kinship that entails obligation and responsibility falls squarely within a particular debate about how to live responsibly, it draws less, I suspect, on contemporary debates of citizenship than it presents an engagement with Transcendentalism. In his reading of Oliver's poetry as an "Emersonian project," Mark Johnson appreciatively calls her "a self-conscious, unembarrassed Romantic" (80). "Emersonian rapture is at the core of her work," he continues, "and informs her sense of what poetry does, her vatic voice, and her adventure of not-knowing" (82). Oliver herself has frequently acknowledged her indebtedness to and love for Emerson's (and other Romantics') work, and Johnson focuses on the field in which Emerson clearly had the greatest impact on Oliver's poetry: nature and the role of the poet. Yet, I suggest that in the—admittedly few—uses of citizenry and citizen as metaphors in her work, and in how Oliver interweaves them with her understanding of human existence in nature and in kinship with non-human life, she also engaged in a conversation with Emerson about meanings and scope of citizenship as a metaphor that transcends the realm of political organization.

The most immediate link to Emerson in "Mornings at Blackwater" may be seen in the poem's obvious call to a seemingly apolitical self-cultivation. Jack Turner has argued that the political potential of Emerson's thinking has been either dismissed outright or that it has been reduced to his concept of self-cultivation (125). Countering either reading, he makes a strong case for what he sees as Emerson's ethics of liberal democratic citizenship. Far from being self-absorbed, Emersonian self-reliance rather "creates an impetus for moral and civic engagement" (Turner 143). I see Oliver's use of the metaphor of citizenship as both tying in with such an understanding of the political potential of self-reliance and its importance for responsible political citizenship, but also with a metaphorization by Emerson himself that points to a more universal responsibility. In his 1878 essay "The Sovereignty of Ethics," Emerson speaks of "man" being made "a citizen of the world of souls: he feels what is called duty; he is aware that he owes a higher allegiance to do and live as a good member of this universe" (405). In light of her own project, Oliver's use of the metaphor of citizenry and citizen, on the one hand, expands the meaning of both terms to cover a sociability beyond political institutions and processes (a metaphorization very much in line with current developments in the broad use of the term); on the other hand, it expands the meaning of connection and responsibility in her own work toward a broader sense of the localized nature, the specific Cape Cod places she so much focuses on as part of a larger social context in which nature and culture interlink, but "neither [as] a naturalist reduction of culture nor a culturalist reduction of nature" (Zapf 139). Despite the individualist focus of Oliver's poetry, her work implies a vision beyond individual emotion and redemption. As Lynn Keller has argued, "poetry can foster an examination of the ethics of our relations with the species with whom we share the planet, and it can attempt—within the limits of what is human-produced—to allow their ways, sounds, and rhythms to enter into our words" (621). Despite or because of its romanticism, this is precisely what Oliver's poetry does.

## Notes

1 | I thank Babette Tischleder for drawing my attention to Haraway's recent work on kinship.
2 | By reading Oliver's autobiographical essay side by side with her poems, I do not suggest a conflation of the speakers, but rather a shared concern with issues of language, relation, and ways of being in the world.

## Works Cited

Bonds, Diane. "The Language of Nature in the Poetry of Mary Oliver." *Women's Studies*, vol. 21, no. 1, 1992, pp. 1-15.
Buell, Lawrence. *The Future of Environmental Criticism: Environmental Crisis and Literary Imagination*. Blackwell, 2005.
Cronon, William. "The Trouble with Wilderness; or, Getting Back to the Wrong Nature." *Uncommon Ground: Toward Reinventing Nature*, edited by William Cronon, Norton, 1995, pp. 69-90.
Davis, Todd. "The Earth as God's Body: Incarnation as Communion in Mary Oliver's Poetry." *Christianity and Literature*, vol. 58, no. 4, 2009, pp. 605-24.
Emerson, Ralph Waldo. "Nature." *The Essential Writings of Ralph Waldo Emerson*, edited by Brooks Atkinson, with an introduction by Mary Oliver, The Modern Library, 2000, pp. 1-39.
---. "The Sovereignty of Ethics." *The North American Review*, vol. 126, no. 262, 1878, pp. 404-420.
Fast, Robin Riley. "The Native American Presence in Mary Oliver's Poetry." *The Kentucky Review*, vol. 12, no. 1, 1993, pp. 59-68. uknowledge.uky.edu
Ferrando, Francesca. "Posthumanism, Transhumanism, Antihumanism, Metahumanism, and New Materialisms: Differences and Relations." *Existenz: An International Journal in Philosophy, Religion, Politics, and the Arts*, vol. 8, no. 2, 2013, pp. 26-32.
Garrard, Greg. *Ecocriticism*. Routledge, 2012.
Graham, Vicki. "'Into the Body of Another': Mary Oliver and the Poetics of Becoming Other." *Papers in Language and Literature*, vol. 30, no. 4, 1994, pp. 352-72.

Haraway, Donna. "Anthropocene, Capitalocene, Plantationocene, Chtululucene: Making Kin." *Environmental Humanities*, vol. 6, 2015, pp. 159-65.

Iovino, Serenella. "Ecocriticism and a Non-Anthropocentric Humanism." *Local Natures, Global Responsibilities. Ecocritical Perspectives on the New English Literatures*, edited by Laurenz Volkmann, et al. Rodopi, 2010, pp. 29-54.

Johnson, Mark. "'Keep Looking': Mary Oliver's Emersonian Project." *The Massachusetts Review*, vol. 46, no. 1, 2005, pp. 78-98.

Keller, Lynn. "Green Reading: Modern and Contemporary American Poetry and Environmental Criticism," *The Oxford Handbook of Modern and Contemporary American Poetry*, edited by Cary Nelson, Oxford University Press, 2012,

McNew, Janet. "Mary Oliver and the Tradition of Romantic Nature Poetry." *Contemporary Literature*, vol. 30, no. 1, 1989, pp. 59-77.

Oliver, Mary. "Staying Alive." *Blue Pastures*. Harcourt Brace, 1995, pp. 63-72.

---. *New and Selected Poems: Volume One*. Beacon Press, 1992. ("Some Questions You Might Ask"; "August"; "Happiness"; "Hunter's Moon—Eating the Bear")

---. "The Perfect Days." *Long Life: Essays and Other Writings*. Kindle edition, DaCapo Press, 2004.

---. *Red Bird*. Bloodaxe, 2008. ("Red Bird"; "Night and River"; "Of the Empire"; "Mornings at Blackwater"; "I Will Try"; "Red Bird Explains Himself")

---. "Sister Turtle." *Upstream. Selected Essays*. Penguin, 2016, pp. 49-61.

---. *Thirst*. Beacon Press, 2006.

Parini, Jay. *Why Poetry Matters*. Kindle edition, Yale University Press, 2008.

Quetchenbach, Bernard. *Back from the Far Field: American Nature Poetry in the Late Twentieth Century*. University of Virginia Press, 2000.

Riley, Jeanette E. "The Eco-Narrative and the Ethymeme: Form and Engagement in Environmental Writing." *Interdisciplinary Literary Studies*, vol. 10, no. 2, 2009, pp. 82-98.

Stevenson, Nick. *Cultural Citizenship: Cosmopolitan Questions*. Open University Press, 2003.

Tsing, Anne Lowenhaupt, and Silvia Yunko Yanagisako. "Feminism and Kinship Theory." *Current Anthropology*, vol. 24, no. 4, 1983, pp. 511-16.

Turner, Jack. "Self-Reliance and Complicity: Emerson's Ethics of Citizenship." *A Political Companion to Ralph Waldo Emerson*, edited by Alan M. Levine and Daniel S. Malachuck, University Press of Kentucky, 2011, pp. 125-51.

Wolfe, Cary. *What is Posthumanism?* University of Minnesota Press, 2010.

Zapf, Hubert. "Cultural Ecology of Literature—Literature as Cultural Ecology." *Handbook of Ecocriticism and Cultural Ecology*, edited by Hubert Zapf, De Gruyter, 2016, pp. 135-53.

# Strange Animals in Stylish Habitats: Marianne Moore's Poetry Revisited

*Sabine Sielke*

## Animals in Style

Much has already been said about Marianne Moore's passion for the animal kingdom and the significance of the various strange animals populating her paradigmatically modernist poetry—creatures ranging from butterflies to snails and reptiles and including an "intramural rat," an "octopus," a "giraffe," and an "arctic ox," among many, many others. Just as much has been made out of this particular affection: poet-critic Randall Jarrell was only one among several of Moore's contemporaries who, in his 1942 essay "The Humble Animal," identified the writer herself with the creatures her writing celebrates with much awe and wonder (qtd. in Mak 873).[1] In the 1950s, Moore went by the label of "pet poet" for some observers—and I have to admit I never quite understood what that meant. At the time Moore famously posed as "poetess" for a series of photographs taken by Esther Bubley—with elephants, zebras, parrots, and chimps at the Bronx Zoo and published by *Life* magazine in September 1953, underscoring how zoos frame our relation with our more or less close kin. And it came as no (big) surprise that Moore, in response to the request of the Ford Motor Company to suggest an effective name for a new model in 1955, came up with a list that included "The Intelligent Whale," "Mongoose Civique," as well as "Turcotinga" ("being a South-American finch or sparrow") and favored suggestion number 43, "Utopian Turtletop" (see Usher). Unfortunately, if understandably, Ford declined, opted for their own coinage "Edsel" instead, and saw the whole enterprise flop. Moore's poetry and her devotion to animals, by contrast, have proven to be quite sustainable, and current literary criticism has both revitalized (see Raphel) and newly politicized the Pulitzer Prize-winning writer. Venturing out to roam the "ecolog[ies] of modernism" (Schuster), readers have recently explored Moore's "zoo-logic" (Colvin), mapped her "eco-" and "animal poetics" (Hutchison; Strømmen), and reinvented the single-minded poet as environmentally-minded conservationist.

Fig. 1. Marianne Moore at the Bronx Zoo. 1953. Courtesy of Esther Bubley Collection, Science & Society Picture Library, London.

Both the old-school "animal-equals-poet" approach and current ecocritical perspectives seem to miss the mark, though, even as they highlight how all our readings are—to a certain degree and somewhat necessarily—driven by contemporaneous ethical, political, or ideological agendas. Still, one may argue, Moore's work seems of particular interest when the "timeless," complex, and fragile interdependence of all life forms has become a timely, a pressing issue indeed. After all, next to climate change, the dramatic decline of biodiversity in recent decades is only beginning to raise the concern it no doubt deserves. That we may never even have heard about some of the endangered species that Moore's poetry features so prominently—such as the pangolin (see Habekuß) or the paper nautilus—certainly enhances the appropriateness of an eco-conscious approach to her writing. Such a perspective on Moore's strange animals is only adequate, I would like to suggest, when we observe her creatures in the stylish habitats the poet created to ensure their survival.

As a strikingly stylish intellectual herself, we need to remember, Moore left sustainable marks on twentieth-century American culture and cultural criticism first and foremost by way of her preoccupation and deep concern with matters of style: in fact, Moore's unconventional take on style, I hold, interrogates and challenges common notions of a concept that for most of its history has remained fairly vague. We may agree, though, that our "styles" seem to lay out the pathways through which we want to or can be approached, the conditions under which we are accessible and, perhaps, available, yet always within limits we deem to set ourselves. For Moore, this "we" unquestionably includes many "stylish" animals which have style in the sense that the idiosyncrasies of their outer appearance and behavior shape the spheres, the habitat in which other animals, including ourselves, are invited to relate to them. For Moore, these "stylish" creatures include "the inextinguishable / salamander" which "styled himself but presbyter" and whose "shield was his humility" (*Complete Poems* 144 [1981]); or the "sea lizards—congregated" in Moore's poem "The Tuatera," "so there is not room to step, with tails laid criss-cross, alligator-style, among birds toddling in and out" (*Complete Poems* 21 [1994]). Accordingly, one of the most salient definitions of Moore's sense of "style" is presented in the apostrophic address of her poem "To a Snail":

> If "compression is the first grace of style,"
> you have it. Contractility is a virtue
> as modesty is a virtue.
> It is not the acquisition of any one thing
> that is able to adorn,
> or the incidental quality that occurs
> as a concomitant of something well said,
> that we value in style,
> but the principle that is hid:
> in the absence of feet, "a method of conclusions";
> "a knowledge of principles,"
> in the curious phenomenon of your occipital horn. (*Complete Poems* 85 [1981])

Projecting style as a "hidden principle," the poet dresses her appreciation in the words of other writers (here Demetrius of Phalerum and Duns Scotus) and engages in an aesthetics that echoes the camouflaging "armored" creatures she so admires. Like the "curious phenomenon" of an "occipital horn," situated at the back of the head, styles, according to Moore, hide more than they expose; they are modes of modesty and mimicry rather than flamboyance.

## Reading as Re-Vision

Of course, just like current ecocritical approaches, my own previous work on Moore has been inspired by a particular agenda and revisionary impulse. When I started to think more intensely about American women's poetry in the early 1980s, I was attracted in particular to the work of Emily Dickinson and Marianne Moore, two poets that revisionist feminist readings had not previously affiliated. While Dickinson had been celebrated by Adrienne Rich, as early as 1976, as a "genius" and "foremother" for women writers ("Vesuvius"

167), Moore had long been considered "in denial" of her gender, engaged as she was in what appeared a cerebral, if not chaste poetics and a "fiddle" with forms that presented us, first and foremost, with curious crafted inanimate objects and odd animate creatures. Characterized by what Geoffrey Hartman read as "an extreme reverence for created things coupled with an extreme distrust of the self" (111), Moore's poems prompted comparisons to "overstuffed cupboards, full of irrelevancies and distractions" (Costello, "'Feminine' Language" 223). For many a critic, though, these gender matters spelt out as matters of sex: somehow assuming that (women's) poetry ought to express (female) sexuality, "more often than not, the suggestion is," as Cliff Mak has it, "that [Moore's] virtuosity comes at the expense of, or as a diversion from, a more fundamentally necessary expression—that of her sexuality" (873). Uneasy with such judgments, I ventured out to show how Moore affirmed style as the faculty of a singular intellect—a preference that is without doubt, to a certain degree, gendered—and how intensely Moore's writing indeed interrogated the precarious position and authority of the female subject.

Before embarking on this project that eventually became my book *Fashioning the Female Subject: The Intertextual Network of Dickinson, Moore, and Rich* (1997), I had a different impulse, however. Studying biology as a second major, I first contemplated examining Moore's deep interest in that field—an interest I shared and, in a chapter on her use of mimicry, came to align with the poet's idiosyncratic concern with style. Characterizing Moore's critical prose in particular, mimicry marks a deferential mode of appreciation in her writing that celebrates style not as an external, but as an existential matter and acknowledges the aesthetic as inextricably tied to the ethical. While my early research came to move gender issues center stage, I did revitalize my passion for the biosciences, making issues at the crossroads of cultural studies and the sciences a focus of my recent work. This work includes new interdisciplinary perspectives on mimicry as well as this essay, dedicated to an admired colleague with whom I have shared part of the way as well as some intellectual and scholarly passions.

I take this revisionary inroad into my argument in part because my contribution to this book re-addresses, in fact reframes one of Moore's poems, "The Paper Nautilus," a text that is both paradigmatic and somewhat singular in her oeuvre. "Re-vision," Adrienne Rich wrote in her seminal essay "When We Dead Awaken: Writing as Re-Vision" (1972), "the act of looking back, of seeing with fresh eyes, of entering an old text from a new critical direction . . . is for us [women] more than a chapter in cultural history: it is an act of survival (35)." Like her exclusionary take on women, Rich's word choice—"survival"—may strike us as perhaps overly strong now; it is a term, however, that gains its urgency from its historical moment, as it does when Margaret Atwood chooses "survival" as the title of her 1972 "thematic guide to Canadian literature." Its many resonances range from evolutionary theory across memory cultures to current concerns with sustainability and may include our care about the survival of poets—and of passionate readers of poetry—who have become an endangered species, too. Even as the currently preferred brevity of (text) messages creates a proximity to poetry and may even remind us of the haiku, and though (Moore's) poems are in line, in some sense, with the art of advertisement, it is the short span of our increasingly fleeting attention that both impedes and shines light on Moore's ultimate definition of poetry as a "place for the genuine" (*Complete Poems* 36 [1981]).

Perhaps accordingly, Moore's favorite fauna are "armored animals" whose evolutionary fitness is due in part to the condition of their skins, to horns or shells that Moore adapted to adorn what I consider the "'battle-dressed' protectiveness" of her own poetics (Sielke 62). Her syllabic poem "The Paper Nautilus" belongs with these "martial arts" (60) which foreground the brittleness and vulnerability of a natural world that, at the same time, so it seems, builds on and keeps mobilizing much strength to persist. The poem certainly fits the framework of recent debates in ecocriticism and animal studies, as it invites eco-conscious perspectives. Yet it also marks the limits of what we, as literary and cultural critics, can make of the relation between literature, human and nonhuman animals, and the environment. "The Paper Nautilus" certainly resists, as I show, presentist re-readings by driving its own morality and poet(h)-ics, thereby challenging the ethics and politics of our revisionism.

Now this is Moore's "The Paper Nautilus" in its final version:

> For authorities whose hopes
> are shaped by mercenaries?
> Writers entrapped by
> teatime fame and by
> commuters' comforts? Not for these
> the paper nautilus
> constructs her thin glass shell.
> 
> Giving her perishable
> souvenir of hope, a dull
> white outside and smooth-
> edged inner surface
> glossy as the sea, the watchful
> maker of it guards it
> day and night; she scarcely
> 
> eats until the eggs are hatched.
> Buried eight-fold in her eight

>     arms, for she is in
>     a sense a devil-
>     fish, her glass ram'shorn-cradled freight
>     is hid but is not crushed;
>     as Hercules, bitten
>     by the crab loyal to the hydra
>     was hindered to succeed,
>     the intensively
>     watched eggs coming from
>     the shell free it when they are freed,—
>     leaving its wasp-nest flaws
>     of white on white, and close-
>     laid Ionic chiton-folds
>     like the lines of the mane of
>     a Parthenon horse,
>     round which the arms had
>     wound themselves as if they knew love
>     is the only fortress
>     strong enough to trust to.
>
>                              (*Complete Poems* 121-22 [1981])

Contemplating titles such as "Second Hercules," "Her Marine Cradle," "A Mermaid," or "A Nest," Moore first published this text as "The Glass-Ribbed Nest" in *The Kenyon Review* in 1940. The poem's moral overtones resonate with its political context, the Second World War. Like Moore's anti-war poem "In Distrust of Merits" (1943), "The Paper Nautilus" has been considered an exception in Moore's work. Its treatment of birth and maternal nurture, in fact the very use of the term "love," has made readers extremely uncomfortable and raised various objections to the poem's sentimentality. Such critique, however, may testify less to the poem's deficiency than to readers' difficulties in dealing with Moore as a woman-identified and politically opinionated, though conservative person. In some sense, Jarrell's famous claim, made in his book *Poetry and the Age* (1953), still seems to apply: "In this world of [Moore's] poems there are many thoughts, things, animals, sentiments, moral insights; but money and passion and power, the brute fact that works, whether or not correctly, whether or not precisely—the whole Medusa-face of the world: these are gone" (182). Yet are they, I wonder? To me, there is no avoiding "money and passion and power" which pretty much make up our habitats and environment, even in Moore's text that keeps pushing us back into the territory of what Lionel Trilling called the "liberal imagination."

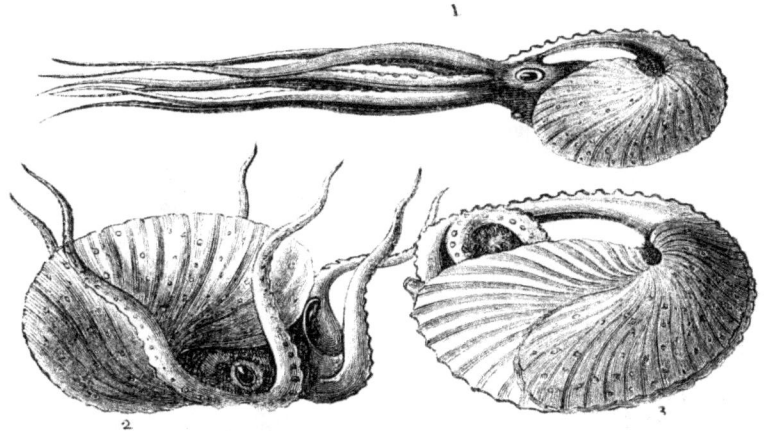

Fig. 2. Paper nautilus. Philip Henry Gosse, *Natural History: Mollusca* (1854).

In what follows, I readdress Moore's "The Paper Nautilus"—a text once crucial for my own feminist revision of Moore's work—with a focus on issues of environmentalism and on how Moore links her interest in biology with her sense of the function of poetry. My previous reading, framed by poststructuralist feminist theory, investigated Moore's sense of the "maternal"—admittedly a debatable term—and explored the ways it ties in with her personal and professional affiliation with other women. Interestingly enough, even though Moore's discourse on the maternal figures predominantly in descriptions of animal behavior, it allows readings inspired by revisionary psychoanalysis. In "The Paper Nautilus," mothering is a process moving from a state of symbiotic or dyadic unity to separation and involving both care and a kind of heroism on the part of caretaker and offspring. Highlighting the marks the nautilus's eggs leave on the surface of its protective shell, the poem values not so much the bodily bond, though, but the persistent traces of proximity that remain. The poem's next to final stanza preserves these marks—beyond the live span of the organisms—as a discourse sensitive to differences within apparent indifference (or sameness), as "flaws / of white on white" that border on silence. Highlighting this poetological self-reflexivity and the complex ethics it drives, the poem avoids reference to the female body; it is thus not about maternity as a "woman's issue." In fact, Moore contemplated, yet ruled out those earlier versions of the text that used the word "mother":

> the watchful
> the tense mother, clutches
> it, scarcely leaving or
> eating till the eggs are hatched.

> the watchful
> animal takes charge of
> it herself and scarcely
> leaves it till the eggs are hatched.   (Rosenbach Museum and Library I.03.23)

Her final version favored the term "maker" instead:

> the watchful
> maker of it guards it
> day and night; she scarcely
> eats until the eggs are hatched.

In this way, the poem ties creation, creativity, and production to *pro*creation and *re*production, drawing an all but original analogy. However, this analogy mutates as Moore links her interest in the biology of a particular organism to the cultural function of poetry as well as its role as a habitat of interpersonal relations. Underlying this analogy is both a strong ambivalence towards maternal power as both shelter and entrapment (and the poem opts for liberation and letting go) and a conservatism that aligns this power with the values of the home (and household matters). This dimension of the poem in turn drives additional moments of ecocritical revision. Presenting us with figures on the move, Moore's "The Paper Nautilus," on the one hand, bespeaks a conservative and conservational agenda that responds to environmental challenges and forces of relocation. On the other hand, the text draws a clear line between the biological life form it explores and her lyrics, which perform the possibilities and limits of poetry and its configurations, first and foremost. Still, our serial revisions do not work against the "nature" of poetry as a form of cultural representation; instead, they are enabled by poetry's figures moving in spaces that are open, if not unlimited. Revisionism responds to this openness and explores layers upon layers of "possibility," to recall Emily Dickinson's definition of poetry as "dwelling" in the realm of the possible (466). At the same time, our revisionist approaches make a conservative move in remembering and reiterating the value of older texts, affirming their sustainability.

## Poetry as Habitat

Now how does Moore's poem "The Paper Nautilus" shape-shift under ecoconscious and ecocritical perspectives? And what additional dimensions of the text does such critique open up? My reading offers four points, ranging from the ethics of popular ecology to a sense of poetry as a habitat and a media ecology for inter- and intra-species exchange. It is based on the insight, drawn from a collaborative project on knowledge ecologies, that the conceptual framework of ecology emphasizes processes of interaction and economies of interdependence. Ecological perspectives, I hold, pinpoint site- and time-specific processes of differentiation, adaptation, and transformation. This approach to a certain degree counteracts the proliferating use of *ecology* as a trendy analogy for rather diverse cultural practices and their media. At the same time, I recognize the value and unavoidability of analogical thinking. In fact, my claim that the conceptual and methodological framework of ecology opens perspectives that account for practices of writing, reading, and sharing of poetry as acts of "environmental protection" is inspired by such thinking.

Now first, there is a sense of wonder and appreciation for living organisms that are fundamentally different from us yet invite a particular mode of "recognition." This recognition of ourselves in the other comes along with anthropomorphism and the consciousness that our present experiences of our immediate environment are of little importance "in the greater scheme of things," as Dana Phillips writes in *The Truth of Ecology* (203). The processes that are significant for the science of ecology today, Hannes Bergthaller underscores in his book *Populäre Ökologie: Zu Literatur und Geschichte der modernen Umweltbewegung in den USA* (2007), happen on a scale beyond the sensorium of human bodies. They certainly include, however, growing concerns with biodiversity and sustainability which is a second point to be made for an eco-conscious reading of Moore's "animated" texts. Third, "The Paper Nautilus" voices a critique of an economy of property and spending and, by extension, of a (neo-)liberalist economic agenda from which the poem itself evolves—at a time when conceptions of neoliberalism find their first formulation (see Hayek). In the poem's own habitat, by contrast, freedom is achieved not by accumulating property, but by relinquishing ownership, by letting go. Fourth and finally, the poem's own agenda makes us curious to learn more about its own cultural ecology. After all, in 1935, botanist Arthur Tansley claimed that any study of organisms needed to include their environment, "the habitat factors in the widest sense," with which they formed an entity he called ecosystem (299).

First on to the work of wonder, appreciation, and anthropomorphism! "Which of us," Moore herself wonders in "O Beast and Jewels," a short piece for *Harper's Bazaar* published in 1963, "has not been stunned by the beauty of an animal's skin or its flexibility in motion?" (*Complete Prose* 573). "The Paper Nautilus" is one among several of Moore's texts that take a bifocal view on animal behavior and make nature resonate with culture and vice versa. Like the fable, Moore's animal poems anthropomorphize the natural world and allow animals to display "certain postures of a man" (*Complete Poems* 119 [1981]). Like La Fontaine's texts, they are primarily "vehicles for [her] philosophy, not studies in natural history" (Moore, *Complete Prose* 595). Unlike fables, however, they guide willing readers into strange worlds that are both imagined *and real*, or as Moore herself put it in a much-quoted passage of "Poetry": into "imaginary gardens with real toads in them" (*Complete Poems* 267 [1981]). We may have seen or even touched a nautilus shell; but until now, science knows very "little," as we can read on the website of the US Fish and Wildlife Service, "about nautilus populations in the wild." Such lack of knowledge makes the precious shell of this rare species serve even better as a vehicle of representation and myth, or more precisely: as a metaphor for metaphor.

Nevertheless and second, the nautilus's biology is suggestive, as it engages matters of biodiversity and sustainability and pulls us away from the text to the animal's own habitat in the surface waters of tropical and subtropical seas. The nautilus or argonaut is a mollusc and one of the few extant species of a group of cephalopods, including squids, cuttlefish, and octopi, which "thrived in the seas 500 million years ago when the earth's continents were still forming" (US Fish & Wildlife Service). Older than dinosaurs, the paper nautilus is the ultimate embodiment of perseverance, survival tactics, and evolutionary fitness. Resembling the octopus, the female is twenty times the size of the male, which was consequently considered its parasite for a long time. Characteristic of the female is that its entrails and mantle are covered entirely by a shell which develops from the membranes of its dorsally located arms.

Fig. 3. Female argonaut in the Sea of Japan. Courtesy of Dr. Julian Finn, Museums Victoria, Melbourne.

Fittingly, the term "paper nautilus" is safely embedded in cultural discourse—and so is Moore's poem. "Paper" makes reference to the "thin, white, brittle shell[s]" the females of the genus *Argonauta* secrete, which primarily enable them to "obtain[] and manag[e] surface-acquired air" (Yong); and of course, this also feeds the poem's self-referentiality. "Nautilus" derives from the Greek Argonauts since it was assumed (and suggested by Aristotle) that the nautilus glides over the sea, using the folds of the skin on its arms as sails. The term refers to the ship in which the Argonauts sailed, the heroes who accompanied Jason in his quest for the golden fleece, and more generally to any adventurer engaged in a journey. Unlike Oliver Wendell Holmes's "The Chambered Nautilus" (1858) which takes the titular animal as a figure for fragmentation, movement, and progress, Moore's poem juxtaposes historical with ontogenetic development (see Costello, "Wild Decorum" 48) and affirms wholeness, stability, nurture, and the "gift of life." At the same time, its mythological connotations make mothering a quest, and reproduction part of a history of seafaring which has traditionally excluded female figures, prompting Margaret Fuller to famously demand that women "be sea captains" (174).

This double context brings to mind Roland Barthes's piece on Jules Verne, "The Nautilus and the Drunken Boat." "[T]he ship," writes Barthes,

> may well be a symbol for departure; it is, at a deeper level, the emblem of closure. An inclination for ships always means the joy of perfectly enclosing oneself, of having at hand the greatest possible number of objects, and having at one's disposal an absolutely finite space. To like ships is first and foremost to like a house, a superlative one since it is unremittingly closed, and not at all vague sailings into the unknown: a ship is a habitat before being a means of transport. (*Mythologies* 66-67)

Reading Verne's Nautilus, Captain Nemo's submarine in *Twenty Thousand Leagues Under the Sea* (1870), as "the most desirable of all cages," Barthes reverberates a traditional symbolism that associates ships and vessels with women and wombs (and which gains an entirely new resonance with the recent refugee crisis). Like Barthes's ship, Moore's shell is "a habitat before being a means of transport."[2]

Third, for an ecologically driven re-reading, the poem's take on matters of economy seems crucial. After all, zoologist Ernst Haeckel in 1870 defined ecology as "the science of the economy, of the household of animal organisms" (qtd. in Jax and Schwarz 150).[3] In coining the word ecology, Haeckel thus explained biological processes in terms of economy, referencing human practices of production, consumption and resource management (see also Bergthaller, "An American Economy"). Moore's poem, which also foregrounds matters of economy, may be read as acknowledging both the history of the concept of ecology and the degree to which the nautilus is endangered by human consumption and environmental pollution. As the marine biologist Robert Kelly explains:

> Nautili are found in international trade primarily for their shells and meat. In addition, their shells are prized by collectors around the world and they are harvested for the aquarium trade. . . . Nautilus species are also threatened by habitat degradation as their native reefs are polluted and destroyed by destructive fishing practices and development.

In hindsight, Moore's poem may even be seen as engaging the liberalist economy that became the driving force during the Anthropocene by juxtaposing the ideology of property (as freedom) with an ethics of gift-giving. More precisely, though, "The Paper Nautilus" juxtaposes two different discursive economies, distinguishing writing as alienated labor from writing as an activity comparable to the labors of reproduction. The poem puts off writers who work merely for pay or sordid advantage ("mercenaries") and sympathizes with a creature that labors apart from the economy of exchange. At the same time, it aligns reproduction with production ("constructs"), thereby dissolving a binarism which is conventionally conceived in analogy to male and female. In this way, the text champions an alternative economy of exchange, apart from entrapments in property, an economy of "giving," "liberty," and "love." Moore's poem thus distinguishes between the realm of the proper that connotes property and appropriation from the realm of the gift, an offer not meant to be returned (Cixous 888-89). Moore herself subscribed to an ethics of non-possessiveness, to "the power of relinquishing / what one would keep" (*Complete Poems* [1981] 144), which clearly challenges the (neo-)liberal claim, reiterated by Hayek in 1944, that property guarantees freedom. Phrases such as "possession is the grave of bliss" or "nothing is worth anything unless it is priceless" adorn the poet's notebooks. "Modesty is a good system," runs a line from Moore's fragments of *La Fontaine's Fables*, "and mercenariness, a bad one" (*Complete Prose* 627). In this way the poem in fact anticipates a perspective that informs the US-American movement of a "popular ecology" which, as Bergthaller has shown, tended to tie ecological processes to notions of a liberal society in ways that challenge the social order: "Again and again, nature is presented as a 'liberal' order, harmonized by the workings of an invisible hand; however, this spontaneous homeostasis must be protected against totalitarian forces" (*Populäre* Ökologie 301-02; translation mine).

The genesis of "The Paper Nautilus," however, underlines how poetry functions within, not separate from economies of exchange, which invites us to, fourth, zoom in on the cultural ecology and interaction from which the text evolved. The poem was occasioned in part by a present, the shell of a nautilus, sent to Moore in 1937 by philanthropist Louise Crane as "a form of interest."

As wealthy heiress to the Crane Paper Company, Louise Crane was a generous sponsor of the arts and culture; she offered Moore monetary support and legal assistance, introduced her to affluent social circles, provided emotional support in times of personal crisis, and became the executer of Moore's estate after the poet's death in 1972. Moore responded to Crane's gift in a letter: "A nautilus has always seemed to me something supernatural. The more I look at it the less I can credit it . . ." (*Selected Letters* 381). Unable to "credit" the nautilus's shell, Moore resists translating its value into monetary terms and labels it "supernatural." Discriminating her own manner of appreciation from that of capitalized/capitalist "INTERESTS," that is, by the degree to which investments pay off, Moore's letter expresses an ambivalence towards the financial "nurture" provided by Crane and blurs its own distinction between disinterested mothering and interested mercenaries, between what Hélène Cixous delineated as the "realm of the gift" and "the realm of the proper." Moore's poem "The Paper Nautilus" eventually turned into a gift for Crane who passed it on to migrant poet Elisabeth Bishop as a souvenir from New York. Finally, dedicating her *Complete Poems* to Crane, Moore offered a gift to someone who had, for decades, generously given to her; for "[d]edications imply giving" to Moore (*Selected Poems* 108). Moving in space as an intermediary, Moore's "The Paper Nautilus" thus affirms an economy of exchange that is both part and apart of our general cultural commerce.

Still, the poem creates its own economy of mutual and unmediated exchange, only part of which can be accommodated to an eco-conscious reading. As the nautilus/writer borrows from her own resources ("she scarcely eats") to feed her offspring, active ("Giving," "guards") and passive constructions alternate ("are hatched," "Buried," "is hid but is not crushed"); thus both nautilus and shell function as subject and make subject and object positions seemingly interchangeable. This "other" economy of exchange fully unfolds towards the end of the poem with its surplus of indefinite pronouns and spatial imagery. While syntactical linearity is equivocated, image and simile, the "close- / laid Ionic chiton-folds / like the lines in the mane / of a Parthenon horse," give prominence to the visual and tactile over the temporal. The term "chiton" denotes both an ancient Greek garment and an order of marine molluscs comparable, yet distinct from the nautilus. Like the "Parthenon horse," the term thus blends nature and culture and suggests a similar sense of difference within indifference already expressed in the phrase "white on white." Comparing nautilus and devilfish (which is an alternative older term for nautilus, yet also denotes fish that feed on cephalopods as well as a group of rays or any other large eight-armed cephalopod), Moore had already prepared the reader for this redundant, yet remarkable doubleness, this indifferent difference of meaning. Like the destabilization of referentiality, the remetaphorization of the maternal advances difference within what seems lacking in difference or common ground precisely where difference seems to reign. In this way, the "flaws / of white on white" left by the nautilus's egg read as marks of a dynamics of exchange distinct from the ordinary economy of discourse and voice—an economy which tends to know white because it knows black, that is, by *différance*. The graft left by the nautilus's eggs, those "wasp-nest flaws / of white on white," by comparison, signifies difference within sameness, separation within connectedness and inscribes a slight, though significant difference into the economy of gain for loss. And yet, Moore's "The Paper Nautilus" ends on a highly ambivalent note. Dominated by the metaphor of the "fortress," the final lines object to a possessiveness, the desire for appropriation and self-identity inherent in maternal care as an affection that cannot let go of its object.

Like Verne's Nautilus, the nautilus's shell is thus an "emblem of closure" indeed. And like the nautical morality Barthes described, "the possessive nature of the man on a ship," which "makes him at once the god, the master and the owner" (67), maternal affection is not separate from the realm of the proper, from possessiveness. According to Barthes's "mythology of seafaring," the only "means to exorcise" possessiveness on the ship is "to eliminate the man and to leave the ship on its own. The ship then is no longer a box, a habitat, an object that is owned; it becomes a travelling eye, which comes close to the infinite; it constantly begets departures." It "can make man proceed," he concludes, "from a psychoanalysis of the cave to a genuine poetics of exploration" (67). Just as they are part of Moore's "martial arts," curiosity and a sense of adventurousness may have been part of her liking of the shell. No longer a natural habitat, it serves to transport new meanings. The "white on white" graft on its surface, the metonymic mark of dyadic relation, traces another economy of signification. Without the absence of the love object, there is no such "poetics of exploration" which itself, though, escapes our framework of eco-politics.

## Conversation, Conservatism, Conservation

When in May 1940, Crane brought a copy of Moore's "A Glass-Ribbed Nest" to Key West, Bishop expressed a particular favor for the poem's final part: "I admire especially," she wrote, "from 'wasp-nest flaws—of white on white,' to the end. The whole poem is like a rebuke to me, it suggests so many of the plans for the things I want to say about Key West and have scarcely hinted at in '[Jeronimo's] House' for example" (qtd. in Kalstone 69). Bishop was well aware of how her own work had "nurtured" Moore's. Like Moore's "glass-ribbed nest," Bishop's "house" is a perishable "love nest" made of paper, of writing in fact. Consisting of eight stanzas of detailed observation, placed in sets of two beside each other, Bishop's poem "Jerónimo's House" forms a kind of nest on the page by itself, leaving blank spaces, "flaws of white on white" in its center(s).

Moreover, both Bishop's and Moore's poems present the interior, the inside space of their house or shell, as images of protection, nurture, and origin of discourse. Bishop's "writing-paper / lines of light" compare to the "flaws / of white on white" on the nautilus's "paper." Unlike Moore, however, Bishop does not project writing as mothering and home as wholeness and enclosure, as a place of "integration too tough for infraction" (Moore, *Complete Poems* 147 [1981]). Bishop's house is a palace, yet no fortress, but a "decentered" dwelling, compartmentalized like a chambered nautilus. Where Moore's poem concludes with a close-up on the textures of affiliation and the closural metaphor of maternal love, Bishop has public "voices of [the] radio" penetrate the apparent privacy of home—a term that has meanwhile achieved complex new cultural capital and figures prominently in postcolonial and diaspora studies, expressing a longing for a place that never was or cannot be remembered. The temper of Bishop's poem is temporariness, discontinuity, departure, displacement ("When I move / I take these things"); her speaker is familiar with homelessness and hurricanes rather than fortresses of maternal affection. Bishop escapes domesticity by imagining new and unfamiliar domiciles, whereas for Moore, "fortitude" is, as David Kalstone claims, "linked to staying home" (89). As it turns out, an ecologically-minded revision of Moore's poem takes us many, perhaps too many, places; it works centrifugally and perhaps harmonizes more with a "distant reading" (Moretti) than with the close-ups we cherish. At the same time, such a revision does not displace, but builds on, adds to, and questions, yet to a certain degree also affirms previous readings, including my own feminist and "engendered" take on it: for the text's overall conservative morale indeed closely relates to eco-conscious concepts of conservation and sustainability. In fact, Moore's "The Paper Nautilus" may help to explain why environmentally conscious and conservative agendas are a likely political match. Evolving in proximity with, if prior to the work of author-critic Lionel Trilling, Moore's poem may indeed foreground the paradoxical potential of a conservative "liberal imagination." By revisiting Moore's work with an eco-conscious mindset we re-enter habitats that may seem strange and foreign territory, yet that invite conversations across political lines—lines that have invaded homes in many cultural habitats; but that certainly is another story—and another analogy. After all, we are meaning-making animals in stylized, if not stylish habitats.

## Notes

**1** | "One can only stand amazed," Cliff Mak rightly observes, "by the frequency with which contemporaries," including William Carlos Williams, Hugh Kenner, and Clement Greenberg, "compared Marianne Moore to different animals" (873). Mak himself argues "that Moore's deferential and more oxygenated model of authority found one of its most effective expressions in Moore's penchant for the comic," and he reads her "slapstick animals" as "the most striking image that the comic comprises in Moore's poems" (874).
**2** | By now, Nautilus is also the name of a Cologne-based magazine for popular science which deals with matters ranging from aerodynamics to its own primary medium, the web, and thus obviously capitalizes on the trope of transport.
**3** | "Unter Oecologie verstehen wir die Lehre von der Oeconomie, von dem Haushalt der thierischen Organismen" ("Über Entwicklungsgang und Aufgabe der Zoologie," 1870). Haeckel offered various definitions; see Zapf, p. 221.

## Works Cited

Atwood, Margaret. *Survival: A Thematic Guide to Canadian Literature*. Anansi, 1972.

Barthes, Roland. *Mythologies*. 1957. Translated by Annette Lavers. Paladin, 1980.

Bergthaller, Hannes. "An American Economy of Nature: Ecology, Liberal Metaphysics, and Aldo Leopold's *A Sand County Almanac*." *American Economies*, edited by Eva Boesenberg, et al., Winter, 2012, pp. 103-20.

---. *Populäre Ökologie: Zu Literatur und Geschichte der modernen Umweltbewegung in den USA*. Lang, 2007.

Bishop, Elisabeth. "Jerónimo's House." 1941. *Poems*, edited by Saskia Hamilton, Farrar, Straus and Giroux, 2011, p. 35.

Cixous, Hélène. "The Laugh of the Medusa." Translated by Keith Cohen and Paula Cohen. *Signs*, vol. 1, no. 4, 1976, pp. 875-93.

Colvin, Christina M. "Composite Creatures: Marianne Moore's Zoo-Logic." *Interdisciplinary Studies in Literature and Environment*, vol. 24, no. 4, 2017, pp. 707-26.

Costello, Bonnie. "The 'Feminine' Language of Marianne Moore." *Women and Language in Literature and Society*, edited by Sally McConnell-Ginet, Ruth Borker, and Nelly Furman. Praeger, 1980, pp. 222–38.

---. "Marianne Moore's Wild Decorum." *American Poetry Review*, vol. 16, no. 2, 1987, pp. 43-54.

Dickinson, Emily. *The Poems of Emily Dickinson*, edited by R. W. Franklin, Belknap Press of Harvard University Press, 1998.

Finn, Julian. "Sinking Aristotle's Sailing Octopus." *Australasian Science*, Nov. 2010, australasianscience.com.
Fuller, Margaret. *Woman in the Nineteenth Century*. 1845. Norton, 1971.
Gilcrest, David W. "Rhetorical Redemption, Environmental Poetics, and the Case of the Campdown Elm." *Interdisciplinary Studies in Literature and Environment*, vol. 8, no. 2, 2001, pp. 169-80.
Gosse, Philip Henry. *Natural History: Mollusca*. Society for Promoting Christian Knowledge, 1854.
Habekuß, Fritz. "Pangolin: Das was?" *Die Zeit*, no. 26, 2017, pp. 37–38.
Hartman, Geoffrey. *Easy Pieces*. Columbia University Press, 1985.
Hayek, Friedrich. *Road to Serfdom*. 1945. Institute of Economic Affairs, 2005.
Hutchison, Sharla. "The Eco-Poetics of Marianne Moore's 'The Sycamore.'" *Interdisciplinary Studies in Literature and Environment*, vol. 18, no. 4, 2011, pp. 763-78.
Jarrell, Randall. *Poetry and the Age*. Faber and Faber, 1955.
Jax, Kurt, and Astrid Schwarz. "The Early Period of Word and Concept Formation." *Ecology Revisited: Reflecting on Concepts, Advancing Science*, edited by Astrid Schwarz and Kurt Jax, Springer, 2011, pp. 149-54.
Kalstone, David. *Becoming a Poet: Elizabeth Bishop with Marianne Moore and Robert Lowell*. Farrar, Straus and Giroux, 1989.
Kelly, Jack. "Rare Nautilus Species Spotted for the First Time in 30 Years." *Into the Blue*, 25 Aug. 2015. marinebiology.co.
Kenner, Hugh. *A Homemade World: The American Modernist Writers*. Knopf, 1975.
Mak, Cliff. "On Falling Fastidiously: Marianne Moore's Slapstick Animals." *ELH*, vol. 83, no. 3, 2016, pp. 873-98.
Moore, Marianne. *The Complete Poems of Marianne Moore*. Viking, 1981.
---. *Complete Poems*. Penguin, 1994.
---. *The Complete Prose of Marianne Moore*, edited by Patricia C. Willis, Viking, 1986.
---. *Selected Letters*, edited by Bonnie Costello, Penguin, 1997.
---. *Selected Poems*. Macmillan, 1935.
Moretti, Franco. *Distant Reading*. Verso, 2013.
Phillips, Dana. *The Truth of Ecology: Nature, Culture, and Literature in America*. Oxford University Press, 2003.
Raphel, Adrienne. "The Marianne Moore Revival." *The New Yorker*, 13 Apr. 2016. newyorker.com/books/page-turner/the-marianne-moore-revival. Accessed 17 Jan. 2018.
Rich, Adrienne. "Vesuvius at Home: The Power of Emily Dickinson." 1976. *On Lies, Secrets, and Silence: Selected Prose 1966–1978*, Norton, 1995, pp. 157-83.
---. "When We Dead Awaken: Writing as Re-Vision." 1971. *On Lies, Secrets, and Silence: Selected Prose 1966–1978*, Norton, 1995, pp. 33-49.

Rosenbach Museum and Library. Marianne Moore Collection. Philadelphia.

Schuster, Joshua. *The Ecology of Modernism: American Environments and Avant-Garde Poetics*. University of Alabama Press, 2015.

Sielke, Sabine. *Fashioning the Female Subject: The Intertextual Networking of Dickinson, Moore, and Rich*. University of Michigan Press, 1997.

Strømmen, Hannah M. "Animal Poetics: Marianne Moore, Ted Hughes and the Song of Songs." *Literature and Theology*, vol. 31, no. 4, 2017, pp. 405-19.

Tansley, Arthur G. "The Use and Abuse of Vegetational Concepts and Terms." *Ecology*, vol. 16, no. 3, 1935, pp. 284-307.

Trilling, Lionel. *The Liberal Imagination: Essays on Literature and Society*. Doubleday, 1950.

US Fish & Wildlife Service. "Chambered Nautilus." fws.gov/international/animals/nautilus.html.

Usher, Shaun. "Utopian Turtletop." *Lists of Note*, 8 Feb. 2012. listsofnote.com/2012/02/utopian-turtletop.html. Accessed 17 Jan. 2018.

Williams, William Carlos. "Marianne Moore." 1925. *Marianne Moore: A Collection of Essays*, edited by Charles Tomlinson, New Directions, 1969, pp. 52–59.

Yong, Ed. "Scientists Solve Millenia-Old Mystery about the Argonaut Octopus." *Discover*, 18 May 2010. blogs.discovermagazine.com.

Zapf, Hubert. "Ecology, Culture, and Literature." *American Studies Today: New Research Agendas*, edited by Winfried Fluck, et al., Winter, 2014, pp. 21-41.

# The Beetles—Greatest Hits: The Rhythm 'n' Sound of Insects

*Bernd Herzogenrath*

Here's how one of Modernisms most famous short stories begins: "When Gregor Samsa awoke one morning from troubled dreams, he found himself changed into a monstrous cockroach in his bed" (Kafka 75). Ever wondered what such a giant insect sounds like? Two pages in, Kafka gives us the answer:

Gregor was dismayed when he heard his own voice . . . . It was still without doubt his own voice from before, but with a little admixture of an irrepressible squeaking that left the words only briefly recognizable at the first instance of their sounding, only to set about them afterwards so destructively that one couldn't be at all sure what one had heard. (77)

Although altered and "de-tuned," Samsa's voice is still human. As Slavoj Žižek has commented on one of Jacques Lacan's *aperçus*: domestic animals, too, because they are so close to humans, live in the dimension of language, and thus are also "infected" by the Symbolic (*Less Than Nothing* 413).[1] And—even if this hurts—cockroaches are domestic animals, albeit not such nice company as dogs, cats, guinea pigs and mini-turtles. In Samsa's case, it also becomes obvious that this domestic animal does not only partake in human language, but also in human pathology—Oedipus looms large in this story (after all, it's Kafka we're talking about here)—next time you talk to your dog and pet her, think about this.

But can we envision insect sounds in a different—in|human—way? What I would like to call *in|human* corresponds to Jeffrey Jerome Cohen's "inhuman" reading of the term *inhuman*, which "signifies 'not human,' of course, and therefore includes a world of forces, objects and nonhuman beings. But *in-human* also indicates the alien within (any human body is an ecosystem filled with strange objects)" (Cohen 271)—a materialist, anti-"human"istic perspective that sees the human inextricably connected to and even emerging from in|human forces.

In the following, I would like to discuss the instance of in|human rhythms in a piece of "bug music" by David Dunn—I wouldn't go as far as calling this a genre in its own right already, but there's a convincing critical mass of recordings and projects that would even justify this move: most and foremost the work of David Dunn himself (see also his *The Sound of Light in Trees*), or Sarah Peebles' *Insect Groove*, but also (and in particular) the work of David Rothenberg, an acclaimed clarinetist who does life improvisations with birds and insects, for example on his CD *Bug Music*, or in his project—together with the late Pauline Oliveros, overtone singer Timothy Hill, and millions of live singing insects—*Cicada Dream Band*.[2] Yet another case in point are the installations of Tomás Saraceno, who, in his project *Arachnid Orchestra*, builds up an interspecies ecology of "musicking" (the term is Christopher Small's), in which spider webs are used as musical instruments, tapping into the structural properties of the spider's silk, but also into the spider's sophisticated mode of communication through vibrations.[3]

## meter | rhythm

In many ways, the twentieth century can be regarded as art's attempts to escape the "tyranny of meter" (Schumann 126; my translation).[4] This phrase is the German composer Robert Schumann's, and he himself tried to free himself from that "law of metric cruelty" (125) by ever finer and braver syncopations (see, for instance, his *Kreisleriana* and *Kinderszenen*).

For the American context, Charles Ives breathes a similar sensibility. Henry and Sidney Cowell report that "Ives's whole approach to his complex rhythms should be understood as an attempt to persuade players away from the straitjacket of regular beats, with which complete exactness is impossible anyhow" (172). Instead, the performance should strive for a "variety of rhythmic tensions and muscular stresses that make constant slight changes of pace" (173)—Ives's "Over the Pavements" may serve as an example here.

It might be argued, though (as, for example, Saxer does), that all these modernist attempts to evade what Vladimir Nabokov has called the "miserable measurement of time" (538) are still marching (in relation to) a steady beat, be it in their scores (which still betray an adherence to "traditional notation"), be it in ever more adventurous deviations from that pulse (see, for example, Messiaen's "added value rhythms," "symmetrical permutations," "non-retrogradable rhythms," etc.). But, is there a way to think rhythm otherwise?

For Gilles Deleuze and Félix Guattari, the "tyranny of meter" is related to it being a nonproductive (or only reproductive) and thus empty periodicity, a static repetition that does not produce difference, a difference they relate to becoming: "Meter, whether regular or not, assumes a coded form whose unit of measure may vary, but in a non-communicating milieu, whereas rhythm is the Unequal or the Incommensurable that is always undergoing transcoding. Meter is dogmatic, but rhythm is critical" (*Plateaus* 313). Metric repetition is thus the repetition of the identical, creating equal units of time, whereas rhythm—real productive repetition, repetition with a difference—involves inequalities, maybe nonlinear logics: intensities that create "incommensurabilities between metric equivalent periods or spaces" (Deleuze, *Difference* 21).

These equivalent metrical periods are what clock-time consists of—as Frank Kermode has so beautifully put it in his *The Sense of an Ending*, "[t]he clock's 'tick-tock' I take to be a model of what we call a plot, an organisation which humanises time by giving it a form; and the interval between 'tock' and 'tick' represents purely successive, disorganised time of the sort we need to humanise" (45). The disorganised time in between, the non-pulsed "time in its pure state" is thus what Deleuze and Guattari refer to as rhythm (Deleuze, *Cinema 2* xi).[5]

In their plateau "On the Refrain," Deleuze and Guattari outline how rhythm and refrain are closely connected to a certain territory and geography, and simultaneously to the forces of deterritorialization, and of becoming. In turn, becoming itself is closely connected to a notion of geography—"[b]ecomings belong to geography, they are orientations, directions, entries and exits" (Deleuze and Parnet 2). Deleuze's concept of "history as becoming" thus reveals a close proximity to the "geohistory" (Deleuze and Guattari, *Philosophy* 95) of Fernand Braudel—"[g]eography wrests history from the cult of necessity in order to stress the irreducibility of contingency" (96). With the concept of *longue durée*, Braudel commented on the geographic aspects of (historical) time itself. According to Braudel, "[h]istory exists at different levels, I would even go so far as to say three levels but that would be simplifying things too much" (74). History—thus Braudel, thus Deleuze—happens at ten, at a hundred levels and time spans (at thousand plateaus) simultaneously. This coexistent and dynamic becoming is to the static succession of being what *locus* is to *datum*, space is to time, and by analogy regards "geography as opposed to history, the rhizome as opposed to arborescence" (Deleuze and Guattari, *Plateaus* 296). History is a rhizome that historiography aims at translating into an arborescent order, with the rhizome standing for the complex interplay of necessity and chance, human and nonhuman, culture and materiality, intention and self-organization.

This notion of geohistory corresponds to a perspective on rhythm of one of the profoundest "escape artists" of the metric tyranny—Olivier Messiaen. In a dialogue with the internationally renowned organist and interpreter of Messiaen's organ works, Almut Rößler, Messiaen puts forward a "time-philosophical" notion of rhythms:

What could be more useful for a musician than to create a link between movement and change.... Of even greater significance, however, will be an awareness of time-scales, superimposed on each other, which surrounds us: the endlessly long time of the stars, the very long time of the mountains, the middling one of the human being, the short one of insects, the very short one of atoms (not to mention the time-scales inherent in ourselves—the physiological, the psychological). Whenever the composer sets the tempo-change machine going, he'll become conscious of these different slownesses, these different quicknesses.... (Rößler 40)

Deleuze and Guattari's own concept of rhythm (and of the refrain) owes much to Messiaen's experimentations. When Messiaen refers to the composer's "tempo-change-machine," he basically talks about a synchronization of nature (that other tempo-change machine) and the composer's activity. Even if Messiaen's notion of nature still smacks of a transcendental concept (a God-centered harmonious *kosmos*), one can easily see how Deleuze and Guattari adapt that idea and relate it to their machinic conception of nature. Nature thus becomes un-natural, inhuman—machinic (or, in|human). From such a perspective, Messiaen's (and also Braudel's) classification of different time scales and time spans relates to the notion of the in|human already mentioned earlier.

## bug music

When discussing a piece by David Dunn now, I will carefully heed Deleuze's advice to not see this endeavor as "a matter of setting philosophy to music, or vice versa," but rather as "one thing folding into another" (*Negotiations* 163).

In 1935, the naturalist Hugh M. Smith observed the following spectacle in Thailand:

Imagine a tree thirty-five to forty feet high thickly covered with small ovate leaves, apparently with a firefly on every leaf, and all the fireflies flashing in perfect unison at the rate of about three times in two seconds, the tree being in complete darkness between flashes.... Imagine a tenth of a mile of river front with an unbroken line of Sonnerati trees with fireflies on every leaf flashing in synchronism, the trees at the ends of the line acting in perfect union with those between. Then, if one's imagination is vivid, he may form some conception of this amazing spectacle. (151)

Smith marveled at this unexplainable wonder—surely, these insects did not possess intelligence that made them intentionally flash in unison? It seems that this spectacle (which is still popular today, for example as a tourist attraction in the Great Smoky Mountains National Park) attracted lots of observers and commentators who published their responses in the journal *Science* in the early twentieth century. As one commentator put it:

If it is desired to get a body of men to sing or play together in perfect rhythm they not only must have a leader but must be trained to follow such a leader. Imagine the difficulty of keeping together on 'Old Hundred' if the notes were started with an interval so long as six or nine seconds between each. Do these insects inherit a sense of rhythm more perfect than our own? (Hudson 574)

The question of how to keep a rhythm without a maestro, conductor or click-track puzzled the naturalists and scientists. Today, it seems that the answer to all this is the concept of emergence, self-organization and spontaneous order. In fact, as Hudson already pointed out, the fireflies—or crickets, for that matter, where the emitted signal is not light but sound—do not perfectly harmonize, unison is not total, but interspersed with slight variations, accelerandos, ritardandos, stringendos, and so on: "Strictly speaking, there was no *measured* regularity in this response and therefore no *true rhythm* . . . . There was present the influence of suggestion on what may be called a "mob-psychology," but there was *no special leader*" (573). In their slightly out-of-sync, non-linear unison, the insects—no matter if fireflies or cicada—are monitoring their collective boundaries rather than individual insects establishing breeding fitness.

Now, with these sounds we enter what Deleuze and Guattari call the "refrain." Taking their cue from their analysis of birdsong (which already shows the more cosmic vision in which they locate their concepts of "rhythm" and "refrain" and which they do not connect to music alone), Deleuze and Guattari state that a refrain is "any kind of rhythmic pattern that stakes out a territory" (Bogue 17). And even if they take birdsong as a primary example, the same relation of song and rhythm to territory can also be seen in "human music"—the *deçî-tâlas (*the 120 Hindu rhythms), the Greek Συρτός (*Sirtos*), the Delta Blues, New Orleans Jazz, or East Coast versus West Coast Hip Hop. The refrain thus is a territorial marker that is always open to its surrounding milieus, which are constituted by different rhythms—rhythm itself is thus the difference between milieus, with chaos being the "milieu of all milieus" (Deleuze and Guattari, *Plateaus* 313). Chaos thus is the pool of the virtuality of rhythms, out of which rhythmic patterns emerge in a self-organizing manner.

David Dunn is a sound artist, ecologist, and researcher who is as interested in the natural world (and its sounds) as he is in science and complexity theory. In fact, quite a lot of his work can be considered "artistic research" in that it is based on active collaborations with scientists, for instance, complexity theorist James Crutchfield.

In his work "Chaos and the Emergent Mind of the Pond" (1991), Dunn entered the acoustic world of underwater life. He recorded the sound of aquatic insects in ponds in New Mexico and Africa, thus fusing insect rhythms of different milieus and territories. In this underwater world, Dunn "hears a rhythmic complexity altogether greater than that in most human music" (Raffles 323). In fact, Dunn's work accomplishes a twist on the standard *musique concrète* aesthetics and ideology. Whereas, in the *objet sonore*, the identification of the sound's origin was to remain concealed, Dunn keeps the representational level of the sound—he wants it to be identified as "something in|of the world"—but he also stresses the uncanniness of these sounds:

While the sounds above water are comfortable and familiar, those occuring [sic] under the surface are shocking. Their alien variety seems unprecedented, as if controlled by a mysterious but urgent logic. The minutiae which produce these audible rasps and sputters remain mostly unseen amongst the tentacles of plants and layers of silt but each contributes to a sonic multiverse of exquisite complexity.

The timbres of these sounds are obviously magnificent, a tiny orchestra of homemade percussion seemingly intoxicated by the infinite diversity of audible colors, but what strikes my ears most readily are the rhythmic structures . . . . Amid a background hum of distant chatter the persistent clicks of several different insects pulsate. Many of these sounds are continuous but elastic, their constancy appears sensitive to the assertions of others. This fabric is punctuated by the intermittent cries of something unseen or the wheezing of larger beetles carrying their air supply between their legs. Steady state bands of sawtooth resonance waft across the distance between schools of insect thought that together form an emergent cognition. This infinitessimal [sic] world seems complete. (Liner Notes)

Dunn's piece is both field recording, composition, and, first of all, a transposition to a human scale of those sounds which are "below the radar," inaudible to the human ear—it takes special technology (in this case, omnidirectional hydrophones) to pick up these patterns, frequencies, rhythms.

By fusing different rhythmic refrains (of different insect ecologies and milieus), Dunn is trying to reflect "in the mix" what he estimates the most striking feature of that underwater invertebrate communication—he basically faces a super-organism, and, ultimately, a consciousness:

there are these emergent rhythms, these elastic pulsations of life, sounding as if the very morphology of these little beings and the pond's macro body were dependent upon this aquatic jazz for the maintenance of time and space: primal drummers collectively engaged in the creation of worlds through jamming together the stridulatory resonance of their viscera. This is a dance between periodicity and chaotic swirl, the expansion and contraction of momentary self-resonance within the mutuality of mind . . . . Perhaps the complexity of these tiny rhythmic entrainments and chaotic cycles of microcosmic heart beats hover around that basin of attraction known as thought and together bring into being an awareness which I cannot fathom. The placidity of the water's surface takes on the sense of a membrane enclosing a collective intelligence. I know that this is not a rational thought but I find it to be irresistible. (Liner Notes)

In a mode strongly reminiscent of Whitehead or Bateson, Dunn asserts:

My direct experience of nature convinces me that the worlds I hear are saturated with an intelligence emergent from the very fullness of interconnection which sustains them . . . . To assert that human consciousness, arising out of a network of material interactions similar to those which give rise to the very existence of all life, is more important than other forms of mind not operating within the human linguistic domain is absurd. (Liner Notes)

Dunn's description of the alien sounds (clicks, sawtooth) is reminiscent of computer music (Dunn is a pioneer of electronic music himself). And indeed, Achim Szepanski, former owner and founder of the labels Force Inc. and Mille Plateaux, has explained that in techno, "you can hear a multitude of noises, shrieks, chirps, creaks, and whizzes. These are all sounds traditionally associated with madness. . . . Techno in this sense is schizoid music" (qtd. in Anz and Walder 140-41). For Deleuze and Guattari, these sounds point towards a becoming-insect, towards a molecular deterritorialization of the territorializing refrains of birdsong:

the reign of birds seems to have been replaced by the age of insects, with its much more molecular vibrations, chirring, rustling, buzzing, clicking, scratching, and scraping. Birds are vocal, but insects are instrumental: drums and violins, guitars and cymbals. A becoming-insect has replaced becoming-bird, or forms a block with it. The insect is closer, better able to make audible the truth that all becomings are molecular (*Plateaus* 308).[6]

In his sonic becoming-insects, then, Dunn deterritorializes the territorial refrains of different insects in order to make expressive the concept that everything is connected, and that mind, or consciousness, is not a human *quale*, but the multiplicity of virtual connections, intra- and interspecies, a style both human and nonhuman: *in|human*.

Finally, Dunn's piece might also be read as a comment on what might be called "Music in the Age of the Anthropocene." With the idea of the human becoming a geological (that is, nonhuman) force itself, art has the responsibility to create an awareness of how we live not only in the world, but also are part of that world. A music that performs these "cosmic dimensions" of the interdependence of human and nonhuman, by focusing on the in|human of the concept "human" might also teach us something in regard to artistic (or musical) form—form as a molar concept tied to the intentionality of a subject that in|forms brute matter:

There is no longer a form, but only relations of velocity between infinitesimal particles of an unformed material. There is no longer a subject, but only individuating affective states of an anonymous force. Here the plan is concerned only with motions and rests, with dynamic affective charges. (Deleuze, *Spinoza* 128)

These rhythmic "relations of velocity" ultimately reveal rhythmic style as the in|human nonlinear pulsation of life—a "life" that escapes conscious control and the all-too-human "tyranny of meter."

## Notes

Parts of this essay have already been published in a longer piece called "in|human rhythms." *Sonic Thinking: A Media Philosophical Approach*, edited by Bernd Herzogenrath, Bloomsbury, 2017, pp. 111-33.

1 | Unfortunately I could not find the phrase in Lacan that Žižek is alluding to, but I remember that Lacan used the highly evocative phrase (in the German translation) "vom Symbolischen durchzittert" ("trembled through by the Symbolic").
2 | See (or, rather: listen to) Gruenrekorder, "Cicada Dream Band," Pauline Oliveros, David Rothenberg, and Timothy Hill, 2014. *Soundcloud*. soundcloud.com/gruenrekorder/cicada-dream-band-pauline-oliveros-david-rothenberg-timothy-hill. Accessed 31 Oct. 2017.
3 | See (or, rather: listen to): Tomás Saraceno, *Arachnid Orchestra: Jam Sessions*, 2015. tomassaraceno.com/projects/arachnid-orchestra-jam-sessions. Accessed 31 Oct. 2017. See also *Arachnid Orchestra: Jam Sessions*, Exhibition Brochure, Nanyang Technological University, 2015. tomassaraceno.com/wp-content/media-library/Saraceno_Arachnid-Orchestra-Brochure.pdf.
4 | See also Saxer.
5 | Deleuze refers to the Proustian idea of "time in its pure state" also in his IRCAM Seminar on music ("IRCAM"). Hence, a vague correspondence between meter—movement-image and rhythm—time image might be proposed.
6 | Compare that Deleuze and Guattari point out that "a musician requires a first type of refrain, a territorial or assemblage refrain, in order to transform it from within, deterritorialized, producing a refrain of the second type as the final end of music: the cosmic refrain of a sound machine" (*Plateaus* 349).

## Works Cited

Anz, P. and P. Walder, editors. *Techno*, Ricco Bilger, 1995.
Bogue, Ronald. *Deleuze on Music, Painting and the Arts*. Routledge, 2003.
Braudel, Fernand. "History and Sociology." *On History*. Translated by S. Matthews. University of Chicago Press, 1982, pp. 64-82.
Cohen, Jeffrey Jerome. "Grey." *Prismatic Ecology: Ecotheory Beyond Green*, edited by Jeffrey Jerome Cohen. University of Minnesota Press, 2014, pp. 270-89.
Cowell, Henry, and Sidney Cowell. *Charles Ives and His Music*. Oxford University Press, 1955.
Deleuze, Gilles. "IRCAM Conference Presentation on Musical Time." 1977. Translated by T. Murphy. *Les Cours de Gilles Deleuze*, 2017, webdeleuze.com.
---. *Spinoza: Practical Philosophy*. Translated by R. Hurley. City Lights Books, 1988.
---. *Cinema 2. The Time-Image*. Translated by H. Tomlinson and R. Galeta. Athlone Press, 1989.
---. *Difference and Repetition*. Translated by P. Patton. Columbia University Press, 1994.
---. *Negotiations*. Translated by M. Joughin. Columbia University Press, 1995.
Deleuze, Gilles, and Félix Guattari. *A Thousand Plateaus: Capitalism and Schizophrenia*. Translated by B. Massumi. University of Minnesota Press, 1987.
Deleuze, Gilles, and Claire Parnet. *Dialogues*. Columbia University Press, 1987.
Dunn, David. Liner Notes to "Chaos and the Emerging Mind of the Pond." *Angels and Insects*, What Next? Recordings, 1992.
Hudson, G. H. "Concerted Flashing of Fireflies." *Science*, vol. 48, no. 1249, 1918, pp. 573-75.
Kafka, Franz. "Metamorphosis." *Franz Kafka: Metamorphosis and Other Stories*. Translated and with an Introduction by Michael Hofmann. Penguin: 2015, pp. 73-126
Kermode, Frank. *The Sense of an Ending: Studies in the Theory of Fiction*. Oxford University Press, 1967.
Nabokov, Vladimir. *Ada, or Ardor: A Family Chronicle*. McGraw-Hill, 1969.
Raffles, Hugh. *Insectopedia*. Vintage Books, 2010.
Rößler, Almut. *Contributions to the Spiritual World of Olivier Messiaen. With Original Texts by the Composer*. Translated by B. Dagg and N. Poland. Gilles & Francke, 1986.
Saxer, Marion. "Die Emanzipation von der metrischen Zeitordnung—eine Utopie? Zeitkonzeptionen in der Musik nach 1945." *Geteilte Zeit: Zur Kritik des Rhythmus in den Künsten*, edited by Patrick Primavesi and Simone Mahrenholz. Edition Argus, 2004, pp. 52-70.

Schumann, Robert. *Gesammelte Schriften über Musik und Musiker*, vol. 1. Georg Wigand's, 1854, pp. 125-26.

Small, Christopher. *Musicking: The Meanings of Performing and Listening*. Wesleyan University Press, 1998.

Smith, H. M. "Synchronous Flashing of Fireflies." *Science*, vol. 82, no. 2129, 1935, pp. 151-52.

Žižek, Slavoj. *Less Than Nothing: Hegel and the Shadow of Dialectical Materialism*. Verso, 2012.

# Robert Lowell's Hidden Cats: From *Lord Weary's Castle* to *Dolphin*

Astrid Franke

In contrast to his female poet friends, Marianne Moore and Elizabeth Bishop, Robert Lowell is usually not considered an animal poet. Yet, as Calista McRae has recently pointed out, "Lowell attends to animals habitually," his "Collected Poems is a bestiary" and "to picture Lowell's poetry without its creatures is to picture a much flatter book" (19-20). This is not only because there are so many of them but also because they give the notoriously self-absorbed poet "a way to evade thoughts of himself" (McRae 20). McRae has thus made a convincing beginning in analyzing the ways in which Lowell uses animals; my own attempt in this paper will be to highlight a few other functions animals have in Lowell's poetry, to order them chronologically, and to suggest that one may detect a few changes in their depiction: some of them are expected, as from the religious symbolism of his early poetry to the realism of the "confessional" phase, and some changes might be less obvious, as the one from feelings of alienation to negotiating multiple or at least fluid selves. I will do so by focusing not so much on Lowell's most famous animals—the skunks and fish that are associated with instinctual life—but on more hidden animals, especially on cats. They are associated with the sexual and the feminine; they also seem to concur with a sick brain or with mental illness: neither entirely wild nor entirely domesticated, they are present whenever Lowell (re)negotiates his sense of self in relation to others.

## A Sick Cat Amongst Christians

In August 1947, Lowell starts to engage in a life-long exchange of letters with Elizabeth Bishop and does so with praise for her "Fish poem." He continues: "Anyway I felt very envious in reading it—I'm a fisherman myself, but all my fish become symbols, alas!" (Lowell, "Dear Elizabeth"). Though not a poem, this line alone says almost everything one needs to know about Lowell's relation to animals at that point in his career: in the complex poems of *Lord Weary's Castle* (1946), serpents, moths, worms, Mr. Edward's famous spider, fish, and the frequent occurrence of whales as Leviathan are steeped in religious symbolism. And so, of course, is Lowell's self-description, for while Bishop simply wrote "I caught a tremendous fish" and then adds significance to that initial statement by giving more and more details, Lowell as "fisherman" makes a (male) profession out of it that is also rife with religious implications: according to Mark 1:17, the brothers Simon and Andrew were asked by Jesus to follow him and become the "fishers of men." Lowell uses this specific Christian imagery and wordplay in "The Drunken Fisherman," a dramatic monologue whose protagonist sounds very much like Lowell, drunk or sober. Lowell's seemingly self-deprecating compliment to Bishop is anything but modest: as a poet, he fishes for readers in the name of a higher power, and his poetic means, such as the use of animals, is clearly subordinated to this purpose. The one exception, it seems, is the cat in "Winter in Dunbarton" a poem that was published in two versions, one in *The Kenyon Review* and the other, slightly altered, in *Lord Weary's Castle*, both in 1947. It is, as Samuel Maio has pointed out, a personal poem in that it deals with "the poet's familial loss" (34), as do the adjacent poems, an elegy to his grandfather, "In Memory of Arthur Winslow," and to his grandmother "Mary Winslow." It is in this personal environment that the cat appears—like the grandparents, it is remembered as dying and dead.

The cat is not a common Biblical animal, nor is it a Christian symbol. In the poem, the cat is surrounded by the signs of passing time such as a melting snow, worms, corruption, and, of course, death, and it is surrounded by Christian vocabulary, such as "Jehovah," "atone," "Christ," and the frequent mentioning of "our father" (26-27). And yet, the medical details of the dying cat do not readily translate into a symbolic, Christian reading:

. . . but my cat is cold, is curled
Tight as a boulder: she no longer smears
Her catnip mouse from Christmas; the germ—
Mindless and ice, a world against our world—
Has tamped her round of brains into her ears . . . . (26)[1]

The mindless germ is a cruel killer and opponent, both to the cat and "our world." It is akin to the cancer or "crab" that killed Lowell's grandfather Arthur Winslow, a biographical fact mentioned in the preceding poem "In Memory of Arthur Winslow" and also in the other poem published in *The Kenyon Review*, "The Cities' Summer Death." Here, we also find that cancer and germ have a similar effect of turning the body rigid and into stone: "Cancer ossifies his features" (953). Through the adjacent poems, the two deaths establish a strange kinship between cat and grandfather. This provides an explanation for one of the changes Lowell made between the first published version of "Winter in Dunbarton" in *The Kenyon Review* in 1946 and the version published in *Lord Weary's Castle*. In the later version, Lowell muted the religious overtones of "our Father" by referring more clearly to "my father" and "his father," disentangling this very idiosyncratic trinity. In one instance, however, a reference to "our Father" is replaced by a reference to the cat: "but the days are short and rot / The holly on our Father's mound" becomes "Belle, the cat that used to rat / About my father's books, is dead" (26). Tillinghast reads the earlier line as referring to Lowell's father and argues: "The *Kenyon Review* version appears to anticipate Lowell's father's death by more than a decade" (211). But given that Robert was an only child, it seems plausible that "our Father" is both Lowell's and his father's father, that is, Robert Lowell's grandfather: from the later poem "Dunbarton" in *Life Studies*, we learn that during his father's long absences, family members and other people routinely refer to Lowell's grandfather as "your father," a relation he adopts himself: "He was my Father. I was his son" (168). Furthermore, as stated above, "Winter in Dunbarton" is adjacent to poems remembering the grandfather's death, so that the mound is likely to be the grandfather's grave. The various poems on the small town of Dunbarton and the grandfather emphasize the importance of the place as a burial ground for members of the Lowell family, including Lowell himself, and as always in Lowell, family history is tightly connected to (American) history. Through the grandfather, Lowell repeatedly addresses aspects of American history such as the gold rush and shady dealings in "real estate" (24), which includes the ground described in "Winter in Dunbarton": "the thankless ground / His father screwed from Charlie Stark and sold / to the selectmen" (26). In "A Prayer for my Grandfather to Our Lady" from *In Memory of Arthur Winslow*, the lines, "Neither our clippers nor our slavers / reached the haven of your peace in this Bay State" and, "Neither my father nor his father" suggest the need to atone for family wrongs and to redeem at least the poet himself (25). It is in this context that the senseless suffering of the cat (and perhaps the grandfather) in the next poem casts doubts about God's willingness to bring peace to this family.

But the replacement of rotting holly on what is in all likelihood his grandfather's grave and the serious dark sounds "short," "rot," "holly" and "mound" by the near-nonsense of "the cat that used to rat . . . is dead" (26) not only changes the mood but also pushes the care for sounds to another level, above (or below) any spiritual concern.[2] Indeed, the cat is introduced through alliteration ("my cat is cold, is curled") and repetition in "catnip" as a suitable word to play with. Likewise, her exit from the poem hovers between horror and humor: "wastes of snow" stare through windows at the "brainless cat" (26), which, in the latter version, appears almost as a punishment for whatever anti-bookish leanings the cat (and the grandfather?) had had. "Belle" clearly stands out in the masculine world of fathers and their historical guilt—if she indicates a leap from faith, it is one to a deliberately weird pun one cannot quite make sense of and therefore reads with a sudden amused discovery about how much sound—and a sick brain—may create moments of anarchy in an otherwise highly ordered and controlled (linguistic) world.[3]

If, ultimately, it is an investment in language and poetry itself that subverts rigid systems of belief, it is not surprising that another animal signaling a departure from the religiously inflected poetry to more secular themes in *Life Studies* is a (toy) parrot or cockatoo in "Thanksgiving's Over," the last poem in *Mills of the Kavanaughs* (1951). The poem is a complicated version of a dramatic monologue with two speakers: the first speaker is Michael who can say of himself "I was dreaming." In this dream, he hears the voice of his dead wife who was apparently declared insane and "shipped" "To the asylum" (105). This catholic woman repeatedly talks about "the parrot" and also owns a celluloid cockatoo, which she breaks at a certain point. In someone as widely read as Lowell, it is not farfetched to assume a deliberate allusion to Félicité's famous parrot in Flaubert's *Un Cœur Simple*, as in both the poem and the novella attention is drawn to the Christian concept of trinity, and here in particular the Holy Ghost is often symbolized by a speechless dove rather than a parrot. In this context, the bird prompts thoughts about religion and mindless chatter or repetition, but also the self-referentiality of literature and poets as parrots, words themselves and their repetition, as well as some women's tendencies to choose undeserving objects of their love, indicating the urgency to love and be loved.

## Compound-Cats in Mental Institutions

In this last aspect, one may see a continuing concern of Lowell's that is picked up in the most famous group of animals in his poetry, a female skunk with her kittens in "Skunk Hour." In her review of Lowell's *Collected Poems*, Marjorie Perloff draws attention to the undertone of "elitism, snobbery and homophobia" towards the three characters standing for the decline of the Maine seaside town in the first part of the poem: the "hermit / heiress," the "summer millionaire," and "our fairy / decorator" (87). She quotes Frank O'Hara's interpretation of the skunks as being implicitly compared to the lovers in "love-cars" whom the speaker spies on—the sentiment expressed here, O'Hara says, is "positively revolting" because he believes Lowell equates the skunks with the lovers (Perloff 88). Alternatively, the mother skunk and the scene as a whole might be read as a metapoetic: "as it swills the garbage in its desperate quest to live and provide for its family, it is doing exactly what Lowell does with his past in *Life Studies*" (Altieri 196). The reason criticism is divided over whether the skunks should be read positively as life-affirming or negatively as a threat to a civilized New England elite is probably that Lowell's attitude toward this elite is divided as well. In the worst of primitivist fashions, he frequently associates himself and his social class with sterility and decline, contrasting with women, animals, and ethnic minorities—all of whom he also admires and tries to associate, even identify, with, not least through dramatic monologues. To see his pattern more clearly, one should, once again, look out for cats!

In *Life Studies*, they can first be found in "A Mad Negro Soldier Confined in Munich." The German town is still in ruins and "the zoo's rubble fumes with cats" (118). The speaker in this dramatic monologue (other dramatic monologues with female speakers in *Life Studies* are "The Banker's Daughter," and "To Speak of Woe That is in Marriage") is an African American soldier confined in a mental institution run by the Americans for disturbed military personal. The poem is a kind of blackface performance, for it is unmistakably a white poet speaking: he refers to his fellow inmates as "black," puns about "the black forest of the colored wards," refers to himself and others as "slaves of habit" and to each "subnormal boot- / black heart" (118) enjoying the tiny portions of food they get. It is in the complicated socio-psychological twists of the blackface tradition that the speaker voices a number of "white" obsessions, in particular a kind of manic hypersexuality that characterized Lowell himself, coupled with an American (but also a Nazi) obsession, miscegenation: "Her German language made my arteries harden— / . . . I had her six times in the English Garden" (118).

The hypersexualization of the black male then is the one context in which to understand the cats: they are the first animals in this poem (followed by pigeons, chickens, and minnows, with the addition of "ant-egg" and "cold turkey") and they are associated with women, madness, and an unconventional use of language: I understand "Cat-houses talk cold turkey to my guards" to mean that brothels or their representatives speak plainly to the guards about what they have to offer—the line displays what the Bostonian poet knows about slang and establishes the connection of this (for Lowell) new linguistic register with cats, prostitution, and miscegenation. The larger context is provided by the ambiguous new beginnings after the defeats of the pope, of King Henri IV, Adlai Stevenson, and Hitler are announced in the four poems in the first part of *Life Studies*. The beginnings are ambiguous because there is both promise and skepticism with regard to a more "democratic" or just better future: there is a clear movement from the Alps to Paris, from the vertical to the horizontal, from a king to a queen, from the Nazis to a mad African American soldier in Munich having sex with a German fräulein. These could be welcomed as progressive changes or mourned for as signs of decline—as with the march of the skunks on Main Street we may not be entirely sure about the implied assessment of a new reality.

Here is one more cat to affirm that there is indeed a pattern: in "Waking in the Blue," we find again a juxtaposition of a Harvard-educated New England elite, the "Mayflower / screwballs" (184), with another ethnic group: the presumably

Irish "Roman Catholic attendants" who study (only) at Boston University and use books such as *The Meaning of Meaning* to sleep on. This is humorous, and what saves it from being quite so condescending is that it makes fun of the book as much as of the student. When he rises from his nap, he "catwalks down our corridor" where the unusual verb aligns him to a cat and its silent (nightly) walks (183). It may also feminize him, particularly as he forms a contrast to the speaker himself: "Cock of the walk, / I strut in my turtle-necked French sailor's jersey / before the metal shaving mirrors," but also to the sea creatures the other inmates of the mental hospital are compared to, namely "seal" and "sperm whale" (183). Compared to the sexualized cats and the "Mad Negro" as Lowell's black mask, "Waking in the Blue" and its catwalking Catholic student and strutting cock amongst a lot of sea creatures express a milder version of social distance: set in an expensive elite mental hospital surrounded by his own social class in New England rather than by traumatized African-American soldiers in an army institution in Europe, Lowell can use the mental hospital as a microcosm where social differences between people decrease and do not appear as threatening any more. He is as distanced to the other inmates as he is to the attendants, all equally treated with mild condescension and associated with animals.

## Finding a Kitten

Seen through the lens of animals in Lowell's poetry, *Near the Ocean* seems closer to the early volumes and their tendency to symbolize or allegorize than to *Life Studies*, where animals may be described in detail without clear symbolism. In "Central Park," the speaker finds

a one-day kitten on the ground—
deprived, weak, ignorant and blind,
squeaking, tubular, left behind—
dying with its deserter's rich
Welfare lying out of reach:
milk cartons, kidney heaped to spoil,
two plates sheathed with silver foil. (392)

It is difficult not to read this as "parable" or "satire" (Williamson 140-41)—a comment on the situation of the poor in America. Lament and satire are dominant modes in this volume where the desire for life is aligned with public life: the first four poems begin in a sexualized mood, as in "Waking Early Sunday Morning," participating or at least observing public events, as in "Fourth of July in Maine" and "The Opposite House," or in a sexualized public as in "Central

Park." Not surprisingly, the sexual aspects in this volume are emphasized through animals (the chinook salmon, bees, and a dog), but the caged lion and the kitten in "Central Park" are to be read as bleak social comment through words like "his slummy cell," "serving a life-term in jail" or "[w]elfare lying out of reach" (392). A further layer of meaning is added if one considers Hart Crane's "Chaplinesque" as an intertext, connected by the kitten in the second stanza:

For we can still love the world, who find
A famished kitten on the step, and know
Recesses for it from the fury of the street,
Or warm torn elbow coverts. (Crane 73-74)

To find a kitten and be able to help it, one may feel chosen, asked to care for a creature more helpless than oneself and this, Crane implies, restores love and helps to make "small adjustments" when times are tough.[4] Not so for the Lowell persona who seems to leave the kitten to die in Central Park, only to end with a typical lament for a general collective "we" (393). It is indeed a strange Lowell who speaks from this volume: as in this poem, he is drawn to public life and political commentary, he seeks it out, like a voyeur in the park who cannot help himself. What he finds, however, according to his poetry, is nothing he can do anything about and all he is left with is recording his powerlessness and his pity. This is true even when he did do something—participating in the March to the Pentagon in October 1967, for instance. Again, however, in his poetry, the emphasis is on his weakness and powerlessness and, as the episode with the kitten demonstrates, there is a danger that his persona is so overwhelmed by indignation over a cruel world that leaves one helpless to change anything that even small gestures of care become impossible or unimaginable.

## A Cat or a Daughter?

This changes in the ensuing volumes, and I want to finish with the return of the cat as it signifies the return of Lowell facing his own illness: there are two sections called "Hospital" in *The Dolphin* (1973), each containing a number of the innumerous sonnets Lowell wrote at the time. While the form is different, some poems hark back to "Mad Negro" and "Waking in the Blue" in that they record the hospital experience of someone who is mentally ill. The poem "Double Vision" also points forward to poems such as "Visitors" and "Home" in *Day by Day* (1977) because certain drugs apparently cause the eponymous effect: "sedation doubles everything I see" (652). And here we may discern an important difference to the earlier stance towards his state of mind and perception:

in the earlier poems, the speaker may acknowledge his stay in a "house for the 'mentally ill'" (183) or admit that "[m]y mind is not right" (191), but that does not seem to qualify his perception of people around him; it certainly does not qualify his condescension towards the outsiders in the village described in "Skunk Hour." But "Double Vision" acknowledges two visions and admits that one or the other may not be shared by others, though it is real to him: "no one is always waiting at the door, / and fills the window . . . sometimes a Burmese cat, / or maybe my Daughter on the shell of my glasses." And later: "The cat walks out— / or does it? The room has filled with double-shadows" (652). Strictly speaking, the speaker not only confesses double visions but also possible hallucinations of things that are not there; alternatively, he cannot believe what he sees and denies its reality, as in: "You can't be here, and yet we try to talk; / . . . / While we are talking I am asking you, / 'Where is Caroline?' And you are Caroline" (652). This new, humble stance towards himself and others is quite courageous and probably only possible to bear with self-deprecating humor. Like the reappearance of a cat, who carried her associations of madness, hospitals, and femininity from earlier volumes into *Dolphin* but has now more of her own life, this indicates a new frankness in acknowledging odd creatures including one's self or selves. For it seems to me that in *Dolphin* and the later volume *Day by Day*, Lowell uses double vision, or, in the case of "Three Freuds" even triple vision to change his way of relating to others and to his "madness": whereas a sick brain or mind previously set him apart and slightly above other people and creatures, he is now no longer superior to them but very much on the same plane, but less mobile and able than they are.

Thus, he records their coming and goings, their shifting shapes and colors, their ups and downs. There is a fluidity that blurs clear distinctions between animals ("Ducks splash deceptively like fish; / Fish break water with the wings of a bird to escape"), between "Home" and hospital, between real things and visions, between inside and outside, between daughter and cat, and also between himself and a cow as "my double" (824-25; 829). In this fluidity, it becomes difficult to hold oneself together or put oneself together again after breaking and to maintain relations with others who may or may not leave. As always in Lowell this, too, is suggested to go beyond a personal observation and beyond a medical diagnosis of mental illness; in the exclamation, "Poor measured, neurotic man— / animals are more instinctive virtuosi" (829), Lowell generalizes the need to control oneself, to adapt and not to let go, as distinctly human. However, knowing that he has not always regarded animals the same way and that he has treated cats (and perhaps other pets and domesticated animals) slightly differently from "wild" animals, we have reason to assume that his attitude towards himself and the world around him has slightly changed over the years: to judge by the double visions of cat and cow, Lowell is no longer preoccupied with desiring and also rejecting a (sexualized) other but has come to accept a plurality of beings that are difficult to control and a bit mysterious—like a Burmese cat.

## Notes

**1** | Unless noted otherwise, I quote Lowell's poems from *Collected Poems* and insert only the page number in brackets.
**2** | In case anyone is wondering: Dr. Seuss's *The Cat in the Hat* was published more than ten years later in 1957.
**3** | Cf. Michael Hofman, who comments on this passage with reference to Ezra Pound's "logopoiea" and Christopher Ricks's "anti-pun" (5).
**4** | Cf. Adrienne Rich's "School Among the Ruins," where a teacher asks the children to offer a young cat some milk, though resources are scarce in the warzone. To help the cat, a creature that presumably does not really need it, is yet important as it is a gesture of care, a bulwark against brutalization and de-civilization, like telling stories, singing, spelling, and remembering names by heart (Rich 22-25).

## Works Cited

Altieri, Charles. "Poetry in a Prose World: Robert Lowell's *Life Studies*." *Modern Poetry Studies*, vol.1, no. 4, 1970, pp. 182-98.
Crane, Hart. *The Collected Poems of Hart Crane*. Edited by Waldo Frank, Liveright, 1933.
Hofman, Michael. "His Own Prophet." *London Review of Books*, vol. 25, no. 17, 11 Sep. 2003, pp. 3-8.
Maio, Samuel. *Creating Another Self: Voice in Modern American Personal Poetry*. 2nd ed., Truman State University Press, 2005.
Lowell, Robert. *Collected Poems*. Edited by Frank Bidart and David Gewanter, Farrar, Straus and Giroux, 2003.
---. "Dear Elizabeth. One Poet Writes to the Other." *The New Yorker*, 20 Dec. 2004. newyorker.com/magazine/2004/12/20/dear-elizabeth. Accessed 16 Mar. 2018.
McRae, Calista. "'Another Armored Animal': Robert Lowell's Allusions to Marianne Moore." *Arizona Quarterly: A Journal of American Literature, Culture, and Theory*, vol. 72, no. 2, 2016, pp. 1-28.
Perloff, Marjorie. "The Return of Robert Lowell." *Parnassus*, vol. 27, no 1/2, 2004, pp. 76-102.
Rich, Adrienne. *The School Among the Ruins: Poems 2000-2004*. Norton, 2004.
Tillinghast, Richard. "Revaluation: Early Poems of Robert Lowell." *Kenyon Review*, vol. 20, no. 3/4, 1998, pp. 205-11.

Williamson, Alan. *Pity the Monsters: The Political Vision of Robert Lowell.* Yale University Press, 1974.

# Zoological Encounters

*Susanne Scharf*

There was a young woman at Yale
Who had to get rid of her whale
'cause the beast wouldn't eat
Simply oatmeal or wheat,
Only catfishes caught with a nail.

In Kansas there was an old wizard
Who just couldn't spot his tame lizard
'cause the pet wouldn't move
With no music to groove.
And all on account of that blizzard.

There was an old lady in Maine
Who sang when she walked her Great Dane.
The size of the dog
Gave people a shock.
To soothe them she hummed the refrain.

There once was a busy Swiss beaver
Who worked to damn Lake Geneva.
That upset a French otter
Who looked out the water:
"Mon Dieu, get out of my reever!"

In the southernmost forest of Spain
Lived a pack of wolves. In vain
They tried to hide
Like Bonnie and Clyde.
They were hunted down—insane!

# Urban Animals

*Babette B. Tischleder*

Athens #1

Athens #2

Athens #2

Athens #4

Berlin-Moabit #1

Berlin-Moabit #2

Berlin, Torstrasse #1

Berlin, Torstrasse #2

Berlin-Hermsdorf

Berlin-Grunewald

Berlin-Moabit #3

Berlin-Moabit #4

Chicago, Near South Side #1

Chicago, South Loop

Chicago, Near South Side #2

Chicago, Wicker Park

Rishikesh #1

Mussoorie

Rishikesh #2

Dehradun, Doon University Campus

Manhattan, 23rd Street Station #1

Manhattan, 23rd Street Station #2

Manhattan, 23rd Street Station #3

Manhattan, 23rd Street Station #4

Brooklyn, East River

Brooklyn, Downtown

Thessaloniki

Almáciga, Tenerife

# Political Ecologies in a Multispecies World

# Notes on Thoreau's Posthuman Democracy

*Johannes Voelz*

## I.

In the closing paragraph of his most famous political essay, "Resistance to Civil Government," Henry David Thoreau sketches out his ideal state:

> I please myself with imagining a State at last which can afford to be just to all men, and to treat the individual with respect as a neighbor; which even would not think it inconsistent with its own repose, if a few were to live aloof from it, not meddling with it, nor embraced by it, who fulfilled all the duties of neighbors and fellow-men. A State which bore this kind of fruit, and suffered it to drop off as fast as it ripened, would prepare the way for a still more perfect and glorious State, which I have also imagined, but not yet anywhere seen. (171)

This passage may sound like the description of an ideal that is distinct from any actual society. But at a closer look, what Thoreau presents are really two states. The first is marked by principles of respect, neighborliness, and aloofness (the latter granted to "a few"). Via a natural process of ripening, decay, and fertilization of the ground—a process largely in line with what he describes in his late essay "The Succession of Forest Trees"—this first state prepares the ground for the second state. This latter state remains so vague (all we learn is that it is "still more perfect and glorious") that we have to take Thoreau at his word when he claims that he "has not yet anywhere seen it." But this last phrase develops its suggestive force not so much because we are asked to imagine something grand about which we know very little, but precisely because of Thoreau's prior differentiation of his two longed-for states. If Thoreau has *not yet* seen ideal state no. 2, we are to infer that he apparently *has* seen ideal state no. 1. Where has he seen it?

Equivocating between the metaphorical and the literal, Thoreau gives us a hint when he says that it is a state that is capable of bearing fruit, of dropping them as soon they ripen, and of preparing the ground for future states.

Without denying the metaphorical, we need to take him literally here: the society Thoreau speaks of, I suggest, is the society he finds in nature. He is, in other words, describing a state that is at once natural and political. The kind of democracy for which he is hoping is not merely modeled on his experiences in nature; being in nature *is* being in a kind of democracy—a democracy which we can call "posthuman." Recently, the concept of the "posthuman" has found itself in conversation with neighboring concepts, such as the "nonhuman" (see Grusin) and the "more-than-human." My understanding of "posthuman" is informed by the idea, expressed paradigmatically by Cary Wolfe, that "'the human' is achieved by escaping or repressing not just its animal origins in nature, the biological, and the evolutionary, but more generally by transcending the bonds of materiality and embodiment altogether" (xv). The concept of the posthuman, in this sense, draws into doubt the possibility of ontologically distinguishing between the human and the nonhuman. I would add, however, that the concept does not obliterate or deny differences between the historical and concrete manifestations of human and nonhuman society. Drawing such lines seems necessary for developing posthumanist forms of critique. Even when we critique (with Wolfe) the notion of the human, we do so from the premise that it is humans only (though not all of them) who entertain such faulty notions. This mixture of ontological dedifferentiation with historically specific differentiation for the purposes of critique makes the posthuman the most useful concept to capture the trajectory of Thoreau's thought.

By and large, Thoreau scholarship has not been willing to consider the idea of "posthuman democracy" in any earnestness. There are, for most influential Thoreau readers, two aspects to his thought, or two modes in his writing: there is Thoreau the political theorist (here, the core texts are "Resistance to Civil Governments" and his anti-slavery and reform papers, such as "Slavery in Massachusetts" and his essays on John Brown), and there is Thoreau the nature writer (ranging from the early Transcendentalist phase of *A Week on the Concord and Merrimack Rivers* to the late naturalist phase of *Wild Fruits*). In one way or another, critics have kept these two aspects apart, or have considered how they cancel each other out (virtually the entirety of Jack Turner's recent collection, *A Political Companion to Henry David Thoreau*, is a testament to this).

To take only three prominent examples: Nancy Rosenblum, one of the most prominent and acute political theorists to have engaged Thoreau at length, recognizes that "his political essays were contemporaneous with his writings about nature, and even the latter contain overt social commentary" (19). But contemporaneity doesn't imply interchangeability. Hence she also argues that "if Thoreau's declarations of solitude and self-reliance seem to cross the boundary out of democratic society, the affront is modulated, and the way back is kept open. In a dialogue in *Maine Woods*, Thoreau has Mount Ktaadn advise him to return home" (20). Home, in Rosenblum's reading, is Concord, or New

England society, but decidedly not nature. Put differently, she associates solitude with nature, and home with democratic society and the human community of his neighbors in Concord. Though she quotes from *Walden*—"[t]he most sweet and tender, the most innocent and encouraging society may be found in any natural object"—for Rosenblum, society can never truly mean anything but human society (20; Thoreau, *Walden* 131).

Shannon Mariotti is another political theorist who takes steps toward recognizing the political dimension of Thoreau's being-in-nature, but then shies away from following through on her insight. Her suggestion is to read Thoreau as democratic precisely in his moments of withdrawal into nature. But the reason she gives ends up pointing away from nature: Thoreau, according to her, thinks of withdrawal as a strategy to "recuperate the critical capacities that are vital to democratic citizenship" (Mariotti 10). If withdrawal is necessary for democracy because it allows the individual to "recuperate critical capacities," being in nature becomes a kind of holiday from democracy, or a reproduction of democratic energies. The expenditure of these energies, however, will have to take place at the social site from which the self had previously withdrawn.

Yet another confirmation of the split between the political and being-in-nature is offered in Jonathan McKenzie's recent provocative study *The Political Thought of Henry David Thoreau: Privatism and the Practice of Philosophy*. McKenzie's main title is misleading since he argues against the notion that Thoreau is a political thinker. In his view, Thoreau is rather a Stoic philosopher who "uses his writings to shape a philosophical personality that can withstand the seductions of democratic political participation" (1). Whereas Rosenblum and Mariotti privilege the political side of Thoreau, McKenzie reduces Thoreau's political interventions to "fits or starts, episodes out of line with the philosophical temperament Thoreau attempts to create throughout his life. Taking political indifference as his apex, Thoreau delves into political activity only when his boundaries of indifference fail him" (25).

Only recently, a small minority of critics has begun to seriously consider the two sides of Thoreau not as antagonistic to one another but as interlinked. Perhaps not surprisingly, these are writers whose allegiance is not with the field of political theory. One exemplar is Laura Dassow Walls, who has been at the forefront of the naturalist strand of Thoreau scholarship for two decades. In her recent biography of Thoreau, she underlines the point (already conceded by Rosenblum and others) that Thoreau engaged in his political interventions at the same time as he pondered how to relate to the natural world.

In the same weeks he was finishing "Resistance to Civil Government," Thoreau put the final touches on *A Week on the Concord and Merrimack Rivers*. "Who hears the fishes when they cry?" he asked in its opening pages. "It will not be forgotten by some memory that we were contemporaries." Their lives, thrown into the hydraulic machinery of the

Billerica Dam, "armed only with innocence and a just cause," were lost, but "I for one am with thee, and who knows what may avail a crow-bar against that Billerica dam?" (Walls 254)

Walls' assemblage of quotes in this paragraph is rich in allusive meaning, even if she doesn't bother to spell it out. For Thoreau, the fish are his "contemporaries." He does not expressly call them his fellow citizens, but he does suggest that, like him, they face an overpowering machinery (the dam, the state) in need of counter-friction. As he puts it in "Resistance to Civil Government": "Let your life be a counter friction to stop the machine" (155). Man and fish, counter-friction and crowbar: unity in resistance. This, too, is a meaning of contemporaneity.

"Resistance to Civil Government" tries to develop a democratic theory based not on procedural consistency or utilitarian expediency, but "on those cases to which the rule of expediency does not apply, in which a people, as well as an individual, must do justice, cost what it may" (150). People are beholden to justice, just like the fish, who are "armed with innocence and a just cause." His essay is an experiment in thinking through a society based not only on resistance, counter-friction, or the crowbar, but simultaneously (contemporaneously) on the "higher law," as New Englanders would come to refer to the priority of the demands of conscience over positive law. And this law, precisely because it is higher, extends beyond humanity, to all living beings.

Walls clearly recognizes all this, but she is quick to differentiate between Thoreau's political and ethical commitments:

> Extending one's ethical community to the nonhuman world was, in 1849, novel, shocking, ridiculous. But Thoreau would give the rest of his life to this revolutionary insight. What he worked out in writing "Resistance to Civil Government" became not only the foundation of his political philosophy but also the gateway to his environmental ethics. (254)

Readers may commend Walls for her caution in distinguishing between a community that is ethical (guided by the question "How should I live?") and one that is political (defined, in democratic terms, by free and open debate among those making up the *polis*). Surely, this distinction ought to make sense. Thoreau (and the individual advocated by him) becomes aware of his ethical responsibility to his neighbors, be they human or nonhuman, but he engages in political deliberation only with his human neighbors (often in a paradoxical style, in which deliberation takes the form of refusal, resistance, and withdrawal). The intuition and purpose of the present article, however, is to push further than this, and to ask whether the posthuman community envisaged by Thoreau may extend beyond the ethical, toward the political.

In *Bird Relics: Grief and Vitalism in Thoreau*, Branka Arsić shifts the perspective from the duality of nature and politics to the vitalist concept of *life*. This shift of perspective goes a long way in unhinging the separation between the ethical and the political because both the ethical and the political become involved in the making of communal life. In reference to Thoreau's call to train the attention on the physical rather than the metaphysical, Arsić writes:

Always democratic in his ontology and epistemology, Thoreau insists that instead of trying to think absolute being, such as God, which is only fantasized and nowhere to be seen, we should "always [look] at what is to be seen" in front of us. This injunction to dedicate our thought to what is corporeally in front of us advocates as an epistemological principle that only earthly creatures are, strictly speaking, knowable to us. Ethically, it suggests, that creaturely life must be of highest value for us, because it is with creatures—human, animal, and vegetal—that we build communities. In fact, precisely because creatures partake of our daily life, which is by definition social, Thoreau can assert that "socialness" is to be experienced in the contemplative encounter with the natural. (313)

Though she is not saying so directly, I infer Arsić to be suggesting that Thoreau's orientation to what is in front of him is not simply an ethical stance that answers the question "How should I behave toward the world around me?" but also a political stance in that the discernment of the world around us produces a common (or shared) world. The political here consists in this production and emergence of a shared world. This resonates with the distinction between *politics* and *the political* (or, in French, *la politique* and *le politique*) in the works of contemporary theorists such as Ernesto Laclau, Jean-Luc Nancy, Jacques Rancière, and Claude Lefort. Roughly speaking, in this debate *the political* refers to the emergence of a new order, whereas *politics* refers to the contestation or administration of an existing order. Thus, when Arsić writes that Thoreau is "always *democratic* in his ontology and epistemology," *democratic* is no mere synonym for *egalitarian, inclusive*, or *non-hierarchical*. Thoreau's ontology and epistemology are rather democratic in the sense that his ontologically and epistemologically grounded acuteness to the given world creates a shared world, and that the coming-into-being of this shared world is itself an instantiation of the moment of democracy.

I am in agreement with much of what I take Arsić to be saying, but as I read Thoreau, life in the wild is imagined as democratic not so much, or not merely, in its emergence as in a particular kind of interaction among the democratic community's members. Nature teaches and allows for an existence that balances kinship and strangeness, contact and distance, responsibility and not being answered to. These are, roughly, the traits that Thoreau, at the end of "Resistance of Civil Government," hopes to find in any political state (as quoted at the outset of this essay): "a State at last which can afford to be just to all men, and to treat the individual with respect as a neighbor; which even would not think it inconsistent with its own repose, if a few were to live aloof from it, not meddling with it, nor embraced by it, who fulfilled all the duties of neighbors and fellow-men" (171). In effect, Thoreau thus reconceptualizes democratic politics: for him, it shouldn't be primarily about the free and open exchange on how to steer the *res publica*—something that is indeed difficult to do with animals and plants (though perhaps not altogether impossible if only we learned to understand their language). Rather, democratic politics is about a shared practice of life based on the insight that people "have other affairs to attend to" than collective self-organization and administration ("Resistance" 155). True democracy, for Thoreau, is what pragmatist Sidney Hook has called "a way of life," a type of conviviality that goes far beyond debates on how to steer the *res publica*.

## II.

The preceding paragraphs have perhaps been unduly abstract. Thoreau himself does not develop the concept of posthuman democracy theoretically, but from the ground up, as it were. It takes shape in the accounts of specific encounters and from the reflections they give rise to. This may explain why *Walden* and his other texts are so full of anecdotes and similar short narrative genres: in these stories of particularity, Thoreau relates experiences of sociality. At some points, it is a sociality in which the human and nonhuman are set on the same plane, as if it were entirely trivial to which species his visitors and neighbors belong. (At other points, Thoreau himself reintroduces a difference between human and nonhuman society, in part to generate a critique of human society with the help of negative contrast; more on that later.)

Perhaps the most memorable of all such stories in *Walden* is his account, in "Brute Neighbors," of his game with the loon. Stanley Cavell, who points to the loon's communicative powers by calling him one of Thoreau's "prophets," rightly considers him "dramatically the most impressive" of all of his natural interlocutors (42). Thoreau begins on an almost sober note: "In the fall the loon (*Colymbus glacialis*) came, as usual, to moult and bathe in the pond, making the woods ring with his wild laughter before I had risen" (*Walden* 233). Thoreau strikes a tone of almost scientific distance, emphasized by the parenthetical inclusion of the loon's zoological name, which makes the loon appear to be part of a natural rhythm. Yet the verbs he uses are decidedly anthropomorphic: not only does the loon moult; he—and I use Thoreau's male pronoun to replicate the effect—also bathes, and his call is identified as laughter. This mixture of natural order and anthropomorphic language gives the naturalist description a touch of the idyllic.

Thoreau's use of the singular may give the impression that he is referring to a particular loon, but the following sentence suggests the he has been speaking of the species. In relating how the seasonal arrival of the loon brings out hunters, we become aware that it is a whole group of loons that has arrived (though the loon is outnumbered by the hunters): "They [the hunters] come rustling through the woods like autumn leaves, at least ten men to one loon" (233). Comparing the movement of the hunters to that of leaves, Thoreau makes a point of including them in the pattern of the natural rhythm. They are less the machine in the garden than just another element of nature. Though a nuisance to Thoreau and the loon alike, the hunters are certainly not elevated above nature. Nor are they any more individualized than the loon.

As an individualized actor the loon only enters *Walden* in the following paragraph, which Thoreau begins with an anecdotal marker of one moment in time: "As I was paddling along the north shore one very calm October afternoon . . . " (234). The loon bursts onto the scene "suddenly" (234), and for the next three pages commands Thoreau's and the reader's full attention. Here, it isn't even a matter of Thoreau having to train his attention on what is already in front of him (as suggested above, in a different context, by Arsić). The loon literally puts himself in this position: he "sail[ed] out from the shore toward the middle a few rods in front of me, set up his wild laugh and betrayed himself" (234). It is the first completion of an implicit call-and-response cycle: Thoreau has been looking for a loon, and rather than finding one, the loon seems to have understood his call and presents himself to him. This establishes the pattern of what Thoreau describes as their "game."

It is a game of hide–and–seek, though the two partners never switch roles. Thoreau himself can seek but cannot hide. The loon, on the other hand, appears, disappears, reappears. It is Thoreau's role to seek in a particular sense: not to find something in its place, but to anticipate where the loon will next appear. "While he was thinking one thing in his brain, I was endeavoring to divine his thought in mine" (235). In other words, the two are playing a mind game. On the part of the loon, this involves outpacing Thoreau's guesswork and thus upsetting his expectations: "Sometimes he would come up unexpectedly on the opposite side of me, having apparently passed directly under the boat" (235).

The loon displays a dexterity and virtuosity that seems to unbind him from the restrictions of the elements. He flies, swims, dives at enormous speed, laughing and calling in two different voices when coming up from the water. This free mobility gives him an edge over his human partner, and yet, despite the obvious inequality, Thoreau takes an aesthetic attitude toward the exchange that emphasizes harmonic balance: "It was a pretty game, played on the smooth surface of the pond, a man against a loon" (235).

The aesthetic quality of this playful battle may be one of harmony but it does not result from the complementary qualities of the two opponents, nor from any kind of symmetry of power, skill, or movement (it is decidedly not a dance). It is rather a hierarchical constellation: the loon is by far superior to the human. Thoreau concedes this quite clearly:

> occasionally, when he had balked me most successfully and come up a long way off, he uttered a long-drawn unearthly howl, probably more like that of a wolf than any bird; as when a beast puts his muzzle to the ground and deliberately howls. This was his looning, —perhaps the wildest sound that is ever heard here, making the woods ring far and wide. I concluded that he laughed in derision of my efforts, confident of his own resources. (236)

The loon's derision poses a riddle. If the loon is superior, why does he deride Thoreau? What exactly are Thoreau's "efforts," and what is really at stake in this game? On some level, the game is part of the structural confrontation between loon and man that was initially introduced via the hunters. Just as the loon starring in this scene is an individualized exemplar of the generalized loon described in the beginning, so Thoreau is an individualized exemplar of the generalized human introduced via the hunters. It is not a matter of Thoreau wanting to shoot the loon (he certainly does not), but of him inhabiting, qua species, the structural position of the hunter. If we imagine Thoreau with a gun, he is no longer in a disadvantaged position and the game the two are playing is a kind of mortal combat. Even without a gun, one might conclude, not unreasonably, that Thoreau's "efforts" consist in a simulation of a hunt.

But the game can also be read differently, as a model for democratic conviviality that makes no demands for egalitarian de-differentiation, symmetry, and mutual understanding. Instead, this kind of sociality recognizes that reading the other's mind can never move beyond uncertainty (which throws the anthropomorphizing language itself into doubt: isn't Thoreau already imputing too much to the loon when he describes his "laugh"?) and further emphasizes that being together can be thought of in terms of a sequence of appearing, disappearing, and reappearing. It is a type of interaction in which distance remains a distinguishing feature, in which co-operation enhances the individuality of both partners, and in which, finally, difference and inequality are tied to the reciprocity of engaging in, and continuing, the game. For even if the two partners to the game are not engaged in a dance, they move together, in difference: the loon presents himself only after Thoreau has paddled out on the lake to find him, and the loon in turn steers Thoreau to the greatest expanse of the lake: "He led me at once to the widest part of the pond, and could not be driven from it" (235).

For the game to continue, the loon, in fact, has to act non-instrumentally, against his purported interest to elude Thoreau's senses—something Thoreau appears not to grasp himself: "But why, after displaying so much cunning, did he invariably betray himself the moment he came up by that loud laugh? . . . He was indeed a silly loon, I thought" (235-36). Under conditions of inequality and asymmetry, silliness (the apparently non-rational) is what makes it possible to stay faithful to the shared project of creating sequences of appearing and disappearing, but the judgment of silliness is also the marker of remaining at a distance from one another, forever incomprehensible. In this dual sense, posthuman democracy is a silly practice.

## III.

Throughout *Walden*, Thoreau tends to imagine the interactions within a posthuman society by anthropomorphizing nature. The loon laughs and derides Thoreau, ants wage a war of epic, historical proportions, and Walden Pond itself is a kind of person who can be meaningfully asked, "Walden, is it you?" (193). In his later years, Thoreau came to identify more and more as a botanist and was recognized as such. In March 1859, Harvard appointed Thoreau to its Committee for Examination in Natural History. "This put him," as Laura Dassow Walls writes, "in a select company of New England naturalists who met annually in mid-July, under the direction of Asa Gray, to conduct the final examination of Harvard's sophomores in botany" (439). Without ever ceasing to approach nature metaphorically and through anthropomorphizing imagery, Thoreau shifted his focus to recording and cataloguing the material minutiae of his natural surroundings. This also brought along a shift in the ways he imagined, and textually constructed, society in nature. Rather than dramatically staging encounters with animals who moved in and out, came close to him only to distance themselves, in his later writings he crafts scenes of encounters with plants by highlighting the epistemological conditions that enable and constitute such encounters. Posthuman democracy thus increasingly becomes a matter of humans' ability to recognize the particularity and even individuality of the natural world. From such recognition follows the awareness that humans are always-already in communion with the natural world.

This can be traced with particular clarity in his late nature essays, such as "Autumnal Tints" (1862). Early on in that essay, Thoreau relates scenes of his sharpening powers of discernment, the result of which is his recognition of natural fellowship. For instance, he writes of his coming to differentiate between different types of grass: "These two were almost the first grasses that I learned to distinguish, for I had not known by how many friends I was surrounded; I had seen them simply as grasses standing" ("Autumnal" 287).

Here, learning to tell apart kinds of grass is a matter of realizing the plentitude of his friends. The temporal structure of these advances in discernment is dual; it concerns being in the present, registering what is in front of him, but it also entails retroactively giving presence to a past, bringing to awareness an old alliance that has been half-forgotten:

> I had walked over those Great Fields so many Augusts, and never yet distinctly recognized these purple companions that I had there. I had brushed against them and trodden on them, forsooth; and now, at last, they, as it were, rose up and blessed me. Beauty and true wealth are always thus cheap and despised. . . . I may say that I never saw them before; though, when I came to look them face to face, there did come down to me a purple gleam from previous years; and now, wherever I go, I see hardly anything else. It is the reign and presidency of the andropogons. (288)

In attributing "faces" to grasses, he reverts to anthropomorphizing, but the effect is not to reduce plants to human-like beings; the face-to-face with plants rather points beyond the limitations of human interaction. Not only humans have faces, and human society is no more than one variant of sociality. The same goes for the activities he ascribes to plants. Grasses "rose up and blessed me," and a particular grass is "the reign and presidency of the andropogons." Taken from religious and political institutions, these images extend principles of social organization beyond human society, not to make nature conform to humanity and thus to rob it of its otherness, but to de-exceptionalize human sociality and strip away its arrogations of superiority.

But as I hinted at earlier, Thoreau is hardly consistent in treating human society as a mere sub-category of generalized sociality. "Autumnal Tints" moves from a sense in which fellowship in nature and human fellowship particularize a single principle of contemporaneity, as if they were set on a spectrum and blended into one another, to an understanding of natural and human sociality as different enough to be compared to, and contrasted from, one another. The point of such contrasts, however, is not to reassert the special place of humanity in creation but rather to critique human society for its shortcomings in comparison to nature. In Thoreau, cultural critique is thus folded into species critique.

The essay shifts into this contrastive mode of critique as the natural specimen Thoreau regards, describes, and praises, are situated in increasing proximity to Concord. The spatial overlapping of nature and civilization reaches its apex in the chapter "The Elm":

> Their leaves are perfectly ripe. I wonder if there is any answering ripeness in the lives of the men who live beneath them. As I look down our street, which is lined with them, they remind me both by their form and color of yellowing sheaves of grain, as if the harvest had indeed come to the village itself, and we might expect to find some maturity and

flavor in the thoughts of the villagers at last. Under those bright rustling yellow piles just ready to fall on the heads of the walkers, how can any crudity or greenness of thought or act prevail? When I stand where half a dozen large elms droop over a house, it is as if I stood within a ripe pumpkin-rind, and I feel as mellow as if I were the pulp, though I may be somewhat stringy and seedy withal. (293)

Here, Thoreau sets up a competitive test. Will his human neighbors "answer" the ripeness of the elm trees' leaves, as they (about this Thoreau is very clear) should? He leaves the answer open rhetorically, but not without signaling to the reader that he, for one, feels "as mellow as if I were the pulp" of a pumpkin. The striking arrogance results from the mix of what I have just called cultural and species critique. In attacking his neighbors in their limitations as members of both nineteenth-century New England society and the human species, he sets himself apart from them in both regards. He is, in other words, closer to the elm tree than the rest.

The remainder of the essay amplifies this contrastive voice:

I see the market-man driving into the village, and disappearing under its canopy of elm-tops, with his crop, as into a great granary or barn-yard. I am tempted to go thither as to a husking of thoughts, now dry and ripe, and ready to be separated from their integuments; but, alas! I foresee that it will be chiefly husks and little thought, blasted pig-corn, fit only for cob-meal,—for, as you sow, so shall you reap. (294)

The crop is better than the humans who harvest it and bring it to market. Yet Thoreau will have no part of the human malaise. He is a different kind of farmer, one who would harvest the thoughts of his neighbors. Nature is superior to the humans that surround Thoreau. And so is he.

That there is indeed a higher kind of farming is affirmed a few pages later.

But Nature . . . is a perfect husbandman; she stores them all [the leaves of different trees]. Consider what a vast crop is thus annually shed on the earth! This, more than any mere grain or seed, is the great harvest of the year. The trees are now repaying the earth with interest what they have taken from it. They are discounting. They are about to add a leaf's thickness to the depth of the soil. This is the beautiful way in which Nature gets her muck, while I chaffer with this man and that, who talks to me about sulphur and the cost of carting. We are all the richer for their decay. (297-98)

Not only is the crop better than its merchant, but nature is also better at farming than humans. Human civilization, on that view, is not part and parcel of nature, but alienated from it: "man is the dwarf of himself," as Emerson put it in *Nature* (42).

Sharp-shooting his cultural critique, Thoreau takes on his distinct tone of satirical wit. In order to target the inferiority of human society, he puns, much like in *Walden*, on the economic terms that structure life in the midst of what historians refer to as the "market revolution" (see Larson). The entire passage is filled with economic language: husbandman, storage, vast crop, harvest, repaying with interest, discounting, riches—Thoreau presents us with the whole economic recycling chain of an agricultural society producing for the market.

But parody and satire are genres that are forever ambivalent, for the forms they imitate and exaggerate in order to deliver their attack are not just ridiculed, they are also repeated and ultimately left standing. Thoreau's witty punning builds on the resignification of the terms of the market system. In altered, reapplied form, these term become legible as the principles of society in nature. An earlier generation of readers—marketplace critics of the 1980s, such as Paul Gilmore and Walter Benn Michaels—saw in such acts of naturalizing capitalist principles the true ideological work of Romantic writing. The fact that the sociality of nature doesn't pose a radical alternative to human society but rather a punning revision may weaken Thoreau's potential for thinking up a utopian alternative to the economic system. But in exchange, it does allow for reconceiving sociality more generally, by extending its outer limits to include all of nature. And it isn't as if the revisionism of punning were critically toothless. The sociality of nature that emerges differs markedly from human society. Human society, based on material profit, egotism, and the need of securing property, hinges, Thoreau writes in *Walden*, on the principle of security. Punning yet again, Thoreau points out that community gets reduced to the provision of defensive *munition*, equating *community* with *immunity*:

> To them the village was literally a *com-munity*, a league for mutual defence, and you would suppose that they would not go a-huckleberrying without a medicine chest. The amount of it is, if a man is alive, there is always danger that he may die, though the danger must be allowed to be less in proportion as he is dead-and-alive to begin with. A man sits as many risks as he runs. (*Walden* 153)

In the society of nature, on the other hand, economic principles come to subvert the risk-averse tendencies of closing down boundaries and protecting the individual from communion with the outside. The society of nature builds on our ethical obligation to recognize always-already existing forms of fellowship, to recognize that where we would draw a line, we have always-already crossed it. But it is also a fellowship that must entail, and insist on, difference and distance, since it rejects building the political on the differentiation of friend and enemy, inside and outside. Difference and distance remain in place once the drawing of categorical boundaries, whether among humans or different species, is abandoned. For only where there is a recognized outside can there be the assumption of remainder-less proximity and identification on the inside. Without the categorical difference between "us" and "them," proximity begins to breathe in distance.

Thoreau's punned-up world remains distinctly worldly—which is why economic categories have their place in it—yet it is a world that depends on the fearful community overcoming its quest for immunity. The political and the ethical are bound up with one another in the task to realize this world, to overstep boundaries while respecting the distance of neighbors and fellows. It is a task, and a world, that is ours.

## Notes

I thank my research assistant Tom Freischläger for his help on this essay.

## Works Cited

Arsić, Branka. *Bird Relics: Grief and Vitalism in Thoreau*. Harvard University Press, 2017.
Cavell, Stanley. *Senses of Walden: An Expanded Edition*. Chicago University Press, 1992.
Emerson, Ralph Waldo. Nature. *The Collected Works of Ralph Waldo Emerson*, edited by Alfred R. Ferguson, et al., vol. 1, The Belknap Press of Harvard University Press, 1971-2013, pp. 3-45.
Gilmore, Michael T. *American Romanticism and the Marketplace*. University of Chicago Press, 1985.
Grusin, Richard, editor. *The Nonhuman Turn*. University of Minnesota Press, 2015.
Hook, Sidney. "Democracy as a Way of Life." *Tomorrow in the Making*, edited by John N. Andrews and Carl A. Marsden. Whittlesey House, 1939, pp. 31-46.
Larson, John L. *The Market Revolution in America: Liberty, Ambition, and the Eclipse of the Common Good*. Cambridge University Press, 2010.
Mariotti, Shannon. *Thoreau's Democratic Withdrawal: Alienation, Participation, and Modernity*. University of Wisconsin Press, 2010.
McKenzie, Jonathan. *The Political Thought of Henry David Thoreau: Privatism and the Practice of Philosophy*. University Press of Kentucky, 2016.
Michaels, Walter Benn. *The Gold Standard and the Logic of Naturalism: American Literature at the Turn of the Century*. University of California Press, 1987.
Rosenblum, Nancy L. "Thoreau's Democratic Individualism." *A Political Companion to Henry David Thoreau*, edited by Jack Turner. University Press of Kentucky, 2014, pp. 15-38.

Thoreau, Henry David. "Autumnal Tints." *Essays: A Fully Annotated Edition*, edited by Jeffrey S. Cramer. Yale University Press, 2013, pp. 281-316.

---. "Resistance to Civil Government." *Essays: A Fully Annotated Edition*, edited by Jeffrey S. Cramer. Yale University Press, 2013, pp. 145-71.

---. *Walden*. Edited by J. Lyndon Shanley. Princeton University Press, 1971.

Walls, Laura Dassow. *Henry David Thoreau: A Life*. University of Chicago Press, 2017.

Wolfe, Cary. *What is Posthumanism?* University of Minnesota Press, 2010.

# Sacred Pact or Overkill? Human-Bison Relations in North American Mythologies

Gesa Mackenthun

The "greening" of the humanities has produced a series of studies that reassess the ecological status of Native Americans (for example Harkin and Lewis; Schweninger; Porter; Cruikshank). This essay will focus on one particular aspect of a scholarly discourse that seeks to correct the popular image of Native Americans as ecologically concerned people: the discussion about the responsibility for the quasi-extermination of the bison and related "charismatic" megafauna during the first human settlement of North America. As I will argue, some critiques of Native Americans' "ecological" attitudes conducted by non-Indian historians and anthropologists tend to revive an earlier colonial myth—that of Indian savagism. The overkill hypothesis is not only coexistent but also consistent with a political backlash on the issues of global climate change and animal well-being. The result of colonial conflict, it ignores the presence of an archive of indigenous stories and epistemologies preserved in the colonial record. From a decolonial perspective, the continuation of discursive practices from classic colonial times is in need of critical revision.

During the 1970s, common concern for the environment forged the strongest tie between white ecologically minded citizen groups and indigenous groups struggling for political representation and participation, as well as for adherence to the treaties and the territorial rights they promised. Next to this transcultural, and soon transnational, Rainbow Coalition there existed innumerable local coalitions like the Black Hills Alliance, which in the early 1980s united environmental activists with members of the Sioux tribes in order to prevent the further exploitation and devastation of the Black Hills in South Dakota, a main target for coal and uranium mining. The recent conflicts about the Keystone XL and Dakota Access pipelines, by which crude oil from the tar sands in Alberta, Canada, will be transported to the refineries in Texas under hazardous environmental circumstances, have brought about a similar coalition of native and non-native environmental activists and farmers who ironically call themselves the Cowboy and Indian Alliance (CIA). A common concern for the environment, then, was and is what binds indigenous and nonindigenous activists together; this liaison has intensified over the decades since the early 1980s. Since the 1990s, scholars have begun to reflect on these developments and associations, lifting the public protest of the previous decades into the ranks of "postcolonial" critical culture studies (see for example Stoler). The intersectional field of postcolonial ecocriticism is presently one of the most vibrant in the humanities (deLoughrey and Handley). Yet, as will be shown in the following sections, a few studies allegedly devoted to understanding the connections between colonial conflicts and the history of the environment seem to be oblivious of the impact of colonization on both human action and the environment, and perhaps latently driven by an antagonism toward present-day cross-cultural coalitions and their common environmentalist causes.

## Pleistocene Progenitors

Our story begins in America's deep past—historically as well as theoretically. Beginning in 1967 and continuing until the present, U.S. academic archaeology has been involved in a passionate debate about human relations to the nonhuman world in Ice Age America. First made prominent by the Arizona archaeologist Paul S. Martin and a productive group of disciples, the hypothesis is that the first Americans, just after having arrived in North America between 12,000 and 10,000 years ago, began to exterminate America's "charismatic megafauna"—a narrative referred to as the Pleistocene Overkill Hypothesis.[1] Calculating the rough temporal concurrence between the demise of the mammoth and other big fauna and the arrival of the first people across Bering Strait, Martin, Jared Diamond, and others promote a causal relation between these two events. Based on fourteen sites where the bones of mammoth and mastodon were discovered in conjunction with Clovis culture hunting implements, they calculate that the newly arrived humans exterminated the megafauna within a few hundred years. Diamond speaks of a continent-embracing "Blitzkrieg" by which Paleo-Indians systematically decimated the animals, thus causing incalculable ecological loss to America's biodiversity. The World War metaphor occludes the weakness of the empirical evidence: the scientists explain the scarcity of sites with the speed of the slaughter that hardly left a trace. In other words, the *absence* of evidence is *proof* of the event having taken place in this or similar form.

The overkill thesis has been questioned from various directions.[2] Donald Grayson and David Meltzer, for example, note that the thesis revives an earlier one from the mid-nineteenth century with which it also shares the absence of Europe in discussions of man-made species extinction. They furthermore argue that Martin's assertion that the lack of supporting evidence is consistent with the overkill model is "turning the absence of empirical support into support for his beliefs. We suggest that this feature of the overkill position removes the hypothesis from the realm of science and places it squarely in the realm of faith" (Grayson and Meltzer, "Requiem" 585). The Native American writer and activist Vine Deloria Jr. likewise wonders that, given the magnitude of the event (the complete eradication of a whole number of species within just a few hundred years), the perpetrators "should have left a little graffiti and picnic litter somewhere" (145). In spite of such fundamental critique, the narrative of the Pleistocene Overkill entered public knowledge and has become a fixed element in trans- or "big" historical surveys of man's ecologically disastrous existence on earth.[3]

Historian Shepard Krech doubts the conclusiveness of the evidence for the Pleistocene Overkill and refers (as others do) to climatic factors as reasons for the extinction of the mammoth and mastodon (40). Yet, he nevertheless includes a chapter on the Pleistocene extinctions in his book *The Ecological Indian* (1999), detailing, to great critical acclaim, the ecological sins of Native Americans. It would have been inconclusive that the Paleo-Indian hunters left such a savory species as the American bison unexterminated. Krech's main argument is that this feat was accomplished by the modern Indians.

## Remembering the Butchery

Forty years earlier and closer to Martin's original assault on the myth of the ecological (Paleo) Indian, Krech's thesis would have come as a great surprise. The general knowledge at that time was that it was whites, not Indians, who drove the buffalo to quasi-extinction. This knowledge is reflected in John Williams' western (or post-western) novel *Butcher's Crossing*, first published in 1960. Reprinted in 2007, fifty-five years after its first publication, the novel is like a reminder of an earlier, now contested, historical consensus. The decade in which it was written also saw the emergence of the Red Power Movement: Vine Deloria's manifesto *Custer Died for Your Sins* debunking Euroamerica's colonial mythology about Native Americans was published in 1969; the American Indian Movement was founded in 1968, just one year after Martin's scientific attack on the indigenous ancestors. Finally, Dee Brown's history of the Plains war, *Bury My Heart at Wounded Knee*, firmly established the narrative of white genocide against Indians and bisons in 1971 (253-55).

Williams's novel is interesting because it culminates in a detailed description of the prolonged butchering of a whole buffalo herd by a white buffalo hunter. Surprisingly, the novel hardly mentions any Native Americans, least of all as agents of the buffalo slaughter. It describes the adventure of a party of fortune hunters who set out from the boomtown Butcher's Crossing in

Colorado to chase down and exterminate a mythical bison herd in the remote mountains of Colorado in 1873. The novel begins with a familiar story of white male existential search for identity but then evolves into a less familiar narrative of human failure and ecological disaster. The key passage of the novel consists of the lengthy description of how the novel's Nietzschean hero-villain, Miller, methodically kills off a herd of about 5,000 bison who can neither see—and thus defend themselves against—the hidden killer, nor escape from a dead-end valley. They let themselves be killed like cows in a stockyard without giving fight. The protagonist is fascinated by the killer's mechanistic, "automaton"-like strategy but also strangely affected by the killed beasts: "One bull had dropped so that its huge head rested upon the side of another buffalo; the head seemed to watch them as they approached, the dark blank shining eyes regarding them disinterestedly, then staring beyond them as they passed" (Williams 137, 138). He is again struck by the first buffalo calf he is about to skin: "He stood looking at the calf, whose open transparent eyes were filmed over blankly with a layer of dust" (143). Before he gets used to the carnage, he at one point dreams of being himself "penned . . . in a corner of blackness from which there was no retreat" (155). But such strokes of empathy with the hunted animal soon disappear, and Andrews, like other young heroes of adventure literature, is being swept along with the events and the fascination of violence, incapable of altering them.

The post-heroic adventure tale—or post-adventure tale?—ends in disaster: the hunters are first unable to return to the city with their thousands of precious hides. Having barely escaped with their lives, the three survivors find the boomtown deserted and the buffalo hides piling up in front of the cabin of the hide trader, who has gone bankrupt and left the town.

*Butcher's Crossing* is a novel about machine-man's senseless butchering of 5,000 bison. It offers a comparatively sober perspective on the history of the westward movement. Without pointing explicitly at a culprit for the bisoncide, the novel suggests a combination of human moral immaturity and western man's unthinking self-subjection to the forces of the market and technology: here the railway, which facilitates the marketing of the skins, and of course the high tech rifles with their "clean" method of killing (137).

First published in 1960, Williams' novel is far from reaching the explicit ecocritical force of Rachel Carson's *Silent Spring* (1962), whose indictment of the chemical industry's destruction of nature was followed only two years later, in the UK, by Ruth Harrison's critique of the mass production of meat in *Animal Machines*. Written at the dawn of the ecological movement, *Butcher's Crossing* avoids any share in a discourse about the nobility and suffering of animals, let alone animal rights; yet it does transport occasional empathy with the nonhuman creature.

Neither does the novel idealize Native Americans as more ecologically minded human beings. This discourse, too, was still in its infant shoes at the time the novel was published. It would develop, in alignment with the environmental and civil rights movements, during the sixties and culminate in the first Earth Day, inspired by Wisconsin senator Gaylord Nelson, which took place throughout the U.S. on April 22, 1970. One year later, the new awareness for the environment would come to be iconized in the famous anti-litter ad "Keep America Beautiful" in 1971, which features Indian actor Iron Eyes Cody spilling his famous single tear for the environment.

## Conspicuous Ambivalence: The Indigenous Art of Killing

Given this prominence of the image, and the political performance, of Native Americans as stewards and protectors of the environment—for instance, in trials for territorial and treaty rights, against nuclear pollution and resource extraction—it came as no small surprise when Shepard Krech III and other scholars began to argue, in the late 1990s, that Native Americans were in large part responsible for the destruction, and sometimes extermination, of American fauna. Krech argues in *The Ecological Indian: Myth and History* (1999) that Native Americans were precisely *not* what the title of his book suggests— "ecological" in the modern sense of the term. Employing ambivalent rhetoric, the book harvests colonial sources to produce abundant evidence of Native Americans' destructive behavior against the nonhuman world. Krech was obviously reacting to what he perceived as an unacceptable romanticization of Native Americans' environmentalist habitus disseminated through the activities of the environmentalist movement. One cannot but agree with Krech when he writes that historically, Native Americans' attitude to the environment was neither "ecologist" nor "conservationist" because they did not use "mathematical or hypothetico-deductive techniques" for thinking about the environment "and its interrelating components in systemic ways," as a scientific ecologist would do. Nor did they promote or practice "careful husbandry and sustainable development," calculating "sustainable yield into the distant future" and deliberately leaving "the environment and resources like animal populations in a usable state for succeeding generations," as a professional conservationist would do (24-26). The thesis is hard to contradict because both "ecological" and "conservationist" are modern Western concepts arising from the capitalist world's rather late, anthropocentric, and still not fully realized, insight that an ecologically feasible practice will be necessary for ensuring the survival of the human species. Employing these terms anachronistically—neither Indians nor non-Indians thought "ecologically," according to Krech's definition of the term, before the 1970s—the book strongly suggests that not only were Native Americans quite unecological, they also strongly if not solely contributed to species extinction, most notably the quasi-extinction of the bison.

Due to its remarkable rhetorical ambivalence, the critical reception of Krech's book was quite mixed.[4] This is not the place for a detailed analysis of the intricate rhetorical strategies used in this book because others have done the work already—of its selectivity of perspective; its use of dramatic detail when evoking native brutality vs. silencing of the violence of white colonists; its effacement of a native perspective and uncritical use of colonial texts; its tendency to arrive at significant historical conclusions based on very thin empirical evidence and hypothetical calculations—to name some of the methods used. I am rather interested in the implicit narrative of Native American savagism that the argument of the book depends on, and that it shares with the older work on the Pleistocene Overkill hypothesis discussed above. Throughout his book, Krech could rely on the ideological force of Martin's earlier but similar narrative that merely projects the mythology of Indian neo-savagism on American antiquity (*The Ecological Indian* begins with a chapter on the Pleistocene extinctions).

One confluence of the two theses is their emphasis on indigenous wastefulness. In Krech's view, Native Americans were savagely wasteful toward nature—a point that Martin and Diamond also make in their *Blitzkrieg* thesis. Though he admits the impact of the capitalist market on the decrease of buffalo in the "final stage" of the decimating process—the rising demands of the leather industry and the use of buffalo leather in "belting for machinery" (139, 141)—Krech calculates that the bison would have been exterminated anyway due to native improvidence and preference for calves and cows. He utilizes the research of William Hornaday, a direct witness of the bisoncide, who in *The Extermination of the American Bison* (1887) seeks to identify the "improvidence" and "wastefulness" of the native lifestyle as reasons for the decline of Native American tribes due to starvation after the buffalo were killed off (Krech 127; Hornaday 527). Yet Hornaday is also the main source for information about the systematic slaughter of the American bison by *white* hunters in the second half of the nineteenth century.[5]

Though he mentions industrial capitalism's effect on the dwindling numbers of buffalo, Krech at the same time mitigates its effects in favor of his narrative of Native American tribes not being able to cope with displacement, starvation, and cultural deracination and thus collaborating with the new system. He rejects the notion that Indians were "corrupted by an irresistible and insatiable European-American marketplace." Rather, "[a]ssigning blame to market forces has been a popular pastime for decades" (Krech 142).

Empirical evidence is in fact incontrovertible in the case of the bison slaughter of the late nineteenth century. As economic historian Scott Taylor shows, the killing of approximately six million buffalo between 1870 and 1890 can be traced to a series of factors, but they are all related to the impact of the capitalist market. Chief among them were the completion of the transcontinental railway that brought hunters into the West and transported buffalo hides eastward,

Fig. 1. "Slaughtered for the Hide." *Harper's Weekly*, vol. 18, no. 937, 12 Dec. 1874, p. 1022. Library of Congress Prints and Photographs Division Washington, D.C.

and especially the demand for buffalo hides in Europe. The beginning of the slaughter (a term Taylor uses) can be traced almost precisely to a new method in Europe (in the UK and in Germany) of turning the thick buffalo hide into patent leather. The demand for hides exploded while the American government was incapable of—and in part unwilling to—regulate the killing of the buffalo. After all, contemporaries considered the decimation of the bison strategically helpful in bringing about the demise of the Plains Indians (Brown 254). While for Taylor, Native American hunting activity is no significant part of the equation, and his research shows that within about a dozen years (1871-83) six million hides were exported to Europe (3), he—an economic historian—leaves out descriptions of the actual scenario. Next to Hornaday's detailed account, that scenario is well documented in contemporary visual culture (see fig. 1 and 2).[6]

Fig. 2. "Pile of American Bison Skulls Waiting to be Ground for Fertilizer. Circa 1870." Burton Historical Collection/Detroit Public Library.

Krech prefers an "anthropological" narrative to a historical one. Using exclusively colonial sources, he refers to the native belief that the buffalo would autochthonously reemerge from the earth every spring, allowing for the conclusion that their numbers would never dwindle (Krech 146-49). On a thin empirical basis, Krech argues that the mythical superstructure of the Plains tribes contributed to their irrational engagement in the slaughter: "Plains Indian ecological spaces would not be within the parameters of a Western ecologist's ecosystem. It is easy to see how a belief of this nature would not encourage conservation of management of a declining resource under conditions like those obtaining increasingly on the nineteenth-century Plains" (149). Krech authoritatively dismisses accounts of Native Americans' *non-wasteful* behavior as being the exception rather than the rule (144-45) while the normative value for measuring indigenous knowledge and practices is, again, the modern Western concept of ecosystem whose criteria are anachronistically held against pre-1900 actors. In its cleanwashing of the evidence, its twisting of counter-evidence into proof of its thesis, as well as its pervasive use of anachronistic concepts and language, the method of *The Ecological Indian* very much resembles that of Paul Martin and his colleagues.

Obliviousness of historical facts and of a non-Western perspective bear considerable ideological potential. Looking at the case historically, the concurrence of the industrial exploitation of animal lives—not only bisons, but also whales were hunted up to the point of extinction—and the beginnings of the mass production of meat for a growing urban population comes to mind. In his muckraking novel *The Jungle*, Upton Sinclair turns his readers' attention to the capitalist waste management, relating how disposable human lives are "wasted" and the market is flooded with spoiled meat while the robber barons fill their pockets. A historically interested discussion of Native American "wastefulness" of bison lives at the peak of the genocidal war against both would have to include this larger context.[7]

## Competing Mythologies

Regardless of the contribution of Native Americans to the late nineteenth-century bisoncide, it was Native Americans who saved the bison from extinction. Ken Zontek shows how even at the climax of the American genocidal war against the Plains Indians and under extremely precarious conditions, individual Native American families—Lakota, Salish—read the signs of the times and started breeding little bison herds; a large amount of the gene pool of today's bison population can be traced back to the herds of these "bison saviors" at the turn of the twentieth century (34). That this is much less known than the savagism myth has to do with the fact that colonial situations produce vastly asymmetrical power relations leading to equally asymmetric and selective documentation. Shepard Krech takes advantage of this fact and the gullibility of his readers trained in the colonial mythology of Indian savagism. His stories about Indian overkill and Indian wastefulness can rely on the earlier narrative of Indian nomadism transported throughout popular culture since the early times of American colonialism and paradoxically coexisting with the romantic narrative of Indian environmentalism. This overdeterminedness with contradictory knowledges is the quintessence of myth, as Barthes and Lévi-Strauss would agree. The neo-savagist myth of the unecological Indian is part of what Mignolo calls the coloniality of knowledge—of the discursive construction of truth under the conditions of coloniality. Modern knowledge, Mignolo argues, is "epistemically imperial"; it "devalues and dismisses epistemic differences" (205).

The myth of Indian savagism was competently analyzed and deconstructed in the 1960s by Roy Harvey Pearce and many scholars after him (see for example Slotkin, Rogin, and Drinnon). Pearce also understood that the myth of savagism included a performative aspect, such as depriving Native Americans of any legal claims to the land that were solved by the U.S. Supreme Court in the 1820s and 1830s, causing domestic and international controversy. Savagism teaches that Indians were nomads—in the words of the Jacksonian James Hall, writing in 1835, a "wandering horde" with no sense of property (Pearce 72).[8] As we know, Jacksonian politics enacted this ideology by the practice of forced removal and deportation—one of the most traumatizing forced migrations in world history. The power of naturalizing mythical stories is to render such contradictions between moral claim and social fact invisible, to employ narrative for smoothing over ambivalence and to imaginatively solve contradictions between social reality and desire. Krech's narrative—full of ambivalence and discrepancies between different claims—more or less successfully enacts this strategy.

The colonial narratives of indigenous bisoncide and mammothcide exist next to documents—some of which (such as Grinnell) were used by Krech—that testify to a benevolent but also complex conceptualization of human-animal relationships, and that transport evidence of Native Americans' strong emotional and epistemological relations to their natural environment—animals, plants, landscapes. Due to the hegemony of colonial over indigenous sources, much of this material is only available in the colonial archive. The Cheyenne stories collected by George Bird Grinnell between the 1890s and 1920s, as well as the memories of John Stands in Timber published by Margot Liberty in 1967, give evidence of the sacred status that the bison had in Plains Indians epistemes. The Cheyenne trace their origins to the actions of a mysterious buffalo woman who introduced humans to valuable cultural techniques and gave them spiritual knowledge. In bearing a child to a human man the buffalo woman is the decisive link between humans and nonhumans; this mythical figure binds the young warrior into a family liaison with her buffalo people and thus prepares him to become an important messenger of culture (Grinnell 87-104). Cheyenne culture, in this reading, is the result of the unified exertions of humans and buffalo. It is through her that humans first learn about the uses of buffalo as the major economic source. Another story, "E Hyoph' Sta," tells of two young men who are sent off by their tribe to end starvation. The creator figure Coyote introduces them first to the use of corn, horses, and other animals for meat and then to the yellow haired buffalo woman who marries one of the men. Coyote requires the woman not to express pity in case the hunters bring a little yellow buffalo calf because the purpose is to furnish these poor people with all kinds of game, including buffalo (Grinnell 248-49). The young men teach their relatives to take only as much meat as is needed (250). But after a while, the woman forgets her pledge and expresses compassion when a few boys wantonly abuse a little buffalo calf, resulting in the disappearance of all the buffalo (251). While the injunction against expressing pity for a suffering creature is disturbing—why is the act of compassion sanctioned and not the boys' violent behavior?—the story can be seen to negotiate the difficult ethical choice that had to be made between respect for one's fellow creatures and the need to escape starvation—a choice around which all societies have built many narratives. Between the lines the story seems to say that individual compassion is not sufficient if it is not transmitted to the younger generation.

Another story is referring to the early days of human life on earth, telling of the decisive race carried out between humans and animals to decide who should be allowed to eat whom. Humans win the race against the buffalo with the help of Magpie and Crow. As a result the buffalo lose their defensiveness and men begin killing and eating them (Grinnell 252-54).[9]

As we can see, the belief among some Plains tribes that the bison originated in the interior of the earth, which Krech uses to their disadvantage, is by far not the only surviving bison story. The indigenous oral tradition transports a differentiated view of the human-bison relationship among the different tribes. They powerfully demonstrate peoples' dependency on the bison—their sacred pact with them, expressed in a complex sense of moral obligation toward these animals, and with a strong injunction against subjecting them to torture and waste.

## Conclusions

People eat animals and have always done so. Especially in areas with a limited availability of agricultural soil, this was necessary for survival. The decisive question is how they imaginatively come to terms with this fact. The neo-savagist myth of the unecological Indian hit the market at a time when the industrialized part of the world had long packaged off its compassion for the suffering creature in aesthetically appealing chunks of meat sold in supermarkets. In the context of capitalist culture's incredible art of abstraction, the myth has two possible effects: first, it absolves its believers from adhering to ecological policies such as limiting meat consumption or exchanging the dependency on fossil fuels in favor of more sustainable ways of producing (or actually saving) energy, by suggesting that, as Vine Deloria states, "at *no* time were human beings careful of the lands upon which they lived" (97). Why should they be now? The myth of the unecological Indian is, in Deloria's words, "symptomatic of a lack of moral fiber and ethical concern for the Earth"—among Indians as among everyone else (97). As Lee Schweninger correctly writes, this may have serious legal consequences because it entails the denial of the core of Native American religious beliefs, which strongly rest on the notion of the sacredness of the land (163). The denial of Native Americans' special feeling of responsibility for the environment is ideologically related to denying the antiquity of their presence in America. Such anthropological and archaeological theories spring from a continuing colonial competition over ancestry, antiquity, and, ultimately, legitimacy.

Secondly, the myth disarticulates the surviving knowledge archive of indigenous societies. It performs a form of cultural monologue or ventriloquism—a "speaking about" instead of a "speaking with." But the existence of this counterhegemonic knowledge archive is essential in mastering the challenges that indigenous people face today. Their struggle for political recognition is fundamentally carried out on a *legal* basis—on the basis of treaties and constitutional rights. But if their claims as to the cultural centrality of the sacredness of the land are weakened because of new "scientific" evidence of their ecological incompetence and even destructiveness, this may have serious consequences for the future of both Indian claims for territorial and political sovereignty and the struggle for a more ecological policy in North America more generally.

Next to being able to identify a myth when we encounter one, it is important to recognize the aspect of its cultural work: which political and economic forces benefit from it? And which of the two sides of the myth—the "green" one of the ecological Indian or the "savagist" one of the unecological Indian—has proven more beneficial to humans and the environment (preservation of fauna and flora habitats, biodiversity, toxic-free existence)? Native American philosopher John Mohawk offers an answer. He concludes his review of *The Ecological Indian* by saying: "It will be difficult for many to understand the harm that Krech finds in an American-generated myth of an ecological Indian as a symbol of a kinder, gentler approach to nature. As with many myths, this one is likely rooted in facts, most of which are not even hinted at in this book." The special legal status deriving from treaties and culturally supported by the knowledge that Indians entertain a special relation to the earth and its nonhuman inhabitants—a relation which parts of modern society began to salvage and rediscover, against the forces of the ruling rationalism concurrent with the colonial encounter—is one of the best moral protections of the environment that all of us have.

## Notes

I would like to thank Helmbrecht Breinig for his helpful and encouraging comments on an earlier version of this essay.

**1 |** Their argument depends on this arrival date. Other archaeologists give much earlier dates—20,000 to 30,000 years ago.

**2 |** See Grayson and Meltzer, "Clovis Hunting," Wroe, et al., and Nagaoka who question the Overkill promoters' reliance on island models (Madagascar, New Zealand) which, they claim, cannot simply be transferred to a huge continent. The literature contains a wealth of empirical discussion impossible to repeat here.

**3 |** Thus, Yuval Harari promotes the thesis as a fact in his fashionable "big history" volume *Sapiens* (2011). Not only does he, like the Overkill promoters, leave out any reference to megafaunal extinctions in Europe during the last Ice Age; his description of the deeds of the human "foragers" is cluttered with terms borrowed from the criminological lexicon: the first settlers of Australia were "conquerors" and "invaders" who "transformed the Australian ecosystem beyond recognition" while the "even larger ecological disaster" would follow in America (72, 76). Without their intervention, "Down Under ... would still be home to marsupial lions, diprotodons and giant kangaroos." In short, the "historical record makes Homo Sapiens"—here accidentally represented only by those groups later to become subject to European settler colonialism, not the ancestors of the settler colonists themselves—"look like an ecological serial killer": "Guilty as Charged" (74, 73). Like Harari, Elizabeth Kolbert, in her no less notorious book *The Sixth Extinction* (2014), skips Europe, "implicates" humans settling in Australia and America, and adds the rather thin evidence of a drop in fungus mass and computer simulation to support the overkill hypothesis (231-34). As with Martin and Diamond, the evidence is bent to fit the thesis, and the ecologically ugly homo sapiens happens to be nonwhite.

**4 |** For a good summary of its reception see Schweninger, pp. 42-51. For a whole volume dedicated to discussing "the Ecological Indian" see Harkin and Lewis.

**5 |** Working on the basis of contemporary military reports and sales statistics, he documents that between 1872 and 1874 about 1,5 million buffalo hides were shipped east by railway and other means; he estimates the number of buffalo "killed *and wasted*" at 1,780,481, and he estimates the total number of bison "slaughtered by whites" in that period at 3,158,730 (Hornaday 499, emphasis added).

**6 |** Here is the witness William Hornaday's assessment of the situation: "During the years 1871 and 1872 the most wanton wastefulness prevailed. Colonel Dodge declares that, though hundreds of thousands of skins were sent to market, they scarcely indicated the extent of the slaughter. Through want of skill in shooting and want of knowledge in preserving the hides of those slain by green hunters, one hide sent to market represented three, four, or even five dead buffalo. The skinners and curers knew so little of the proper mode of curing hides, that at least half of those actually taken were lost. In the summer and fall of 1872 one hide sent to market represented at least three dead buffalo. This condition of affairs rapidly improved; but such was the furor for slaughter, and the ignorance of all concerned, that every hide sent to market in 1871 represented no less than *five* dead buffalo" (494-95, emphasis added). Without wanting to join the tedious numbers game of the revisionist historians, it's tempting to combine the numbers given by Taylor and Hornaday: we would arrive at about 24 million bison killed by mostly white hunters in twelve years for the hide and leather market. Krech and Flores offer the total number of 30 million bison in 1500 (Krech 126, 136).

7 | The transformation of organic lives into the abstractions of canned and dried convenience food would deserve an essay of its own. See Mackenthun, "Night of First Ages" for a few ideas. The idea of "wasted lives" is Zygmunt Bauman's.

8 | Andrew Jackson's Secretary of War Lewis Cass, writing in 1830, also helped popularize the image of the Indian as nomad, although it cannot have escaped his attention that all the tribes about to be removed to areas beyond the Mississippi did practice advanced forms of agriculture. Yet he claims: "[t]he new race of men, who landed upon these shores, found that their predecessors had affixed few distinctive marks of property in the forests where they roamed" and that "[l]ike the bear, and deer, and buffalo of his own forests, an Indian lives as his father lived, and dies as his father died. . . . His life passes away in a succession of listless indolence." Therefore, the Indian "is perhaps destined to disappear with the forests" (Cass 372-73).

9 | Stands In Timber fuses the two stories; the race between man and buffalo becomes part of the process of defining the family relations between the two groups (19-24).

## Works Cited

Bauman, Zygmunt. *Wasted Lives: Modernity and Its Outcasts*. Polity, 2004.

Brown, Dee. *Bury My Heart at Wounded Knee*. Bantam, 1972.

Cass, Lewis. "Remarks on the Policy and Practice of the United States in their Treatment of the Indians." 1827. *Concepts in American Cultural History from the Colonial Period to the End of the 19th Century*, edited by Bernd Engler and Oliver Scheiding, WVT, 2005, pp. 370-74.

Cruikshank, Julie. *Do Glaciers Listen? Local Knowledge, Colonial Encounters, and Social Imagination*. British Columbia University Press, 2005.

Deloria, Vine, Jr. *Red Earth—White Lies: Native Americans and the Myth of Scientific Fact*. Fulcrum, 1997.

DeLoughrey, Elizabeth, und George B. Handley, editors. *Postcolonial Ecologies: Literatures of the Environment*. Oxford University Press, 2011.

Diamond, Jared. "The American Blitzkrieg: A Mammoth Undertaking." *Discover*, 1987, pp. 82-88.

---. "Blitzkrieg and Thanksgiving in the New World." *The Third Chimpanzee: The Evolution and Future of the Human Animal*. Harper Perennial, 2006.

Drinnon, Richard. *Facing West: The Metaphysics of Indian-Hating and Empire-Building*. University of Minnesota Press, 1980.
Echo-Hawk, Walter. *In the Courts of the Conqueror: The 10 Worst Indian Law Cases Ever Decided*. Fulcrum, 2012.
Feit, Harvey A. "Myths of the Ecological Whitemen: Histories, Science, and Rights in North American-Native American Relations." *Native Americans and the Environment: Perspectives on the Ecological Indian*, edited by Michael E. Harkin and David Rich Lewis, University of Nebraska Press, 2007, pp. 52-94.
Grayson, Donald K., and David J. Meltzer. "A Requiem for North American Overkill." *Journal of Archaeological Science*, vol. 30, 2003, pp. 585-93.
Grayson, Donald K., and David J. Meltzer. "Clovis Hunting and Large Mammal Extinction: A Critical Review of the Evidence." *Journal of World Prehistory*, vol. 16, no. 4, 2002, pp. 313-59.
Grinnell, George Bird, editors. *By Cheyenne Campfires*. 1926. Reprinted ed., Nebraska University Press, 1962.
Grossman, Zoltan. "Unlikely Alliances." *Unsettling America: Decolonization in Theory and Practice*. 11 June 2013, unsettlingamerica.wordpress.com
Harari, Yuval Noah. *Sapiens: A Brief History of Humankind*. 2011. HarperCollins, 2015.
Harkin, Michael E. and David Rich Lewis, editors. *Native Americans and the Environment: Perspectives on the Ecological Indian*. University of Nebraska Press, 2007.
Hornaday, William T. *The Extermination of the American Bison*. Government Printing Office, 1889. Project Gutenberg, gutenberg.org
Kolbert, Elizabeth. *The Sixth Extinction: An Unnatural History*. Henry Holt, 2014.
Krech, Shepard, III. *The Ecological Indian: Myth and History*. 2000.
Mackenthun, Gesa. "Night of First Ages: Deep Time and the Colonial Denial of Temporal Coevalness." *Crossroads in American Studies: Transnational and Biocultural Encounters*, edited by Frederike Offizier et al., Winter, 2015, pp. 177-214.
Martin, Paul S. "Prehistoric Overkill." *Pleistocene Extinctions*, edited by Paul S. Martin and H. E. Wright. Yale University Press, 1967, pp. 75-120.
Mignolo, Walter D. *The Darker Side of Western Modernity: Global Futures, Decolonial Options*. Duke University Press, 2011.
Mohawk, John C. "Review of *The Ecological Indian*." *Great Plains Research: A Journal of Natural and Social Sciences*, 2001. Digital Commons, University of Nebraska, digitalcommons.unl.edu
Nagaoka, Lisa. "The Overkill Hypothesis and Conservation Biology." *Conservation Biology and Applied Zooarchaeology*, edited by Steve Wolverton and Lee Lyman. University of Arizona Press, 2010, pp. 110-38.

Porter, Joy. *Native American Environmentalism: Land, Spirit, and the Idea of Wilderness*. 2012. University of Nebraska Press, 2014.

Ranco, Darren J. "The Ecological Indian and the Politics of Representation: Critiquing the Ecological Indian in the Age of Ecocide." *Native Americans and the Environment: Perspectives on the Ecological Indian*, edited by Michael E. Harkin and David Rich Lewis. University of Nebraska Press, 2007, pp. 32-51.

Rogin, Michael Paul. *Fathers and Children*. Vintage, 1975.

Schweninger, Lee. *Listening to the Land: Native American Literary Responses to the Landscape*. University of Georgia Press, 2008.

Sinclair, Upton. *The Jungle*. 1906. Bedford St. Martin's, 2005.

Slotkin, Richard. *Regeneration Through Violence*. Wesleyan University Press, 1973.

Stands in Timber, John. *Cheyenne Memories*. Edited by Margot Liberty. University of Nebraska Press, 1967.

Stoler, Ann Laura, editor. *Imperial Debris: On Ruins and Ruination*. Duke University Press, 2013.

Williams, John. *Butcher's Crossing*. 1960. New York Review Books, 2007.

Wroe, Stephen, et al. "Megafaunal Extinction in the Late Quarternary and the Global Overkill Hypothesis." *Alcheringa*, vol. 28, no. 1, 2004, pp. 292-31. *Taylor & Francis Online*, tandfonline.com

Zontek, Ken. *Buffalo Nation: American Indian Efforts to Restore the Bison*. University of Nebraska Press, 2007.

# Hands: Transdifferent Encounters between Human and Nonhuman Animals

*Helmbrecht Breinig*

Folsom: Cary was suggesting that in *The Lice* and *The Carrier of Ladders* you sometimes take on the voice of the culture in a kind of negative way. I'm wondering if sometimes too the voice in those books is not that of the other animals, if your desire throughout your work is not in part to accomplish what is both impossible and absolutely necessary, that is, to give voice to the voiceless beings, to those creatures that cannot speak their rage. Do you at times feel your voice coming not from the human culture but instead from the silent herds being destroyed by that human culture?

Merwin: It would be very presumptuous to agree to that, but insofar as I dare to suggest a formula for myself or anyone else, I think it's very important to remain open to that possibility, to welcome it, and to evoke it if possible. Otherwise, what else is there? Otherwise, one is there in an ego-bound, historical, culturally brainwashed, incredibly limited moment. One can't perceive anything because one has no perspective at all. The opposite—the nearest thing I can imagine to what I would think of as a sound or even healthy approach and attitude toward existence as a whole (as distinct from the endless separation of the human species from the rest of existence that leads to evaluating the one at the expense of the other)—would be Blake's "How do you know but ev'ry Bird that cuts the airy way, / Is an immense world of delight, clos'd to your senses five?" It works both ways, one both can be and can never be the bird.

—Ed Folsom and Cary Nelson, "'Fact Has Two Faces': An Interview with W.S. Merwin"

## I.

Quite a number of people have tried to be like other animals, to project themselves into animals' minds, to even become an animal or animal-human.[1] One of the most fascinating texts in this regard is J. Baker's *The Peregrine*, a book about his following and observing peregrine falcons to a point where he would become like one himself: "Learn to fear. To fear is the greatest bond of all.

The hunter must become the thing he hunts. What is, is now, must have the quivering intensity of an arrow shuddering into a tree. Yesterday is dim and monochrome. A week ago you were not born. Persist, endure, follow, watch" (13). Another radical approach to getting close to an animal's experience is Charles Foster's experiment to physically imitate as much as possible of the life of a badger, an otter, a fox, a red deer, and a swift—all of this based on the knowledge that we share with these animals much, if not most, of our evolutionary history, and hence our physiological makeup, our sensory equipment. We can use this shared background in a common physical environment: "The animals and I speak a shared language: the language of the buzzing of our neurons. Often they speak in a difficult—though never quite incomprehensible—dialect. When it is difficult to make out what is being said, context helps. The context is always the land" (Foster 18). The experiences of these and other humans who have made an effort to get into some animal's skin, as it were, can be highly rewarding, but except in shamanistic, drug- or ecstasy-induced states of awareness, they are characterized by the simultaneous presence of quite contradictory, human and nonhuman, impulses and valuations. They are experiences of transdifference.

The concept of transdifference, which was first formulated in the context of a doctoral program on cultural hermeneutics at the University of Erlangen-Nürnberg, has been applied to a variety of scholarly problems. To my knowledge, all of them come from the fields of social science, psychology, gender studies, and literary or cultural studies.[2] What has been ignored thus far is the field of human-animal relations. And yet, it is a fact that humans are also animals, that people try to think and feel with (other) animals, project forms of feeling and thinking on them, identify with them, problematize the kinds and degrees of difference between them and themselves, imagine themselves as animals, or as part animal, part human in shamanistic practices and the mythology of many cultures, desire animals even erotically, and communicate with them on an eye-to-eye level. This fact makes it inevitable that there also arise situations of interspecies transdifference.

Let me begin by quoting our definition of the term of 2006, which I still consider as valid and usable:

The term *transdifference* refers to phenomena of a co-presence of different or even oppositional properties, affiliations or elements of semantic and epistemological meaning construction, where this co-presence is regarded or experienced as cognitively or affectively dissonant, full of tension, and undissolvable. Phenomena of transdifference, for instance socio-cultural affiliations, personality components or linguistic and other symbolic predications, are encountered by individuals and groups and negotiated in their respective symbolic order. (Breinig and Lösch 105)

The term as defined here refers to sociocultural or psychological situations and processes, and to forms of textual meaning construction. How, then, can it be applied to transspecies phenomena? And yet, such phenomena are not completely different from those encountered exclusively in what is deemed to be a human world. The symbolic orders, that is, the totality of sign systems, meaning construction, and valuation concerning humans and nonhumans overlap.

In chapter 16 of Stowe's *Uncle Tom's Cabin* we find the following scene: Ophelia, a New England woman and abolitionist on a visit at the plantation of her cousin St. Clare, a slaveholder, finds St. Clare's little daughter Eva playing with the slave Tom, the novel's protagonist. Eva finally sits down on his knee. Ophelia is disgusted: "'How can you let her?'" she asks, "'it seems so dreadful.'" St. Clare, whose own position is somewhere between South and North, answers:

You would think no harm in a child's caressing a large dog, even if he was black; but a creature that can think, and reason, and feel, and is immortal, you shudder at. . . . You loathe them as you would a snake or a toad, yet you are indignant of their wrongs. . . . You would send them to Africa, out of your sight and smell, and then send a missionary or two to do up all the self-denial of elevating them compendiously. (Stowe 154)

Both cultural discourses, that of the North and that of the South, are based on a hierarchy, but in the South the slaves are considered less than human, which makes physical intimacy possible because it does not affect the symbolic order. The North sees them as humans, but as the racial, that is, primarily, the physical, Other, and would rather relocate them than have them as neighbors demanding recognition and respect.[3]

All this we know. We have developed a cultural discourse that accommodates human otherness and accepts difference both on the inter- and the intragroup level. The changes that have occurred since the nineteenth century have been studied extensively. And we know that there still exist forms of transcultural interaction that are directed at converting and assimilating the Other. We might also notice some interesting differences among the differences: in the nineteenth century, Native Americans were to be assimilated or else obliterated—or maybe assimilation is another form of obliteration? Blacks, on the other hand, were constructed as being unassimilable, indelibly different, and therefore exploitable as slaves (that is, not to be obliterated), or else to be removed to where they did not disturb the cultural order.

Vestiges of this traditional cultural order based on difference are at work in inter-group relations to this very day, as the current discourse on race in the United States and elsewhere makes abundantly clear. But the boundaries of difference have changed, and therefore experiences of belonging on both sides, of interethnic transdifference, have become much more common than in Stowe's time. It is important to remember that transdifference does not obliterate difference but rather presupposes it. One case that exemplifies the black-vs.-white differentiation and hierarchization discussed here is that of Anatole Broyard, a famous twentieth-century literary and cultural critic working for the *New York Times* and the *New York Review of Books*. For decades he was an influential member of the white cultural establishment. Only years after he had died in 1990, Henry Louis Gates revealed that Broyard had been an African American—according to the historically established racial distinctions in the US—who had used his apparent whiteness to pass as white during his military service and ever after. His career would have been unthinkable without this act of passing. As I have shown elsewhere (Breinig and Lösch 41-46), this identity construction must have been accompanied by cognitive and affective dissonance and hence taken place in a condition of transdifference lasting for many decades, a condition Broyard tried to cope with by undergoing psychoanalysis for many years. Not surprisingly, his transdifferent existence became the material of fiction.[4]

Now, it should not be assumed that humans can actually undertake or undergo a similar step beyond hierarchical difference into a new, transdifferent identity by passing as another animal—except through flights of the imagination, shamanistic role changes and the like. What can be changed, though, is our self-awareness, our mental and emotional identity formation. How about our dealing with the dog, the snake, the toad? Isn't there a parallel tendency to either make them almost human—dogs standing in for children, conversation partners, objects of love—or else to push them down the ladder of closeness, even those that are genetically just as closely related to humans as canines, for instance pigs or cows? And isn't this done in order to make it discursively and emotionally bearable to turn such animals into objects of industrial mass murder, to convert them into food? What we need is a cultural theory that does not restrict attention to human affairs but takes the other animals into account as well, and also our cultural practices regulating our dealings with them. And their dealings with us.

In his comparative analysis of modern theories of culture, Andreas Reckwitz favors a praxeological approach over the textualist theory so much in use in recent decades because the concept of cultural practice can include anything from the use of tools and bodily hygiene to forms of economic exchange, or, indeed, the production of and response to texts, theories, systems of meaning. I believe that both approaches, the textual and the praxeological, are complementary and that we should not abandon the notion of a discursive construction of reality. While, with regard to the examples mentioned above, we can explore the textualist/discursive foundation of racism, the praxeologist approach can describe the cultural practices of slavery, forced assimilation, and so forth. In the case of other animals, such an approach can be made to relate back to the discourse of what Peter Singer has called "speciesism," and also to the practices of how animals are used, or, more generally, to human interaction with what was traditionally called nonhuman nature. Zoologists have a non-constructivist praxeological definition of culture that is meant to cover the whole range of practices by animals, including the human animal: culture is "a system of socially transmitted behavior" (Van Schaick et al. 105). This definition can be applied to nonhuman animals because, as we now know, many species have distinct and historically variable cultures including forms of partnership, childcare, the development and use of tools, and sign systems. Such recent insights are convincingly used to make a case for animal rights, that is, in the rapidly expanding discipline of animal ethics. But how can these insights affect our self-awareness vis-à-vis individuals from other species?

## II.

I will explore this question further by using a piece of fiction (not fantasy!) as my example. In his short story "Hands" (1983), Gregory Blake Smith has a first-person narrator named Smith tell of his encounters with a raccoon, encounters that drive him to questioning the limits of humanness and animalness.[5] It is a story about interpersonal and, indeed, interspecies contact and communication, about identity, difference and transdifference.

Right from the start, where we expect information about the characters involved, we are confronted with a number of questions. Like the author, the narrator is named Smith, and the possibility of their being identical in postmodern fashion is thus raised but never developed any further. Smith is called "Smitty" by his sister who visits him over the weekends—why doesn't she use his first name (which we never learn about)? The sister's name is Jaxxlyn, a first name so uncommon that we may be tempted to see it as either a last name or an invention (the narrator's?). She "hates her last name" (Smith 123), but unless it should be Jaxxlyn we do not get to know it. Her identity and identity status seem to be uncertain as well.

The story begins with a proclamation of humanness as cultural praxis: "Here in New England we sit in chairs" (121). But the next being that is mentioned after the collective human implied in the "we" is the raccoon: "It's from my porch rocker that I watch the raccoon. He usually comes at dusk, that time of half dog and half wolf, when the downturned leaves seem to glow with the sunset and the upturned ones glimmer with moonlight" (121-22). "He," not "it"—and so he shall be referred to in this paper. The metaphors, however, indicate an in-between state of things, not hybridity, but a simultaneousness of different modes of being—transdifference.

The raccoon, whom the narrator does not give a name—a nice touch of anti-Adamic non-anthropocentrism—always comes at dusk to pilfer the narrator's garbage, and the latter is not sure of how he should take this intrusion of the wild into his world of civilization. As it turns out, he is not sure about what is wild and what is civilized, about the animal and the human. His neighbor Moose suggests shooting the raccoon and selling the fur, but, as his name indicates, he may be on the other side of the divide himself. If there exists such a divide. "I tell him I'm not sure I want to kill him. '*Him?*' he says. 'How d'you know it's a *him?*' And he spits on my woodstove so the cast iron sizzles and steams" (122). He seems to refer to the uncertainty of gender identification but might inadvertently also hint at the question of a possible personhood of the raccoon, the animal antagonist—or protagonist?—of this story. Moose, who calls the animal "it"—"'But if you want it trapped I can trap it'" (122)—would be incapable of such considerations, but the narrator is not.

The raccoon gets more and more at ease during his visits. Clearly, he has agency and, indeed, he is one of the four actors in this story: the narrator, his sister, his neighbor, and the raccoon. There are other beings that appear to be capable of motivated action, notably "my moaning tree," that seems to comment on Moose's crudity and hard-heartedness: "Outside, my moaning tree sends up a regular howl" (122). Thus, we get this introductory constellation:

My name is Smith. I'm a chairmaker with a tree that's grown itself around a telephone pole and a raccoon that's taken a fancy to my garbage. I've never minded the name Smith. I like the ancestral whiff of fashioning and forging in its single syllable. And I don't mind the moaning tree and its outrage over the telephone poles that have been stabbed into the landscape like stilettos, rubbing its insulted bark in the slightest breeze and howling when the wind blows in earnest. But the raccoon has unsettled me and I don't know why. My sister—who hates her last name and is being driven psychotic by my moaning tree—is not bothered by the raccoon. (123)

In her condescending big-city way Jaxxlyn finds the raccoon "*cute*" and wonders how he might be able to open the trash can (123). "Hands, I tell her, and I feel a faint panic at the word. They've got hands. And I hold my own hands up in the gloom, the backs reddish with dusk, the palms silver with moonlight" (123), just like the leaves mentioned above. His own in-between nature, his own animality, as well as the racoon's features of humanness make him experience an identity crisis that renders him incapable of making the eight Queen Anne chairs some lady has ordered.

My cabriole legs aren't right. I can't strike the balance between knee and foot. It's never happened like this before. I get out Hogarth's *Analysis of Beauty* and look his S's over, and I print S S S S S on my graph paper, write my own name: Smith, Smith, Smith, Smith, but when I go to draft my Queen Anne leg I can't balance the knee to the foot, the foot to the knee, the S's top orb to the bottom. I . . . end up tossing a sheaf of rejected legs into the stove. That night the raccoon dines on pumpkin and old cantaloupe. (124)

The association of chair legs with body parts seems to make the work of his own hands transcend categorial differences. Later, when the narrator has temporarily re-achieved his mental and artisanal balance, the customer who ordered the chairs seems to confirm this closeness: "I let her run her wealthy fingers across the soft wood, up and down the smooth legs. She shivers and says it feels alive still. 'Doesn't it feel alive still?' she says" (127). Plant and (human) animal, alive and dead remain different, but these distinctions have become instable, and it is possible to feel like belonging to both sides at the same time.

Earlier, in the second section of the story, the narrator takes action by invading the territory of the raccoon on his own terms. That is, he goes into the woods in order to get lumber for his chairmaking. Not surprisingly, "[a]t the sight of my bucksaw, my moaning tree groans" (124). He feels like "trespassing," "being where I only half belong" because "I *poach* my lumber" (124, my italics), a term usually applied to illegally catching game or fish, thus indicating another categorial border crossing. In a sense he does the same as the raccoon. He crosses old stone walls now again grown over by the forest and "indecipherable" (124). Thus, his foray is less an invasion into human territory than into the wilderness: "There is a feeling of low menace all around" (125). Nonetheless, he also manages to find the raccoon's den in a beech tree, well-built and padded, and he lauds him as another artisan. He also finds the raccoon's "cache of junk, bottle caps and aluminum can rings. Then . . . a piece of old coffee cup I'd broken in the summer" (126) and other objects he had thrown out, for instance "an old ballpoint, a spoon, screws" (126). "Are you a user of spoons, too, raccoon? I finally say out loud"—and with poetic assonance. "And screws? And pens? Are you a writer of sonnets? I say" (126). The raccoon's border-crossing transcends the foraging for food and amounts to an acquisition of human cultural objects. The narrator's remarks are meant facetiously, condescendingly, but he will soon drop this attitude. From now on, narrator and raccoon seem to be playing a game. The former steals his old ballpoint back and plans to come again.

In the third section of the story the narrator relates how, after having stolen back one object every day, he finds himself in better shape to continue his work on the chairs. He and the raccoon continue to steal each other's things, and finally the raccoon steals the ballpoint pen back. But when the narrator comes to his den and reaches in to take it back again, the raccoon is home and attacks him. "I hear a hiss, a growling sibilance, and just before I fall see two leathery hands gripped around my wrist and a furry mouth set to bite" (128). The raccoon "peers fiercely down at me from his hole. His eyes are black and fanatical, and he seems to say: 'All right? All right? Understand? All right?'" (128), while the wounded narrator can only utter "*Violence!*" (128).

In the fourth section the narrator relates how, after having been ill with his wounds and the rabies shot, he tries to reach a final balance. He tells his scornful neighbor Moose "I don't want to shoot the raccoon, I want to trap him. And once I've trapped him I want to let him go" (129). At first the raccoon ignores the trap, and the narrator has feverish conversations with him in his dreams. "*What do you want?* I whisper to the raccoon in my sleep. *What do you want?* '*What do you want?*' the raccoon whispers back. '*What do you want?*'" (129). Only when the narrator gives up watching the raccoon from his chair and hides in the wintery shrubbery until he is "iced over, a snowy stump among the evergreens . . . my hands clubbed," the raccoon comes, looks for him and probably locates him among the junipers (130). And the story ends with an acknowledgment of their common animalness-humanness:

> For a moment we are poised, balanced, the one against the other. He blinks, acknowledging my presence in the snow, and then with an air of genteel reciprocation, turns and walks straight into the trap.
> When I reach him he has his paws up on the trap's sides, the fingers outstretched on the fencing. He peers up at me as if to see if I'll take his hands as evidence after all. . . . When I bend over him our breaths mingle in the cold gray New England air. (130)

The raccoon has *paws* according to the ordinary terminology we apply to nonhuman animals, but given the fact that they are characterized by fingers, the narrator corrects himself by calling them *hands*. For a moment we may be tempted to read the phrase 'if I'll take his hands' as an acknowledgment that he is ready to shake hands with his antagonist. And 'evidence' what for? It can only refer to an insight into their common nature, an acknowledgment of sharing properties with one another, while either one remains who or what they are. Strangeness persists—why would the raccoon collect discarded objects? It seems to be part of his or his species' culture, just like the New England habit of sitting in chairs is part of a regional human culture. The raccoon seems to be capable of complex forms of communication, in tune with what we have come to know about the "languages of animals" (Meijer). What is more, he seems to represent a symbolic order in his own right, involving material possessions, perhaps aesthetics, and certainly ownership values. Mutual communication, the sharing of not only body parts but also values, are factors that are strong enough to make the narrator feel panicky (Smith 123), as if doubting his own identity. He realizes that he is both human and animal and thus experiences transdifference in this unusual constellation.

He thus stands between his neighbor who considers the raccoon as vermin that can be turned into a marketable object by killing "it," and his sister who calls the raccoon "cute," wants to treat him as a pet, and tries to make him accept human closeness by offering him water in a bowl that she plans to move ever closer to the house so that "the raccoon gets used to being with us" (126). Her symbolic order seems to be similar to that of Stowe's Ophelia; she is trying to convert the wild animal into a "dog, even if he was black." Each of the human characters remains anthropocentric since there is no way of letting go of a human perspective. Jaxxlyn sees the raccoon in sentimentally anthropomorphic terms and Moose uses anthropomorphism ironically—"'You might open up a motel . . . seeing as what you already got yourself a rest'rant'" (124). Neither of them ever questions the symbolic order that puts animals below humans and at their disposal. The narrator, however, wonders whether his obviously anthropomorphic negotiations with the raccoon may not be an acceptance of a dual nature of each. Jaxxlyn lets the moaning tree affect her because, again, she anthropomorphizes it and insists that its assumed suffering creates anguish for her. Her anthropomorphism doesn't equal sympathy or pity. With the same cold-heartedness that makes her wish the tree to be cut down she likens the raccoon to the skunk that her friend in Manhattan keeps as a pet: "'Of course he's been desmelled or whatever they do to them'" (123). The narrator also seems to constantly anthropomorphize the raccoon: "He tosses a wary look at me" (122); "He . . . tosses me a scornful look" (124); or, when Jaxxlyn tries babytalk on the raccoon, "The raccoon and I exchange looks. He knows, I think to myself" (127), referring to the stealing game he is playing with the animal; "His eyes are black and fanatical" (128); "This time it's contempt in his face when he catches sight of me through the windowpane" (129). But why should scorn, fanaticism, contempt be beyond the range of animal behavior and feelings? The narrator projects emotions on his antagonist, and there is no way of telling whether his assumptions are correct. What we can see, however, is that his relationship with the raccoon amounts to a contest of gazes, and the gaze, as we know from Jean-Paul Sartre and others, is associated with power and control.[6] That is, the narrator is always afraid of losing control over his interaction with the natural world.

What we have here, then, is an example of "thinking with animals," to use the title of Lorraine Daston and Gregg Mitman's edited volume *Thinking with Animals: New Perspectives on Anthropomorphism*. And, as the editors tell us, anthropomorphism, "the belief that animals are essentially like humans" (2) is never far from its inverse, zoomorphism: "The yearning to understand what it would be like to be, say, an elephant or a cheetah scrambles the opposition between anthropomorphism and zoomorphism, that is, between humanizing animals and animalizing humans" (8). But in the narrator's case, his is not so much a desire to overcome the boundary between species but the fear that such boundaries are more permeable than we normally assume. When he poaches wood and invades the raccoon's place he takes over the latter's forms of behavior. His errand into the wilderness is ambivalent: after all, he is moving through territory that was once converted from a pristine state into farmland and scripted over with a system of stone walls that is now "indecipherable" (Smith 124), obliterated by nonhuman nature whose vanguard is the raccoon. In a sense, both narrator and raccoon are exchanging the gifts of the natureculture each of them comes from. Indeed, to use Donna Haraway's term (*Companion Species*) is their meeting place, the dancefloor of transdifference.

The raccoon is the narrator's Other, but is he alien or just different? The distinction between alterity and alienity has been explored by a number of scholars, notably Bernhard Waldenfels, whose phenomenological perspective produces a clear differentiation between the two terms. Horst Turk has used a more flexible approach. For him, the Other is not really alien as long as it remains within the same system. It is the *alter* of the *ego*. Thus, members of Western societies appear as different—*other*—to each other, but not as alien, whereas for classical Greece the barbarian stood outside the system of language, literature, culture and hence was considered *alien* (Turk 173). However, as Turk realizes, the order of things classifying the respective systems of the own and the Other has always been subject to change in terms of historic development or individual, experience-based insight. Thus, European cultures have seen a constant process of acceptance and hence "alterization" of the alien, but the reverse has also happened (175-76). Self and Other, own and alien, are not simply contrastive but relational categories.[7] The distinctions between identity and alterity or alienity are constantly renegotiated. This affects interpersonal and intercultural relations, as we have seen in the debate on race, but does it also influence interspecies contacts? What the story describes is a process of de-alienization, a familiarization that results in the establishment of trust—why else would the raccoon walk calmly into the trap? He has become less *alien*, perhaps just *alter* in a world of living beings shared by him and the narrator. The hands of the raccoon are "leathery" (Smith 128), but hands, nonetheless, while the cold makes the narrator's hands "clubbed" (130), and thus more pawlike.

But there is no identification between the two. In many respects both remain quite different. The narrator experiences his symbolic order as shifting, his sense of hierarchy crumbling, and yet this order is still in place and results in his realization of transdifference, which may be a core experience in our encounters with other animals. The undissolvable co-presence of his affiliations with the human and the nonhuman is symbolized by his own hands, "the backs reddish with dusk, the palms silver with moonlight" (123) like the leaves of the trees that connect wilderness and civilization. This way the story refers to the interconnectedness of all forms of life, including a tree moaning in the wind.

This view is possible not only by a poetic, but also by a factual, scientific approach. As Native American (Potawatomi) biologist and writer Robin Wall Kimmerer has put it:

> Doing science with awe and humility is a powerful act of reciprocity with the more-than-human world. I've never met an ecologist who came to the field for the love of data or for the wonder of a p-value. These are just ways we have of crossing the species boundary, of slipping off our human skin and wearing fins or feathers or foliage, trying to know others as fully as we can. Science can be a way of forming intimacy and respect with other species that is rivaled only by the observations of traditional knowledge holders. It can be a path to kinship. (Kimmerer 252)

Kinship, not sameness. But hands are offered in many varieties.

## Notes

1 | Henceforth, "animals" is used here in the sense of "other animals."
2 | Cf. the survey of various pertinent or problematical applications of our concept in Breinig and Lösch, "Transdifference."
3 | This scene was first pointed out to me by Susanne Opfermann, whose masterful study *Diskurs, Geschlecht und Literatur* has much to say about the symbolic order of that period.
4 | See for instance Philip Roth's fictional treatment of such a biography in his novel *The Human Stain*. Roth denied that Broyard served as a model for his protagonist.
5 | The story was first published in the *Kenyon Review*, New Series, vol. 5, no. 1, 1983, pp. 110-117, and is included in Smith's collection *The Law of Miracles and Other Stories*, University of Massachusetts Press, 2011, pp. 64-73. My quotations come from the reprint in Michael J. Rosen, *Company of Animals* (1993).
6 | See for instance Christina Judith Hein's discussion of power, the gaze, and the construction of self and Other in her *Whiteness, the Gaze, and Transdifference in Contemporary Native American Fiction*, 51-59.
7 | See Klaus Lösch's comprehensive discussion of "The Other and Its Description" in his essay on "Das Fremde und seine Beschreibung." See also the relevant passages in my chapter on "Identity and Alterity" (Breinig, *Hemispheric Imaginations* 27-30).

## Works Cited

Baker, J.A. *The Peregrine*. 1967. Intr. Robert Macfarlane. New York Review Books, 2005.

Breinig, Helmbrecht. *Hemispheric Imaginations: North American Fictions of Latin America*. Dartmouth College Press; University Press of New England, 2017.

Breinig, Helmbrecht, and Klaus Lösch. "Transdifference." *Journal for the Study of British Cultures*, vol. 13, no. 2, 2006, pp. 105-22.

---. "Forschungsfelder der Transdifferenz: Identität, Leiblichkeit und Repräsentation." *Identität und Unterschied. Zur Theorie von Kultur, Differenz und Transdifferenz*, edited by Christian Alvarado Leyton and Philipp Erchinger. transcript, 2010, pp. 37-58.

Daston, Lorraine, and Gregg Mitman, editors. *Thinking with Animals: New Perspectives on Anthropomorphism*. Columbia University Press, 2005.

Folsom, Ed, and Cary Nelson. "'Fact Has Two Faces': An Interview with W.S. Merwin." *Conversations with W.S. Merwin*, edited by Michael Wutz and Hal Crimmel. University Press of Mississippi, 2015, pp. 44-80.

Foster, Charles. *Being a Beast*. Profile Books, 2016.

Haraway, Donna J. *When Species Meet*. University of Minnesota Press, 2008.

---. *The Companion Species Manifesto: Dogs, People, and Significant Otherness*. Prickly Paradigm Press, 2003.

Hein, Christina Judith. *Whiteness, the Gaze, and Transdifference in Contemporary Native American Fiction*. Winter, 2012.

Kalof, Linda, and Amy Fitzgerald, editors. *The Animals Reader: The Essential Classic and Contemporary Writings*. Berg, 2007.

Kimmerer, Robin Wall. *Braiding Sweetgrass*. Milkweed Editions, 2013.

Lösch, Klaus. "Das Fremde und seine Beschreibung." *Phänomene der Fremdheit – Fremdheit als Phänomen*, edited by Simone Broders, Susanne Gruß, and Stephanie Waldow. Königshausen & Neumann, 2012, pp. 25-50.

Meijer, Eva. *Die Sprachen der Tiere*. Matthes & Seitz, 2018.

Opfermann, Susanne. *Diskurs, Geschlecht und Literatur: Amerikanische Autorinnen des 19. Jahrhunderts*. Metzler, 1996.

Reckwitz, Andreas. "Kulturelle Differenzen aus praxeologischer Perspektive: Kulturelle Globalisierung jenseits von Modernisierungstheorie und Kulturessentialismus." *Kulturen vergleichen: Sozial- und kulturwissenschaftliche Grundlage und Kontroversen*, edited by Ilja Srubar, Joachim Renn, and Ulrich Wenzel. Verlag für Sozialwissenschaften, 2005, pp. 92-111.

Singer, Peter. "Animal Liberation or Animal Rights?" *The Animals Reader: The Essential Classic and Contemporary Writings*, edited by Linda Kalof and Amy Fitzgerald. Berg, 2007, pp. 14-22.

Smith, Gregory Blake. "Hands." *The Company of Animals*, edited by Michael J. Rosen. Doubleday, 1993, pp. 121-30.

Stowe, Harriet Beecher. *Uncle Tom's Cabin*. 1852. Edited by Elizabeth Ammons. Norton Critical Edition. Norton, 1994.

Turk, Horst. "Alienität und Alterität als Schlüsselbegriffe einer Kultursemantik: Zum Fremdheitsbegriff der Übersetzungsforschung." *Kulturthema Fremdheit*, edited by Alois Wierlacher. Iudicium, 1993, pp. 173-197.

Van Schaik, Carel P., et al. "Orangutan Cultures and the Evolution of Material Culture." *The Animals Reader: The Essential Classic and Contemporary Writings*, edited by Linda Kalof and Amy Fitzgerald. Berg, 2007, pp. 104-110.

Waldenfels, Bernhard. *Phenomenology of the Alien: Basic Concepts*. Translated by Alexander Kozin and Tanja Stähler. Northwestern University Press, 2011.

# Immanence is Bliss:
# The Ecological Imagination in Thomas Pynchon's *Gravity's Rainbow*

Magda Majewska

Beginning with its very first sentence, "A screaming comes across the sky," which announces the fall of a German V2-rocket on London, the specter of annihilation haunts Thomas Pynchon's *Gravity's Rainbow* (1973). While the first nightmarish scenes of the novel confront readers with the precariousness of human life, the ending invokes the imminent possibility of annihilation of all life on the planet, human and nonhuman alike. This may happen in a nuclear Holocaust or it may be the ultimate outcome of a much slower process that increasingly transforms life into dead matter, organic substance into plastic waste.

As the novel progresses, the view that all forms of life existing on Earth are entangled becomes more and more pronounced. We are not only consistently reminded that we share the Earth with other creatures but that we share with them a materiality that renders us equally vulnerable to the destructive potential humankind has generated. All efforts to set humanity apart, to disentangle its affairs from nature and the fate of fellow creatures, prove equally disastrous and illusionary. And the novel suggests that it is only through the recognition of the entanglement that binds human and nonhuman life together that humankind might avert a course that is both destructive to other life forms and self-destructive. It is because of this existential entanglement or interconnectedness of all being that the choice between life and death, between affirmation of life and promotion of death—the ultimate ethical choice that *Gravity's Rainbow* forces us to face—cannot rest on a fundamental distinction between human life and other life forms. In this sense, Pynchon's vision is both ecological and non-anthropocentric.

While critics generally recognize that *Gravity's Rainbow* has a "strongly ecological thrust" (Buell 429), this dimension of the novel has rarely been explored in detail.[1] In the following, I would like to outline those aspects of the novel that highlight its ecological investment. I attempt to address this dimension by centering on two different yet related narrative levels. First, by showing how the novel's critique of instrumental rationality, which informs its engagement with modernity as a historical process that takes a toll on both human and nonhuman life on earth, is linked with its ecological critique. Second, by showing how the novel's more abstract and theoretical ideas reverberate in scenes that depict particular encounters between humans and nonhuman life forms.

## I.

In the complex narrative that enfolds between the nightmarish scenario of the novel's beginning and the apocalyptic scenario suggested at its end, Pynchon explores the logic at the heart of Western culture, particularly modernity. While the action of the novel concentrates mainly on events taking place shortly before and shortly after the end of WWII, its time frame expands to early European and Euro-American colonization, on the one hand, and to the 1960s and 70s, when modernity assumed its late capitalist form, on the other. The logic explored can be best characterized as instrumental rationality and indeed there are striking correspondences between Pynchon's cultural critique and the critique articulated by Max Horkheimer and Theodor Adorno in *Dialectic of Enlightenment* (1944) as well as in the writings of Herbert Marcuse. As a quantitative, efficiency-oriented approach to life, instrumental rationality turns nature into a mere raw material for production and treats all living beings as means rather than ends. The totality of a culture that is operating according to instrumental reason is what Pynchon (with Marcuse) calls "the System"— including a capitalist economy, technological and scientific progress, ever more effective means of destruction, and modern ways of governance. The novel leaves no doubt that the System is as much fueled by human greed and need for control as it is self-destructive, turning not only plant and animal life to waste but also endangering the survival of the human species:

> Taking and not giving back, demanding that "productivity" and "earnings" keep on increasing with time, the System [is] removing from the rest of the World these vast quantities of energy to keep its own desperate fraction showing a profit: and not only most of humanity—most of the World, animal, vegetable and mineral, is laid waste in the process. . . . Living inside the system is like riding across the country in a bus driven by a maniac bent on suicide . . . (Pynchon 412; first ellipsis is mine).

A paradigmatic product of this system is plastic, a material that exemplifies its self-destructive aspects in both symbolic and practical ways. Pynchon retraces the major steps in the science and technology of plastic, from the kick-off of organic chemistry after August Kekulé's groundbreaking discovery of the structure of the benzene molecule in the mid-nineteenth century, through the inception of methods of polymerization, to the large-scale production of synthetic polymers such as synthetic dyes, synthetic rubber, and plastic by petrochemical cartels like the IG Farben, which accelerated during WWII.

The production of plastic depended on the discovery that raw materials extracted from coal and petroleum can be used for the synthesis of new molecules. The fact that plastic is an entirely man-made material, whose components are derived from nature but cannot be reintegrated into the natural cycle, assumes a larger symbolic significance in the novel. Attesting to the human ability to manipulate nature in accordance with human desires, plastic promises transcendence of natural mortal life. As the fictional chemist Jamf, employed by IG Farben, teaches his students: "You have two choices . . . stay behind with carbon and hydrogen . . . or move *beyond* . . . move beyond life, toward the inorganic. There is no frailty, no mortality—there is Strength, and the Timeless" (580; second ellipsis is mine). It is exactly the "immortality" of plastic—its non-biodegradability—that makes the self-destructive dimension of the human endeavor to transcend nature so palpable.

There is, moreover, a close link (both literal and metaphorical) between plastic and the V2-rocket—the emblem of human capacity to annihilate life. On the one hand, rocket technology largely depended on plastics; on the other hand, the V2-rocket, being the first man-made object to enter space, holds the promise of defying gravity and thus overcoming human boundedness to nature. As the character Enzian observes: "Beyond simple steel erection, the Rocket was an entire system *won*, away from the feminine darkness, held against the entropies of lovable but scatterbrained Mother Nature" (324).

The logic of instrumental rationality that both the rocket (or war technology in general) and plastic symptomatically represent is opposed, in *Gravity's Rainbow*, to a vision of life as an interconnected whole.[2] This vision has a symbolic equivalent in the Uroboros, a serpent holding its tail in its mouth. Ironically, it was the image of the Uroboros, which came to Kekulé in a dream, that inspired him to conceive of the benzene molecule as a ring—a discovery that laid the foundations for plastics technology. As Pynchon's narrator remarks: "The Serpent that announces 'The world is a closed thing, cyclical, resonant, eternally-returning,' is to be delivered into a System whose only aim is to *violate* the Cycle" (412). The plastic motif thus connects the critique of instrumental rationality with a distinctly ecological perspective, from which plastic appears above all as a violation of the life cycle and a threat to the ecosystems of the planet.

Both perspectives can be related to the historical context from which *Gravity's Rainbow* emerged. While the novel's critique of instrumental rationality is indebted to the theories of the Frankfurt School and other cultural-critical discourses that inspired the counterculture of the 1960s, its ecological investment can also be seen in light of the awakening of an ecological consciousness in the 1960s and 70s. In his enlightening essay on the ecocritical dimension of the novel, Thomas Schaub argues that "the environmental frame is one of the most explicit openings through which we can see *Gravity's Rainbow* as a text from a specific historical period" (60). As Schaub demonstrates, *Gravity's Rainbow* is highly resonant with groundbreaking ecocritical works of the 1960s, such as Rachel Carson's *The Silent Spring* (1962). Carson locates the sources of environmental destruction in chemical corporations, tracing the development of the chemical industry to WWII. Schaub suggests that "Pynchon's representations of cartelized capital, chemistry, and rocket technology in the prewar decades and wartime years are deeply influenced by the discourse of environmental dissent from which they emerge" (63). Indeed, Schaub argues, "*Gravity's Rainbow* may be understood as the culmination or *summa* of three decades of intense environmental dissent" (60). The environmental dissent involved the perception of plastic as an environmental threat. As Jeffrey Meikle contends in *American Plastic*, it was the apprehension of a nuclear disaster in the first decades of the Cold War period that led to a growing awareness that life on Earth can come to an end and hence a recognition of the threat posed by plastic.

## II.

About a hundred pages into the novel, a flashback takes us back to one of the first documented cases of human-caused extinction of a species in modern history: the extermination of the dodo bird endemic to Mauritius in the seventeenth century. According to the information provided by the Oxford University Museum of Natural History, which holds the most complete remains of a dodo specimen in its collection, the first documented encounter of the dodo took place in 1598 when Dutch sailors arrived on Mauritius. The last confirmed sighting of a dodo was in 1662.

The decimation of the dodo is generally attributed to several factors such as hunting, the introduction to the island of pigs, dogs, and rats who fed on its eggs, and the destruction of its habitat.[3] All that we know of the dodo, based on contemporary accounts, is that it was a flightless bird nesting on the ground with no natural enemies and thus a particularly easy prey for the humans and for the animals they brought along with them. When the Dutch departed from Mauritius in 1710, after several attempts at establishing a permanent settlement there had failed, the dodo was considered extinct. As the novel's narrator remarks, it took "about a human lifetime" to remove an entire species from the face of the earth (Pynchon 110).

The focalizer in Pynchon's story is the Dutch ancestor of the novel's character Katje, Frans Van der Groov, "who went off to Mauritius with a boatload of . . . hogs and lost thirteen years toting his haakbus through the ebony forests, wandering the swamps and lava flows, systematically killing off the native dodoes for reasons he could not explain" (108). The colonial enterprise—on its own terms a failure—left a trail of destruction on Mauritius, including the devastation of its native rain forest. Hinting at the ironic disproportion between the effects of human actions and the limitations of human understanding, the narrator points out that Frans remains unaware that the dodoes are a unique species and that he is helping to "exterminate a race" (110). Neither he nor the seventeenth-century culture to which he belongs seem to have a concept of extinction yet. As Katje observes at some later point in the novel, Frans believed that the world held an endless supply of dodoes.

Though he is hunting them obsessively, Frans "left the dodoes to rot, he couldn't endure to eat their flesh" (109). One reason for the animosity that the dodo inspires in him and his companions is its deviation from standards of beauty and suitability established by his culture: "the stupid, awkward bird, never intended to fly or run at any speed—what *were* they good for?" (108). Indeed, the bird's appearance, its disproportionately large beak that didn't seem to serve any particular purpose, and its incapability to fly, ostensibly puzzled Europeans who often described them as "awkward" or "clumsy" (see Fuller). Revealing the hubris inherent in the imposition of human aesthetic standards on animals, Frans muses whether "a more comely beak, a fuller feathering, a capacity for flight, however brief" might have prevented the dodo's demise (110). As Frans reports in one of the letters he sends home, some of his fellow men felt inclined to kill the dodoes off because "[t]hey saw the stumbling birds ill-made to the point of Satanic intervention, so ugly as to embody an argument against a Godly creation" (110). For readers familiar with American colonial history, this calls to mind depictions of Native Americans by Puritan settlers, and Pynchon invites us to draw such connections.

Pynchon shows the extinction of the dodoes as deeply intertwined with colonial history, linking it metonymically to the devastation of natural environments and the decimation of populations that inhabited them in the course of European colonization. It is one of several historical events related in the novel that confirm its often-expressed idea that the culture of Western modernity, driven by the desire for imperial dominance, control of nature, and economic profit, is essentially a culture of death.

By choosing to frame the extinction of the dodoes in terms of genocide, as he explicitly does by referring to it as the "extermination of a race," Pynchon moreover suggests that there are historical and ideological connections between violence committed against fellow humans and against nonhumans in the course of modernity. Within the architecture of the text, the story of the dodoes foreshadows the genocide of the Herero people by German colonial forces in South-West Africa between 1904 and 1907, which is one of the thematic centers of *Gravity's Rainbow* as well as of Pynchon's first novel *V.* (1963). (While Pynchon does not directly represent the Holocaust, the Herero genocide can be read as its synecdoche.)

Violence directed against a specific category of beings is always preceded by symbolic distinctions that render them disposable or exploitable. Pynchon sees a prototype of such hierarchical distinctions in the discrimination between the "elect," the chosen ones, and the "preterite," those who are passed over or damned, central to the religious doctrine of Calvinism. Elect vs. preterite is one of the dominant symbolic oppositions running through the novel, analogous to the opposition of "Them" and "Us," the System and its victims, the "winners" and "losers" of historical processes. Used mostly in an abstract or metaphorical sense, "preterite" applies to all the disenfranchised and exploited humans as well as the nonhumans that appear in the text. In the story of the dodoes, the elect/preterite distinction appears within a specifically religious context, since Calvinism informs the worldview of the Dutch.[4]

If the colonizers are "impersonating a race chosen by God" (110), as they believe they do, the dodoes are by definition preterite. Frans proposes that "their tragedy is to be the dominant form of Life on Mauritius, yet incapable of speech" (110). In the words of the narrator: "No language meant no chance of co-opting them into what their round and flaxen invaders were calling Salvation" (110). Frans, however, is increasingly troubled by "the scale and frenzy of the hunting" (110) and begins to envision a conversion of the dodoes. It remains open whether it is compassion that allows him to see the dodoes in a different light or whether remorse and loneliness have blurred his perceptions; but observing the dodoes gathered in large numbers at the shore and listening to their voices, Frans comes to the conclusion that the birds are not only capable of meaningful communication but that they display a capability for "rational discourse" (111). This passage in the text simultaneously invests the dodoes with agency by showing them engaged in a communicative exchange and mocks Frans's attempts to interpret it within the lines of his ideological framework. His recognition that the dodoes have their own means of communication may be his redeeming quality, but what he allows himself to hear is that they ask for admittance into the community of believers. Frans's perspective is of course deeply anthropocentric, as Pynchon's narrator is quick to point out: what could "salvation" possibly mean in relation to animals other than the promise of an afterlife or giving their otherwise senseless deaths a meaning? In any case the dodoes are dead.

Pynchon's critique of Protestant (or generally Christian) theology as a worldview that is deeply anthropocentric, and that denies life on Earth a value in-and-of-itself, presents one aspect of a larger critique directed against human dreams of transcendence. The secular version of such dreams is the wish to overcome the limitations that nature imposes on human life through technological control. As Pynchon reminds us throughout the novel, denying the immanence of human life has repercussions for human relations to other life forms but also for the human ability to affirm life as such.

## III.

Transcendence vs. immanence and election vs. preterition provide the symbolic framework of yet another episode in the novel that centers specifically on human-animal relations. This episode is set within the context of Puritan settlement and takes place at approximately the same time as the dodo episode. Again, the focalizer of the story is the ancestor of one of the novel's major characters. This time it is Tyrone Slothrop's—the novel's main protagonist's—"first American ancestor" (554), William. After having arrived on the *Arbella* (364), William makes his living as a pig farmer and regularly leads a herd of pigs to a slaughterhouse in Boston. Interestingly, the narrator introduces William Slothrop as a "peculiar bird" (554), which may be taken as an allusion to the dodo story, indicating both similarities and dissimilarities between William and Frans.

What makes William "peculiar," setting him apart from fellow Puritans, is his growing affection for the pigs: we learn that his trips to Boston are motivated less by the prospect of monetary gain than by his growing appreciation of the time spent in the pigs' company: "He enjoyed the road, the mobility, the chance encounters of the day—Indians, trappers, wenches, hill people—and most of all just being with those pigs. They were good company" (555). To William, the pigs display qualities much different from those ascribed to them by his culture: "Despite the folklore and the injunctions of his own Bible, William came to love their nobility and personal freedom, their gift for finding comfort in the mud on a hot day" (555). After having left them at the slaughterhouse, he sadly recalls "their happy sounds, their untroubled pink eyelashes and kind eyes, their smiles, their grace in cross-country movement" (555).

It is noteworthy that the pigs are described in most tender terms. Considered unclean and a lower form of animal life in Christianity and Western culture in general, the pig moreover functions as "a totemic sign of the preterite throughout GR," as Steven Weisenburger puts it (273-74). Eventually, William rejects the cruelty of a world where the pigs are predestined for slaughter and, in a heretical tract titled *On Preterition*, calls the dualism of the Calvinist doctrine and the idea of special election into question. In the words of Thomas Moore, the heresy of William "is to argue that election emerges dialectically from preterition and for the sake of it; that election is not ontologically *other*" (136). William even goes so far as to claim that there is no Christ without Judas, that one cannot exist without the other, and that loving Christ must entail loving Judas, too. Above all, William claims that to love creation means to love *all* of creation. Puritan authorities in Boston ban the tract and William is forced to leave the Massachusetts Bay Colony for England.

But before that happens, his fondness of the pigs notwithstanding, William leads them to their death. And the pigs, unaware of what is awaiting them, follow him each time: "his Gadarene swine . . . rushed into extinction like lemmings, possessed not by demons but by trust for men, which the men kept betraying . . . possessed by innocence they couldn't lose . . . by faith in William as of pig, at home with the Earth, sharing the same gift of life" (Pynchon 555; first ellipsis is mine).

Pynchon refers here to an act of exorcism performed by Jesus in the town of Gadara, where he frees a man possessed by demons by transferring them into a herd of two thousand swine. The swine then rush from a cliff into the sea and die (Mark 5:1-20; Matthew 8:28-34). The allusion to the story of the Gadarene swine provides an interesting subtext to the story of William and the pigs, since this passage of the New Testament was used within the Christian theological tradition to illustrate the point that humans and animals have no rights in common and that Christians are not morally obliged to consider the rights of animals.[5]

As I have argued earlier, Pynchon opposes hierarchical notions of value with regard to life by insisting on its existential interconnectedness. This perspective, we may call it ecological, demands respect for all forms of life as well as for the Earth as a shared home. In this particular episode, however, Pynchon engages also specifically with the question of morality, that is, with our behavior concerning others with whom we engage in the social realm. William's pigs are not possessed by demons but "by trust for men." The pigs are not just objects of human actions and considerations; they are also subjects of a mutual relation, which involves trust on their part. William's moral obligation to the pigs arises from the very fact that the pigs trust him. Trust as the foundation of any sociality demands reciprocity; therefore the betrayal of trust cannot be regarded as morally irrelevant. By accentuating trust—a capacity that humans and animals have in common—Pynchon implicitly makes the case for an interspecies morality: humans and swine are bound together across the boundaries of species by the demand for trust.

A few pages later, William's descendant Tyrone encounters a solitary pig in the devastated landscape of postwar Germany and for a short time forms with her a relation based on trust, cooperation, and friendship. In this case, it even seems that Tyrone is the one who trusts and follows, and the pig is the one who cares for him: "Slothrop keeps waking to find the pig snuggled in a bed of pine needles, watching over him. It's not for danger, or out of restlessness. Maybe she's decided Slothrop needs looking after" (575). Such instances of connectivity among creatures offer rare glimpses of hope in *Gravity's Rainbow*. The pig's "faith in William as another variety of pig, at home with the Earth, sharing the same gift of life," presents us with a model of being-in-the-world which resonates throughout Pynchon's text. It poses an alternative to the transcendental vision that informs not only human relations towards fellow creatures, but to the Earth.

As one character recognizes, "the Earth is a living critter" (590). This can be taken to mean that the Earth is the totality of interconnected matter, in which both the animate and the inanimate are in a constant process of transformation. From the perspective of the System, which is operating according to the logic of instrumental reason, the earth is just the inanimate raw material that can be taken, exploited, and manipulated in order to serve human interests, be it economic profit or the need for dominance and control. Sharing the gift of life and being at home with the Earth requires humans to accept that they are subject to the same natural processes as other species and thus to come to terms with their own mortality. Pynchon follows Nietzsche and his own contemporary Norman O. Brown in the assumption that the inability to be content with being alive, with accepting one's own embeddedness within a larger whole, stems from the fear of death.[6] Humans, therefore, are never "innocent" in the way that the pigs are.

Because life and death are part of the same process, the "flight from death"—the driving force behind civilizational progress—can only lead to human alienation from inner and from external nature. As a consequence, life becomes an object of control or administration and nature is increasingly turned into dead matter. While the novel's worldview is ecological and non-anthropocentric, as I have claimed in the beginning of this essay, it is at the same time deeply humanistic, since Pynchon is trying to envision modes of being that would allow humans a fuller existence. In the words of Paul Bové: "Pynchon's deepest humanism requires of humanity—if it wishes to remain itself—a constant vigilance, a steady stream of defectors who accept the necessary role of death not in the overcoming of life but in its maintenance, who see that life and death are enfolded" (677). William, though a minor character (if judged by the time allotted him in the narrative), assumes the role of the defectors' guiding spirit. As N. Katherine Hayles writes, by realizing "that the distinction between the elect and the preterite implies a fragmentation of an original unity," William belongs among the "lone visionaries of *Gravity's Rainbow*, who try to tell the world that what we perceive as opposites are really parts of an interconnected whole" (176).

In the present time of the novel, his descendant Tyrone wonders whether William "could have been the fork in the road America never took, the singular point she jumped the wrong way from. Suppose the Slothrop-ite heresy had had the time to consolidate and prosper? Might there have been fewer crimes in the name of Jesus, and more mercy in the name of Judas Iscariot" (Pynchon 556)? William's inclusive vision of life appears both as a lost opportunity (for America as well as for Western culture) *and* as a possibility that still remains open. As he wanders shortly after the end of WWII through the German Zone, a territory occupied by but not yet divided among the Allied powers, Tyrone reimagines the Zone as a potential site of departure into a new direction:

It seems to Tyrone Slothrop that there might be a route back—maybe that anarchist he met in Zurich was right, maybe for a little while all the fences are down, one road as good as another, the whole space of the Zone cleared, depolarized, and somewhere inside the waste of it a single set of coordinates from which to proceed, without elect, without preterite, without even nationality to fuck it up. (556)

In *Gravity's Rainbow* the Zone functions both as an actual geographical and an imaginative space.[7] As "a geographical slate momentarily wiped clean," as Steven Weisenburger puts it, where social and political hierarchies are suspended, it invites visions of a new beginning (177-78). Slothrop shares the longing for a "route back" with several other characters in the novel, such as the descendants of the Herero people, who have been displaced from their land to the Zone due to colonization and who have been disconnected from their culture, which understood individual lives as part of a natural cycle of life and death. Their leader Enzian voices the hope that "[s]omewhere, among the wastes of the World, is the key that will bring us back, restore us to our Earth and to our freedom" (Pynchon 525).

Such images are resonant with T.S. Eliot's *The Waste Land*, expressing the hope that among the waste of a world in ruins new life might spring. But for the Hereros, as for all others, the route back to an original unity is foreclosed, just as the extinction of the dodoes is irrevocable. And the Zone, for all the promise it holds in Slothrop's imagination, is the site from which the new geopolitical order of the Cold War emerges—continuing the destructive course modernity has taken and even escalating the human capacity for destruction. But while there is no way back, there still is a chance to turn around a historical process that seems to point in one direction only, coming to its logical conclusion in the destruction of the natural world and the annihilation of humankind.

## IV.

In the remaining paragraphs I would like to discuss the novel's investment in an ecological perspective as it is expressed through its main character, Slothrop. In view of the novel's eco-critical dimension, it is quite significant that the potentiality that the Zone represents to Slothrop is connected to the heretical vision of his ancestor William. What Slothrop sees is not just a possibility opening up in human history but in history as a process in which the fate of nonhuman life is embedded. Moving throughout the Zone, Slothrop becomes increasingly aware of its nonhuman inhabitants. The image of the Zone quoted above can be related to an earlier passage, where hope concerning the future is expressed less in political or social than in ecological terms. As Slothrop stands at the former rocket-launching site in Peenemünde, he notices the effects of war on the natural environment, such as trees turned into "stalks of charcoal" (502). In a series of images the passage juxtaposes human-caused destruction with the regenerative powers of nature:

Wild summer ducks up exploding, wet and showery, out of green reeds—they swing aft over the boat and descend in its wake, where they bob quacking in two-foot excursions. High in the sunlight, a white-tailed eagle is soaring. Smooth-lipped bomb and shell craters hold blue see water. Barracks have had their roofs blown away . . . . But trees, beech and pine, have begun to grow in again where spaces where cleared and leveled for housing or offices—up through cracks in the pavement, everywhere life may gain purchase, up rushes green summer '45, and the forests are still growing dense on the upland. (501-02)

Subjected in his infancy to a conditioning that linked his sexual reflexes to a particular synthetic polymer used later in rocket technology, Slothrop is the archetypal victim of a System that turns life into an object of control. As an effect of this conditioning (unbeknownst to him), Slothrop's erections are correlated with the fall of V2-rockets on London. After this correlation becomes apparent to Slothrop and after he begins to have suspicions about his childhood conditioning, he deserts the US army and embarks on a very personal mission to solve the mystery of his connection to the rocket. Nothing, however, brings him closer to his goal.

His personal trajectory can be understood both as a regression in psychoanalytical terms and as a reversal of Nietzsche's *principium individuationis*. Seen from a psychological perspective, Slothrop's ego or personality gradually disintegrates, because he is increasingly unable to make sense of his past and therefore to project himself into the future. He begins to live in a state of perpetual present, and while this state does not allow him to properly function as a person within human society (or meet the demands of being a "character" in the novel), it makes him all the more attuned to nature. Like Orpheus, Slothrop is able to communicate with other living beings and likewise he becomes fragmented and scattered in the end.

Before we witness his final disintegration or dispersal into nature, we follow Slothrop through a series of disguises he takes on in order to hide from the agents of the System, above all from the behaviorist Pointsman, who wants to build his career on Slothrop's case. If caught, Slothrop will share the fate of the dogs that Pointsman—one of the prominent representatives of instrumental rationality in the novel—subjects to experiments in his laboratory. Each of these disguises is related to some aspect of Slothrop's identity. At some point he switches the costume of "Rocketman"—which signifies, albeit in a comic manner, his identification with the rocket (the ultimate symbol of human destructiveness)—for the costume of the pig hero Plechazunga, offered to him by a group of children in a German village during carnival. The costume marks a stage in Slothrop's development in which he all but disappears from the map of human affairs, and seems most content with being "just another variety of pig" (555).

One morning he wakes in a hollow between a stand of beech and a stream. It is sunrise and bitter cold, and there seems to be a warm tongue licking roughly at his face. He is looking here into the snout of another pig, very fat and pink pig. She grunts and smiles amiably, blinking long eyelashes. "Wait. How about this?" He puts on the pig mask. She stares for a minute, then moves up to Slothrop and kisses him, snout-to-snout. Both of them are dripping with dew. (573)

The long passage that follows shows Slothrop and the pig travelling and sleeping side by side. They are two fellow creatures, equally invested in finding food and shelter and equally enjoying each other's company. His encounter with the pig is one instance of Slothrop's growing capacity to communicate with other creatures, and thus to grant them a viewpoint or a subjectivity. This capacity is also linked to a specifically ecological sensitivity, as the following passage demonstrates:

Trees, now—Slothrop's intensely alert to trees, finally. When he comes in among trees he will spend time touching them, studying them, sitting very quietly near them and understanding that each tree is a creature, carrying on its individual life, aware of what's happening around it, not just some hunk of wood to be cut down. Slothrop's family actually made its money killing trees, amputating them from their roots, chopping them up, grinding them to pulp, bleaching that to paper and getting paid for this with more paper. "That's really insane." He shakes his head. "There's insanity in my family." He looks up. The trees are still. They know he's there. They probably also know what he's thinking. "I'm sorry," he tells them. "I can't do anything about those people, they're all out of my reach. What can I do?" A medium-size pine nearby nods its top and suggests, "Next time you come across a logging operation out here, find one of their tractors that isn't being guarded, and take its oil filter with you. That's what you can do." (552-53)

The passage, in a manner quite characteristic for Pynchon, combines a macroscopic narrative level with a microscopic one. On the macroscopic level, the exploitation of nature is once again shown as inextricably connected with colonization and capitalism (or modernity at large), as Slothrop's Puritan ancestors quite literally turn trees into money. But the passage also draws our attention to the particularities and singularities of each being (which disappear under larger categories such as "humans" or "trees") and thus to the immense richness of forms in which life manifests itself.

As Paul Bové suggests, in *Gravity's Rainbow* creation itself imposes an ethical duty "upon a never innocent and never to be transcendent humanity" (677). Meeting this ethical demand requires a mode of perception free from the logic of instrumental rationality, which allows humans only to look at the natural world as raw material or object of scientific inquiry. As embodied by Slothrop, this mode of perception also challenges the exclusive attribution of consciousness to humans, granting nonhuman life (and matter) different forms of consciousness and experience. As I remarked earlier, Pynchon equally insists on the materiality of human bodies, which connects them to the Earth. This is why the attempt to escape the Earth, directly connected to its destruction by humans in the novel, is a suicidal mission. "*Gravity's Rainbow* should be seen as a celebration of love, but not merely human love, which quickly becomes masculinist games, but of love of creation, a deeply ecological sense of the location of human fate in that of the universe" (Bové 677).

In the last scenes that show Slothrop as a distinguishable entity, he "likes to spend whole days naked, ants crawling up his legs, butterflies lighting on his shoulders, watching the life on the mountains, getting to know shrikes and capercaillie, badgers and marmots," until he finally "becomes a crossroads, a living intersection" (Pynchon 623, 625).

His subsequent dispersal, fragmentation, scattering over the Zone, reported by the narrator, is an ambivalent image. It can be read as a triumph (since he is beyond the control of the system) or as a defeat (he cannot participate in society in any meaningful way). But seen from the vantage point of the novel's investment in finding alternative modes of being-in-the-world, Slothrop—as a figure of the text—can be read as a "new set of coordinates from which to proceed" (556). These "coordinates" diverge from principles of spatial ordering that stand at the center of projects of modern rationality whether it is colonialism, science, or warfare. The alternative coordinates from which to proceed replace the ideals of ordering, fixating, and dominating with ideas of transgressing, dispersing, blending, embedding, and uniting in difference. These are the coordinates at once of a postmodern literary aesthetic, and of a trans-species, ecological ethics.

**Notes**

1 | Notable exceptions are Thomas Schaub and Chris Coughran.
2 | In Pynchon's extensive metaphorical scheme the two perspectives are associated with Nietzsche's famous dialectical pair, where the Apollonian stands for the human attempt to control nature—both internal and external nature—and the Dionysian represents an understanding of life as an endless cycle of generation and decay, in which human lives are embedded. On this point see Tabbi.
3 | As Pynchon points out, the Dutch stripped large portions of the native ebony trees from the island, leaving the rainforest depleted (110).
4 | This is another connection to American Puritans.
5 | St. Augustine interpreted the story as a confirmation "that to refrain from the killing of animals and the destroying of plants is the height of superstition" (qtd. in Singer 126). Thomas Aquinas cited the biblical passage in support of the argument that Christians are not morally obliged to consider the rights of animals, since Jesus sacrificed two thousand swine in order to save a human soul (Sorabji 181; 195-98).
6 | On the influence of Norman O. Brown on Gravity's Rainbow see Wolfley and Majewska.
7 | As Hanjo Berressem has pointed out, all spaces in the novel are at once geographical/historical and imaginative or mental (121).

**Works Cited**

Adorno, Theodor W., and Max Horkheimer. *Dialectic of Enlightenment.* 1944. Verso, 1997.
Berressem, Hanjo. *Pynchon's Poetics: Interfacing Theory and Text.* University of Illinois Press, 1993.
Bové, Paul A. "History and Fiction: The Narrative Voices of Pynchon's *Gravity's Rainbow*." *Modern Fiction Studies,* vol. 50, no. 2, 2004, pp. 657-80.
Brown, Norman O. *Life Against Death: The Psychoanalytical Meaning of History.* 1959. Wesleyan University Press, 1985.
Buell, Lawrence. *The Dream of the Great American Novel.* Harvard University Press, 2014.
Carson, Rachel. *The Silent Spring.* Houghton Mifflin, 1962.
Coughran, Chris. "Green Scripts in *Gravity's Rainbow*: Pynchon, Pastoral Ideology and the Performance of Ecological Self." *ISLE: Interdisciplinary Studies in Literature and Environment,* vol.16, no. 2, 2009, pp. 265-79.

Fuller, Errol. *Dodo: From Extinction to Icon*. Harper Collins, 2002.
Hayles, N. Katherine. *The Cosmic Web: Scientific Field Models and Literary Strategies in the Twentieth Century*. Cornell University Press, 1984.
Majewska, Magda. *Die Lust im Text: Der postmoderne Roman und die sexuelle Befreiungsbewegung in den USA*. 2017. Freie Universität Berlin. PhD dissertation.
Marcuse, Herbert. *One Dimensional Man: Studies in the Ideology of Advanced Industrial Society*. Beacon Press, 1964.
Meikle, Jeffrey. *American Plastic: A Cultural History*. Rutgers University Press, 1995.
Moore, Thomas. *The Style of Connectedness:* Gravity's Rainbow *and Thomas Pynchon*. University of Missouri Press, 1987.
Oxford University Museum of Natural History. oumnh.ox.ac.uk/the-oxford-dodo. Accessed Sep. 2018.
Pynchon, Thomas. *Gravity's Rainbow*. Viking, 1973.
Schaub, Thomas. "The Environmental Pynchon: *Gravity's Rainbow* and the Ecological Context." *Pynchon Notes*, no. 42/43, 1998, pp. 59-72.
Singer, Peter. *Animal Liberation*. Harper Collins, 1990.
Sorabji, Richard. *Animal Minds and Human Morals: The Origins of the Western Debate*. Cornell University Press, 1993.
Tabbi, Joseph. "'Strung into the Apollonian Dream': Pynchon's Psychology of Engineers." *NOVEL*, vol. 25, no. 2, 1992, pp. 160-80.
*The New Oxford Annotated Bible*, edited by Michael Coogan, Oxford University Press, 2007.
Weisenburger, Steven. *A* Gravity's Rainbow *Companion: Sources and Contexts for Pynchon's Novel*. University of Georgia Press, 2006.
Wolfley, Lawrence. "Repression's Rainbow: The Presence of Norman O. Brown in Pynchon's Big Novel." *PMLA*, vol. 92, no. 5, 1977, pp. 873-89.

# The Decline of Humanity in a Post-Animal World: The Animal Motif in Cormac McCarthy's *The Road*

Yvonne Wiser

> Cold. Desolate. Birdless.
> —MCCARTHY, THE ROAD

You cannot undo the reading of *The Road*. Standing on the beach of a wintery North Sea, I was struck by the despair and the remembrance of how I felt being immersed in the dystopian world of the novel. There, earth became uninhabitable and the dark, lifeless ocean the protagonists have to find on their quest for a better life, symbolizes this desolation perfectly. Here, the ocean was wild, brown in color and the waves were of a threatening massiveness that I felt totally exposed to. Nonetheless, there were birds all around, seagulls swimming on the water, sparrows hunting for breadcrumbs on the beach and plenty of dogs chasing balls joyfully. Also, a fishing boat was in sight, connecting to the life in the ocean, if also in a deadly endeavor. The animals and their human companions on the beach embodied comfort and ease facing the power of the elements. They brought me back to the present moment, here and now, full of life. There is no such solace in *The Road*. The protagonists, a father and his son, both unnamed, undertake a pilgrimage to the mythologized South because their home region became lifeless: "The landscape the man and the boy travel is the corpse of the world" (Huebert 73). Cormac McCarthy artistically enhances the symbolic dimensions of the novel and their relevance to modern-day life by obfuscating the reason for the post-apocalyptic scenario. Most likely, a nuclear war has taken place, as the predominance of ashes and the greyness of all elements as well as the seemingly complete eradication of all animal life suggest.

I will approach my interpretation of McCarthy's 2006 novel as a high school teacher and also consider students' views about it in this essay. *The Road* is a dystopian science fiction novel and has, by genre, "strong didactic functions" as Hannah Stark attests (71). It "can be read as a warning about impending environmental catastrophe" (Stark 71). Because the topic and the language are rather accessible, it is a good choice for classroom reading matching the curriculum of a 10th grade in a German high school. My students were very captivated by the novel and wrote extensive reading journals. The quest for what is left of humanity in this dystopian world fascinated my students, as will be shown later.[1] They saw humanity equivocally represented in the son and dwelled long on the relationship to his father. The students focused on what they found in the novel because "[un]deniably, it is the human that is at the heart of the text" (Stark 80).

In my analysis, I will go beyond human existence and suggest that—even though only one animal appears in the diegetic present—animals as such *do* play a vital role in this novel. The animal motif in *The Road* has only been very peripherally mentioned in the criticism of the novel, and animals have never been the sole focus of an analysis.[2] Considering the plethora of animals appearing in other McCarthy novels, this virtual absence of animals seems to be a conspicuous deviation from his former writings.[3] As mentioned, most readings of *The Road* focus on the anthropocentric world without considering the meaning of absence. There are exceptions though. For example, David Huebert states that "[a]nimals—luxuriantly recalled but fundamentally absent from the present—create a melancholy, astonishing lack at the affective core of *The Road*. Animals, therefore, serve as a crucial part of what Kevin Kearny calls the central "hole in the text" (80). In my view, "luxuriantly" is an exaggeration because the animal motif is used by McCarthy most sparsely, predominantly as memory sequences or rather "memory flashes" because those are always extremely brief. Huebert's reference to Kearny also needs to be met with skepticism due to the latter's equation of the absence of a rationale for the apocalypse with a "hole."[4] Also, if the nature of the apocalypse is unknown, the fact that there are a few human survivors and almost none from the animal kingdom, has to be seen as a literary means defying rational explanations as scientists stated more than once that human survival depends on the survival of animals as well.[5] Though I acknowledge Huebert's and Kearny's awareness that the absence of animals has to be taken into account, I would like to propose a different terminology: seeing the predominant absence of animals on the actual diegetic level—this means as "physically appearing" within the storyline—as a blank space rather than a "hole" offers new insights into the notion of humanity constructed in the novel. This blank space should be seen as characterized by the aforementioned physical absence, but also by its mirror quality which provides humans the opportunity to reflect on themselves or which reflects back on them without their understanding. I will show that McCarthy uses the motif of an absence of animals to portray a decline of humanity and nonetheless as a plead for humanity and the preservation of our planet.[6]

## Animals as the Novel's Framework

Due to the conventions of the genre "dystopian science fiction" as such—and especially representations in films—animals are often represented as monsters. Instead, animals are extinct in the world of *The Road*. They neither represent a threat, nor do they embody evil, as might be deducted from Andrew Keller Estes's observation that "the world of *The Road* is the site of a Manichaean struggle between good and evil" (185). The Manichaean struggle is reserved for the human race alone. In the world of *The Road*, only the human animal turns into a cannibalistic monster, forming the "extremes of human avarice" (Frye 171).

In a beautiful contradiction to the physical absence of beastly monsters, McCarthy nonetheless starts the novel with the appearance of a strange creature in a dream—a monster after all. The introduction of the main characters is accompanied by a dream sequence including this conventional epitome of evil: the father is being led into a cave by his son. There, he is confronted with a monster.

> They stood in a great stone room where lay a black and ancient lake. And on the far shore a creature that raised its dripping mouth from the rimstone pool and stared into the light with eyes dead white and sightless as the eggs of spiders. It swung its head low over the water as if to take the scent of what it could not see. Crouching there pale and naked and translucent, its alabaster bones cast up in shadow on the rocks behind it. Its bowels, its beating heart. The brain that pulsed in a dull glass bell. It swung its head from side to side and then gave out a low moan and turned and lurched away and loped soundlessly into the dark. (McCarthy 7-8)

This encounter with a primordial, monstrous creature leaves the reader befuddled because in this early stage of the reading process one lacks the context to understand its symbolic meaning. At this point, it can only be taken for surface value: the dream is about a blind creature living deep in the earth, reminiscent of species of the deep sea, which is not aggressive towards human intruders, but turns its back to them.[7] It seems to be frustrated ("it gave out a low moan") and disappears into the dark. The son is not further mentioned and the reaction of the man after the encounter remains unknown. This passage is immediately followed by the novel's next short section and leaves the reader in the dark about the aforementioned monster or the man's feelings about his dream. Instead, the actual plot starts and the novel's setting is established. It should be emphasized, however, that McCarthy opens the novel with the description of an animal. Doing so, he evokes the existence of an animal kingdom in the depth of the earth, even if this might be only the subconscious desire of the protagonist that becomes manifest in his dream. From section two on, we are confronted with an almost completely animal-free surface.

Starting the novel with the protagonist's confrontation with a monster creates the setting of a conventional science fiction novel or film. Any action element is spared though, and instead resigned passiveness lingers, which again defies our expectation of the clashes of species as shaped by the genre. This Tiresias of the deep does not want to have anything to do with humans, not even as prey. The blind animal turns its back to mankind. Although described as extinct on the earth, McCarthy here evokes the idea that down below, in the deep, there might be something waiting.

The least known species are still those of the deep sea. Even though the ocean in *The Road* is devoid of life and the deep sea remains unmentioned, fish play an important metaphorical role in the novel, once again despite their actual physical absence from the diegetic world. McCarthy ends his novel—after the death of the father and the son finding "a new family"—by dedicating the complete last section not to the future of the boy, but to trout. What interests most at this point is the fact that McCarthy ends the novel with these animals at all, which, as I have argued, establishes a frame around the story and thereby endows animals with great symbolic significance.

## The Desire of the Present: The Rare Appearance of Actual Animals

Before exploring the implications of the post-animal world of the novel in more depth, it is necessary to focus on the only living nonhuman creature mentioned in the course of the actual storyline of the father's and son's odyssey: a dog. Once more though, even in the case of this singular animal that supposedly exists in the characters' world, my thesis of the employment of animals as a blank space, a space that only enables reflection, applies here. The dog, in fact, does not actually enter the stage as a physical entity, but only through the perception of the characters, and the reader learns about it through the mediation of their senses. The dog is introduced by the reference to the sound of its barking which catches the attention of the father and the son:[8]

Then in the distance he heard a dog bark. He turned and looked toward the darkening town. It's a dog, he said. A dog? Yes. Where did it come from? I don't know. We're not going to kill it, are we Papa? No. We're not going to kill it. He looked down at the boy. Shivering in his coats. He bent over and kissed him on his gritty brow. We wont [sic] hurt the dog, he said. I promise. (McCarthy 62)

What seems to be remarkable in this scene is that the (rare) sound of a dog immediately triggers the son's nurturing and life-preserving instincts. Hence the physically absent dog serves as a blank space reflecting the father's humanity, which is shown here by refraining from killing the dog. The son's diligent reminder to the father that they do not eat what is close to them, may it be the dog or other humans, is the general symbol for the protagonist's preservation of humanity. Another reading of this passage could point at seeing the dog as a possible pet. Erica Fudge suggests that "[t]o begin to think about the animals we live with is, thus, to begin to undo a humanist construction of the human" which she defines as "dominant, controlled and powerful" (109). Therefore, the reverberation that the sound of the dog, a possible pet, leaves behind, could reflect an alternative understanding of humanity, one based on empathy.

How human are the humans in *The Road* and what can even be called "humanity" in this inhospitable setting? The predominant topic in the novel is certainly the deterioration of humankind and, concomitantly, humanity. Most of the survivors turned cannibals, hence their so-called humanity is lost.[9] Father and son try to consciously draw the demarcation line by repeating and living up to the son's concern "We wouldnt [sic] ever eat anybody, would we?" (McCarthy 93).

Nonetheless, their fight seems futile. The hostile environment is taking over and diminishes their chance for staying humane step by step. If it has been man-made, which is suggested by the text, the apocalypse that preceded the world of *The Road*, cannot be classified other than "insane" for it deprived men from all resources.[10] Clearly, the Aristotelean answer to what humanity entails, "reason," has therefore been invalidated in the world of *The Road*. That is why I would rather like to apply the criteria of what makes a human as it has been drafted in James Gormandec's *New York Times* article "Considering the Humanity of Nonhumans." Gormandec distills four essences of humanity—the sense of "I," autonomy, self-awareness, and a sense of future. McCarthy deconstructs all these criteria: he denies his protagonists the sense of "I" by not granting them names and hence setting them up as types from the start. How much autonomy do father and son have who are so completely absorbed by surviving? There is some autonomy left by their decision not to become cannibals and by granting one drifting man they encounter, Ely, temporary company and a share of their food. This altruism is unique though and the father hardens in the course of the novel and shows no mercy with the thief he leaves behind naked and doomed to die. The son, still in contact with his humanity, feels pity and sorrow: "He was just hungry, Papa. He is going to die." The father only replies laconically, "He will die anyway" (184). He, the adult, forecloses the possible autonomous decision of the son to share their food. Hence, it can be said that the son, being so dependent on his father, is a human-in-progress and does not have a real chance for autonomy yet. Self-awareness is not completely lost with the main characters, but almost forgotten. It is constituted by their belief in their humanity, but already detached from the physicality. There is a touching scene where both are confronted with their mirror image: "They came upon themselves in a mirror and he almost raised the pistol. It's us, Papa, the boy whispered. It's us" (95). It's the boy, not the father, who shows self-awareness here. The last category Gormandec suggests to define humanity, the sense of future, is obviously questioned. The need to survive dooms the characters in the here and now of finding food and subsequently destroys their sense of future.[11]

## Animals as Relics of the World Gone

There are numerous animal references to allude to the pre-apocalypse world of the past. Two classes of animals, birds and bony fish, will be taken as examples here. Foremost, birds are mentioned throughout the novel, even though often in connection with fish. One passage seems to be especially significant to me due to its explicit connection of flora and fauna. Meandering through the wasteland, father and son come to an abandoned house: "They approached slowly up the drive. No tracks in the random patches of melting snow. A tall hedge of dead privet. An ancient birdsnest [sic] lodged in the dark wicker of it" (78). Here, the mentioning of the "privet" as the most content garden plant of long elapsed ("ancient") times which exists today, is most telling. In the pre-apocalyptic world, privets were home to myriads of birds, feeding from its berries and hence they were any gardener's nightmare because the seeds got distributed to places beyond the assigned demarcation ground of the garden's hedge. Humans planted the hedges with a purpose, nature did not comply with the assigned and demarcated destiny.

In the now of *The Road* the birds are gone, birds of all families, including sea birds. The sea in the novel is an "anti-fantasy of a lifeless ocean" (Huebert 76)—and ascribed with an enumeration of three words: "Cold. Desolate. Birdless" (McCarthy 153).[12] This list has to be understood as a progression because the absence of birds is mentioned only a few pages later more extensively, which by itself represents a remarkable accumulation of animal references in a rather small passage of the novel: "In the morning he rekindled the fire and they ate and watched the shore. The cold and rainy look of it not so different from seascapes in the northern world. No gulls or shorebirds" (156). Once more, the denial of a complete sentence structure shows animals appearing as—what I call—"memory flashes." Through the progression suggested by the former passage and by means of positioning the last mention of "No gulls or shorebirds" at the end of the entire section as an impression that keeps lingering, the author uses the blank space left behind from a past filled with life to emphasize the barrenness of the world even more. Humankind in the last quote is again reduced to the mere fulfillment of primary needs.

In addition, the painful absence of birds is strengthened by re-occurring images of them in the dreams of the father, which can be seen as "moments of the earth's lost biodiversity" (Huebert 79). The "profound celebration of life" (Huebert 68) here results from the juxtaposition of the pre- and the post-apocalyptic world. Both times, the source for these images from the former world stems from the father's dreams and memories, our only glimpse of the times before the catastrophe. The first mentioning of the birds is contrasted with the desolate present of the book:

He dreamt of walking in a flowering wood where birds flew before them he and the child and the sky was aching blue but he was learning how to wake himself from such siren worlds. Lying there in the dark with the uncanny taste of a peach from some phantom orchard fading in his mouth. He thought if he lived long enough the world at last would all be lost. Like the dying world the newly blind inhabit, all of it slowly fading from memory. (McCarthy 18)

This passage confirms my thesis of the blank space constituted by the absence of physically appearing animals because the desolate present triggers a memory of what is no longer, and the dire reality is juxtaposed with the painful memory of a more livable world which is symbolized by an animal.

Another section that mentions two specific bird species further emphasizes this: a falcon and cranes are the subject of a subsequent memory of the father which is, once again, paired with the element of water and the absence of life in it. First, there is a discussion between father and son about a lake they are seeing. Representing hope, the son asks, "Do you think there could be fish in the lake," and the father answers soberly, "No. There is nothing in the lake" (19). This nothingness triggers the memory of the aforementioned birds: "In that long ago somewhere very near this place he'd watched a falcon fall down the long blue wall of the mountain and break with the keel of its breastbone the midmost from a flight of cranes and take it to the river below all gangly and wrecked and trailing its loose and blowsy plumage in the still autumn air" (19-20). Here, the section ends, but the setting stays the same at the beginning of the next section, though brought back into the post-animal reality: "The grainy air. The taste of it never left your mouth" (20). There are no birds to be seen anymore and the three looming verbs of the bird memory "fall," "break," and "wreck" are revealed to be messengers of doom.

Later in the novel, we can find a similar reminiscing: "Once in those early years he'd wakened in a barren wood and lay listening to flocks of migratory birds overhead in that bitter dark. Their half muted crankings miles above where they circled the earth as senselessly as insects trooping the rim of a blow. He wished them godspeed [sic] till they were gone. He never heard them again" (42). Here, McCarthy not only equates the former memory once more with the coming end ("in that bitter dark," "half muted," "senselessly"), but he reinforces the usage of the animal- and, more specifically, the bird-motif for showing the disappearance of animal life from the world as such, the doom fulfilled. The father's "wish for godspeed" gets a different connotation from the knowledge of what has happened later: the wish also meant a last salute to a species which should save itself from the world humans were in the process of destroying, signified by the "barren woods." Hence, the absent birds come to embody the extinction process which is so encompassing that it even affects the character's language, as will be presently shown.

Before animals become a cognitive void, they not only disappear physically, but the ability to name what is lost and, by that, the memories are also fading. The following passage describes a depressing moment in a bleak and empty world:

Then he spread the sheet of plastic on the ground and got the coats and blankets from the cart and he took off their damp and muddy shoes and they sat there in silence with their hands outheld to the flames. He tried to think of something to say but he could not. He'd had this feeling before, beyond the numbness and the dull despair. The world shrinking down about a raw core of parsible [sic] entities. The names of things slowly following those things into oblivion. Colors. The name of birds. Things to eat. Finally the names of things one believed to be true. More fragile than he would have thought. How much was gone already? The sacred idiom shorn of its referents and so of its reality. Drawing down like something trying to preserve heat. In time to wink out forever. (66)

Here, McCarthy catapults animals into the non-restorable realm of oblivion. The extinction of animals is followed by the extinction of memory and names in the diegetic world of the novel. When the referents are gone, the signifiers, too, lose their power. And with the memory of human beings gone, humanity as such will die as well.

As mentioned above, McCarthy ends his novel with a pastoral memory sequence focusing on trout. Earlier in the novel, the trout-motif appears twice in connection with the father, in terms of a pastoral memory connected to the father's pre-apocalyptic life. The first passage bespeaks his former connectivity with nature. The vehicle of this connection is the character's gaze, just like in Hemingway's "Big Two-Hearted River," where the trout are also seen by the protagonist: "Nick looked down into the clear, brown water . . . and watched the trout keeping themselves steady in the current with wavering fins. As he watched them they changed their positions" (163).[13] The father in *The Road* reminisces a pastoral moment juxtaposing the present desolation with his past: "He stood on a stone bridge where the waters slurried into a pool and turned slowly in a gray foam. Where once he'd observed trout swaying in the current, tracking their perfect shadows on the stones beneath" (McCarthy 26).

His second memory of a whole world and environment is focused on a similar picture. "He'd stood at such a river once and watched the flash of trout deep in a pool, invisible to see in the teacolored [sic] water except as they turned on their sides to feed. Reflecting back the sun deep in the darkness like a flash of knives in a cave" (34). Once again, we find the visual faculty as the bond between the character and nature, resulting in a moment of pastoral bliss. The remembered trout serve as a reflecting surface, brightening up the dark waters just like their absence, the blank space in the presence of *The Road*, reflects its desolate character by pointing at such memories. By that, McCarthy does, as Nora Kestermann states, "de-mythologize the pastoral" (7) as such and also its iconic American embodiment in Hemingway's story. All "memory flashes" of animals looked at here represent pastoral moments devoid of action, in which the father relates to nature via his senses. These are moments of relaxation and freedom from obligation, which could have been used for transcending the moment and giving way to Thoreauvian contemplation as an expression of a humanity which is lost in the present of *The Road*.

## The Unexpected Lures of *The Road*

The reader of *The Road* has to cope with this calamitous present of the novel somehow. Here, the still ongoing quest for humanity, which especially the son embodies, becomes particularly important. This was the biggest incentive for groups of young students to take up the challenge of reading and analyzing this novel in an ESL-classroom. I am indebted to students from the high school I was teaching at the time, Goetheschule in Neu-Isenburg, for picking this novel for a 10th-grade English class in the first place and another 10th-grade class which I taught in the schoolyear 2016/2017. Both times, the response of the students to this—for young readers[14]—rather challenging book was very positive. The students coped very well with the language level but suffered (at first) from the laconic style and the rather monotonous storyline of the book.[15] Nonetheless, the students were very diligent readers. Students also worked on extensive reading diaries and in my conclusion I will present some of the results to demonstrate the lure of this book for younger readers.[16]

The absence of animals was not an explicit topic in class, yet some students did notice this aspect as constituting *The Road*'s world: the world is characterized as "it's wet all the time [and] no animals or human beings appear anymore" (student A, 7). Especially the absence of animals in the ocean was noted: "In the world, there aren't any animals which are still alive" (student B, 27). Other students added that "the bones of the animals and the boat are an empty vessel of the old world, which shows that the old world is lost.... The sea which stands for life has nothing left for the man and the boy" (student C, 83) and "normally, the sea stands for life, but it's dead" (student D, 16).

After facing the annihilation of nature, the plea for humanity in the book became my students' focus. This humanity was recognized especially in the way the boy still makes ethically impeccable decisions regarding other men and the dog: "I think it's nice to see how the boy is the light in the darkness of this new world" (student C, 45). "There was no humanity in the father character. But the more we could see the humanity in the boy. [It can be seen in the fact] how much he worries about other people and what a moral instinct he has" (student B, 8). This student also mentions that "cruelty" against animals contradicts humanity. Another student reflects on a scene, in which the father takes revenge on a thief by abandoning him without food or clothes against the son's protest: "The boy represents hope for the world's future and the proof that humanity still exists" (student C, 93). Also, one student sees the dog as a catalyst for the son's "caring" humanity; student F writes: "I thought the most heart-wrenching moments were when the [son] cried for the little boy and the dog."[17] . . . [H]e is also always ready to help and he cares a lot for others" (45).

## The Decline of Humanity

With *The Road*, Cormac McCarthy has written a most impressive plea for humanity or rather a testament that in a post-apocalyptic and hence a post-animal world humanity will be at least hard to keep up if not impossible. I have shown the need to include the animal motif into discussions about the possibility of humanity in *The Road*. Reflecting on our world, Stephen Joyce states "the survivors of the apocalypse will no longer be human because what we mean by 'human' is a construct of our civilization and once that civilization is gone so too will all the innate morality we like to ascribe to ourselves" (9). It has been shown in this essay that McCarthy uses animals as a blank space within the novel to exacerbate this thought. No humanity survives without animals.[18] To illuminate this, I would like to introduce one last passage of the novel, its ending.

Here, the father dies and the son ventures out alone only for a short time. He finds another family which takes him in. After the son is convinced that the father of this family, who has observed him for a while, is one of the "good guys" and that they have maintained the ethical code of "you don't eat people" (McCarthy 201), he joins them. After a funeral ritual, which again can be seen as one of the criteria that define humanity according to Gormandec, they leave. We do not learn any more and are left in the dark about the son's future and also the future of humanity. The following section concludes the novel:

Once there were brook trout in the streams in the mountains. You could see them standing in the amber current where the white edges of their fins wimpled softly in the flow. They smelled of moss in your hand. Polished and muscular and torsional. On their backs were vermiculate patterns that were maps of the world in its becoming. Maps and mazes. Of a thing which could not be put back. Not be made right again. In the deep glens where they lived all things were older than man and they hummed of mystery. (203)

This section feels like a coda because it is detached from the actual plot and the characters. Why does McCarthy end his novel with this image? Can it be interpreted as a look into a better future or the swan song for a lost world? The fact that the boy's future is not even alluded to can be read as a likely loss of future. McCarthy rather reminisces on trout, starting with "[o]nce there were . . . " and the ascription of "maps of the world in its becoming" that "could not be put back" is—in my view—a clear indication of a pessimistic ending. As the monster in the beginning, the only realm McCarthy points us to in which animals might still survive is in "the deep glens where they lived [and] all things were older than man" (203). There, also the blind monster might wait with them and other animals for a post-human thriving epoch after humans become extinct because they could not uphold their humanity.[19] "Cold. Desolate. Birdless." (153). That is how the world in *The Road* has become.

My experience at the North Sea beach was that it was cold, but full of life. And there were birds—still.

## Notes

**1 |** Although the human animal has committed the widest range of atrocities from the beginning of time, I will stick to the disputed term *humanity* and use it for my argument. I still see it as a necessary word to express ideals and hopes connected to our species. Taking the definition in the Merriam Webster as an example, which states the term's meaning as "compassionate, sympathetic or generous behavior," I see "humanity" as the promise for capabilities our species does have to do good. The fact that humans did widely not live up to these possibilities and even perverted them does not invalidate this promise per se.

**2 |** Examples for the necessity to complement the otherwise incredibly comprehensive criticism on *The Road* can be Rebecca Gigg's essay on the book, where she discusses the extinction of animals, but doesn't dwell on the general topic of animals as such. Also, scholar Hannah Stark presents a very thorough analysis of the anthropocentric world of The Road, in which she observes the extinction of flora and fauna (73), but does not consider the animal motif further. In her study on "The American Pastoral and

Its De-Idealization," Nora Kestermann dedicates a section of her book to McCarthy's novel. While she analyzes specific animal motifs, she never broadens the view to other absent species (227). And even though Kestermann pointedly describes the "absence of purpose" and "the absence of meaning" as characteristic for the novel, the category of "absent animals" is itself conspicuously absent from her argument (219). As a last example to be mentioned, Stephen Joyce fittingly describes the world of *The Road* as characterized by four "physical aspects . . . : darkness, cold, barrenness, and hunger" (6). This "barrenness" would also seem to entail the absence of animals, but rather than exploring this aspect in more depth, Joyce leaves it at a general phrase regarding fauna and flora ("[t]here are barely any signs of growth of life") and instead places the emphasis on the "presence of things" (7).

3 | For a thorough analysis of the usage of the animal motif in McCarthy's fiction published before *The Road*, see Willis R. Sanborn's book on the topic.

4 | Kearny writes: "I argue that the 'real' cause of the apocalypse exists as a hole in the text that parallels a potential hole in human existence: the complete absence of human futurity and the absence of life itself" (161).

5 | Paul Ehrlich et al. write about the "Long-Term Biological Consequences of Nuclear War" that after numerous nuclear strikes "[t]he diversity of many natural communities would almost certainly be substantially reduced, and numerous species of plants, animals and microorganisms would become extinct" (1298). This obviously would have consequences for humans: "From the human perspective . . . [a]n accelerated loss of these genetic resources through extinction would be one of the most serious potential consequences of nuclear war" (1298). Hence, a survival of humans in a post-nuclear apocalypse world could only be temporary.

6 | No one has conveyed the meaning of *The Road* as an environmentalist's statement better than George Monbiot in his seminal 2007 *Guardian* article "Civilisation Ends with a Shutdown of Human Concern: Are We Ready?" where he calls the novel "the most important environmental book ever written." Monbiot shrewdly connects McCarthy's depicted "world [which] lost its biosphere" with the collapse of "all pre-existing social codes." Although this is not elaborated on any further, I am indebted to his thoughts in the following.

7 | Who can blame it, considering that even in our times "[h]umans were breaking the backs of animal culture and society with violence, even while seeking to conserve precious wild life" (XVIII) as the ecologist G. A. Bradshaw writes. Humans are the problems for animals, not vice versa. According to Smith, an earth and environmental sciences professor at the University of Portsmouth in the U. K., "[n]ature flourishes when humans are removed from the equation, even after the world's worst nuclear accident" (qtd. in Wendle).

8 | Sound is also largely absent from the world of *The Road*. Hence, the meaning of this particular sound is manifest and the metaphorical dimension of the animal motif for the more humane pre-apocalyptic world evident. The world of the novel lets the senses wilt

for there are no stimuli: no sounds, no colors, no pleasant surfaces or animal fur is left to satisfy tactile needs.

9 | For a thorough analysis of the cannibal motif compare Huebert's comprehensive essay "Eating and Mourning the Corpse of the World: Ecological Cannibalism and Elegiac Protomourning in Cormac McCarthy's *The Road*."

10 | In the reception of *The Road*, natural disasters such as a volcanic eruption or a huge earthquake are also considered as possible causes of the catastrophe, but details in the novel and the symptoms of the post-apocalypse contradict these interpretations.

11 | This short list may be amended by other categories which scientists like G. A. Bradshaw bring up in their work, such as showing empathy, mourning rituals or funeral practices, which are also considered in *The Road* as my concluding reflections on the ending will show.

12 | McCarthy ascribes the beach with remnants of birds and fish to intensify the animal- and hence lifelessness of the former "cradle of life": "They trekked out along the crescent sweep of beach, keeping to the firmer sand below the tidewrack. They stood, their clothes flapping softly. Glass floats covered with a gray crust. The bones of seabirds. At the tide line a woven mat of weeds and the ribs of fishes in their millions stretching along the shore as far as eye could see like an isocline of death. One vast salt sepulchre. Senseless. Senseless" (157).

13 | The second mentioning of the trout also follows this pattern: "Nick looked down the river at the trout rising. They were rising to insects come from the swamp . . . As far down the long stretch as he could see, the trout were rising" (Hemingway 166).

14 | In Germany, 10th-grade high school students are usually between 15 and 16 years old.

15 | A typical judgement about the reading process sounds like this: "At the beginning, I thought that this book will be very boring because nothing special happened. But the more I read, the more I wanted to read on."

16 | In the following, I will quote from five reading journals which the students provided me with for the writing of this essay. The names have been anonymized and the students' consent to the publication of their thoughts has been given.

17 | In the respective passage, the boy thinks that he has seen a boy and he expresses a big desire to see and stay with this other boy to enlarge his social circle beyond his father.

18 | Paul R. Ehrlich et al. suggest in their essay "Long-Term Biological Consequences of Nuclear War" that "[i]n any large-scale nuclear exchange between the superpowers, global environmental changes sufficient to cause the extinction of a major fraction of the planet and animal species on the Earth are likely" (1299).

19 | A good example for the reverse scenario is what happened around Chernobyl and other sites of former disasters as John Wendle writes in *The National Geographic*: "In places plagued by guerrilla warfare, nuclear fallout, and chemical weapons, wild animals have rebounded in great numbers on land we have made too polluted—or too dangerous—for human habitation."

## Works Cited

Allen, Mary. *Animals in American Literature*. University of Illinois Press, 1983.

Bradshaw, Gay A. *Elephants on the Edge. What Elephants Teach Us about Humanity*. Yale University Press, 2009.

Ehrlich, Paul A., et. al. "Long-Term Biological Consequences of Nuclear War." *Science*, New Series, vol. 222, no. 4630, 1983, pp. 1203-1300.

Estes, Andrew Keller. *Cormack McCarthy an the Writing of American Spaces*. Rodopi, 2013.

Frye, Stephen. *Understanding Cormac McCarthy*. University of South Carolina Press, 2009.

Fudge, Erica. *Pets*. Routledge, 2015.

Giggs, Rebecca. "The Green Afterword. Cormac McCarthy's *The Road* and the Ecological Uncanny." *Criticism, Crisis and Contemporary Narrative*, edited by Paul Crosthwaite. Routledge, 2010, pp. 201-17.

Gormandec, James. "Considering the Humanity of Nonhumans." *The New York Times*, 9 Dec. 2013. nytimes.com.

Hemingway, Ernest. "Big Two Hearted River: Part I and II." 1925. *Ernest Hemingway: The Complete Short Stories*. Simon & Schuster, 1987.

Huebert, David. "Eating and Mourning the Corpse of the World: Ecological Cannibalism and Elegiac Protomourning in Cormac McCarthy's *The Road*." *The Cormack McCarthy Journal*, vol. 15 no. 1, 2017, pp. 66-85.

Joyce, Stephen. "The Double Death of Humanity in Cormac McCarthy's *The Road*." *Transatlantica*, vol. 2, 2016, transatlantica.revues.org/8386.

Jingjing, Guo. "McCarthy's The Road and Ethical Choice in a Post-Apocalyptic World." *Comparative Literature and Culture (CLCWeb)*, vol. 17, no. 5, 2015 docs.lib.purdue.edu/clcweb/vol17/iss5/2/

Kearny, Kevin. "Cormac McCarthy's *The Road* and the Frontier of the Human." *Literature Interpretation Theory*, vol. 23, no. 2, 2012, pp. 160-78.

Kestermann, Nora. *The American Pastoral and its De-Idealization in Two Contemporary American Novels*. Pro Business, 2015.

Lundblad, Michael. "Introduction: The End of the Animal—Literary and Cultural Animalities." *Animalities: Literary and Cultural Studies Beyond the Human*, edited by M. Lundblad, Edinburgh University Press, 2017, pp. 1-21.

McCarthy, Cormac. *The Road*. 2006. Cornelsen, 2011.

Monbiot, George. "Civilization Ends with a Shutdown of Human Concern: Are We Ready?" *The Guardian*. 30 Oct. 2007, theguardian.com.

Stark, Hannah. "'All the Things He Saw and Did Not See': Witnessing the End of the World in Cormac McCarthy's *The Road*." *Critical Survey*, vol. 25, no. 2, 2013, pp. 71-84.

Wendle, John. "Chernobyl and Other Places Where Animals Thrive Without People." *National Geographic*, 9 Oct. 2015, news.nationalgeographic.

# Uninvited Collaborations with Nature

*Nina Katchadourian*

Renovated Mushroom (Tip-Top Tire Rubber Patch Kit)
*Cibachrome, 27.25 x 39.5 inches, 1998*

For many years, I've made works that I loosely think of as uninvited collaborations with nature." The *Mended Spiderwebs* series came about during a six-week period in June and July in 1998 which I spent on a small Finnish island called Pörtö. In the forest and around the house where I was living, I searched for broken spiderwebs which I repaired using red sewing thread. All of the patches were made by inserting segments one at a time directly into the web. Sometimes the thread was starched, which made it stiffer and easier to work with. The short threads were held in place by the stickiness of the spider web itself; longer threads were reinforced by dipping the tips into white glue. I fixed the holes in the web until it was fully repaired, or until it could no longer bear the weight of the thread. In the process, I often caused further damage when the tweezers got tangled in the web or when my hands brushed up against it by accident.

The morning after the first patch job, I discovered a pile of red threads lying on the ground below the web. At first I assumed the wind had blown them out; on closer inspection it became clear that the spider had repaired the web to perfect condition using its own methods, throwing the threads out in the process. My repairs were always rejected by the spider and discarded, usually during the course of the night, even in webs which looked abandoned. The larger, more complicated patches where the threads were held together with glue often retained their form after being thrown out, although in a somewhat „wilted" condition without the rest of the web to suspend and stretch them. When I exhibit the work, each "Rejected Patch" is shown next to the photograph showing the web with the patch as it looked on site.

A bicycle tire patching kit found in the tool shed was used to patch up a group of mushrooms that had small tears on the caps. (previous page)

Mended Spiderweb #19 (Laundry Line)
*Cibachrome, 20 x 30 inches, 1998*

Mended Spiderweb #8 (Fish Patch)
*Cibachrome, 20 x 20 inches, 1998*

**With and Beyond Nonhumans:**
**Encounters, Empathy, Entanglements**

# "Strange Matings" and Cultural Encounters: Octavia Butler's Fiction as "Companion Species" to Theory

*Maria Holmgren Troy*

"Strange matings" is a quotation from African American science-fiction writer Octavia Butler's fifth novel, *Wild Seed* (1980), and it also serves as the title of the second book entirely devoted to Butler and her works.[1] This is indeed an apt title since there are intimate as well as hostile encounters between humans and other species in many of her narratives from the Clayarks (a quadruped hybrid human-alien species) in her first published novel *Patternmaster* (1974) to the Ina (or vampires) in her last novel, *Fledgling* (2005). Through these always cultural and often biological exchanges, Butler's fiction explores the problems and possibilities of hybridity in ways that match and, I would argue, sometimes surpass theoretical formulations of the concept. There is never an option for her human protagonists to settle with the notion of the "Sacred Image of the Same," to borrow an expression from Butler's third novel, *Survivor* (1978); they have to find ways of dealing with Others—other races or ethnicities and/or other species—and with the outcomes of these encounters in terms of physical and mental changes and hybrid offspring. In this article, I will examine a few examples of cross-species encounters in Butler's fiction and discuss the theoretical resonances and implications of these fictional boundary crossings.

At the end of the 1980s, Butler had already published nine novels and a few short stories, so her fictional explorations of cultural and biological hybridity were well underway when Homi Bhabha's postcolonial theories of hybridity and cultural translation appeared at the beginning of the 1990s. Reading Bhabha's early discussions of these notions parallel to Butler's fiction is an enlightening project in many ways, as they deal with similar, if not the same, dynamics and ideas. There are also many correspondences between Butler's fiction and Donna Haraway's theoretical work—unsurprisingly, since Haraway overtly draws on Butler's fiction in her theorizations, which are also highly relevant to the issues under consideration here. An instance of Haraway directly commenting on and borrowing from Butler's fiction is the phrase "the sacred image of the same" that Haraway employs in her writing from the late 1980s onwards (see *Primate* 378; *Simians* 226; *Modest Witness* 243; "Species Matters" 21), a phrase, which, as indicated, she has borrowed from one of Butler's novels.

Rather than reading Butler's fiction through the theoretical lenses provided by Bhabha and Haraway the aim of this article is to put fiction and theory side by side and read them as a kind of textual "companion species," to appropriate Haraway's phrase. As Haraway puts it, "to focus on companion species is for me one way to refuse human exceptionalism without invoking posthumanism. In human-animal worlds, companion species are ordinary beings-in-encounter" ("Species Matters" 18). What I want to avoid here is privileging theoretical writing over Butler's fictional explorations of ideas and processes: in other words, I want to avoid theoretical exceptionalism.[2]

In what follows, I will focus on two of Butler's short stories: "Bloodchild" (1984) and "Amnesty" (2003).[3] Each story centers on the interaction between humans and an alien species that is very different from humankind. In both cases, the aliens are in positions of power—a scenario that challenges the notion of human exceptionalism and recurs in most of Butler's fiction—and the human characters have had to negotiate with them in order to survive and retain some degree of human agency.[4] Nevertheless, the interaction between humans and aliens has led to something new and different for both species, which in many ways could be said to flesh out what Bhabha calls "the process of cultural hybridity," a process that, he proposes, "gives rise to something different, something new and unrecognisable, a new area of negotiation of meaning and representation" ("Third" 211). As I will demonstrate, Butler's stories emphasize the physical and emotional costs and benefits of the process of cultural hybridity, which is never abstract in her fiction and always has a direct impact on the bodies of her protagonists. Reading Butler's stories side by side with Haraway's and Bhabha's theories without privileging one over the other, as companion species or "ordinary beings-in-encounter," I would argue, helps the reader to achieve a greater understanding of both theory and fiction as well as the cultural dynamics with which they both engage.

## "Displaced Again from the Center of the Universe": Challenging Human Exceptionalism

In "Bloodchild," the protagonist Gan, a male human teenager, has been born and raised on a planet where a large insect-like people called Tlic are in charge, and the humans, called Terrans, live in the Preserve, protected by Tlic officials. Selected human men serve as hosts for the eggs of female Tlic, as Tlic grubs have a much better chance of survival if they develop in a human host rather than in a native animal. From the day he was born, Gan has been raised to become a host for the eggs of T'Gatoi, who is an important Tlic government official and a close friend of the family. Gan has seen this arrangement as natural until he witnesses the horrific, gory process of her removing grubs before they actually consume their human host on the evening of his own first impregnation, which constitutes the present of the story. The historical background of the current human-Tlic interrelationships emerges in bits and pieces in the first-person narrative of the human protagonist and can be regarded as a story of failed human colonization, or perhaps rather a story of migration in which, as Butler puts it in her afterword to "Bloodchild," the humans have had to "pay the rent" for a new "livable space" (31-32).

The other short story, "Amnesty," takes place on Earth at a time when an alien species has been present for decades. The human protagonist of this story is a woman called Noah, who works as a translator for the aliens. These are even less humanlike than those of "Bloodchild": they resemble plants, weeds, or bushes, and consist of various kinds of organisms with different functions: for example, manipulation of physical objects and bodies, seeing, and creating visual displays. Noah refers to them as Communities, and she works for one specific Community. Having settled on Earth, the Communities live in bubbles in the deserts, where they mine for minerals in ways that humans are unable to. The human governments made peace with the newcomers after these governments' failed attempt to exterminate the Communities during their early settlement, which instead gave the aliens control of half of the human weapons of destruction. The Communities, in a human economy that has been globally depressed since their arrival, have become employers of humans who are desperately trying to find work in order to support themselves and their families. In the story's present, Noah's job as Translator is to prepare a group of humans to work for the Communities by answering the humans' questions and dealing with their concerns, prejudices, fears, and hate.

In both short stories, the newcomers—Terrans in "Bloodchild" and the Communities in "Amnesty"—do not have the option to leave the planet to which they have migrated. In the first story, the question of the Terrans' leaving is not brought up at all. It is made clear that "there was no 'away.' Not in the Preserve. Certainly not outside ("Bloodchild" 19). In "Amnesty," Noah explains to the group of humans that the aliens, the Communities, cannot leave, and that it is impossible to drive them away: "There's no 'away' for them—not for several generations anyway. Their ship was a one-way transport. They've settled here and they'll fight to keep the various desert locations they've chosen for their bubbles" ("Amnesty" 167). As she emphasizes, it is out of the question that humankind can win such a fight since the Communities have already shown their superior strength in the military confrontation mentioned above.

That the notion of human exceptionalism is undermined by the presence of the Communities is spelled out in the dialogue between Noah and the group of humans. One of the men says that even though the Communities have been on earth longer than he has been alive, he thinks that "[i]t feels wrong that they exist." He muses, "that's because we've been displaced again from the center of the universe. We human beings, I mean. Down through history, in myth and even in science, we've kept putting ourselves in the center, and then being evicted" (157). Noah is pleasantly surprised by his observation: "I noticed the same thing. Now we find ourselves in a kind of sibling rivalry with the Communities. There is other intelligent life. The universe has other children. We knew it, but until they arrived here, we could pretend otherwise" (158). In other words, Noah is happy to confirm the refutation of human exceptionalism, but also the ambiguous feelings about the realization that human beings are not the center of the universe. In *When Species Meet* (2008), Haraway defines human exceptionalism as "the premise that humanity alone is not a spatial and temporal web of interspecies dependencies" (11). In "Amnesty," Noah's use of the phrase "sibling rivalry" signals that she sees the interspecies dependencies as fundamental, since she casts them in familial terms.[5]

The human protagonists of the two stories, Gan and Noah, are intellectually, physically, and emotionally involved in a hybrid culture that has evolved from the encounter and subsequent extended interaction between the two species: Terrans and Tlic; humans and Communities. Like Haraway, they are "committed to inhabiting both the trouble and the vitality of the contact zones of companion species, where the situated work and play of myriad critters, including people, make history" ("Species Matters" 18). In an interchange at the beginning of "Amnesty," Noah is taken care of by one Community, who is her employer, after a physically demanding encounter with another Community, a subcontractor who wants to use Noah's services. While her employer thinks that she should not put herself in harm's way since it is impossible to change either species' view of the other, Noah argues that she can "a little . . . . Community by Community, human by human" (155). Aware of the Communities' superior strength and ability to destroy humanity, she insists, "I want to vote for peace between your people and mine by telling the truth. I don't know if my efforts will do any good, in the long run, but I have to try" (155). When Gan is asked by other Terrans whether he has ever been afraid of T'Gatoi he tells them that he was "caged within [her] many limbs only three minutes after [his] birth" and he tells Tlic the same thing "when T'Gatoi suggests a young Terran child for them and they, anxious and ignorant, demand an adolescent" ("Bloodchild" 8). The reason for the Tlic to demand an adolescent would be to shorten the time that they will have to wait for the human to be able to serve as a host for their eggs. Gan believes that even his "brother who had somehow grown up to fear and distrust the Tlic could probably have gone smoothly into one of their families if he had been adopted early enough" (8-9). Here again, the relationship between the two species is expressed in familial terms: "families" and "adopted." Like many other of Butler's protagonists, as for instance Alanna in *Survivor* (1978) and Lilith in *Dawn* (1987), Gan and Noah serve as negotiators, physical go-betweens, or bridges between the two species.

## Embodied Encounters

There are, however, significant differences between the two protagonists' histories and situations. Whereas Gan has been aware his whole life that he will become the host for T'Gatoi's eggs and does not have any misgivings about this role until he witnesses her removing grubs from a man on the eve on his own insemination, Noah's history is one of alien abduction, or a captivity narrative.[6] Part of the second wave of abductees, she was abducted by the Communities when she was eleven years old, at a time when the two species were unable to communicate with each other, and held in the Mojave Bubble for twelve years. To begin with, "human beings were captives of uncertain ability, intellect, and perception" (153), and subject to a number of different experiments—some of which were injurious, poisonous, and even lethal. As Noah explains to the group of humans, the Communities abducted and experimented on humans because they "wanted to understand us and communicate with us. . . . They wanted to know how we got along with one another and they needed to know how much we could bear of what was normal for them" (160). When asked if that was what the Communities told her, Noah answers that they did, "but not until some of them and some of us, the surviving captives, had managed to put together a code—the beginnings of a language—that got communication started" (161). Noah tells the group of humans that she does not hate the Communities for what they made her go through as a captive, but that she "did once, especially when they were beginning to understand us a little, and yet went right on putting us through hell. They were like human scientists experimenting with lab animals—not cruel, but very thorough" (161). The simile here says a great deal. There are obvious parallels between the attitudes of the species in power: the human captives are forced to take the powerless and vulnerable position of "lab animals" despite the Communities' increasing knowledge of their physical constitutions and intellectual capabilities.

However, the Communities are not actually the ones to inflict most pain while Noah is a captive in the Mojave Bubble; as she explains, "most of the time, the people actually hurting me were other human beings. The aliens used to lock groups of two or more of us up together for days or weeks to see what would happen" (164). The outcomes of these "cell-mate experiments" were, among other things, rapes, pregnancies, and killings. When, years later, the Communities finally ask the captives whether they would like to stay with them voluntarily or leave, Noah is the first to leave, only to be immediately captured, held for a long time, and tortured by the FBI, who erroneously believe that she is withholding valuable information about the Communities' technology. Noah describes this part of her history as worse than her captivity in the Mojave Bubble: "The only difference between the way they treated me and the way the aliens treated me during the early years of my captivity was that the so-called human beings knew when they were hurting me" (170). She emphasizes that "[i]t mattered more than I know how to tell you that this time my tormentors were my own people. They were human. They spoke my language. They knew all that I knew about pain and humiliation and fear and despair. They knew what they were doing to me, and yet it never occurred to them not to do it" (172). So after eventually being released and having physically healed from the mistreatment in jail, Noah returns, being "not only the first to leave the Mojave Bubble, but the first to come back to offer to work for the Communities" (175). As she puts it, "I had a small part in helping them connect with some of the lawyers and politicians" who worked with the Communities to establish legal relationships, such as functioning employer-employee contracts, between the two species (175). In other words, Noah is involved in the development of the legal and political relations between humans and aliens, and, as a captive, she helped in developing a common language together with the Community who is now her employer: "Noah had met her current employer before she turned twelve. It was one of the Communities who never injured her, one who had worked with her and with others to begin to assemble a language that both species could use" (173). As Haraway puts it in *Primate Visions* (1989), "Butler's is a fiction predicated on the natural status of adoption and the unnatural violence of kin" (378). Although "adoption" may be overstating or misrepresenting the relationship between Noah and her employer, which she secretly regards as friendship, Noah's story in "Amnesty" highlights "the unnatural violence of kin," the intraspecies violence: the ways in which humans hurt each other for different reasons or no reasons at all.

In "Bloodchild," the two species have lived together for at least two human generations, and both species are physically vitalized by the interchange with each other. Not only have humans proved to be superior hosts to Tlic grubs, they gain health and longevity by partaking of sterile Tlic eggs, which also offer a pleasant short-term intoxication. The history Gan and the reader have access to dates from after the Terrans' arrival on the planet, when the Tlic initially regarded them as animals and kept them in pens, and the humans called the Tlic worms and killed as many of them as they could. Gan lives in a society that has evolved beyond those initial hostilities between the two species, and he has no sense of a time and a place without the Tlic. Thus, "Bloodchild" shows what it means to deny, in Bhabha's terms, "the essentialism of a prior original or originary culture"—what it means that "all forms of culture are continually in a process of hybridity" ("Third" 211). In *Simians, Cyborgs, and Women* (1991), Haraway comments on the fact that characters in Butler's fiction do not have access to origins, and argues that "[f]rom the perspective of an ontology based on mutation, metamorphosis, and the diaspora, restoring an original sacred image can be a bad joke" (226-27).

"Bloodchild" further corroborates Bhabha's claim that hybridity "is the 'third space' which enables other positions to emerge. This third space displaces the histories that constitute it, and sets up new structures of authority, new political initiatives, which are inadequately understood through received wisdom" ("Third" 211). I would argue that Gan's body as a host for Tlic grubs has everything to do with a conception of hybridity as a material, rather than purely discursive, kind of "third space." Moreover, like the Communities in "Amnesty," the Tlic grubs growing in a human body could also be regarded as yet another challenge, in line with Haraway's theories, to the idea of the human being as an isolated entity.

At the end of the short story, after Gan has been impregnated with T'Gatoi's eggs, the dialogue between the two turns on what could potentially lead to a new development in the relationship between the two species. T'Gatoi insists that Terrans should be protected from the sight of Tlic "birth," which means when the grubs come to full term and, in a best-case scenario, are removed from the human host before they eat him. She says, "I had never known a Terran to see a birth and take it well. Qui [Gan's brother] has seen one, hasn't he?" (28). While Gan acknowledges that this is what has alienated his brother, he argues that Terrans should not be protected, which he doubts is possible, but instead be shown more than once when they are children: "Gatoi, no Terran ever sees a birth that goes right. All we see is . . . pain and terror and maybe death" (28-29). T'Gatoi maintains that Tlic birth is and has always been private at which point Gan stops arguing due to the tone of her voice: "that and the knowledge that if she changed her mind, I might be the first public example" (29). He knows, however, that he has "planted the thought in her mind. Chances were it would grow, and eventually she would experiment" (29). The interchange brings to mind not only Bhabha's formulations about cultural hybridity as a third space that "enables other positions to emerge" ("Third" 211), but also a passage in *The Location of Culture*: "The borderline engagements of cultural difference may as often be consensual as conflictual; they may confound our definitions of tradition and modernity; realign the customary boundaries between the private and the public, high and low; and challenge normative expectations of development and progress" (2). The depiction in "Bloodchild" of the private as political (in keeping with the feminist slogan from the 1960s: "the personal is political") also shows what Bhabha describes as "a shift of attention from the political as a pedagogical, ideological practice to politics as the stressed necessity of everyday life—politics as a performativity" (*Location* 15). T'Gatoi is a government official, a politician, and what Gan plants in her mind is potentially "a new political initiative," which is "inadequately understood through received wisdom" and which may displace the established practices around Terrans and Tlic's reproductive interaction.

Although the reproduction of one of the species is not an issue in the interaction between the two species in "Amnesty," physical interchanges certainly are. By accident, both humans and Communities discover that when a human is enfolded by a Community, both experience pleasure and comfort: "The first enfoldings happened because they were convenient ways of restraining, examining, and, unhappily, poisoning human captives. It wasn't long, though, before unoccupied humans were being enfolded just for the pleasure the act gave to an unoccupied Community" (172). Despite the Communities' inability to "understand at first that their captives could also take pleasure in the act," it is what Noah thinks about as "the perverse security and peace of being enfolded" that kept her alive during her twelve years in captivity (172). Noah explains to the group of humans that to the Communities "[w]e are one interesting and unexpected thing . . . an addictive drug" (179). After some distressed comments from the group following her statement, Noah clarifies that those Communities "who are having trouble adjusting to this world are calmed and much improved if they can enfold one of us now and then. . . . [E]nfolding one of us calms them and eases what translates as a kind of intense biological homesickness" (180). In *When Species Meet*, Haraway connects touch to world making: "Touch does not make one small; it peppers its partners with attachment sites for world making" (36). In Butler's "Amnesty," it is touch, the enfolding, that makes the world livable for both species.

As indicated, the Communities are very different from humans in every way. The story begins with a description of one of them: "The stranger-Community, globular, easily twelve feet high and wide . . . . It looked, Noah thought, a little like a great, black, moss-enshrouded bush with such a canopy of irregularly-shaped leaves, shaggy mosses, and twisted vines that no light showed through it" (149). Later Noah explains to the group of humans that "[e]ach Community contains several hundred individuals—an intelligent multitude. But that's wrong too, really. The individuals can't really survive independently, but they can leave one community and move temporarily or permanently to another" (162). Indeed, the idea of the Community in this story challenges the idea of the subject as an isolated bounded entity.

More than anything, the Community brings to mind Haraway's discussion, in the 1995 Foreword to *The Cyborg Handbook*, of *Mixotricha paradoxa* that lives in the termite's gut. She explains that *Mixotricha paradoxa* is "a nucleated microbe with five distinct kinds of internal and external prokaryotic symbionts . . . which live in various degrees of structural and functional integration with their host. About one million "individuals" of the five kinds of prokaryotes live with, on, and in the nucleated being that gets the generic name *Mixotricha*. . . . All the associated creatures live in a kind of obligate confederacy" (xviii). Hence, "[t]his little filamentous creature makes a mockery of the bounded, defended, singular self out to defend its genetic investments" (xvii). Butler's Communities do the same, but on a larger scale and in direct interaction with human beings.

## "I Loved Watching Her Move": Interspecies Regard

As should be obvious by now, communication between such different species is not depicted as easy. Lacking hearing, the Communities speak between themselves by using electrical display that humans are unable to read, and the common language that has been developed to enable humans and Communities to speak to each other is described as a "painfully created" touch and sign language (150). The Communities prefer large gestures when the human they communicate with is out of reach and "unlikely to hit or kick anyone . . ." (152). At first, Noah believed that they like the large gestures because they could not see very well, but she has subsequently learned that they actually like to watch people move: "In fact, the Communities had developed a real liking for human dance performances and for some human sports events—especially individual performances in gymnastics and ice skating" (152). In *When Species Meet*, Haraway makes a connection between embodied communication and dance: "An embodied communication is more like a dance than a word." She continues, "The flow of entangled meaningful bodies in time—whether jerky and nervous or flaming and flowing, whether both partners move in harmony or painfully out of sync or something else altogether—is communication about relationship, the relationship itself, and the means of reshaping relationship and so its enactors" (26). The tactile communication between two very different species, and one species' appreciation of the physical movements and cultural expressions of another species could perhaps be seen in Bhabha's terms of the "borderline work of culture [that] demands an encounter with 'newness' that is not part of the continuum of past and present. It creates a sense of the new as an insurgent act of cultural translation" (*Location* 7), and, as he explains elsewhere, his notion of hybridity comes from this idea of cultural translation ("Third" 211).

In "Bloodchild," verbal communication between the two species is not brought up as an issue, but physical closeness plays an important part. The Tlic like humans' body heat, which is emphasized at the beginning of the story, with Gan sipping an egg and lying against "the long, velvet underside" of T'Gatoi, who will impregnate him at the end of what he calls his "last night of childhood" (3). Gan is used to the close proximity of T'Gatoi since he has experienced it since the day he was born. Despite being an important Tlic official and in charge of the Preserve, she and Gan's mother have been friends all his mother's life, and T'Gatoi regards Gan's mother's house as "her second home" (4). As Gan explains, "She simply came in, climbed onto one of her special couches, and called me over to keep her warm. It was impossible to be formal with her while lying against her and hearing her complain as usual that I was too skinny" (4). Later on, he watches as "T'Gatoi whipped her three meters of body off her couch . . . . She had bones—ribs, a long spine, a skull, four sets of limb bones per segment. But when she moved that way, twisting, hurling herself into controlled falls, landing running, she seemed not only boneless, but aquatic—something swimming through the air as though it were water. I loved watching her move" (9). As is the case with the Communities' appreciation of human movement, species difference does not block Gan's appreciation of the way the Tlic looks and moves. Indeed, "Bloodchild" is a story of love between individuals from two different species, between Gan and T'Gatoi. It resonates with Haraway's statement in *When Species Meet*: "Significantly other to each other, in specific difference, we signify in the flesh a nasty developmental infection called love. This love is a historical aberration and a naturalcultural legacy" (16). Haraway, of course, refers to the relationship between dogs and humans, while Butler envisions a more intimate love relationship between two species that are, at the same time, more alien to each other than dogs and humans. It is also a relationship where the nonhuman species is clearly in charge and has more power than the human one.

In these two science-fiction short stories, then, Butler depicts the complexity of cultural encounters through her protagonists' interactions with both aliens and humans. These interactions involve all senses, as well as intellect and emotions, and have a variety of impacts on their bodies and their social and political surroundings. Both protagonists' sense of themselves and of others as well as of the world they live in have been shaped in close contact with another species. They demonstrate, as Haraway puts it in *When Species Meet*, that "[a]ccountability, caring for, being affected, and entering into responsibility are not ethical abstractions; these mundane, prosaic things are the result of having truck with each other. . . . Touch, regard, looking back, becoming with—all these make us responsible in unpredictable ways for which worlds take shape. . . . Touch and regard have consequences" (36). In *The Location of Culture*, Bhabha suggests that "[a]s literary creatures and political animals we ought to concern ourselves with the understanding of human action and the social world as a moment when *something is beyond control, but it is not beyond accommodation*" (12). It is such worlds, such moments, that Gan and Noah inhabit, where humans are not in control, and where survival means accommodation to another species.

To conclude, in "Bloodchild" and "Amnesty," as in so many of her other stories, Butler challenges human exceptionalism and investigates processes of hybridity and cultural translation in ways that highlight the affective and physical impact of those processes on both her human and alien characters. As I hope to have demonstrated, showing interspecies regard, in the sense of regarding theory and science-fiction stories as mutually illuminating, benefits the reader as it helps gaining a deeper understanding of the ideas presented in both kinds of texts. Thus, as a kind of "companion species" to Haraway's and Bhabha's theories, the worlds Butler creates in her short stories and novels help us imagine and rethink intercultural and interspecies relationships in our world—in the past, the present, and the future.

## Notes

**1** | *Strange Matings: Science Fiction, Feminism, African American Voices, and Octavia E. Butler* (2013) edited by Rebecca J. Holden and Nisi Shawl. It is a hybrid collection of different kinds of texts by different types of authors: novelists, poets, playwrights, fans, scholars, and others. The first book is Gregory Jerome Hampton's monograph *Changing Bodies in the Fiction of Octavia Butler: Slaves, Aliens, and Vampires* (2010). Since 2013 Florian Bast's *Of Bodies, Communities, and Voices: Agency in Writings by Octavia Butler* (2015) and Gerry Canavan's *Octavia E. Butler* (2016) have been published.

**2** | Together with Andreas Jacobsson, a colleague at Karlstad University, I am currently embarking on a project called "Science Fiction, Cultural Encounters, and Interculturality" in which we will use Butler's works as philosophically motivated sources of knowledge for rethinking cultural encounters in science fiction.

**3** | Due to my objective in this article, I will not engage with criticism on the two short stories. There are, moreover, not that many in-depth discussions of Butler's short stories. For further reading on "Amnesty," I recommend Thomas Foster's article on "Amnesty" and *Dawn* (1987), "'We Get to Live, and So Do They': Octavia Butler's Contact Zones;" and Claire P. Curtis's article on "Amnesty" and "The Book of Martha" (2003), "Theorizing Fear: Octavia Butler and the Realist Utopia." In addition to my own 2002 article on "Bloodchild," see Elyce Rae Helford's "'Would You Really Rather Die than Bear My Young?': The Construction of Gender, Race, and Species in Octavia E. Butler's 'Bloodchild,'" and Kristin Lillvis' "Mama's Baby, Papa's Slavery?: The Problem and Promise of Mothering in Octavia E. Butler's 'Bloodchild.'"

**4** | Negotiations of different kinds play important parts in Butler's works, which I have highlighted in the titles of two of my articles: "Negotiating Culture, Gender and Genre: Octavia E. Butler's 'Bloodchild'" (2002) and "Negotiating Genre and Captivity: Octavia Butler's *Survivor*" (2011). Her characters' negotiations often resonate with Bhabha's understanding of the concept: "Subversion is negotiation; transgression is negotiation; negotiation is not just some kind of compromise or 'selling out' which people too easily understand it to be" ("Third" 216). As the titles of my articles indicate, Butler captures the complexity of negotiation in her fiction on many different levels, such as character, gender relations, theme, and genre.

**5** | In *Primate Visions*, which was published at the end of the 1980s, Haraway observes that "Octavia Butler's speculative/science fiction is preoccupied with forced reproduction, unequal power, the ownership of self by another, the siblingship of humans with aliens, and the failure of siblingship within species" (378). It is interesting that Haraway also sees the relationship between humans and aliens in Butler's fiction as that between siblings.

6 | In "Aliens and Indians: A Comparison of Abduction and Captivity Narratives," Michael Sturma examines similarities between the two kinds of narratives. In "Negotiating Genre and Captivity: Octavia Butler's Survivor," I compare aspects of Butler's novel with two well-known Indian captivity narratives.

## Works Cited

Bast, Florian. *Of Bodies, Communities, and Voices: Agency in Writings by Octavia Butler.* Universitätsverlag Winter, 2015.
Bhabha, Homi. *The Location of Culture.* Routledge, 1994.
---. "Third Space: Interview with Homi Bhabha." *Identity: Community, Culture, Difference,* edited by Jonathan Rutherford. Lawrence and Wishart, 1990, pp. 207-21.
Butler, Octavia E. Afterword. *Bloodchild and Other Stories.* 2nd ed., Seven Stories Press, 2005, pp. 30-32.
---. "Amnesty." 2003. *Bloodchild and Other Stories,* pp. 147-84.
---. "Bloodchild." 1984. *Bloodchild and Other Stories,* pp. 1-29.
Canavan, Gerry. *Octavia E. Butler.* University of Illinois Press, 2016.
Curtis, Claire P. "Theorizing Fear: Octavia Butler and the Realist Utopia." *Utopian Studies,* vol. 19, no. 3, 2008, pp. 411-31.
Foster, Thomas. "'We Get to Live, and So Do They': Octavia Butler's Contact Zones." *Strange Matings: Science Fiction, Feminism, African American Voices, and Octavia E. Butler,* edited by Rebecca J. Holden and Nisi Shawl, Aqueduct Press, 2013, pp. 140-67.
Hampton, Gregory Jerome. *Changing Bodies in the Fiction of Octavia Butler: Slaves, Aliens, and Vampires.* Lexington Books, 2010.
Haraway, Donna. *Modest_Witness@Second_Millennium: FemaleMan©_Meets_ OncoMouse™: Feminism and Technoscience.* Routledge, 1997.
---. *Primate Visions: Gender, Race, and Nature in the World of Modern Science.* 1989. Verso, 1992.
---. *Simians, Cyborgs, and Women: The Reinvention of Nature.* Routledge, 1991.
---. "Species Matters, Humane Advocacy: In the Promising Grip of Earthly Oxymorons." *Species Matters,* edited by Marianne DeKoven and Michael Lundblad, Columbia University Press, 2012, pp. 17-26.
---. *When Species Meet.* University of Minnesota Press, 2008.

Helford, Elyce Rae. "'Would You Really Rather Die than Bear My Young?': The Construction of Gender, Race, and Species in Octavia E. Butler's 'Bloodchild.'" *African American Review*, vol. 28, no. 2, 1994, pp. 259-71.

Holden, Rebecca J., and Nisi Shawl, editors. *Strange Matings: Science Fiction, Feminism, African American Voices, and Octavia E. Butler*. Aqueduct Press, 2013.

Lillvis, Kristen. "Mama's Baby, Papa's Slavery?: The Problem and Promise of Mothering in Octavia E. Butler's 'Bloodchild.'" *MELUS*, vol. 39, no. 4, 2014, pp. 7-22.

Sturma, Michael. "Aliens and Indians: A Comparison of Abduction and Captivity Narratives." *Journal of Popular Culture*, vol. 36, no. 2, 2002, pp. 318-34.

Troy, Maria Holmgren. "Negotiating Culture, Gender and Genre: Octavia E. Butler's 'Bloodchild.'" *Collusion and Resistance: Women Writing in English*, edited by Kerstin Shands, Södertörns Högskola, 2002, pp. 200-09.

---. "Negotiating Genre and Captivity: Octavia Butler's *Survivor*." *Callaloo*, vol. 33, no. 4, 2010, pp. 1116-31.

# More Than Human? Dracula's Monstrosity

*Susanne Scholz*

Bram Stoker's *Dracula* (1897) has often been read as an evolutionist fantasy, showing the vampire as the superior species replacing humans at the top of the food chain (Arata; Hurley; Senf; Spencer). In the logic of Darwinian theory, this does not necessarily mean that he is more than human in any positive sense; rather, the creature which adapts better to the dismal conditions prevalent in late-nineteenth-century London is regarded as an atavistic regression, a predator successful in a struggle for existence precisely because he has no moral scruples. A monster as the superior species: this is the evolutionist nightmare *Dracula* envisages. Judith Halberstam claims that the gothic mode "produces monsters as a kind of temporary but influential response to social, political, and sexual problems" (95); so it should come as no surprise that the figure of Dracula tropes degeneration anxieties of various kinds—fears of sexual contagion, aristocratic decadence, "racial" pollution. If, as Nina Auerbach has suggested, every culture gets the monsters it deserves (1), and if the gothic is the cultural means of articulating this symptomatic shape, the high frequency with which animalistic features or mixtures of man and beast appear in nineteenth-century literature betokens, in the wake of Darwin's findings, fears of the animal within and a growing anxiety about man's position at the top of the evolutionary ladder.

Essentially, the gothic always has an anthropological point to make. In this case, it concerns the challenge to the border between man and animal, which produces imaginary monsters. Halberstam identifies hybridity as a production mode of monstrosity, thriving on the transgression of borders: between man and animal, life and death, male and female. Anxiety about the stability of boundaries is acted out, in the gothic mode, by condensing visual traits of the allegedly monstrous deviancy into one body (Halberstam 88). Animal features and the framework of evolution which positions the human animal at its apex are thus instrumental in othering threats to British (bourgeois) society in the manner of what Halberstam has called a "technology of monstrosity" (86-106). Characteristically, these monstrous mixtures of kind often occur within a scientific framework and are geared to make sense of the surface of a scientific object by classifying its visible traits. This semiotic system, however, is destabilized by the blatant unreliability of observers. Not only does every culture get the monsters it deserves, but every single spectator *sees* the monster he or she is afraid of. In the following chapter, I will investigate the animalistic imagery made use of to describe the vampire in Stoker's *Dracula* and Friedrich Wilhelm Murnau's *Nosferatu*—predator, atavistic degenerate, parasite—in order to show how the gothic mode and its technologies of monstrosity negotiate anthropological anxieties prevalent in late-nineteenth-century Britain.

## Predator: Victorian Invasion Anxieties

In the case of *Dracula*, the vampiric object of investigation seems to move through different frames of perception. In the radically multiperspectival narrative of the novel, every observer renders his or her own account of Dracula's monstrosity, producing various and often incompatible versions which are coordinated and made coherent through the editorial efforts of Mina Harker. She thus intradiegetically provides a chronology of events that helps track down the vampire while extradiegetically producing the text of the novel we read.

The first encounter with the count takes place in Transylvania, where Jonathan Harker has travelled in order to validate a contract for a house in London. In tune with the premodern setting of the Transylvanian castle and the clash of cultures which Harker's diary elaborates on, he fears Dracula as a blood-sucking remnant from a long-buried, archaic past, and his proposed move to London as a threat of invasion by demonic forces:

then I saw something that filled my very soul with horror: There lay the Count, but looking as if his youth had been half renewed, for the white hair and moustache were changed to dark iron-grey; the cheeks were fuller, and the white skin seemed ruby-red underneath; the mouth was redder than ever, for on the lips were gouts of fresh blood which trickled from the corners of the mouth and ran over the chin and neck. Even the deep, burning eyes seemed set amongst swollen flesh, for the lids and pouches underneath were bloated. It seemed as if the whole awful creature were simply gorged with blood; he lay like a filthy leech, exhausted with his repletion. . . . This was the being I was helping to transfer to London, where, perhaps for centuries to come he might, amongst its teeming millions, satiate its lust for blood, and create a new and ever-widening circle of semi-demons to batten on the helpless. (Stoker 59-60)

Jonathan's renditions of Dracula's monstrosity draw on boundary transgressions from a moral or even religious rather than a scientific register. Being situated outside the frame of his modern, enlightened England, he accepts "truths" that are impossible at home: that phantoms, ghosts, and demons exist, that men can dematerialize or move like lizards. Harker's journal moves into the romance mode as soon as he has crossed the Danube and thus left his European frame of reference, but by trying to see things through the eyes of his implicit addressee Mina, he manages to reflect on the strangeness of what surrounds him.

Jonathan's journal provides the only direct relation of Dracula's own version of his story. Although inflected by Jonathan's feelings of alienation vis-à-vis the archaic customs and primitive manners in this country beyond the forests, he strives to faithfully record the count's self-narrative. When Dracula boasts to him about his Boyar ancestry, the count voices some of the worst fears besetting Victorians at the end of the nineteenth century:

We Szekely have a right to be proud, for in our veins flows the blood of many brave races who fought as the lion fights, for lordship. Here, in the whirlpool of European races, the Ugric tribe bore down from Iceland the fighting spirit which Thor and Wodin gave them, which their Berserkers displayed to such fell intent on the seaboards of Europe, ay, and of Asia and Africa too, till the peoples thought that they were the werewolves themselves had come. Here too when they came they found the Huns, whose warlike fury had swept the earth like a living flame; till the dying peoples held that in their veins ran the blood of those old witches, who, expelled from Scythia had mated with the devils in the desert. Fools, fools! What devil or what witch was ever so great as Attila whose blood is in these veins?' He held up his arms. 'Is it a wonder we were a conquering race.' (Stoker 35-36)

Dracula here clusters together all the warlike races which history and mythology imagine as threatening European civilization: Vikings and Berserkers from the North, Huns, Scythians, Amazons from the East and South, all of them creatures which are traditionally described as dreadful mixtures of human and beast. Without alluding to his own animality, which is repeatedly pointed out by Jonathan Harker (29), Dracula proudly locates the ancestral agency, which conquered all these beastly threats in his blood, and figures this blood as the fountain of his aristocratic sense of entitlement and superiority. Harker comments on this with a mixture of admiration and anxiety: "Whenever he spoke of his house he always said 'we,' and spoke almost in the plural, like a king speaking. I wish I could put down all he said exactly as he said it, for to me it was most fascinating. It seemed to have in it the whole history of the country" (35).

Here, as elsewhere in the story, Jonathan Harker figures as the average middle-class Victorian, whose hopes for bourgeois domestic contentment lie in fending off the dangers incorporated in Dracula. What Victorian readers and modern viewers tend to forget, however, is that the warrior hero of these stories was a fighter against the Turks, a bulwark at the outer borders of Christendom. His enemies were Muslims and the spectacle of impaled bodies that film versions of the novel so elaborately stage speaks of anti-Islamic violence.

In the light of late-nineteenth-century worries about the Ottoman empire, he is thus an ally rather than an enemy. The novel, however, stages him as a monstrous transgressor, a mad mixture of rabid animal and demonic invader, threatening European integrity from the East. In this political frame of reference, the danger embodied in Dracula refers to a festering political conflict with the Ottoman Empire, which had implicated Britain ever since the Crimean War of the 1850s. Eleni Coundourotis places *Dracula* in the context of the British debates about Turkish atrocities in Bulgaria in 1876 (149-50). Britain had until the mid 1870s been traditionally pro-Ottoman because it saw in the Ottoman Empire an important bulwark against Russia's ascendancy and it had significant economic interests in Turkey. After the Bulgarian massacre, public opinion turned, and the Ottomans were again seen as a danger but also, in the melange of symbolic and realist representations so characteristic of orientalist discourse, as the ultimate menace to Western civilization, pictured in charges of monstrosity, excessive violence, and autocratic rule: "Wherever they went, a broad line of blood marked the track behind them; and, as far as their dominion reached, civilization disappeared from view. They represented everywhere government by force, as opposed to government by law . . . . This advancing curse menaced the whole of Europe" (Gladstone 13).

In the novel, however, it is the violence against these enemies of Christendom that turns excessive, marking out Dracula as some kind of borderline figure, fighting for Christendom but violating its basic rules of peacefulness—necessary but shunned. The novel never explains how Dracula turned from a human warrior into a vampire, how he became a *Nosferatu*, an Undead, a creature of the night. Prequels in various film versions link this transformation to the bloody fight against the Ottomans, sometimes inserting a love interest, often imagining some kind of sacrilege against the Eucharist. Thus they link the Christological meanings of sacrificial blood and everlasting life in a dark savior figure that turns into an Anti-Christ whose blood, like that of Christ in the Eucharist, bequeaths perpetual life (Mulvey-Roberts 132).

Dracula obviously sees his blood as the physical bearer of his martial prowess. At the same time, he feels that he has reached the end of a time when blood signified honor and valor: "The warlike days are over. Blood is too precious a thing in these days of dishonorable peace; and the glories of the great races are as a tale that is told" (Stoker 37). Since the world has changed, Dracula must change with it, follow the trail of civilization and adapt to its new functional logic (as indicated in his preoccupation with maps, the Baedeker, Bradshaw's guide, Whitaker's almanac, law lists and other products of bureaucratic modern Britain).

After centuries in which this exceptional creature has lurked in the dark recesses of Transylvania, the backyard of Europe, Dracula has come to a point in his own story where he has to leave his Transylvanian comfort zone and develop new feeding ground elsewhere. His long-planned effort to remove to London speaks of a deeper understanding of historical and cultural value changes in Europe on the part of the count. Interestingly, however, his immersion in the new modern logic of the West holds on to an old signifier of his power. What the novel stages, on an ideological level, is a re-coding of the symbolic value of blood as the count moves from the East to the West, from a sign of valor in a heroic, aristocratic paradigm to a signifier of "racial" and sexual purity in a scientific logic. While blue blood turns to bad blood, the predator image remains: Dracula's warlike transgression transforms into a subtler form of attack as he moves West, from combat to contagion. His planned invasion of England is thus essentially both a biological and a political one.

## Degenerate, Atavistic Alien, Undead

Many of Stoker's works feature returns from a distant past (*The Snake's Pass, The Mystery of the Sea, The Jewel of Seven Stars, The Lair of the White Worm,* and of course *Dracula*), suggesting a preoccupation with history, deep time, and the alleged aging of the world, but also with concerns more close to home and to the Victorian subject, such as the return of the repressed, archaic or racial atavisms or the revenge of the evolutionary throwback. Almost all of his other works share with *Dracula* the sense of impending danger which needs to be staved off by a joining of the forces of civilization, usually in the form of Christian masculinity. Lisa Hopkins even makes the point that "there is a sense in which he wrote *Dracula* many times over and called it a variety of different things" (1).

Although the figure of the undead or the vampire has existed for a long time in (not only) eastern European folk lore, Stoker's inclusion of the creature in an evolutionary logic of species development seems to make it more threatening in one sense, but also more containable. This results in a transfer of the creature from the order of unspeakable monster or sacrilegious transgressor to the classificatory order of science which makes sense of its "aberrations" (feeding habits, reproduction, preferred habitat and climate, nocturnal activities, etc.) in the light of a zoological logic. Given the predominance of evolution theory as an explanatory model for biological as well as social transformation phenomena throughout the second half of the nineteenth century, it comes as no surprise that the border that the creature Dracula transgresses is envisaged as a species border. All the animal characteristics that Harker has described, the "blazing eyes," the "long, sharp canine teeth" (33, 29) suggest that he is somewhere lower down in the evolutionary scale than his modern pursuers. At the same time, his shape-shifting capacities and his extended life span, which allows him to learn the languages, manners, and mores of his host country, make him conspicuously more adaptable to changing circumstances and thus a contender for the highest rank of the species hierarchy. In the eyes of his adversaries in London, he is a threat not because he has fallen from God's grace but because he might supersede the human animal at the top of the food chain. While he figured as a great warrior and threateningly eerie aristocrat in the romance-cum-travel narrative written down by Jonathan Harker, Dracula is re-fashioned as an atavistic return and consequently rendered in terms of animality and abjection as soon as he enters the perceptive frame of Western Europeans. While he appears to be a human being, he also displays traces of the beast. This hybrid creature, however, not only transgresses the borders between man and animal but, as Van Helsing finds out later, also that between living and dead (Stoker 252-56). In the eyes of his pursuers, he is thus at the same time more and less than human, less than a subject and more than an object: "The abhuman subject is a not-quite-human subject, characterized by its morphic variability, continually in danger of becoming not-itself, becoming other" (Hurley 3-4). The gothic text here produces a version of mankind's dark other, and whatever the monster looks like, it is intimately bound up with the self-image of the human.

Not only is Dracula's effort to find new feeding ground in London represented in evolutionary terms, his looks and his behavior are also perceived through an evolutionary lens. In the multiperspectival narrative of the novel, it is not only the two doctors, John Seward and Abraham Van Helsing, who classify the count in evolutionary terms, but also the representatives of the Victorian bourgeoisie, Jonathan and Mina Harker, whose physiognomic readings of Dracula contribute largely to the readers' perception of the count's evil nature:

His face was a strong—a very strong—aquiline, with high bridge of the thin nose and peculiarly arched nostrils; with lofty domed forehead, and hair growing scantily round the temples, but profusely elsewhere. His eyebrows were very massive, almost meeting over the nose, and with bushy hair that seemed to curl in its own profusion. The mouth, so far as I could see it under the heavy moustache, was fixed and rather cruel-looking, with peculiarly sharp white teeth; these protruded over the lips, whose remarkable ruddiness showed astonishing vitality in a man of his years. For the rest, the ears were pale and at the tops extremely pointed; the chin was broad and strong, and the cheeks firm though thin. The general effect was one of extraordinary pallor. (Stoker 24-25)

Jonathan Harker here reads Dracula's face as a medium of his inner disposition but he is unable to interpret what he sees in any sensible way. He also comments on further signs of animality: "there were hairs in the centre of the palm" (25). Obviously, this is not a human being but a monster which feeds on blood, leaves no mirror image and keeps Jonathan captive in a strange place. Maybe the shock of realization vis-à-vis this abject creature is too great, in any case, all Jonathan can convey is his somatic reaction to what he sees: "a horrible feeling of nausea came over me" (25). This first physiognomic vision of Dracula, written while Harker is still in Transylvania, foregrounds the subjective nature of these descriptions, which strive to remain factual, but never manage to just render what is seen. It almost suggests that Jonathan's nausea brings forth the animality described so vividly, just as Mina's physiognomic gaze seems to produce the evil face she sees when they encounter the rejuvenated count in London: "[Jonathan] gazed at a tall, thin man, with a beaky nose and black moustache and pointed beard.... His face was not a good face; it was hard, and cruel, and sensual, and his big white teeth, that looked all the whiter because his lips were so red, were pointed like an animal's" (183).

Mina clearly reads the face as a character chart, every facial feature is commented on by a value judgement which inserts what is seen into a classificatory scheme which deduces moral interpretations from facial features ("hard, ... cruel, ... sensual"). While the description relies on the orientation physiognomic knowledge promises to provide in the urban jungle, the novel's technique of displaying the unreliability of its narrators suggests that marks of degeneration always lie in the eyes of the beholders. For modern, scientifically minded, Britons, evolution and its dark side, degeneration, seem to be the only patterns in which the figure of Dracula makes sense.

Physiognomic readings in the nineteenth century almost invariably lead to ethnic classifications, so many scholars have commented on the Jewish features in Dracula's face. Especially his nose seems to fulfil all the expectations for a Jewish nose, due to its "beakiness" (Stoker 138) or "strong aquiline" (Halberstam 91-93; Mulvey-Richards 132-40; Karschay 127, 257; Fischer 29-47). He also displays the specific "nostrility" that is attributed to the Jewish nose in domestic ethnographies of the time, such as, for example, Joseph Jacob's entry for "nose" in the *Jewish Encyclopedia* of 1906 (see also Fischer; Dornhofer). Dracula's "peculiarly arched nostrils" (Stoker 24) are commented on early in Jonathan's description, and again later, where they appear in a rather menacing way—like a dragon blazing fire—to the Crew of Light: "the great nostrils of the aquiline nose opened wide and quivered at the edge" (Stoker 300-01). Pascal Fischer has argued that the facial signifier of the aquiline nose can signify both Jewishness and aristocratic descent. In both cases, it is deployed here as a sign of alien extraction or foreign influence, a means of othering the count, as William Hughes suggests, "All are signifiers in a discourse which constructs a perceived cultural or racial Other as both degenerate and potentially infectious" (94).

Dracula's red eyes have also been identified as, variously, markers of his Jewishness and his animality or even devilishness. Mulvey-Roberts comments on red-eyed Jews in English literature and establishes a symbolic link with the notion of the Evil Eye: "The eye of the Jew has been stigmatized as red, mesmeric and demonic through its association with the Evil Eye, a superstition that is referred to in Dracula and used in traditional depictions of the devil, an embodiment of evil that was also associated with Jews" (134). For Lucy, Dracula's red eyes are a means of hypnotic control (Stoker 104-05), while for the four men fighting against Dracula in Carfax, they signify his satanic powers. Harker earlier comments on "the red light of triumph in his eyes" accompanying "a smile that Judas in hell might be proud of" (58). Along the lines of well-worn "racial" stereotypes, the text here conflates the paradigmatic ethnic Other (the Wandering Jew) with a vision of evil, thus again drawing on a mixture of scientific and symbolic frames of reference.

Halberstam points out that, in the light of Victorian degeneration anxiety, monstrosity in late-nineteenth-century gothic is represented "as a mixture of bad blood, unstable gender identity, sexual and economic parasitism, and degeneracy" (91). All of these, it should be added, are represented in animal imagery, which serves to mark off the respective bearers of these traits as threatening "others" which need to be contained, or, even better, excluded. In the specific scientific mindset of the late nineteenth century, with evolution theory serving as the dominant model to describe social and physical difference in terms of development and progress, fundamental otherness is frequently imagined as species difference. As the narrative proceeds, however, it becomes clear that these scientific efforts to capture Dracula in the net of zoological classification do not suffice to contain him.

As the two doctors fashion the evidence against Dracula into a case narrative, more degeneration markers emerge. Van Helsing and Mina make use of the findings of criminal anthropology (another technique of capture drawing on animalistic features) to classify Dracula, but also to predict his next moves in order to hunt him down. "The Count is a criminal and of criminal type. Nordau and Lombroso would so classify him" (Stoker 362). Again, it is Mina's gaze and common knowledge which bring up these classificatory patterns. In *Criminal Man*, Lombroso identifies bushy eyebrows as signs of a thievish disposition and a beaky nose and pronounced canines as signs of a murderer: "[thieves] are notable for their thick and close eyebrows," and "the nose [of the habitual murderer] is often hawklike and always large; the jaw is strong, the cheekbones broad; and their hair is dark, abundant, and crisply textured. Their beards are scanty, their canine teeth very developed, and their lips thin" (51). Darwin also identifies projecting canines as an atavistic remnant (41). Henry Havelock Ellis's description of the face of the "born criminal" draws on similar features:

> The eye of the habitual homicide is glassy, cold, and fixed; his nose is often aquiline, beaked, reminding one of a bird of prey, always voluminous; the jaws are strong; the ears long; the cheek-bones large; the hair dark, curling, abundant; the beard often thin;

the canine teeth much developed; the lips thin; nystagmus frequent; also spasmodic contractions on one side of the face, by which the canine teeth are exposed. (90)

While these animal signs in Dracula's face suggest a reading based on a semiotic system developed by ethnology and criminal anthropology, there is maybe an alternative (or additional) way of making sense of them, one harking back to an earlier version of physiognomics. In his *De humana physiognomia* (1597), Giambattista Della Porta pursues a zoological approach by discovering typical analogies between animal characteristics and human faces and giving them moralistic readings: a "foxy" face signifies cunning, for instance (Baumbach 36-38). Dracula's hawk-like nose and the wolfish eyes might thus be seen as remnants of older forms of physiognomic knowledge, but what is more interesting is that they are literalized in the supernatural qualities of the count, for example in his ability to change into animal shapes. In Transylvania, he appears in the form of wolves before he is even met in human shape by Jonathan Harker. He crawls down the wall like a lizard and feeds like a leech; later in England he leaves the ship in the shape of a great wolf dog and reappears in the form of a myriad of rats disturbing the Crew of Light who are in search of Dracula's lair. The rats' as well as the wolf's red eyes are commented on; Coppola's film version elaborates on this by match cuts which turn the bite holes on Lucy's neck into the wolf's red eyes (00:51:07-10). His most iconic animal apparition is of course the bat, whose bad press as a satanic creature reaches back as far as Aesop's fables, and whose leathery wings have appeared throughout the Middle Ages as attributes of *Frau Welt* and other allegories of sin, the devil and the dragon, which is, as Steinborn points out, a large snake with bat wings (Steinborn 231-39; Daly 257, 305). A coiled dragon is also the heraldic sign of Dracula's historical model, Vlad Tepes (Mulvey-Richards 139).

What these animals have in common is that they are predators—they assimilate easily to changing circumstances, they are creatures of the night, and they allegedly feed on blood. In the fantastic storytelling of the novel, they not only metaphorically stand for qualities attributed to the count, but they are the count's operating shape in certain situations, usually of danger, where they literalize his alleged animal characteristics. Turning figurative into literal meanings is one of the characteristic features of the fantastic mode, thus enhancing the respective figure with superhuman capacities which even increase the danger emanating from it—not least because it thus gains a head start in the race for the top position on the evolutionary ladder. Obviously, in the symbolic hierarchy of the animal kingdom, these are never noble animals: wolf, bat, leech, and rat are evil creatures by moral standards, and (maybe with the exception of the wolf) parasites from the more modern perspective of urban hygiene and public health.

As Dracula moves through the various perceptive frames provided by the different observers and narrative modes of the novel, his monstrosity gets overwritten and new layers are added with every stage. While he figures as a blood-sucking demon in Jonathan's Transylvanian romance and as ruthless invader and menace from the East in a political context, he is predominantly seen as an atavistic return, a more animalistic version of man, or a new species striving to dethrone man at the top of the food chain as soon as he has entered the perceptual frame of the West. At the same time, as the narrative proceeds, it becomes obvious that scientific methods of containing the beast by producing more and more scientific knowledge about it will not suffice. Both the creature and the methods of capture get ever more hybrid, mixing symbolic and scientific registers. Only when premodern techniques of defense such as garlic, the cross, holy water, and the consecrated host come into play can the vampire count be defeated. This includes an acknowledgment of his position as warrior, aristocrat, and feudal lord, as well as the recognition that supernatural powers defying scientific logic do indeed exist. It is Van Helsing, the non-British, Catholic, "Renaissance Man"-type of scientist—himself a hybrid of sorts, who is capable of integrating the different strands of knowledge and act on them.

While Dracula's face and shape seem to be made up of the characteristics of different animals, they always remain those of a human being. Whether this is a signal of his extreme dangerousness because his hunters deal with a case of perfect mimicry, or whether it is a sign that he ultimately remains a human being—as the restoration of his soul in his death scene suggests—remains unresolved. This fundamental humanity of the count seems abandoned in Friedrich Wilhelm Murnau's film version of the novel, *Nosferatu*, whose visual representation plays much more on the alleged hybridity of satanic creatures (Steinborn 237-39), between human and animal, dead and undead.

### Parasite: Murnau's *Nosferatu: A Symphony of Horror* (1922)

Friedrich Wilhelm Murnau's 1922 silent film version of *Dracula*, while adopting the basic narrative lines of Stoker's novel, invests its central figure with animal features which hark back to more ancient taxonomies. Providing an actualization of Stoker's Victorian novel in Weimar Germany, it fashions the vampire count as a parasitic force infiltrating the social body of the fictive Northern German city of Wisborg. It largely abandons the scientific framing of the quest and the united efforts of the professional men to hunt down the menace, and foregrounds the triangular relation of Hutter, his wife Ellen and Count Orlok, the eponymous *Nosferatu*. In Murnau's version of the threat of contagion coming via ship from the East, there is no heroic Crew of Light willing to defend the social body at all costs. Ellen is the sole opponent conscious of the impending danger, and her feat of defending Wisborg is accomplished not by positive action but through sacrifice. Murnau here changes some of the basic constellations of the novel—modern science versus pre-modern magic, feudal reign versus the modern nation (figured in the "band of brothers" fighting for the good cause)—and puts the burden of blame on the greedy estate broker Knock (played by the well-known Jewish actor Alexander Granach), while the task of salvation rests with the quasi-virginal Ellen. Clearly introduced as Hutter's wife by the intertitles, the relationship is represented as childish and somewhat asexual, so that Ellen qualifies as the "woman with a pure heart" mentioned in the *Book of Vampyres*, who must sacrifice herself in order to rid the world of the monster.

A title card quoting from the *Book of Vampyres* that natives have provided Hutter with, claims that Nosferatu springs "from the seeds of Belial" and "liveth and feedeth on human bloode. This unholy creature liveth in sinister caves, tombes and coffins which are filled with cursed dirt from the fields of the Black Death" (*Nosferatu* 00:17:05). Consequently, the film's representation of the vampire draws on premodern animal symbolism (to be found, for example, in medieval bestiaries) which the expressionist film visualizes in an almost allegorical way. In contrast to Dracula, he is not prepared (or unable) to adapt to Wisborg society and infiltrate it via courting its women and subverting its moral codes. Rather, he enters Wisborg with a pack of rats bringing the plague to the city. "His clawlike fingers, hairless cranium, bat-like ears and pointed front teeth resemble a rodent" (Mulvey-Roberts 140); he is, as it were, the prime rat, the paradigmatic parasite bringing death to the city. "The implications of Orlok's physiognomy," Mulvey-Roberts continues, "bear the unmistakable mark of the Jew, especially since the actor Max Schreck wore a prosthetic to achieve an exaggerated hooked nose" (Mulvey-Roberts 140). The association of Jew and parasitic bringer of illness is thus made via the animalistic rat-like features of Orlok. It draws on a long-established defamation of Jews as social parasites feeding on the bodies of their host countries, draining them of vital energy and weakening the social corporation (Kaes 112).

In the context of the political debates and anxieties in Weimar Germany, the strong anti-Semitic associations of the figure of Count Orlok come as no surprise. Artur Dinter sets the tone when he exhorts the German people "to throw off and exterminate the Jewish vampire which it nursed with its heart's blood" (Dinter, qtd. in Kaes 112). In *Nosferatu*, the diatribe on the infiltrating, corrupting, maybe hypnotic and remote-controlling power of Jews in German culture was acted out in the form of invasion horror, and while the film itself remains ambivalent (after all, both the script writer Henrik Galeen and one of the main actors, Alexander Granach, were Jews), the visual reservoir it mobilizes ran riot in the film industry of the later 1920s as well as in cultural discourse as a whole (Kaes 108-13; Mulvey-Roberts 129-78).

Within the film narrative, Orlok is never even recognized as a danger by the populace of Wisborg, his destruction falls to Ellen alone. The expulsion of the (Jewish) scapegoat from the community, however, is exemplarily exercised with the figure of Knock, Orlok's local contact in Wisborg, who, having gone mad with the advent of the count and committed to an asylum, where he lives on flies, is blamed for the arrival of the plague and has to flee the wrath of an enraged mob.

While they are cast as predators in the evolutionary logic of the day, Dracula's and Nosferatu's *modus operandi* is in fact parasitic: they effect a transformation from within, a visible change of the (often female) host which leads to a weakening of the social body through infiltration and infection. Blood functions as an agent and a symbol for this corruption, suggesting a foreign agency weakening the vital power (or purity) from within. Parasitism, as Ross G. Forman has shown, is a very versatile signifier, allowing for a semantic spectrum that covers issues of political influence as well as infectious attacks on the individual and the social body. The relationship of parasite and host is often imagined as almost symbiotic, and it transforms the host body (or personality) from within. "The parasite, in short, not only resides within the body, but also alters its relationship to the world" (Forman 925). Orlok's attempts to seduce Ellen establish a symbolic link between the pure female body and the social corporation, which is also made explicit by Dracula: "Your girls that you all love are mine already; and through them you and others shall yet be mine" (Stoker 326). Just as Dracula transforms Lucy into a sexual predator and thus changes her relationship to her fiancé and the group of men setting out to rescue her, Orlok's choice of Ellen as a victim and her willingness to sacrifice herself cast her as a representative for the whole of the social body that is threatened by pollution, miscegenation, and disintegration.

## Conclusion: Gothic Anthropology

Animal lore and the relation between man and beast have always been a fertile ground for technologies of monstrosity; yet under the specific scientific conditions of the nineteenth century, man himself turns into an animal, albeit (ideally) a morally and socially refined one. This epistemological shift troubles cultural discourse immensely and spawns a myriad of hybrids: werewolves, ape-men, snake-women and others. In contrast to those more obviously chimeric formations, the anthropological projection figure of the vampire makes use of a parasitic mode: the hybridity of the creature is not immediately visible from the outside; for all practical purposes, he moves through society like a human being. Both Stoker and Murnau use the figure of the vampire in order to articulate anxiety about the vulnerability of the social body prone to attacks from blood-sucking aristocrats, greedy capitalists, (Jewish and other) migrants and invaders from the East. Mapping the individual body onto the social structure, the vampire's attack brings pollution, contagion, and ultimately dissolution to the pure body of the community. It does so by corrupting the social body and its individual members, turning them into power-hungry, greedy or over-sexualized predators eating up the social structure from within. Like most cultural productions in the fantastic mode, vampire fantasies unfold a black anthropology, submitting the human and his/her body to transformations that test their integrity and throw into relief what it means to be human. Both Dracula and Nosferatu posit the readiness of virtuous humans to sacrifice themselves for the good of the community against the selfishness of the predator. Their anthropological utopia thus dreams up a moral community of social animals that vanquish the monstrous Hobbesian wolf.

## Works Cited

Arata, Stephen. *Fictions of Loss in the Victorian Fin de Siècle*. Cambridge University Press, 1996.
Auerbach, Nina. *Our Vampires, Ourselves*. Chicago University Press, 1995.
Baumbach, Sibylle. *Shakespeare and the Art of Physiognomy*. Humanities E-Books, 2008.
*Bram Stoker's Dracula*. Directed by Francis Ford Coppola. Columbia Pictures, 1992.
Coundourotis, Eleni. "Dracula and the Idea of Europe." *Connotations*, vol. 9, no. 2, 2000/2001, pp. 143-59.
Daly, Lloyd W. *Aesop without Morals: The Famous Fables, and A Life of Aesop*. Yoseloff, 1961.
Darwin, Charles. *The Descent of Man*. Gibson Square Books, 2003.
Della Porta, Giambattista. *De humana physiognomonia*. Sutorius, 1601.
Dornhofer, Daniel. "Palestine Reclaimed: Rassekunde und Zionismus unter dem Eindruck des Ersten Weltkriegs." *Transversal: Zeitschrift für Jüdische Studien*, vol. 2, 2013, pp. 59-75.
Ellis, Henry Havelock. *The Criminal*. Patterson Smith, 1973.
Fischer, Pascal. "Die gebogene Nase: Bedeutungszuschreibungen von Matthew Lewis' *The Monk* bis Bram Stokers *Dracula*." *AAA: Arbeiten aus Anglistik und Amerikanistik*, vol. 37, no. 1, 2012, pp. 29–47.
Forman, Ross G. "A Parasite for Sore Eyes: Rereading Infection Metaphors in Bram Stoker's *Dracula*." *Victorian Literature and Culture*, vol. 44, 2016, pp. 925-47.
Gladstone, William Ewart. *Bulgarian Horrors and the Question of the East*. John Murray, 1876.

Halberstam, Judith. *Skin Show: Gothic Horror and the Technology of Monsters.* Duke University Press, 1995.

Hopkins, Lisa. *Bram Stoker: A Literary Life.* Palgrave Macmillan, 2007.

Hughes, William. "Terrors that I Dare Not Think Of": Masculinity, Hysteria and Empiricism in Stoker's *Dracula.*" *Dracula: The Shade and the Shadow: Papers Presented at "Dracula 97," a Centenary Celebration at Los Angeles, August 1997,* edited by Elizabeth Miller, Desert Island Books, 1998, pp. 93-103.

Hurley, Kelly. *The Gothic Body: Sexuality, Materialism and Degeneration at the Fin de Siècle.* Cambridge University Press, 1996.

Jacobs, Joseph, and Maurice Fishberg. "Nose." *Jewish Encyclopedia: The Unedited Full-Text of the 1906 Jewish Encyclopedia.* jewishencyclopedia.com/articles/11598-nose. Accessed 11 May 2018.

Kaes, Anton. *Shell Shock Cinema: Weimar Culture and the Wounds of War.* Princeton University Press, 2009.

Karschay, Stephen. *Degeneration, Normativity and the Gothic at the Fin de Siècle.* Palgrave Macmillan, 2015.

Lombroso, Cesare. *Criminal Man.* 1876. Edited and translated by Mary Gibson and Nicole Hahn Rafter, Duke University Press, 2006.

Mulvey-Roberts, Marie. *Dangerous Bodies.* Manchester University Press, 2016.

*Nosferatu, eine Symphonie des Grauens / Nosferatu: A Symphony of Horror.* Directed by Friedrich Wilhelm Murnau. Prana Film, 1922.

Senf, Carol A. *Science and Social Science in Bram Stoker.* Greenwood Press, 2002.

Spencer, Kathleen. "Purity and Danger: *Dracula,* the Urban Gothic, and the Late-Victorian Degeneracy Crisis." *ELH,* vol. 59, 1992, pp. 197-225.

Steinborn, Anke. "Nosferatu: Ein expressionistisches Bewegtbild-Bestiarium." *Komparatistik Online,* vol. 20, 2013, pp. 229-43.

Stoker, Bram. *Dracula.* 1897. Edited by Maurice Hindle, Penguin, 2003.

# "Revealing the Wellsprings of Power":
# An Essay on the Social Function of Humor in
# "The Wonderful Tar-Baby Story"

*Christa Buschendorf*

Animals in fables often serve as masks that allow discussions of such sensitive topics as power relations in society. African American folk tales reflect the stark power differential that exists between master and slave within the institution of slavery. Circulating among slaves, the tales created a counter world in which the weaker animal—if only temporarily—is shown to outwit the physically stronger one. Many of the African American animal stories have come down to us in the written version of Joel Chandler Harris, a white southern journalist who started collecting them when, as a youth, he worked as a printer's devil for Joseph Addison Turner, editor of the weekly newspaper the *Countryman*, on Turnwold Plantation near Milledgeville, Georgia, between 1862 and 1866. A few tales appeared in the Atlanta *Constitution* in the late 1870s, and as they received considerable attention, Harris decided to publish the first collection of the so-called Uncle Remus tales in 1880. It was above all the narrative frame that turned *Uncle Remus: His Songs and His Sayings* into one of the most popular and eventually one of the most controversial literary anthologies ever produced in the United States. Harris created the constellation of the old storyteller Remus, an ex-slave who after emancipation stayed on the plantation of his former master, and the young son of the family, who would eagerly listen to the black man's fables about "Brer Rabbit" and "Brer Fox" (to name but the two most prominent animals). Apart from the lively debate among folklorists on how much these tales owed to the rich tradition of African animal fables, controversy centered on the author of the collection, on the character of Remus, and on the relation between frame and animal stories. There were (mostly white southern) readers who readily shared in what they considered Harris's nostalgia for the Old South, and there were (mostly black) readers who criticized what they regarded as Harris's paternalism, if not blatant racism. While some saw the figure of "Uncle Remus" as the incarnation of the wisdom of black humor, others saw in him the embodiment of the stereotype of the "happy darky" of nineteenth-century minstrelsy. Some argued that one could read the frame independently from the animal tales; others maintained that the two levels were closely interrelated and that the frame stressing the harmonious communication between the former slave and the slave-holder's grandchild not only contributed to the romanticization of slavery and race relations after the era of Reconstruction, but also necessarily corrupted the subversive message of the animal tales. The emasculated narrator, they claimed, toned down the belligerent spirit of the tales, and the innocuous humor of the frame offset the liberating force of the tales' aggressive wit. In contrast to the late-nineteenth-century popularity of the Uncle Remus tales (in the first year of its publication, *Uncle Remus: His Songs and His Sayings* went through four editions), in the twentieth century many Americans became familiar with Remus and the characters of the animal stories through the commercially successful, highly distorted, genuinely racist version of the 1946 Walt Disney film *Story of the South* and its various releases.

Whereas the general public's interest in the Uncle Remus tales has diminished, scholarship has renewed its efforts of interpretation since the late twentieth century and has produced valuable criticism that transcends the dichotomies mentioned above. Biographical studies of Harris's life and letters paint a much more complex portrait of the author, highlighting his critique both of modernism and of southern racism. The understanding of the figure of Remus has undergone radical change as his character is also granted more complexity. And the relation between narrative frame and animal stories has been declared more complicated on the basis of the observation that the presence of the trickster is not limited to the animal stories. Thus, Uncle Remus's benignity is recognized as a mask behind which lurks a sophisticated trickster outsmarting his audience just as successfully as Brer Rabbit outwits his adversaries. In addition, the author himself has been said to act like a subversive trickster by undermining what at first sight might appear as an idealized image of southern society before and after the Civil War. Consequently, Harris's often-quoted statement from the introduction of the *Complete Tales* that Remus "had nothing but pleasant memories of the discipline of slavery" should be read together with allusions to his suffering under slavery and the harsh living conditions in the Jim Crow South. Likewise, Harris's portrayal of Remus as an amiable, simple-minded old man must be supplemented by his depiction as a shrewd and manipulating individual, characteristics he, like Brer Rabbit, needs in order to survive under the conditions of poverty. Yet, if we accept that Remus's character is more ambivalent than readers of the nineteenth century had assumed, then we must be prepared to reassess his humor as well.

The fact that the animals in the Uncle Remus tales are addressed as "Mr." or "Brer" indicates that they are anthropomorphized. Moreover, as I will argue, the storytelling focuses less on anthropological themes than on social issues. At the same time, the stories often take up common structural patterns of African animal tales, such as the type of the trickster out-tricked. Once in a while, the fables insist, even the smartest trickster-hero is outwitted. So is Brer Rabbit in one of the most popular and most frequently anthologized of the Uncle Remus tales, "The Wonderful Tar-Baby Story." It answers to the probing question of the little boy whether Brer Fox ever managed to catch Brer Rabbit, to which Uncle Remus replies that Brer Fox came mighty close one day. The more intriguing questions the story itself poses are, first, what makes Brer Fox's trap so efficient that Brer Rabbit is caught in it, and, secondly, what are the mechanisms of humor that make this episode especially successful?

Brer Fox, who in the previous story was outmaneuvered by Brer Rabbit, is determined to catch him this time, and out of tar and turpentine he fabricates a contraption he calls "Tar-Baby," places the doll in the middle of the road and hides nearby to see what will happen. Brer Rabbit approaches full of self-confidence, onomatopoetically revealing his "sassy" trickster self in the buoyant sound of his gait: "lippity-clippity, clippity-lippity" (*Uncle Remus* 7). Upon discovering Tar-Baby, he stops immediately and in an explicit reference to his animal shape is said to sit on his hind-legs, a posture expressing both caution and curiosity with regard to the unknown figure before him. Then he politely addresses the stranger with a friendly greeting and a conventional remark about the fine weather, and when he does not receive an answer extends the salutation by politely inquiring about Tar-Baby's health, once more to no avail. In his third attempt to make conversation, Brer Rabbit suggests he could talk louder in case Tar-Baby was deaf. His patience diminishing, Brer Rabbit next changes to an admonishing tone, then he threatens, and finally, carried away by anger, he starts hitting Tar-Baby—and gets stuck. He demands that Tar-Baby let him loose, but only gets ever more glued to her as he is threatening and hitting more aggressively. When even Brer Rabbit's head gets stuck, Brer Fox comes out of hiding, laughs excessively and finally, in allusion to the foregoing episode, invites him to dinner again, assuring him that this time, he will take no excuse from Brer Rabbit. At this moment of heightened suspense, Uncle Remus interrupts his narration, and when the little boy wants to know whether "the fox [did] eat the rabbit" (11), claims that this is how far the story goes, that he might, and then again he might not.

Compared with other tales about Brer Rabbit and Brer Fox in the collection, "The Wonderful Tar-Baby Story" differs in two significant aspects. First, the contest between the mighty fox and the smart rabbit is not fought directly. Instead, the stronger of the two creates a device whose outward appearance does not reveal its connection with the predator; he probably calculates that the clever rabbit can be defeated more easily when he is less vigilant than in a direct skirmish with the enemy. Second, in contrast to an ending typical of the genre, which usually concludes with the unequivocal victory of one of the contestants and often with the death of the defeated, the outcome of this tale is left open. It takes a second story, "How Mr. Rabbit was too sharp for Mr. Fox"—separated from "The Wonderful Tar-Baby Story" by a tale about Brer Possum and Brer Coon—to assure the little boy that the rabbit managed to escape yet another time. Since we know Remus to be an excellent storyteller, we may assume that apart from the outcome of the second story, there should be a moral of the tar-baby tale conveyed through the story itself. And indeed, as the following close reading argues, the point of the meeting between Brer Rabbit and Tar-Baby—arranged by Brer Fox—is about the confrontation of the slave with the effigy of slavery.

Tar-Baby may be defined as blackness that sticks. In the context of slavery, Tar-Baby embodies the concept of the slave as fabricated by the master, namely a nonhuman black body. Opposed to the image of the slave as a black commodity is the slave's self-image exemplified by Brer Rabbit, a lively and intelligent creature, who possesses the very features the dominating class of masters denies him. Apart from the peril of physical death, the trap that Brer Fox produces represents the most serious danger the institution of slavery keeps in store for the slave, namely, succumbing to the master's definition of the slave as subhuman. As the encounter between Brer Rabbit and the image of objectified blackness shows, even the most self-confident slave can get into trouble if he allows himself to be provoked by lack of recognition. The interaction between Brer Rabbit and Tar-Baby stages the capitulation of the slave to his master's notion of the slave: in the encounter, despite (or rather because) of desperately battling against it, Brer Rabbit becomes more and more attached to his counter-image, until, in the end, he is inseparable from Tar-Baby. No wonder, Brer Fox laughs until he can laugh no more.

But how exactly is the trickster tricked into being stuck up with Tar-Baby? Again, the foundation of the slave's self-assertion is recognition, which, in the master-slave constellation, is systematically denied to him. Applying concepts of relational sociology, we can read this constellation as a figuration of two interdependent groups, in which the group of high-powered slave masters (the established) are able to define the image of the powerless group of slaves (the outsiders), who due to their relative weak position in the figuration lack the possibility of retribution. According to Norbert Elias's theory of established-outsider relations, the superior group maintains its superiority, for example by attaching the label of lower value to the group of outsiders. While the technique of stigmatization secures the existing power differential, it simultaneously confirms the relative powerlessness of the outsiders to whom the bad image sticks.

In speaking to Tar-Baby, Brer Rabbit experiences the very denial of recognition to which he is used in communication with the slave master, but which he does not expect from what he takes to be a fellow slave. Thus,

Brer Rabbit's anger is triggered, when he comes to the conclusion that Tar-Baby's silence is a sign of disrespect toward "'specttubble fokes" like himself (7). At this point, the relation between Brer Rabbit and Tar-Baby undergoes a figurational change. Brer Rabbit turns into a member of the established within the group of outsiders. As such, he is offended by Tar-Baby's unruly behavior not simply because he feels resentment at the lack of respect of a fellow slave, but—on a deeper level—because Tar-Baby, who appears to be either uncivilized, or deaf and dumb, or, even worse, subhuman, displays the very qualities that confirm the low opinion the established have of the outsiders. Brer Rabbit fears social and psychological contamination. Considering how much strength the outsider needs to continuously battle the label of unworthiness attached to him by the established, Tar-Baby's anomic behavior is a fundamental threat to Brer Rabbit's hard-earned self-respect and must be overcome by all means. But being disrespected makes Brer Rabbit particularly vulnerable in this situation, and due to this psychological weakness he chooses the wrong tactics. Instead of keeping a safe distance, he reacts emotionally, and giving in to his rage leads to the mistake of engaging physically with Tar-Baby.

Ultimately, Brer Fox's potent weapon is the socio-psychological mechanism of slave oppression itself. Confronted with the embodiment of the slave as objectified blackness that the slave must repudiate in order to survive, Brer Rabbit's defense is weakened and he loses self-control. The trickster figure of the rabbit is an African American hero who, notwithstanding his general powerlessness, represents the victory over the denigrating image imposed on the group; but he can be out-tricked when he is provoked by the very icon that not even the most self-confident trickster has the power to defeat once and for all. The master exerts symbolic violence upon the slave by denying him human dignity; the slave who misrecognizes this type of violence is more likely to succumb to it. Thus, the slave stands in constant danger of coming up to the tar-baby image the master constructed for the very purpose of keeping him in the position of subordination. Brer Rabbit's physical attachment to Tar-Baby, which at the end of the story leaves him as immobile as his counter-image, can be read as a compelling symbol of the long-lasting psychological effects of oppression. This is the poignant warning of "The Wonderful Tar-Baby Story" which remains valid in Jim Crow America, when the image of the slave as black commodity is substituted by negative stereotypes that serve the same goal, namely to keep Blacks in their place.

Granted its special significance, it does not come as a surprise that "The Wonderful Tar-Baby Story" stands out by its exceptional title: no other tale of the collection is singled out by the adjective "wonderful" (or any other adjective characterizing the story itself, for that matter). Furthermore, it holds a special position in the collection following right after the introductory story, in which "Uncle Remus initiates the little boy" through an episode about an exchange of dinner invitations between Brer Rabbit and Brer Fox. By emphasizing manners, the first story reveals that civilized behavior is but a thin veneer that only insufficiently covers the relentless battle of survival. To the theme of fight for survival the presentation of tar-baby adds the issue of race relations as power relations, and both aspects shape the readers' perception of the subsequent tales.

The concepts of relational sociology such as Pierre Bourdieu's symbolic violence or Elias's established-outsider relation lay bare the complex power dynamics at play in "The Wonderful Tar-Baby Story." Yet, as Bourdieu pointed out, it is not only the discipline of sociology, but also the literary genre of comedy which is capable of "revealing the wellsprings of power." Bourdieu exemplifies his thesis of the affinity between sociology and comedy by referring to literary techniques of unmasking in Molière's comedies, as for example, parody or caricature. While the comic devices with which the tar-baby story operates differ in part from the ones employed by Molière, they undoubtedly also contribute to disclosing hidden power structures.

What, then, are the sources of laughter in the tar-baby story? The humor derives from the dynamics of the encounter between Tar-Baby and Brer Rabbit itself, which employs several stock elements of the comic situation. Our sense of the comic is frequently triggered by contrast or incongruity. Thus, we laugh at role reversals, for example, when the judge becomes a defendant, as in Kleist's famous novella *Der zerbrochene Krug*, a turnaround that also implies the reversal of high and low and wisdom and foolishness. In the case of the tar-baby story the folk hero Rabbit, esteemed for his wit, is turned into a fool by falling for a trick worthy of his own ingenuity. An essential precondition of the trickster's fall is his misconception of the situation into which he is transposed. The hero's ignorance correlates with the reader's knowledge about his erroneous judgment, a discrepancy that is yet another source of laughter. As Freud claimed in *Jokes and their Relation to the Unconscious*, we turn into the laughing third when, as observers, we enjoy our superiority vis-à-vis a figure commonly considered superior. This type of amusement may be enhanced if the trickster is confronted with the malice of the inanimate. The obstinacy of Tar-Baby exasperates Brer Rabbit the more as it contradicts the trickster's ideal of flexibility. In the beginning, Brer Rabbit displays the virtue of elasticity by suggesting reasons for Tar-Baby's silence and immobility. The comicalness of the situation derives from the trickster's lack of control over it. Again, as a laughing third, the reader observes how Brer Rabbit, frustrated with Tar-Baby's persisting stubbornness, loses his mental flexibility, and in the increasing physical rigidity of his reactions to his counterpart, he resembles more and more the lifeless contraption with which he tries to come to terms. According to Henri Bergson's theory of laughter, Brer Rabbit's desperate struggle with the obstinacy of the inanimate object is funny, because it changes into an expression of the mechanical. Bergson considers the latter a fundamental malfunction of living. To Bergson, then, laughter is a social act, whose function consists of a warning that for the sake of society—understood as a living organism—the individual must preserve his or her mental and physical elasticity. Among the comic means that demonstrate such mechanical malfunctioning in comedy, Bergson lists repetition. In "The Wonderful Tar-Baby Story" the skillful narrator Remus uses repetition for two purposes. He builds up tension by repeating the phrase "Tar-Baby stay still, en Brer Fox, he lay low" (7). Secondly, he highlights Brer Rabbit's increasingly automated reaction, which in the end leaves him immobile. One of the reasons for the great success of the tar-baby story then is the ingenious congruence of theme and comic technique: the slave master's invention of the slave as reified blackness comes to embody the malice of the object which, in turn, evokes the mechanical reactions of a commonly supple trickster figure. The comicalness of the situation is further enhanced by the element of parody, another prominent means through which comedy unmasks the wellsprings of power. In the course of his interaction with Tar-Baby Brer Rabbit demands—more and more aggressively—not only respect but reverence: "'Ef you don't take off dat hat en tell me howdy, I'm gwineter bus' you wide open,' sezee" (9). At this point he turns into a parody of the slave master and, at the same time, alludes to the various African American artistic genres that focus on the parody of whites.

In addition, the mésalliance of Tar-Baby and Brer Rabbit brings to mind Mikhail Bakhtin's theory of the popular culture of laughter with its focus on the corporeal as the eccentric body. In the tar-baby story, the body appears grotesque because it combines a lifeless object with a living creature. However, the merging of the incongruous in the grotesque figure does not have the immediate liberating effect Bakhtin ascribes to the carnivalesque reversal of hierarchies that imply a defeat of power. Nevertheless, the social space presented in the black animal fable resembles the realm of Bakhtin's concept of carnival in that it emphasizes basic bodily needs (the fables' contests center on food and sex), questions power structures from below, and uses black vernacular, which in Harris's Uncle Remus tales is juxtaposed to the Standard English used by the narrator and the little boy in the frame. To Bakhtin, the vernacular of folk culture is the language of life, of physical work, of everyday life, and as such it also constitutes the language of the lower literary genres of the comic. Just like the focus on bodily functions and the undermining of social hierarchies, the black vernacular contributes to the subversion that the genre of the animal fable has in common with the culture of carnival.

It is important to note that Remus's use of the vernacular is highly sophisticated; the verbal skill and creativity his storytelling displays is yet another great source of humor. For example, Remus employs a clever play on words by making use of the multiple meanings of the verb "to be stuck (up)." When Brer Rabbit's "head got stuck," the Fox addresses him as follows: "'Howdy, Brer Rabbit,' sez Brer Fox, sezee. 'You look soter stuck up dis mawnin',' sezee, en den he rolled on the groun', en laft en laft twel he couldn't laff no mo'" (5-6). In this passage, the Fox refers to the obvious fact that the Rabbit is literally glued to Tar-Baby's sticky surface; but the word could also be understood figuratively, as articulating the Fox's triumph that Brer Rabbit is in a fix, in a desperate situation. At the same time, the phrase points back to its earlier usage by the Rabbit, who evokes yet another connotation of the word when he accuses Tar-Baby of being uppity, conceited: "Youer stuck up, dat's w'at you is." At this very moment the Rabbit changes from friendliness to arrogance himself, threatening that he is "gwineter kyore you, dat's w'at I'm gwineter do" (7). What a brilliant rhetorical device to communicate the analogy between Tar-Baby and the defeated Rabbit by repeating one word that thereby turns into a pun!

"The Wonderful Tar-Baby Story" seems to confirm the proverb, he laughs best that laughs last. However, Brer Fox's excessive laughter derives from malicious joy. According to Baudelaire, the laughter based on schadenfreude is founded on a sense of superiority vis-à-vis the person at whom we laugh. In his *Essence of Laughter*, Baudelaire suggests that the conviction of one's own superiority is the hallmark of inmates of "madhouses" and that laughter is one of the most frequent expressions of insanity. Therefore, he argues, we recognize in laughter motivated by arrogance the very element of the ridiculous that it targets. The laughter of the spiteful victor is in itself laughable and, thus, we may suspect, will not last. And it is indeed short-lived, as the reader discovers in the sequel to "The Wonderful Tar-Baby Story," when the animal trickster regains his wit in direct confrontation with his enemy and once more proves to be "too sharp for Mr. Fox." In this episode, the oppressed is shown to exploit both his knowledge about the oppressor's cruelty and the latter's ignorance about the harsh living conditions of the oppressed. Thus the Rabbit succeeds in persuading the Fox that the most torturous method to kill him would be to "fling [him] in dat briar-patch" (18). Having escaped, "Brer Rabbit was bleedzed fer to fling back some of his sass, en he holler out: 'Bred en bawn in a briar-path, Brer Fox—bred en bawn in a briar-patch!'" (19). In other words, to Brer Rabbit the thorny environment is not life-threatening, because he has been shaped and toughened by the hostile social setting of slavery. By accepting the challenging conditions of his socialization and proudly embracing his roots, Brer Rabbit is able to shed the stigmatizing image of the tar-baby and regain his subversive power. As the laughing third we will anticipate Brer Fox's failure to kill Brer Rabbit, rejoice with the triumphant trickster and, consequently, laugh at the out-foxed master.

However, the lesson of the episode also highlights the suffering of the oppressed. Thereby it exposes the other side of the comic, namely the tragic or melancholy spirit of the African American animal fables. Or, in Remus's words, "ef deze yer tales wuz des fun, fun, fun en giggle, giggle, giggle, . . . I'd a-done drapt um long ago. W'en it come down ter gigglin' you kin des count ole Remus out" (*Complete Tales* 355). The tales share the tragicomic sensibility characteristic of African American humor. While they provoke our laughter at the comic aspects of the everyday struggle of the outsider, they simultaneously sadden us through the depiction of the relentless brutality to which the trickster, far from relying merely on the verbal violence of "signifyin'," resorts in many stories. Above all, the tragic element of the tales lies in the fact that its hero, notwithstanding his numerous triumphs over his powerful enemies, can only achieve temporary relief from the burden of oppression. The systemic power imbalance between the established and the outsiders remains intact. And yet, the emotional release, even if impermanent, is stronger because the genre of the fable allows to express the affects through the hyperbolic mask of animality, or even bestiality. The animals, despite being highly anthropomorphized, stay, as it were, pre-moral creatures who are not at all plagued by a bad conscience after having committed murder. The animal guise then has a double function. From the viewpoint of the slave, it stages the reversal of master-slave power relations, and, in addition, it allows the slave to vent the pent-up anger and frustration with a maximum of aggression. In combination with the classic elements of the animal fable, techniques of the comic are the major literary means of the tales' subversive expression of resistance. What makes the tar-baby story—and all the other tales about Brer Rabbit—so "wonderful" is that the genre, by creatively staging the animal trickster's tragicomic battles, not only reveals the wellsprings of power but keeps alive the long tradition of African American struggles for freedom.

## Bibliographical Note

"Revealing the Wellsprings of Power" is an article by Pierre Bourdieu in *Political Interventions: Social Science and Political Action*, edited by Frank Poupeau and Thierry Discepolo, translated by David Fernbach, Verso, 2008, pp. 133-36. Remarks on Bourdieu's concept of symbolic violence are based on his books *Masculine Domination*, Stanford University Press, 2001, and *Pascalian Meditations*, Polity, 2000, both translated by Richard Nice. For Norbert Elias's theory of established-outsider relations, see Norbert Elias and John L. Scotson, "Towards a Theory of Established-Outsider Relations" (1976), *The Established and the Outsiders, The Collected Works of Norbert Elias*, vol. 4, edited by Cas Wouters, University College Dublin, 2008, pp. 1-36. On the social function of laughter, see Elias's unfinished, "Essay on Laughter," edited by Anca Parvulescu, *Critical Inquiry*, vol. 43, 2017, pp. 281-304. I would like to thank Johannes Kohrs for bringing Elias's essay to my attention.

Apart from drawing on Sigmund Freud's seminal *Jokes and their Relation to the Unconscious*, translated by James Strachey, Routledge & Kegan Paul, 1960, I also applied Henri Bergson's notion of the social function of laughter, published in *Laughter: An Essay on the Meaning of the Comic* (*Le Rire*, 1900), translated by Cloudesley Bereton and Fred Rothwell, 1911, Green Integer, 1999. For concepts of the grotesque body, the carnivalesque, and the vernacular, I refer to Mikhail Bakhtin, *Rabelais and His World*, translated by Helene Iswolsky, Indiana University Press, 1984; see also Dorothy J. Hale, "Bakhtin in African American Literary Theory," *ELH*, vol. 61, no. 2, 1994, pp. 445-71. Charles Baudelaire's concept of laughter, which stands in the tradition of the superiority theory of the comic, can be found in English translation in *The Essence of Laughter, and Other Essays, Journals, and Letters*, edited by Peter Quennell, Meridian, 1965. I owe my remarks on Baudelaire's reflections to Bernhard Greiner's instructive summary in *Die Komödie. Eine theatralische Sendung: Grundlagen und Interpretationen*, revised ed. Francke, 2006; Greiner's discussions of theories of the comic also include references to Karlheinz Stierle's concept of the humor of action, which sharpened my observations on the "Tücke des Objekts" (malice of the object).

The following studies shaped my understanding of African American Humor and the African American animal fable: Henry Louis Gates, Jr., *The Signifying Monkey: A Theory of African American Literary Criticism*, Oxford University Press, 1988; Glenda R. Carpio, *Laughing Fit to Kill: Black Humor in the Fictions of Slavery*, Oxford University Press, 2008; Lawrence W. Levine, *Black Culture and Black Consciousness: Afro-American Folk Thought from Slavery to Freedom*, Oxford University Press, 1977; Mel Watkins, *On the Real Side: Laughing, Lying, and Signifying—The Underground Tradition of African-American Humor That Transformed American Culture, from Slavery to Richard Pryor*, Touchstone, 1994; Gretchen Martin, *Dancing on the Color Line: African American Tricksters in Nineteenth-Century American Literature*, University of Mississippi Press, 2015.

For pragmatic reasons, quotations from the tales are taken from Joel Chandler Harris, *Uncle Remus. With 79 Illustrations by A.B. Frost*, Schocken Books, 1965. Harris's introduction was published in *The Complete Tales of Uncle Remus*, compiled by Richard Chase, Houghton, Mifflin, 1955. Besides Walter M. Brasch's biography *Brer Rabbit, Uncle Remus, and the 'Cornfield Journalist': The Tale of Joel Chandler Harris*, Mercer University Press, 2000, the following biographical studies were particularly valuable with regard to a complex portrait of the author: Wayne Mixon, "The Ultimate Irrelevance of Race: Joel Chandler Harris and Uncle Remus in Their Time," *Journal of Southern History*, vol. 56, no. 3, 1990, pp. 457-80; Robert Cochran, "Black Father: The Subversive Achievement of Joel Chandler Harris," *African American Review*, vol. 38, no. 1, 2004, pp. 21-34.

For a survey of the early scholarship on Harris, I consulted *Critical Essays on Joel Chandler Harris*, edited by R. Bruce Bickley, Jr., G.K. Hall, 1981; for an instructive analysis of the rhetoric of the tales, see Lee Pederson, "Language in the Uncle Remus Tales," *Modern Philology*, vol. 82, no. 3, 1985, pp. 292-98; Eric J. Sundquist's chapter on Chesnutt and Harris was indispensable for the understanding of the multiple trickster figures, *To Wake the Nation: Race in the Making of American Literature*, Harvard University Press, 1993. In developing my argument, I profited most from recent scholarship that emphasizes the complexity of the Uncle Remus tales, in particular, Christopher Peterson, "Slavery's Bestiary: Joel Chandler Harris's Uncle Remus Tales," *Bestial Traces: Race, Sexuality, Animality*, Fordham University Press, 2013, pp. 50-73. For a study of the psychosocial conditions of nineteenth-century white readers' reception of the tales, see the illuminating article by Jennifer Ritterhouse, "Reading, Intimacy, and the Role of Uncle Remus in White Southern Social Memory," *Journal of Southern History*, vol. 69, no. 3, 2003, pp. 585-622; for an enlightening article on Disney's adaptation of the Uncle Remus tales, see Daniel Stein, "From Uncle Remus to Song of the South: Adapting American Plantation Fictions," *Southern Literary Journal*, vol. 47, no. 2, 2015, pp. 20-35; and, finally, while I argue that, despite the storyteller Uncle Remus, the animal tales express a radical spirit of resistance, one should be aware of the fundamental critique of Harris's and Disney's distorted appropriations of the African American tradition, which has been eloquently voiced, for example, by Alice Walker in her essay "Uncle Remus: No Friend of Mine," *Georgia Review*, vol. 66, no. 3, 2012, pp. 635-37; cf. also Ellen Johnson, "Geographic Context and Ethnic Context: Joel Chandler Harris and Alice Walker," *Mississippi Quarterly*, vol. 60, no. 2, 2007, pp. 235-55.

Fig. 1. William Wegman, *Cinderella*. 1992. Reproduction courtesy of William Wegman.

# Empathy with the Animal

Christine N. Brinckmann

I.

In her short story "Painwise," the science fiction author James Tiptree, Jr. describes creatures endowed with an excess of empathy.[1] These "empaths" seek to be exclusively in the presence of happiness, since they immediately assume both the pleasurable and the painful feelings of others. They often struggle to distinguish their own thoughts from those of other beings, and they say what their dialogue partner was in fact going to say or wanted to say. There are three kinds of empaths: the golden-yellow bushbaby monkey, soft, relaxed, and pliant, like a child in a fur coat too large for it; the butterfly with enormous compound eyes, feathered antennae, and sheer rainbow wings; and the boa constrictor, tightly wound, smooth, and cool, with a wedge-shaped head and ice-gray eyes.

"Touch, taste, feel" is the empaths' motto. Now and then, three of them come together to organize a "lovepile," an amorous heaping of a "great palatal-olfactory interplay" in which they blend tastes and smells as well as other unnameable euphoric sensations. The mutual aim is to taste all the contradictory haptic textures and materials of the three heterogeneous partners. At the same time, the reciprocal assumption of feelings engenders a kind of self-pleasure that only processes of empathy allow, and thus an immense increase in desire. For in infinitely spiraling reactions to reactions, a cumulative mise-en-abîme, everyone feels like everybody else, and everyone feels the feelings in everybody else, and everyone feels themselves amidst the feeling of all of these feelings.

James Tiptree, Jr. sounded out various aspects of the phenomenon of empathy, taking them to the telepathic, erotic, and unreal extreme in her story. In reality, empathetic processes are far more ephemeral, and it is generally not hard to distinguish between oneself and another person. But in reality, too—particularly in moments of heightened sensuality and in the reception of works of art—a sort of emotional understanding of another being occurs, and the other being can be of an entirely different composition than oneself. Empathy does not rely on similarity.

## II.

The inexhaustible attraction of the zoo may be explained in part by way of empathetic processes. Even nature lovers who would rather set the animals free cannot deny the appeal of the direct encounter, the mirroring, and the involuntary comparison with the animal. They look at the lion and sense themselves muscular and covered in silk fur the color of sand—or small, weak, upright, and naked by comparison; or they look at the birds and know what it feels like to stand on two plastic sticks with talons that are much too long and folded up when in flight—or to wear shoes that fit well and provide a firm grip on the ground. In each case, empathy shoots out towards the animal, announces what it would be like if . . . and then, relenting, permits the return of the subjective sense of one's own body—undermined, changed, strengthened, enriched.

Visitors to the zoo are particularly fascinated by the faces of the animals with their alien physicality and their supposed expression of character. These faces are compared to human physiognomies and anthropomorphized. One imagines slipping into these other faces or tries to project them onto one's own face. What would it be like if my eyes were so close to one another—a mien of distrust or of penetrating, resentful attention; if the nostrils were so broadly flared—a mien of wild, dull thoughtlessness; if quick eyes could become entirely round, the limp corners of the mouth could hang down, bony lips were opened by a crack. This is a source of amusement and delight not only for children.

The empathetic experience usually goes no farther than this pleasurable play of the imagination, and the zoo experience generally stops with the visual comparison. It is different from the case of Tiptree's empaths, who wish to touch, taste, and feel, and thus to intensely taste-with, feel-with, and indeed think-with the other. In our world, the distance between the self and the other may be reduced when we empathize, but it remains fundamentally there. We do not confuse ourselves with the others. And when, now and then, we encounter disagreeable bodily conditions—in animals that are infested with vermin or have running eyes—we quickly break out of the shared experience and react with pity, horror, or disgust. In such cases, empathy forms only a short transitional stage towards understanding the condition of the other being.

## III.

Images, statues, and particularly photographs and films can likewise trigger empathetic processes, but the encounter takes a different course than it does in reality. Even though only limited sensory data are available—images have no smell and are not three-dimensional—similar attainments of shared feeling can occur. The extent to which a work stimulates empathy is thus of tremendous relevance for aesthetics, as Theodor Lipps already emphasized in 1903. For Lipps, such acts of empathy are not only triggered by humans and other creatures but also by architecture in its palpable power relationships of burden and support, and in its colors, lines, and rhythms. Even if Lipps may have overestimated their potential for a general theory of art, these are interesting observations in which the phenomenon manifests itself as something very basic.

Every conceivable variant of empathy can have importance for a filmic response theory, in particular empathy with persons and other beings in whom stories or emotional developments may be observed. Film, in its frontal attention to animated faces and its deploy of movement that exhibits the play of muscles, engenders more impulses for emotional and somatic empathy than do other representations, and thus has a more powerful capacity to involve its viewers. The motionless attention directed entirely at the screen, liberated from any need to act, also makes the cinema an ideal site for empathetic understanding. Compared to the novel, film has highly specific means to intensify the relationship between the recipient and the characters.

The reactions of spectators are at the center of contemporary film theory, in particular in discussions from the standpoint of cognitive psychology, a psychology in which "empathy" is of increasing importance as a keyword. Lipps' aesthetic observations on *Einfühlung* were a starting point for German approaches to viewer responses. With the English term "empathy," Anglo-American psychological research took another path, with an empirical orientation towards the natural sciences. Their findings now make it possible for reception theory to dispense with the potentially misleading and overused term "identification," and in its place to draw on a nuanced terminology to describe many variations of the integration of the viewer into a film.

This progress is due to two books in particular: Murray Smith, *Engaging Characters: Fiction, Emotion, and the Cinema*, and Ed S. Tan, *Emotion and the Structure of Narrative Film: Film as an Emotion Machine*. Both works were apparently written contemporaneously but largely independently of each other—one in England, the other in the Netherlands—yet they address quite similar processes and arrive at comparable models and conclusions. While Smith was coming from the perspective of the humanities, drawing on the discipline of psychology to support his investigations, Tan's starting point was the other way around, as a psychologist active in the field of narrative film theory.

Empathy is viewed in this context as a basic factor in filmic understanding, one that takes on a number of forms. Smith distinguishes between "emotional simulation," in which the spectator puts himself in the shoes of his or her fictional counterpart to test out how a situation is experienced, and "affective mimicry," in which gestures and facial expressions evoke the other subject's sensations directly (although usually in a weaker form). The two phenomena have in common that they occur involuntarily and swiftly, and that they dissipate with equal speed.

The simplest form of affective mimicry, the interior imitation of feelings, reacts on an expressive scale of the so-called basic affects: fear, surprise, rage, disgust, grief, joy, interest (the list varies slightly from school to school). These facial equivalents of affects appear to be universally comprehensible, presumably being based on an inborn code (Ekman). We are able to quickly interpret facial expressions that are indignant, frightened, or distorted with rage, and we react with a sort of distant echo of the same affect. More complex emotions—envy, shame, disappointment, and so forth—can also be comprehended empathetically, but require a higher degree of cognitive cooperation and insight into the situation, since they are experienced and expressed differently in different cultures. At the physical level, motor mimicry corresponds to affective mimicry, involving parallel muscular activity to bodily exertions observed in other beings. Motor mimicry ranges from subliminal innervation to slight, intuitive, at times anticipatory mirror movements when another person is perceived, and sometimes to more substantial, more extensive muscular imitation.[2] One need think only of the soccer fans whose feet twitch in front of the television when a player needs to kick the ball, or of the mother who opens her own mouth when spoon-feeding a baby—though here empathetic mimesis is often mixed with gestural demand.

The various forms of empathy elicit more or less the same emotions and motor impulses in the audience as in the counterpart observed. This is not the case, however, with other forms of viewer response. In the register of sympathy or its opposite, antipathy, independent feelings can rise up among the viewers—for example being moved, amused, revolted, or touched by pity at the sight of a person experiencing fear. These responses are dependent on spontaneous affection and narrative point-of-view, as well as moral approval and shared view of life. Over the course of a film, sympathy tends to solidify gradually into allegiance or partisanship for certain characters, but empathetic and sympathetic forms of reaction can also occur simultaneously. They often have a strengthening effect on one another, and they occasionally contradict each other: it is thus possible at the cinema to both hope and fear that the murderer will be caught.

## IV.

But back to empathy with the animal. Motor mimicry appears frequently in animal films, particularly in shots that illustrate the play of the muscles so clearly that one senses analogies to the pattern of one's own body. In horse shows, for example, frontally filmed hurdle races trigger little empathy, whereas the opposite is the case with side views that show us the work of the four legs and hooves: a trivial observation, but one that attests to the fact that it is possible to empathize with foreign anatomies (also the reason why millipedes make us nervous).

At least as important as an advantageous angle is the anticipatory understanding of what an animal is planning to do. Leaping over a hurdle requires momentum and precision, a particular dynamism to be dealt with according to the obstacle and also in relation to one's stature. Watching the horse jump, we mix our own experiences of jumping with the facts of the animal's musculature and volume, and we experience the successful jump as a triumph over gravity in which we inwardly participate.

Empathy of this kind reacts to the animal as animal, independent of the anthropomorphizing processes animal films often strive to arouse. Animal films draw first on impulses of the sort described above for the real-world zoo experience: similarities between animal physiognomies and human expressions lead to intuitive projective attributions. They can occur freely since most animals lack, or seem to lack, the capacity for affective expression. One knows, of course, what it means when a predator shows its fangs or a dog wags its tail; but in general the facial expressions and body language of animals remain opaque. Thus the anthropomorphizing can proceed apace without taking animal conditions into account, filling in the blanks with human emotions.

## V.

The American art photographer and video artist William Wegman has worked almost exclusively with his beloved dogs. His Weimaraner "Man Ray" achieved great photographic prominence in the 1970s, and other dogs followed. More recently, Wegman has created a book version of *Cinderella*, lavishly illustrated with photographs, in which all of the characters are embodied by hybrid creatures with costumed human bodies and canine heads. Cinderella, the serving girl who will marry the prince, wears the floor-length, long-sleeved, dowdy dress of a simple maiden, and looking out from this dress is the head and the sturdy furry neck of a Weimaraner with the characteristic lop ears, wrinkled forehead, and worried-looking eyes (fig. 1, preceding this essay). The prince is a costumed

Weimaraner as well, as are the stepmother and stepsisters; appearances are also made by cats (as cats) and other breeds of dogs (as carriage horses).

Comparing female and male characters, a certain disparity, a "gender trouble," becomes evident. Dog ears that hang down can be read as hairstyling, as an equivalent to feminine curls, and thus the female characters are at first glance more credible than the male ones. But on closer inspection, the hairy surfaces and strong necks disrupt the illusion. Above all, there is something disturbingly unfeminine in the black lips, half-hidden beneath the muzzle, instead of the red mouth associated with femininity. The result is that the young women, Cinderella and her sisters, appear almost like transvestites. Equally disruptive are the deep canine wrinkles, running counter to youthful beauty. The male characters, by contrast, seem more convincing in this respect and less grotesque. But at the same time they are less interesting and on the whole seem weaker than the women, as they are so similar to them: the heads and necks of male dogs differ little from the heads and necks of bitches.

From the perspective of empathy, the appeal of Wegman's approach lies in the opposing impulses that the images trigger. On the one hand, the dogs are anthropomorphic fictional characters animated by attributes, situations, and modes of action, as well as the accompanying emotions with which we involuntarily supplement them. Thus, one reacts to these characters effortlessly with affective mimicry. On the other hand, at the level of the animal faces a resistance arises, because reality and appearance are too divergent. With the faces one is grasped by a direct response to the animal as animal. One can experience empathetically the sturdy neck musculature, for example, as well as the fact that the dogs have probably been forced to stand upright, and one can feel their discomfort in human clothing. Or one reacts, as at the zoo, to the animal compared to and contrasted against humans, thus attributing to the Weimaraners a disposition that is in part anxious, in part devoted, somewhat supercilious, and both obstinate and good-natured—and all of this entirely apart from the roles they play in the fairy tale. Whereas anthropomorphizing is easier to achieve with "normal" animal stories in which the fictional characters are either seen as actual animals or, in the case of drawings, are already given strongly human traits (Mickey Mouse expresses the basic affects entirely), a viewing of Wegman's hybrids prompts a deep ambivalence or a conception of the characters that, tipping to and fro, remains unsettled.

There are instances—pinnacles of the approach—in which the various elements flow together in a way that is witty and moving. Occasionally Wegman makes use of the typical posture of canine interest, in which the head is extended crookedly forward, the ears perked up slightly, the eyes rounded to express the attention and enthusiasm of his characters: Cinderella sews herself a dress for the ball, and the Weimaraner seems ardently concentrated on the sewing machine. Or the red-rimmed dog eyes and the anxious wrinkles stand for pain and distress: Cinderella lies on her bed, her ears pressed tousled between pillow and blanket, and cries herself to sleep.

Whereas Wegman's photo books are colorful and luxuriant and his art photos are choice and perfect, his early video works limit themselves to a meager, flat black-and-white.[3] The technical absence of luster that was specific to the simple video cameras of the era is accepted here, perhaps even consciously made use of. Each video presents a concept, a small idea, never played out for longer than necessary, and each video seems to complete itself spontaneously: laconic sketches of two or three minutes with an air of modesty that can deceive the viewer into overlooking how subtle they are.

*Man Ray, Do You Want To?* from 1973 shows, against a neutral background, the dog's head and neck reacting to his master's questions. The dog's understanding of language and imaginative freedom to make choices are assumed. Questions like "Man Ray, do you want to see Jane?" or "Do you want to go to the beach?" permit the dog to listen attentively and signal his understanding through small gestures and sounds. An admonishing "Man Ray!" calls him back to order when he begins to turn away; shaking the head seems to signify rejection, raising the muzzle a heightened interest, winking a waiting position, and licking the lips an incipient boredom. When the dog finally stands up, Wegman quickly says, "Let's go," and the little film is over. The concept is achieved: to give expression to the gulf between animal and human communication by overtaxing plausibility and thus to deconstruct the anthropomorphizing impulse. At the same time, the loving connection to the animal and the intensive communication between dog and master attest to the fact that anthropomorphizing is not needed at all.

Still more ascetic is Wegman's three-minute video *Two Dogs and Ball* (also known as *Dog Duet*) from 1974, which does without sound altogether. A frontal view is shown of two Weimaraners, a smaller one and a larger one, sitting next to each other in front of a dark wall and moving their heads, eyes, and ears simultaneously. Their expressions appear identical—attentive yet annoyed, arrogant yet slightly duped—but the smaller dog appears to be more obtuse than the larger one, and the movements of one are sometimes delayed a few fractions of a second after the movements of the other. Their gazes apparently follow an object that means something to them even though they are unable to grasp what is happening, and without their interest being sufficient to prompt them to stand up. The title already gives away what sort of object is involved (and the tennis ball appears at the end of the piece), but for the spectators the real situation pales in comparison to the mysterious, nearly telepathic simultaneity of the two animals. They almost seem to follow a choreography. Yet they lack rhythmic grace, so that the impression that prevails is one of useless effort, undignified pathos, and misunderstanding. Unintended comedy as the consequence of relatively complicated head movements ensues when the dogs turn in various directions. Contributing to this effect is that they are pointed at the camera—and thus at the viewer—but are reacting to something that exists invisibly in the space near, behind, and above the camera: in a visual void.

As in the previous film *Man Ray, Do You Want To?* Wegman plays with the viewers' knowledge of the pro-filmic situation coming into conflict with the perception and comprehension of what is shown. What is more, one reads feelings into the animals that are in no way appropriate. One endows these feelings with an anthropomorphic charge, but then slides away from them, defeated by the absurdity and minimality of what is shown, until ultimately reacting again to the reality of the dogs as dogs.

## Notes

The English version of this essay first appeared in *Color and Empathy: Essays on Two Aspects of Film* (2014) by Christine N. Brinckmann and is reprinted with permission by Amsterdam University Press; translated from German by Ben Letzler.

1 | "James Tiptree, Jr." is the pen name of the author Alice Bradley Sheldon. The short story "Painwise" is included in her *A Thousand Light Years from Home*.
2 | On this, see my essay "Motor Mimicry in Hitchcock" (1999) in *Color and Empathy: Essays on Two Aspects of Film*. Amsterdam University Press, 2014, pp. 135-44.
3 | All video works mentioned here are included in *William Wegman: Video Works 1970-1999*.

## Works Cited

Ekman, Paul. *Emotion in the Human Face*. 2nd ed. Cambridge University Press, 1982.
Lipps, Theodor. *Grundlagen der Ästhetik*. Leopold Voss, 1903.
Smith, Murray. *Engaging Characters: Fiction, Emotion, and the Cinema*. Oxford University Press, 1995.
Tan, Ed S. *Emotion and the Structure of Narrative: Film as an Emotion Machine*. Lawrence Erlbaum, 1996.
Tiptree, James, Jr. "Painwise." *A Thousand Light Years from Home*. Ace Books, 1973, pp. 117-45.
Wegman, William, et al. *Cinderella*. Schirmer/Mosel, 1993.
*William Wegman: Video Works 1970-1999*. Microcinema International, 2006.

# Martin Usborne's Dogs: On Entangled Empathy in *The Silence of Dogs in Cars* and *Where Hunting Dogs Rest*

*Claudia Lillge*

The fact that artists maintain affinities to specific animals is well-known. Most of the paintings by Jean-Baptiste Oudry (1686-1755) show hunting scenes and hunted animals. Rosa Bonheur (1822-99) concentrated on livestock and wildlife; Wilhelm Kuhnert (1865-1926) was fascinated by lions, and Paul Klee (1879-1940) preferred to paint fish. The London-based photographer Martin Usborne (1973–) cannot hide the fact that his camera's eye frequently focuses on specific animal species as well. Similar to the American Magnum photographer Elliott Erwitt (1928–), Usborne prioritizes dogs, which he has spotlighted to date in three photo books published in quick succession.

Although the three volumes—*My Name is Moose: Modern Life Through a Dog's Eyes* (2011), *The Silence of Dogs in Cars* (2013), and *Where Hunting Dogs Rest* (2015)—depict a wide variety of dogs in disparate contexts and settings, all three publications engage in reflections on human-animal encounters, interactions, and relationships. The following considerations track this artistic trail in the two more well-known and well-received volumes, *The Silence of Dogs in Cars* and *Where Hunting Dogs Rest*, and discuss how they are aesthetically designed, what functions they contain, and what effects they provoke.

## The Silence of Dogs in Cars

A unique feature of photography is that the subject is not captured through an act of symbolic representation (as in literature) but rather initially and primarily as an *index* pointing to a related reality. Usborne's work combines typical features of narrative texts with photography's indexical qualities by consistently placing the photographed animals in specific narrative settings and by providing textual or *para*-textual comments. Therefore, Usborne's work always deals with real canines as well as with symbolic and/or abstract content designed to be communicated beyond the portrayed dogs.

*The Silence of Dogs in Cars* produces, for example, a specific feeling that the artist associates with his earlier childhood and visually depicts through the series of photos.

> I was once left alone in a car at a young age. I do not know when or where or for how long—possibly at the age of four, perhaps outside a supermarket, probably for fifteen minutes only. The details do not matter. The point is that I wondered if anyone would come back. The fear I felt was strong: in a child's mind, it is possible to be alone forever. (Usborne, *Silence*)

Angst, and psychological research largely agrees here, is clearly a complex and multifaceted phenomenon; in contrast to fear, according to common psychological understanding, angst is neither centered on an object nor is it clearly defined; rather it constitutes a "psychic reality" (Tuschling 46).[1]

The same is true for Usborne, who in the afterword to his photo book admits: "I should say that I was a well-loved child and never abandoned, and yet it is clear that both these experiences arose from the same place deep inside me: a fear of being alone and unheard" (*Silence*). This is noteworthy in terms of the emotional settings the photographer selects for his photos in order to communicate the experience of abandonment.

A biographical synchronism is decisive for the choice of his aesthetic subjects; simultaneously to the experience of his early fears of separation and abandonment, Usborne developed a long-lasting empathy for animals: "Around the same age, I began to feel a deep affinity with animals—in particular their plight at the hands of humans. I saw a television documentary that included footage of a dog being put into a plastic bag and being kicked. What appalled me most was that the dog could not speak back" (*Silence*). Childhood angst and empathy with an animal's fate are superimposed and create an emotional "contact zone" centered on both the powerlessness and defenselessness of children *and* animals (Haraway 205). This intersection results in thirty-nine photographs which, for the purpose of an aesthetic embodiment, do not portray children but dogs left behind in cars. "The dog in the car is a metaphor, not just for the way that animals (both domestic and wild) are so often silenced and controlled by humans, but for the way that we so often silence and control the darker parts of ourselves: the fear and loneliness that we would rather keep locked away" (Usborne, *Silence*).

In most cases, the dogs are portrayed alone in the car. Only two of the photos include pairs of dogs. The lighting, the locations in which the vehicles are parked, and the specific settings evoke a clear similarity to photographs from Gregory Crewdson's *Twilight* series (1998-2002), which, through their

Fig. 1. Martin Usborne, *The Silence of Dogs in Cars* (Lula)

Fig. 2. Martin Usborne, *The Silence of Dogs in Cars* (Prospero)

Fig. 3. Martin Usborne, *The Silence of Dogs in Cars* (Lottie)

enigmatic nature and style, generate fluid boundaries between dream and reality, thereby appealing to the unconscious (fig. 1).²

Usborne favors a range of perspectives for placing the dogs in his photographs. Medium shots and close-up perspectives alternate; some dogs are photographed from above, others present a frontal view. A dog's gaze is sometimes fixed on a point outside the frame, or may be focused on their reflection in the car window. Some dogs display an "inward look," others appear to be looking directly at the observer (fig. 2).

A decisive factor of Usborne's work is that it invites the viewer to enter into the negotiation of an emotional process. Anyone who associates the experience of being locked into an automobile with feelings of powerlessness can not only identify with feelings of *angst*, anger, grief, or hopelessness, but can also recognize these feelings in the physiology of the dogs themselves (fig. 3). Nonetheless, complementary fears or feelings are not only projected onto animals but highlighted through the medium so that they can be simultaneously reflected and overcome. To speak with Hartmut Rosa, Usborne's photographs fulfill the qualities of a "sphere of resonance" (472). In other words, the photographs provide stimuli for a "mutuality of 'touching' and 'being touched'" as well as for a specific form of "entangled empathy" between human and nonhuman animals (Rosa 284-85).³

## *Where Hunting Dogs Rest*

It is well-known that particularly artists, who explicitly express the political dimensions of their work in the service of animal rights, often work in the field of photography (specifically in documentary photography) in order to make their audiences aware of many different contexts in which animal abuse occurs. Usborne, who is known as an animal rights activist, can also be placed in the lawyer-driven animal justice genre, at least with his second, well-known volume of photos. Two years after the appearance of *The Silence of Dogs in Cars*, the British artist once again brought dogs in front of his camera in *Where Hunting Dogs Rest*, in this case he specifically features hunting dogs used in rabbit hunting in the Southwest of Spain—dogs who are either abandoned or brutally killed at the end of the hunting season.

Before giving further attention to this work by Usborne, I would like to examine what a "hunting dog" really is. There are two very different approaches to answering the question. One method turns to lexicons on dogs or relevant resources describing canine breeds, which classify "working dogs" with a view to their specially developed hunting skills. The other approach, which serves my following argumentation more completely, follows two tracks:

it first provides a general definition of "hunting" and is then followed by an attempt to understand the "idea" of a hunting dog.

"The hunt or chase," as the philosophers Jens Tuider and Ursula Wolf point out, "includes the standard definition of catching the scent, tracking the prey and bagging the game" (33). As Roland Borgards more precisely expresses, the hunt is a highly "ambivalent situation": "On the one hand, it is a natural phenomenon: falcons hunt blackbirds, antlions hunt ants, chimpanzees hunt smaller monkeys. On the other hand, it is part of an elaborate human culture, which distinguishes human and nonhuman animals" (7). In his *Meditations on Hunting* from 1944, the Spanish philosopher José Ortega y Gasset leaves no doubt that humans who hunt animals are at a clear disadvantage vis-à-vis the animals they hunt. In the end, animals are able to meet the hunter's pursuit with a series of counter responses.

They possess, for example, a "fleetness of foot that simplifies flight," a "keen sense of smell that warns [them]," a "sharp sense of sight that sweeps the horizon" as well as the "gift of being able to remain hidden." Ortega outlines these momentary deficits of the hunter with precision: "the human does not possess the animal's superior instinct to make itself invisible and no complementary instinct" and "even reason . . . fails in the attempt to capture the wary game" (107-09). The clear aspect that upsets the imbalance of power that gives wildlife the advantage collapses with the invention of a "go-between" positioned between humans and animals:

One day, however, [the human] . . . had a brilliant idea in order to scent the overly cautious prey, he took refuge in the tracing ability from a different animal and borrowed its skill. With that dogs joined the hunt, and that is the singular, recognizable and real 'progress' in hunting. This progress does not consist in the direct application of reason, but rather much more in the fact that humans recognized their inadequacies and inserted an animal between his reason and the prey. That would not have been possible if the dog itself was not a hunter. The human actually did little more that improve the hunting instincts inherent in the dog and accommodated himself to the situation for the sake of cooperation . . . . As a result, the human includes the hunting skills of the canine in his own hunt and therefore raises hunting to a perfection of form that corresponds to the discovery of polyphony in music. (Ortega y Gasset 109-10)

The euphoria clearly recognizable in Ortega's account, in which the Spanish philosopher celebrates the "invention" of the hunting dog, is countered in literature and the arts by a whole range of animal portraits that problematize and display the ambiguous position of hunting dogs. Especially because hunting dogs characteristically oscillate between human and nonhuman realms, I would like to argue that they are particularly equipped to stimulate aesthetic displays of and reflection on human-animal relationships.

Back to Usborne: In order to visualize the annual abandonment or execution of thousands of hunting dogs in the South of Spain, the British photographer selects an artistic approach which not only combines several image traditions and intermedial connections, but also explores how the relationship of aesthetics and animal ethics can be newly determined.

The hunting dogs in Usborne's photographs are presented as complete or partial portraits and possess a special charm (fig. 4 and 5). The absence of movement and liveliness, which most of them convey, is striking. Usborne pairs almost every photograph of a hunting dog with a landscape photo or a static location. These primarily sparse and raw or empty scenes portray ravines, rivers, city outskirts and streets or even trees in the cool tones of harmonious, earth-bound colors that appear to resonate with the respective animal photo. The hunting dogs are frequently discarded in those remote locations or hung head down from trees. Usborne's works encounter these acts of animal abuse and execution by not only presenting the hunting dogs in an aesthetic context but also by the photographic staging that, in spite of the tragic condition of the animals, succeeds in communicating their previous grace and charm. At the same time, this effect is not simply the result of a photographic presentation, but also of a style that takes up conventions of painting.

With a view to the aesthetic presentation of his photo portraits, Usborne attempts to produce an unmistakable link to the painter who is connected in a singular way with southern Spain, Diego Velázquez. In particular, the color schemes of the photos, including the application of model-orientated lighting and chiaroscuro effects, are reminiscent of Diego Velázquez's paintings. At the time of Velázquez, the Spanish Galgos, the predominant breed in Usborne's photos, enjoyed its highest level of prestige. Owning one was the privilege of royalty. Therefore, the reference to Velázquez in Usborne's work implies also a historic transition that communicates the considerable loss of stature that hunting dogs have experienced over the centuries. The tradition of still life paintings that Usborne reproduces (fig. 6 and 7),[4] also appears in the compositions of his photographs. The term "still life" generally refers to the artistic "exhibition of static, mostly small objects, plants and immobile life forms in an intentionally arranged setting" (Schütz 17).

The two oranges in the lower right half of the photo in fig. 7 call that context to mind as does the position of the dog on a stage-like podium in front of a canvas background. Of course, we recognize the style of the painted hunting still life that includes, for example, dead rabbits, grouse and partridge or pheasants. In such traditional still lives, however, hunting dogs seldom appear unless they are present to guard the bagged prey.

Fig. 4. Martin Usborne, *Where Hunting Dogs Rest*

Fig. 5. Martin Usborne, *Where Hunting Dogs Rest*

Usborne takes up and at the same time varies the traditions of still life painting, because his photographs set the hunting dog in the place of the lifeless game. The dog is no longer the agent of death for a different animal, but he is threatened with death himself. Exactly this impression is fostered by the "mortifying" impact of photography, an effect emphasized by Philippe Dubois and others (Dubois 164). Usborne found all of the animals he photographed in animal rescue sanctuaries which care for abandoned animals. The final photo in the series contains the only dead animal. It is significant that here the subject is not a dead dog, but a lifeless rabbit. Therefore, Usborne formulates not only a visual critique that is centered on the violent killing of hunting dogs. His interventionist project also calls attention to the overarching problem of hunting practices, especially the pursuit hunt, which has not been forbidden in Spain to date.

## Conclusion

In summary, cultural artifacts can suspend boundaries between humanity and the animal world. Exactly in that way, they motivate us to consider what is actually "human" and what is "beast" and from what perspective we determine our relationship to animals. At the same time, literature and the arts provide a place to encounter the cultural discomfort emanating from animals: a disquiet that confronts us with concepts of the supposed "property," "related," "other," or "stranger" and draws our attention to the ambivalent and contradictory logic of human-animal relationships. Specifically, the representations of dogs lead us a significant part of the way towards the center of this tension and uncertainty. In the end, dogs are not simply "boundary beasts" (Borgards 486). In the main, however, they introduce defined cross-over spaces in which not only human-animal differences, but above all resonating interspecies relationships or moral and emotional belonging can be negotiated.

## Notes

1 | All translations are mine.
2 | Usborne explains: "Nearly all the images are taken at dusk or dawn, never in broad daylight, and often with multiple lights. The question I always ask myself after taking an image is not: Does this look good? But rather: Does this feel right? The emotional impact is paramount" (*Silence*).
3 | Lori Gruen defines "entangled empathy" as: "An experiential process involving a blend of emotion and cognition in which we recognize we are in relationships with others

Fig. 6. Klever Schule, "Stillleben mit Schnepfe und Orange"

Fig. 7. Martin Usborne, *Where Hunting Dogs Rest*

and are called upon to be responsive and responsible in these relationships by attending to another's needs, interests, desires, vulnerabilities, hopes, and sensitivities" (3).
4 | Fig. 6: Klever Schule, "Stillleben mit Schnepfe und Orange." Second half of the nineteenth century. Oil on canvas.

## Works Cited

Borgards, Roland. "Tier." *Phantastik: Ein interdisziplinäres Handbuch*, edited by Hans Richard Brittnacher and Markus May, J. B. Metzler, 2013, pp. 482-87.
Borgards, Roland. "Tiere jagen." *TIERethik*, vol. 7, no. 2, 2013, pp. 7-11.
Dubois; Philippe. *Der fotografische Akt: Versuch über ein theoretisches Dispositiv.* Philo Fine Arts, 1998.
Gruen, Lori. *Entangled Empathy: An Alternative Ethic for our Relationships with Animals.* Lantern Books, 2015.
Haraway, Donna. *When Species Meet.* University of Minnesota Press, 2008.
Krüger, Gesine. "Geschichte der Jagd." *Tiere: Kulturwissenschaftliches Handbuch*, edited by Roland Borgards, J. B. Metzler, 2016, pp. 111-21.
Ortega y Gasset, José. *Meditationen über die Jagd.* 1944. Dürckheim, 2012.
Rosa, Hartmut. *Resonanz: Eine Soziologie der Weltbeziehung.* Suhrkamp, 2016.
Schütz, Karl. "Die Geschichte des Stilllebens." *Das flämische Stillleben: 1550-1680*, edited by Wilfried Seipel, Luca, 2002.
Suter, Robert. *Par Force: Jagd und Kritik.* Konstanz University Press, 2015.
Tuider, Jens, and Ursula Wolf. "Gibt es eine ethische Rechtfertigung der Jagd?" *TIERethik*, vol. 7, no. 2, 2013, pp. 33-46.
Tuschling, Anna. "Psychologie der Angst." *Angst: Ein interdisziplinäres Handbuch*, edited by Lars Koch, Metzler, 2013, pp. 41-51.
Usborne, Martin. *The Silence of Dogs in Cars.* Kehrer, 2012.
Usborne, Martin. *Where Hunting Dogs Rest.* Kehrer, 2015.

# Paws of Courage: The Heroization of Dogs in Contemporary American Culture

*Simon Wendt*

On 27 May 2004, the dog handler Sgt. Herman Haynes and his German Shepherd Dog Frenke received the first DOGNY Heroic Military Working Dog Award for their military service in Iraq and Afghanistan (Bauer 288). Since it was sponsored by the American Kennel Club, this award might be dismissed as a peculiar ritual among dog lovers who feel that "man's best friend" does not receive the appreciation it deserves. But a closer look at American culture in the twenty-first century reveals that the heroization of dogs is not exceptional at all. In fact, it is so ubiquitous that it begs for a scholarly analysis.

This chapter therefore explores how dogs are heroized in twenty-first-century U.S. culture, focusing on nonfictional accounts of dogs serving in military and quasi-military contexts. By doing so, it seeks to combine heroism studies and Human-Animal Studies to explore interactions between humans and animals and the ways in which humans use animals to make sense of their world. Animals help in constructing identities and hierarchies within human society, which is why studying representations of animals and human interactions with them reveals much about the social and historical contingency of human norms and values. Based on these premises, the chapter asks what the heroization of dogs can tell us about American notions of the heroic, related norms and values, and the relationship between animals and humans more generally. Up to this point, scholars have not attempted to address such issues. Of course, there are numerous examples of new and innovative research on animals and their role in American society, including representations of animals in U.S. culture and the role of animals in military conflicts (see, for example, Dubino et al.; Grier; Möhring et al.; Nocella et al.; Ohrem). Yet, despite hinting at the connection between animals in war-related heroism discourses, scholars have largely neglected the heroization of animals in general and that of dogs in particular. This exploratory essay thus adds much to our understanding of both American heroism and human-animal interactions in the United States by analyzing the significant ways in which animals are invested with meaning.

## Human Heroism, Heroism Research, and Human-Animal Studies

Scholars of heroism have not explicitly addressed animals, but their writings tend to suggest that heroism is a notion of extraordinariness that is confined to humans. Heroes embody the norms, values, and beliefs of social groups within human societies, which makes them essential for the formation of collective identities. As symbols of dominant norms and identities, they become sources of authority and are frequently used to legitimize social, cultural, and political hierarchies. For many centuries, for example, only military commanders were regarded as heroes, while ordinary soldiers were not. Similarly, women and people of color were (and, to some extent, still are) deemed "unheroic" by nature, thus cementing dichotomous views of society that revolve around white male privilege. However, despite the fact that heroism tends to be a stabilizing force in human societies, it is constantly debated and reevaluated. Consequently, it is historically contingent, since the significance attributed to heroism and the qualities that people deem heroic change according to time and place (Campbell; Drucker and Cathcart; Kendrick; von den Hoff et al.).

It is important to stress that heroism is a cultural construct. Heroes are the product of intricate heroization processes that involve various "hero-makers" who communicate with multiple audiences (Drucker and Cathcart; Rollin; Strate). Representation and narration are therefore key to understanding these processes, although defining heroism remains a vexing problem. Cultural anthropology might offer a methodological solution because it takes as a point of departure the very same terms that are used by the people and societies it studies. When viewed from this perspective, people themselves define what heroism is by employing such terms as "hero," "heroism," and "heroic" when describing actions or individuals they regard as exceptional or extraordinary (Meyer). At the same time, even in cases where the term "hero" is not applied, processes of heroization can be analyzed by focusing on the particular attributes that are deemed heroic at a particular moment in time.

Despite the fact that cultural studies and cultural history have thoroughly examined various processes of meaning-making in the United States, surprisingly few scholars have examined American heroism. Just as problematic, those who do, including historians, frequently affirm rather than critically examine hagiographic traditions of hero-worship. A classic example is Arthur Schlesinger Jr.'s 1959 essay on the "decline of heroes." In it, he lamented: "Ours is an age without heroes" (341). According to Schlesinger, post-1945 U.S. society regrettably objected to heroes and hero-worship, without which he believed America to be doomed (341). While today's historians tend to be less pessimistic than Schlesinger, they frequently engage in the same type of normative hero-making. In addition, most of the heroization processes these and other scholars study continue to revolve around white and male hero figures. And even when non-white and female hero figures are addressed, uncritical traditions of hero-worship loom large. This is particularly true in the case of military heroism. Many scholars merely attempt to unearth the "unsung" heroism of previously neglected groups of soldiers, implicitly or explicitly imploring readers to acknowledge their exploits on and off the battlefield (Wendt).

If the study of heroism focuses on meaning-making and the constructed nature of this phenomenon, it makes sense to explore how Human-Animal Studies might help us better understand both human heroism and human-animal relations. Human-Animal Studies has become a growing field of scholarly inquiry in recent decades. In light of the fact that many of its practitioners focus on processes of meaning-making in the various ways in which the lives of animals and humans intersect, it is worth investigating whether and how various forms of heroization have affected or help us shed light on this complex interrelationship. As Margo DeMello reminds us, Human-Animal Studies are an interdisciplinary endeavor "that explores the spaces that animals occupy in human and social and cultural worlds and the interactions humans have with them" (4). While Human-Animal Studies scholars do not necessarily focus on animals, a number of them try to understand how studying animals' behavior as well as their emotions and forms of communication can shed fresh light on human behavior. Viewed from this perspective, animals are frequently used to perpetuate race, gender, and class hierarchies within human societies. Probably most importantly, Human-Animal Studies scholars question long-held beliefs about the binary opposition between nature and human culture. From their vantage point, animals are not mere "things" but can have "human" characteristics and must be regarded as active agents in human-animal contexts (Hurn 2-6). For the purposes of this chapter, DeMello's astute observation that animals "exist as mirrors of human thought," which allows humans "to think about, talk about, and classify ourselves and others" (14), hints at what an analysis of the heroization of animals might teach us about both our notions of heroism and interpretations of animals and human-animal relations.

## American Military Heroism

If one wants to understand the heroization of dogs in the U.S. military and in American quasi-military contexts, it is essential to have a better understanding of human war heroes and their functions in American history. In general, there are more continuities than discontinuities with regard to the importance accorded to martial valor, the particular attributes that were ascribed to heroic soldiers, and the norms and values they were and are believed to embody. In Western cultures, warrior heroes and heroic military leaders have been worshiped for millennia, but important changes took place in the nineteenth century (Kendrick). In a process whose earliest manifestations could be observed on the North American continent, heroism was simultaneously nationalized and democratized. Warrior heroes and heroic military leaders became admired symbols of nationhood, and the official recognition of martial valor was no longer confined to the upper echelons of the military hierarchy. During the wars that U.S. soldiers fought after American independence, more and more common servicemen received praise for successfully defending the young republic, a process of democratized heroization that was reflected in the introduction of the Medal of Honor in 1862, the first permanent American award for valor on the battlefield. As in the past, American fighters who received this coveted award were admired as daring risk takers who embodied manly honor, but their recognition as national heroes was now contingent upon their willingness to sacrifice their lives for the nation (see Kendrick; Hagemann; Zabecki; Schwartz, "George Washington;" Schwartz, *George Washington*; Pettegrew; "Awards"). On the eve of World War I, Americans tended to associate war heroes with a catalogue of attributes that revolved around cherished masculine qualities and national loyalty. "True" heroes were devoted to honor, duty, and the nation; they showed physical courage, endurance, and strength in the face of mortal danger; and they deliberately risked their lives to save comrades in battle or fought against impossible odds to defeat the enemy (Goldstein; Madigan; Cockerham; Anderson).

The changing nature of modern warfare, however, caused military officials to reconsider some of these attributes when establishing an array of new military awards after the Great War to boost soldiers' morale. Support troops, for instance, had always played a role in warfare, but their numbers rose exponentially in the large-scale military conflicts of the twentieth century. In addition, the Cold War saw the emergence of modern strategic weapons systems such as intercontinental missiles, which required highly trained noncombat personnel. Like support troops, however, these servicemen had few opportunities to distinguish themselves through displaying physical courage or some form of daring on the field of battle. To recognize the service and the achievements of such noncombat forces, the military introduced numerous awards that were given for heroism in peacetime, meritorious service, or for particular proficiency with weapons and equipment. Since few of these awards are actually given for martial valor, the line between martial heroism and military service has been somewhat blurred in the twentieth and twenty-first centuries ("Awards;" Baucom; Zabecki).

## The Heroization of Dogs in Twenty-First-Century American Culture

To what extent, then, does the heroization of dogs in military and quasi-military contexts mirror or divert from the heroization of human soldiers in the twenty-first century? Before answering this question, it is useful to briefly look at the history of dogs in the U.S. armed forces. Dogs have long been part of human societies in North America. Native Americans used them for sentry and pack duty long before the arrival of European explorers. American colonists used dogs for herding, hunting, and protection (Lemish 5-6). But already during the Colonial era, some dogs and a few other animals, including cats and birds, became companions rather than animals to be used for economic purposes or for hunting. After the Civil War, Americans began to develop an interest in pure-bred dogs and other animals specially bred for mere pleasure. As part of this process, more and more middle-class citizens reconsidered their relationship to animals, condemning cruel treatment and advocating kindness toward animals (Grier 11-13).

With regard to the use of dogs in military contexts, however, they played only a minor role in the U.S. armed forces until the late twentieth century. In stark contrast to its European counterparts, the American military was slow to integrate dogs into their operations at home and abroad. They were rarely used during the Revolutionary War, and even during the Civil War, dogs were visible primarily as regimental mascots. The first time canines played a considerable role in the armed forces was during World War I, when the Red Cross trained dogs to comfort wounded soldiers. While European armies also used them for messenger and sentry jobs, as well as for scout duties, the U.S. army had no military canine program. When the United States entered World War II, dogs were popular as pets who received no or only little formal training. Obedience training schools were established only in the early 1940s, and even American police departments rarely used dogs in their work. 1942 marked an important turning point because of the efforts of private pet owners who established the project "Dogs for Defense," which consisted of a large network of owners, trainers, and kennel clubs that sought to prepare privately owned dogs for military duty. Only then did the U.S. armed forces become interested in recruiting military working dogs. Between 1942 and 1946, thousands of canines were used as scouts and messengers, as well as for patrol duty. In part because of the mixed results of this experiment, few dogs were used during the military conflict in Korea. In the 1960s, military officials briefly considered and financed research on developing "superdogs" for military purposes. Ultimately, however, the research program neither produced the desired superior ambush detection dogs, nor did it convince military officials to use dogs on a larger scale. During the Vietnam War, only about 1,500 dogs were used for scouting and sentry duties. After 1975, the first dogs were trained to detect narcotics and explosives, a skill that became important for both the U.S. military abroad and American police forces at home. But even during Operation Desert Storm, few dogs saw action (Lemish 8-247). It was only during the late twentieth century and early twenty-first century that the U.S. military as well as police forces used dogs on a regular basis and in larger numbers. Search and rescue dogs, bomb sniffing dogs, and therapy dogs have become more prominent since 9/11 and the Iraq War, which partly explains the deluge of nonfiction books on their "heroism" that has appeared since 2000.

Against the backdrop of the increasing visibility of this particular group of dogs, the remaining part of this chapter analyzes three popular nonfiction books that contribute to the heroization of dogs in the twenty-first century: Lisa Rogak's *Dogs Who Serve: Incredible Stories of our Canine Military Heroes* (2016), Nancy Furstinger's *Paws of Courage: True Tales of Heroic Dogs that Protect and Serve* (2016), and Nona Kilgore Bauer's *Dog Heroes of September 11th: A Tribute to America's Search and Rescue Dogs* (2011). All three books were written by experienced nonfiction authors who are adept at using storytelling and interviews to create emotional tales that presumably appeal to both pet owners and those who do not harbor particular affections for animals. According to Amazon rankings and reviews, these books sold well, which makes them a good place to begin an exploratory investigation into the heroization of military working dogs.

Lisa Rogak's *Dogs Who Serve* is a heavily illustrated volume on dogs who serve in the U.S. military. The term "hero" is only used in the book's title, but Rogak's narrative emphasizes various qualities that tend to be considered heroic, and she utilizes photographs to visualize some of those qualities. For example, a number of photographs show dogs with soldiers who are holding or aiming their rifle, evoking traditional notions of heroic courage to confront the enemy, while others remind readers of soldiers' and dogs' selfless sacrifice and sense of duty. At the same time, *Dogs* repeatedly stresses the special bond that connects canines and their handlers within the military.

From the start, the text strongly affirms the idea of a strong U.S. military and related notions of American nationalism, which leaves little room for ambiguity or critique. Answering the question of why Americans crave for stories about "Military Working Dogs" (MWDs) on the very first page, Rogak asserts that they do because these dogs "represent everything that is great about the U.S. military" (1). Further into the text, she describes her goal as helping "readers to appreciate and learn a little bit more about the absolute love and devotion that these dogs show towards their jobs and human partners and that they serve their country without question" (8). Anthropomorphizing these dogs by suggesting that they have an inborn devotion to their work and their country, Rogak projects the qualities of human war heroes onto MWDs, which serves to normalize both the idea of patriotic loyalty and national belonging.

The book's eight chapters present the various stages of training and deployment that dogs undergo during their career in the military, repeatedly affirming the particular norms and values that Rogak stresses in her introduction. More importantly, these chapters largely smooth over the brutal realities of modern warfare, or they emphasize canines' important role in helping humans overcome the traumatic experiences of military combat. Dog trainers and dog handlers, Rogak writes in the chapter on basic training, are asked to "build the finest canine soldiers they can manage" (19). This focus on training and military dogs' superior abilities as bomb-sniffing dogs or as patrol dogs is stressed again and again throughout the text, suggesting that these animals are to be regarded as heroic because of their superior skills. At the same time, the chapters on "Stress Relief" and "At Your Service" provide much information on the ways in which therapy dogs "selflessly" assist "active-duty military personnel" (107) who were maimed or injured during combat. Selfless service, sacrifice, and devotion to duty—qualities these dogs are said to possess—similarly echo human notions of the heroic that are closely associated with military service.

The numerous photos that accompany the text do not necessarily enhance the "heroic" reputation of the dogs whose stories are told in the book, but they do serve to project an image of the U.S. armed forces that revolves around cute puppies and playful dogs during various stages of their training and deployment. While a few images show dogs that display aggressive behaviors as part of their training as sentry or patrol dogs, the vast majority of the images show male and female soldiers smiling or laughing while playing or cuddling with the dogs they have been assigned to. The supposedly "non-heroic" aspects of war, including destruction, trauma, and death, are ignored, or only vaguely hinted at, as is the case in the concluding section of the book, in which therapy dogs are said to have helped maimed soldiers overcome their traumatic war experiences. At the same time, all of these images speak to the strong human-animal bond that Rogak and the handlers she interviewed repeatedly discuss in the narrative. Ultimately, the combination of text and photographs serves to construct an image of human-animal camaraderie and to reaffirm traditional notions of the heroic, both of which present a sanitized version of the U.S. armed forces and the American military that leaves little room for a critique of the nation's warrior hero tradition.

The second example to be discussed here, Nancy Furstinger's *Paws of Courage*, reveals an even more deliberate attempt to heroize dogs that serve in the military. Through more than 20 stories about heroic dogs, most of which were taken from the American context, the experienced author Furstinger mixes fact and fiction to create emotional and action-packed profiles of dogs that she asserts have accomplished heroic feats. These stories, as the book's dust jacket tells readers, not only teach "us the meaning of bravery," but also "our four-legged friends' courage, devotion, and loyalty." Portraying dogs from the past and the present, the book introduces one such character as Chips, who "guarded tanks" in the European theater during World War II and "displayed fierce determination during the 1943 invasion of Sicily" by overpowering several enemy soldiers. "With a burst of courage," Furstinger writes, "Chips took matters into his own paws. He broke away from John, ignoring his handler's orders to halt. Chips raced into the shack, seized one of the gunners, and forced him and the other three enemy soldiers to surrender" (30). In Furstinger's telling, Chips's life clearly was "one of heroism and honor" (29). "Fearless Warrior" Layka, who searched for explosives and enemy soldiers during the Afghanistan War, was just as heroic. When she lost a leg after being fired at by the enemy, she was awarded an unofficial "medal of heroism for action under fire" (47). Another canine amputee, "Lucca: Courageous Marine," also displayed extraordinary courage during her service in the Iraq War, when she saved the life of her handler. Even after having been maimed, Lucca inspires "human wounded warrior amputees with her amazing story when she visits veterans and military hospitals" (62). Unlike Rogak, Furstinger does not explicitly praise the U.S. military or extols the virtues of patriotism, which might be in part due to the fact that she also discusses non-American examples in her book. What is similar, however, is the reaffirmation of traditional notions of heroism, the attempt to project them onto dogs, and repeated references to the strong bond between military working dogs and their handlers (e.g. 47, 60).

Many of the images that are used in *Paws of Courage* underline the text's arguments that the dogs they introduce to readers are truly heroic, either showing them with unofficial medals that were given to them by military personnel, or by showing them in action, for example, skydiving with their handlers or being on patrol. In contrast to Rogak's book, there is much less cuddling and more focus on the work the dogs perform, but Furstinger similarly suggests that these animals are "true" heroes and heroines whose extraordinariness is partly fueled by the special relationship that exists between them and the humans they work with.

The final example to be discussed here is the tenth-anniversary edition of Bauer's *Dog Heroes of September 11th*. It is the most ambivalent way of heroizing dogs, since it most explicitly attempts wedding tributes to these animals' search and rescue work with notions of patriotic heroism, while simultaneously revealing uncertainty as to whether dogs actually deserve to be called heroes. Ever since Islamist terrorists highjacked commercial airliners to attack the twin towers in New York City and the Pentagon in Washington, D.C., the police officers, firefighters, medics, and ordinary citizens, who either tried to help the victims or confronted the terrorists, became part of a deeply nationalistic heroism discourse (Thompson). Bauer's text taps into this discourse, singling out dogs as the one group that has yet to be commended for its patriotic contributions in the aftermath of 9/11. In this vein, Bauer dedicates the book "To all of the heroic canines who served their country following the September 11, 2001, terrorist attacks and who continue to serve whenever and wherever they are needed" (1). These dogs, Bauer writes in her introduction, deserved "to be recognized and honored for their service to America during those tormented days" (18).

However, despite such unambiguously patriotic statements, Bauer concedes that the complex and highly ambivalent process that elevates dogs to heroic status is one that can involve contradictory and competing views. "With almost one voice," she writes, "most of the K-9 handlers said they do not consider their canine partners heroes: their dogs are just doing a job they love, and they do it for the love of the people at the end of their leashes. It is America on the end of the leash now, and it is America that has crowned these canines as our heroes" (18). From this perspective, dogs are not heroes because they do not understand the danger or extraordinariness of their actions, although Bauer flatly dismisses that critique, arguing that citizens' collective desire to see them as heroes trumps any nature-versus-culture arguments. Surprisingly, despite the fact that those closest to the dogs portrayed in Bauer's book question her attempt to heroize their partners, Bauer does not elaborate on this inconsistency. Instead, she leaves it up to the readers to draw their own conclusions: her short profiles of various search and rescue dogs are based on interviews with their handlers, many of whom engage critically with the question of whether dogs' actions can be regarded as heroic. While putting much emphasis on patriotism, then, this book inadvertently provides important insights into popular notions of heroism and related views of animals' behavior and thinking.

As stated by Bauer in her introduction, the dog handlers she interviewed engage critically with their dogs' performance and related notions of the heroic. John Gilkey, the handler of a Labrador Retriever named Bear, states: "Bear is not a 'hero': Those firefighters and police officers are heroes ... they knew they might not be coming back and still climbed into those towers" (37). Another handler from New Jersey concurred. "My dog is not a hero," Lorrie Clemmo said about her Border Collie Blitz. "He is my partner and my search tool. He loves his job and does it mainly to please me. The real heroes are the ones who lost their lives, especially the men and women who took down the plane over Pennsylvania" (43). Still another handler, Jane David, provided a much more nuanced assessment of the performance of her Labrador Retriever Kita:

If Kita was capable of self-reflection, I don't believe she would describe herself as a hero. She would see herself as a dog who just loves doing her job. However, I think that disaster search dogs are indeed heroic because they overcome their instinctive fear of a hazardous environment, trusting in their handlers to keep them safe while they follow the command to search. They are high-spirited and bold and show great fortitude and heart in carrying out their work. (79)

These dog handlers' statements are revealing because they attest to the fact that those who work with search and rescue dogs tend to reserve the hero status for humans, who they believe either faced greater danger or contemplated the prospect of their own death. Dogs, by contrast, are not granted real agency, since their "heroism" is described as a form of play and as a seemingly natural inclination to please their human handlers and to trust human judgment. Bauer's book can therefore tell us much about human interpretations of dogs as "tools," notwithstanding the fact that human handlers develop a strong emotional bond with their dogs. It also demonstrates that the heroization of humans and animals speaks to a deep-felt need to affirm identities and values that are believed to be threatened, as was the case after 9/11. "Heroic" dogs therefore serve important functions that reflect the uses of human heroism in American culture.

The numerous photographs that accompany Bauer's text serve a similar purpose. In stark contrast to the first two examples, these images show the destruction, despair, exhaustion, and anguish that the terrorist attacks caused in New York. However, since almost all photographs feature dogs that search for victims at ground zero, they underscore the sense of hopefulness and pride that some handlers voiced in their interviews with Bauer. One handler from New Jersey stated: "My dog's search work made me realize how proud I was to live in this great and free country. These dogs worked tirelessly, never quitting. They were our companions, our working partners and our strength" (34). Despite potentially opening old wounds when viewed years after 9/11, then, these images use dogs to do both, to heal these wounds and to remind citizens of what made and makes America great. In addition, countless photos show handlers or firefighters petting dogs or playing with them, interrupting the potentially disturbing images that show the havoc the terrorist attacks had caused. Just like firefighters or first responders, search and rescue dogs became powerful symbols of hopeful patriotism and entrenched notions of heroic self-sacrifice and service.

## Conclusion

While this chapter could only scratch the surface of what has become a pervasive phenomenon in twenty-first-century American culture, it hints at how studying the heroization of dogs can enhance our understanding of both notions of the heroic in U.S. society and human-animal relations. Conceptualizing dogs as heroes appears to reaffirm traditional ideas about human heroism and the norms and values they entail, including patriotism and such personal qualities as courage and self-sacrifice. But doing so reveals as much about what humans think about animals and their role in human societies. Men and women who are considered heroic are frequently believed to have accomplished exceptional feats as a consequence of a "heroic impulse," that is, a moment in which they spontaneously react to a dangerous situation, refraining from pondering the consequences of their actions (Mechling). In the case of dogs, however, it appears that even, or especially those who work with dogs on a daily basis do not consider these qualities to be heroic. From their perspective, animals are not heroes because of their inability to see the implications of what would otherwise (that is in humans) be regarded as extraordinary deeds. Ultimately, the agency that these animals are granted in the narratives about their actions remains limited, suggesting that those representations of animals primarily fulfill human psychological needs. What appears to make military working dogs particularly useful in this regard is that they tend to accomplish pro-social feats, which means that they save rather than destroy lives. The fact that these are the lives of humans rather than those of other animals is crucial, since rescuing other animals' lives without human supervision appears to be much less noteworthy.

More research will be needed to fully comprehend the heroization of dogs and other animals in American culture. In the case of military dogs, for instance, a number of biographies of canine "heroes" have been published, including one on Lucca, the German Shepherd that is mentioned in this chapter (Goodavage). In addition, there are numerous books not only on heroic dogs, but on other "heroic" animals and their role in military campaigns (see, for example, Cawthorne; Cooper; Frankel; Le Chêne). Moreover, these heroization processes are not confined to written texts. Already in the 1990s, Disney produced a film on the World War II dog Chips, and the twenty-first century has seen the release of a number of films on "heroic" canines in military and non-military contexts, including *Max* (2015) and *Max 2: White House Hero* (2017). Analyses of these films and comparisons between them and pre-1990s television series such as *Lassie* and *Fury* might reveal new insights into the ways in which the heroization of animals has changed over time. Finally, a comparative and transnational perspective on this phenomenon might shed fresh light on human efforts to elevate animals to heroic status, given that the status of animals and their cultural uses differs considerably in the Americas, Europe, Asia, and Africa.

## Works Cited

"Awards, Decorations, and Honors." *Encyclopedia of American War Heroes*, edited by Bruce H. Norton, Checkmark Books, 2002, p. xxvii.

Anderson, Jeffrey W. "Military Heroism: An Occupational Definition." *Armed Forces & Society*, vol. 12, no. 4, 1986, pp. 601-04.

Baucom, Donald. "Awards, Decorations, and Honors." *The Oxford Companion to American Military History*, edited by John Whiteclay Chambers II et al., Oxford University Press, 1999, pp. 67-68.

Bauer, Nona Kilgore. *Dog Heroes of September 11th: A Tribute to America's Search and Rescue Dogs.* Rev. ed. Kennel Book Clubs, 2011.

Campbell, Joseph. *The Hero with a Thousand Faces.* 1949. Fontana Press, 1993.

Cawthorne, Nigel. *Canine Commandos: The Heroism, Devotion and Sacrifice of Dogs in War.* Ulysses Press, 2012.

Cockerham, William C. "Green Berets and the Symbolic Meaning of Heroism." *Urban Life*, vol. 8, no. 1, 1979, pp. 94-113.

Cooper, Jilly. *Animals in War: Valiant Horses, Courageous Dogs, and Other Unsung Animal Heroes.* Lyons Press, 2002.

DeMello, Margo. *Animals and Society: An Introduction to Human-Animal Studies.* Columbia University Press, 2012.

Drucker, Susan J., and Robert S. Cathcart, editors. *American Heroes in a Media Age.* Hampton Press, 1994.

Dubino, Jeanne, et al., editors. *Representing the Modern Animal in Culture.* Palgrave Macmillan, 2014.

Frankel, Rebecca. *War Dogs: Tales of Canine Heroism, History, and Love.* Palgrave Macmillan, 2014.

Furstinger, Nancy. *Paws of Courage: True Tales of Heroic Dogs That Protect and Serve.* National Geographic, 2016.

Goldstein, Joshua S. *War and Gender: How Gender Shapes the War System and Vice Versa.* Cambridge University Press, 2001.

Goodavage, Maria. *Top Dog: The Story of Marine Hero Lucca.* Dutton, 2014.

Grier, Katherine C. *Pets in America: A History.* University of North Carolina Press, 2006.

Hagemann, Karen. "Of 'Manly Valor' and 'German Honor': Nation, War, and Masculinity in the Age of the Prussian Uprising Against Napoleon." *Central European History*, vol. 30, no. 2, 1997, pp. 187-220.

Hook, Sidney. *The Hero in History: A Study in Limitation and Possibility.* 1945. Transaction Publishers, 1992.

Hurn, Samantha. *Humans and Other Animals: Cross-Cultural Perspectives on Human-Animal Interactions.* Pluto Press, 2012.

Kendrick, M. Gregory. *The Heroic Ideal: Western Archetypes from the Greeks to the Present.* McFarland, 2010.

Klapp, Orrin. "The Creation of Popular Heroes." *American Journal of Sociology*, vol. 54, no. 2, 1948, pp. 135-41.

Le Chêne, Evelyn. *Silent Heroes: The Bravery and Devotion of Animals in War*. Souvenir Press, 2010.

Lemish, Michael G. *War Dogs: A History of Loyalty and Heroism*. Brassey's, 1999.

Madigan, Edward. "Courage and Cowardice in Wartime." *War in History*, vol. 20, no. 1, 2013, pp. 4-6.

Mechling, Jay. "Heroism and the Problem of Impulsiveness for Early Twentieth-Century American Youth." *Generations of Youth: Youth Cultures and History in Twentieth-Century America*, edited by Joe Austin and Michael Nevin Willard, New York University Press, 1998, pp. 36-48.

Meyer, Silke. "Helden des Alltags: Von der Transformation des Besonderen." *Die Helden-Maschine: Zur Aktualität und Tradition von Heldenbildern*, edited by LWL-Industriemuseum, Klartext-Verlag, 2010, pp. 28-40.

Möhring, Maren, et al., editors. *Tiere im Film: Eine Menscheitsgeschichte der Moderne*. Böhlau, 2009.

Nocella II, Anthony J., et al., editors. *Animals and War: Confronting the Military-Animal Industrial Complex*. Lexington, 2014.

Ohrem, Dominik, ed. *American Beasts: Perspectives on Animals, Animality, and U.S. Culture, 1776-1920*. Neofelis, 2016.

Pettegrew, John. "'The Soldier's Faith': Turn-of-the-Century Memory of the Civil War and the Emergence of Modern American Nationalism." *Journal of Contemporary History*, vol. 31, no. 1, 1996, pp. 49-73.

Rogak, Lisa. *Dogs Who Serve: Incredible Stories of our Canine Military Heroes*. Thomas Dunne Books, 2016.

Rollin, Roger R. "The Lone Ranger and Lenny Skutnik: The Hero as Popular Culture." *The Hero in Transition*, edited by Ray B. Browne and Marshall W. Fishwick, Bowling Green University Popular Press, 1983, pp. 14-45.

Schlesinger, Arthur, Jr. "The Decline of Heroes." *Heroes and Anti-Heroes*, edited by Harold Lubin, Chandler Publishing, 1968, pp. 341-51.

Schwartz, Barry. "George Washington and the Whig Conception of Heroic Leadership." *American Sociological Review*, vol. 48, no. 1, 1983, pp. 20-24.

Schwartz, Barry. *George Washington: The Making of an American Symbol*. Free Press, 1987.

Strate, Lance. "Heroes and/as Communication." *Heroes in a Global World*, edited by Susan J. Drucker and Gary Gumpert, Hampton Press, 2008, pp. 19-45.

Thompson, J. William. *From Memory to Memorial: Shanksville, America, and Flight 93*. Pennsylvania State University Press, 2017.

von den Hoff, Ralf, et al. "Das Heroische in der neueren kulturhistorischen Forschung: Ein kritischer Bericht." *H-Soz-Kult*, 28 July 2015, hsozkult.de/literaturereview/id/forschungsberichte-2216.

Wendt, Simon. "Introduction: Reconsidering Military Heroism in American History." *Warring over Valor: How Race and Gender Shaped American Military Heroism in the Twentieth and Twenty-First Centuries*, edited by Simon Wendt, Rutgers University Press, 2019, pp. 1-19.

Zabecki, David T. "Medals and Decorations." *The Encyclopedia of World War I: A Political, Social, and Military History*, edited by Spencer Tucker, vol. 1., ABC-CLIO, 2005, pp. 766-68.

## Acknowledgements

Babette Tischleder is grateful to Andrew Gross for his perceptive editing of the introduction and to Shruti Belliappa for her invaluable advice on style. The multispecies exchange with Bill Brown, Alan Kasper, Kazoo and Reba during our daily morning walks in sun and in snow has been a great inspiration for thinking beyond the human. All my canine friends, including Bianca and Bloo, smart strays from Chalkidiki, have taught me the art of living in the present and the joy of exploring puddles, pebbles, waves, and other analog media.

Birgit Spengler would like to thank Neil Cormier for pausing to ponder trees, Hildegard Spengler for *The Secret Life of Trees*, Maya, Matti, Heike, Hildegard, and Gerhard Spengler for helping make the final selection. Many thanks also to Eva Mangieri for research and proofreading assistance.

Babette and Birgit would like to thank Katharina Wierichs at transcript for her editorial support and generosity, Helmbrecht Breinig for keeping secrets and providing conceptual advice, and Caroline Bürmann for her sharp eye, careful proofreading, patience, and invaluable and untiring support in arranging the manuscript for publication.

# Biographical Notes

## Editors

**Birgit Spengler** is professor of American Literature at the University of Wuppertal. Her publications include *Vision, Gender, and Power in Nineteenth-Century American Women's Writing* (2008), *Literary Spinoffs: Rewriting the Classics, Re-Imagining the Community* (2014), and "The Body-That-Is-Not-One: Exception and Belonging on the US-Mexican Border in *The Bridge*" (2016).

**Babette B. Tischleder** is professor of North American Studies and Media Studies at the University of Göttingen. Her books include *The Literary Life of Things: Case Studies in American Fiction* (2014) and the coedited volume *Cultures of Obsolescence: History, Materiality, and the Digital Age* (2015). Her current work is concerned with the ways that critical and creative practices tackle present ecological troubles and our endangered futures, as in her recent essay "Neither Billiard Ball nor Planet B" on Latour and literary worlding in the Anthropocene.

## Contributors

**Helmbrecht Breinig** is professor emeritus of American Studies at the University of Erlangen-Nürnberg and founding director of the Bavarian American Academy. He has published widely in the fields of American fiction and poetry, intercultural American studies, Native American literature and cultural theory. Recent books include: *Hemispheric Imaginations: North American Fictions of Latin America* (2016); *das auge des raben schwarz: Tiergedichte aus der englischsprachigen Welt* (2016); *Mark Twain: Eine Einführung in sein Werk* (2011).

**Christine Brinckmann**, professor emerita from Zürich University, began to make experimental films in 1979. The DVD-booklet *The Primal Scene* including her films and a number of essays appeared in 2008. Her academic publications focus on film history, film style, narratology, documentary film, experimental film, feminism, the aesthetics of color and empathy. Her books include the collection of essays *Die anthropomorphe Kamera* (1997) and *Color and Empathy. Essays on Two Aspects of Film* (2014). She is coeditor of *montage/av*.

**Christa Buschendorf** was professor of American Studies at Goethe University Frankfurt from 1998 to 2015. Her recent publications include *Power Relations in Black Lives: Reading African American Literature and Culture with Bourdieu and Elias* (2018); "Grappling with German Atheism and Pessimism: The Reception of Schopenhauer in the United States" (2017); and she conducted and edited conversations with Cornel West on *Black Prophetic Fire* (2014).

**Judith Fetterley** is a Distinguished Teaching Professor Emerita at the University at Albany/State University of New York. She is the author of *The Resisting Reader: A Feminist Approach to American Fiction* and *Writing Out of Place: Regionalism, Women, and American Literary Culture*. Since retiring she has opened a garden design business, Perennial Wisdom, and become a Master Gardener. She is currently at work on *Out in the Garden*, a memoir of her life as a gardener.

**Astrid Franke** is Professor of American Studies at Tübingen University. Her publications include *Keys to Controversies: Stereotypes in Modern American Novels* (1999), *"Pursue the Illusion": Problems of Public Poetry in America* (2010), and various articles on literature and inequalities.

**Ulla Haselstein** is professor of American Literature at the John F. Kennedy-Institute for North American Studies at the Freie Universität Berlin. Her book publications include *Die Gabe der Zivilisation* (2000), *The Cultural Career of Coolness* (2013) and *Gertrude Steins literarische Porträts* (2019, forthcoming).

**Bernd Herzogenrath** is professor of American literature and culture at Goethe University of Frankfurt/Main, Germany. He is the author of *An Art of Desire. Reading Paul Auster* (2001), *An American Body/Politic: A Deleuzian Approach* (2010) and the editor of a.o. *Film as Philosophy* (2017).

**Maria Holmgren Troy** is Professor of English and Director of the Research Group for Culture Studies (KuFo) at Karlstad University, Sweden. Troy is currently involved in a book project under contract with Manchester University Press on Nordic Gothic fiction together with three other Swedish scholars, and she is the co-author of *Making Home: Orphanhood, Kinship, and Cultural Memory in Contemporary American Novels* (2014).

**Nina Katchadourian** is an interdisciplinary artist and an associate professor on the faculty of NYU Gallatin. Her work includes video, performance, sound, sculpture, photography and public projects. Her video *Accent Elimination* was included at the 2015 Venice Biennale in the Armenian pavilion, which won the Golden Lion for Best National Participation. A solo museum survey of her work entitled "Curiouser" was on view at the Blanton Museum of Art in Austin, Texas (2017); the monograph *Curiouser* is available from Tower Books. Her work is in collections including The Metropolitan Museum of Art, Morgan Library, San Francisco Museum of Modern Art, Margulies Collection, and Saatchi Gallery.

**Karen L. Kilcup** is the Elizabeth Rosenthal Excellence Professor of English, Environmental & Sustainability Studies and Women's and Gender Studies at the University of North Carolina at Greensboro. She is author of several dozen essays on American literature and author or editor of eleven books, including two forthcoming monographs: *Who Killed American Poetry?: From National Obsession to Elite Possession* (2019) and *"Stronger, Truer, Bolder": Nineteenth-Century American Children's Writing, Nature, and the Environment* (2020).

**Claudia Lillge** teaches English and Comparative Literature Studies at Goethe-University Frankfurt/Main. Her publications include *Arbeit: Eine Literatur- und Mediengeschichte Großbritanniens* (2016), the edited volume *Die Brontë-Methode: Elizabeth Stoddards transatlantische Genealogie und das viktorinanische Imaginäre* (2009), and the special issue *Tiere sehen* (2018).

**Gesa Mackenthun** teaches American Studies at Rostock University. Her publications include *Fictions of the Black Atlantic in American Foundational Literature* (2004), *Metaphors of Dispossession* (1997), the coedited *Sea Changes. Historicizing the Ocean* (2004), and an eight-volume edited series on *Cultural Encounters and the Discourses of Scholarship* (Waxmann). Her forthcoming book deals with constructions of American antiquity.

**Magda Majewska** is assistant professor of American Studies at Goethe Universität Frankfurt. Her book, *Die Lust im Text: Der postmoderne Roman und die sexuelle Befreiungsbewegung in den USA*, is forthcoming from transcript.

**Katja Sarkowsky** is Chair of American Studies at Augsburg University. Her publications include *AlterNative Spaces: Constructions of Space in Native American and First Nations Literatures* (2007), *Narrating Citzenship and Belonging in Anglophone Canadian Literature* (2018), and the edited volume *"Cranes of the Rise": Metaphors in Life Writing* (2018).

**Susanne Scharf** is an independent Americanist and art historian. She is writing her dissertation on the German-American art collector Hugo Reisinger (1856-1914) and has contributed to the proceedings *George Bellows Revisited: New Considerations of the Painter's Oeuvre* (2016) and to several exhibition catalogues, among them *Hopper to Rothko: America's Road to Modern Art* (2017) and *Es war einmal in Amerika: 300 Jahre US-amerikanische Kunst* (2018).

**Susanne Scholz** is Professor of English Literature and Culture at the University of Frankfurt/Main. Her major book publications include: *Body Narratives: Writing the Nation and Fashioning the Subject in Early Modern England* (2000); with Daniel Dornhofer (eds.), *Spectatorship at the Elizabethan Court* (2013); *Phantasmatic Knowledge: Visions of the Human and the Scientific Gaze in English Literature, 1880-1930* (2013), and *Handbuch Literatur und Materielle Kultur* (2018), edited with Ulrike Vedder.

**Sabine Sielke** is Chair of North American Literature and Culture and Director of the North American Studies Program and the German-Canadian Centre at the University of Bonn. Her numerous publications include *Reading Rape* (2002) and *Fashioning the Female Subject* (1997), the series *Transcription*, and 20 (co-)edited books as well as numerous essays on poetry, (post-)modern literature and culture, literary and cultural theory, gender and African American studies, popular culture, and the interfaces of cultural studies and the sciences.

**Kirsten Twelbeck** teaches as interim professor for American Studies at the University of Regensburg. Her publications include *No Korean is Whole, Wherever He or She may be* (2002) and *Beyond the Civil War Hospital. The Rhetoric of Healing and Democratization in Northern Reconstruction Writing, 1861-1882* (2014).

**Johannes Voelz** is Heisenberg-Professor of American Studies, Democracy, and Aesthetics at Goethe-Universität Frankfurt. He is the author of *Transcendental Resistance: The New Americanists and Emerson's Challenge* (2010) and *The Poetics of Insecurity: American Fiction and the Uses of Threat* (2018).

**Simon Wendt** is Associate Professor of American Studies at Goethe University Frankfurt. His research interests revolve around African American history, gender history, memory, nationalism, and the history of heroism. He is author of *The Spirit and the Shotgun: Armed Resistance and the Struggle for Civil Rights* (2007) and (co-)editor of *Warring over Valor: How Race and Gender Shaped American Military Heroism in the Twentieth and Twenty-First Centuries* (2019) and *Black Intellectual Thought in Modern America: A Historical Perspective* (2017).

**Yvonne Wiser** teaches English, Politics and Economics at Goetheschule in Neu-Isenburg. She published encyclopedia articles on Mary E. Wilkins Freeman, Charlotte Perkins Gilman and Elizabeth Stuart Phelps (2000) and edited *Elizabeth Stoddard: Stories* (2003) with Susanne Opfermann.

GPSR Authorized Representative: Easy Access System Europe, Mustamäe tee 50, 10621 Tallinn, Estonia, gpsr.requests@easproject.com